Ninja Foodi Cookbook #2020

600+ Incredible and Irresistible Ninja Foodi Recipes for Your Whole Family: The Ultimate Cookbook for Beginners

(600 Recipes)

Darlene A. Wilson

Table of Content

MEAT — 130

DESERTS — 227

DESCRIPTION

The Ninja Foodi is one of the best kitchen revolutions, it allows you to make a wide variety of healthy meals with various different components using just a single pot. You can quickly cook your desired meat on the bottom while adding veggies on top using the reversible rack. Each individual part of your meal will get an even and fine texture in the end that will provide a fine and satisfying meal.

I cannot stress this enough, the versatility of the Ninja Foodi is what makes them so unique. Using the TenderCrisp tech, you will be able to turn simple recipes like soups and stews into amazing Wonders! Alternatively, using the pressure cooking feature, you will simply cook stews, chilis, casseroles, and even desserts! The list goes on. As a matter of fact, the crisping lid also allows you to bake biscuits too!

The Ninja Foodi is one of that rare appliance that actually allows you to directly cook frozen meals, saving a lot of time. The pressure method can easily defrost and tenderize frozen meat, while the Crisping Lid will allow you to get a fine crispy finish.

Yes, you read that right! Using the Ninja Foodi and its patented Air Crisping technology, you can even create restaurant style BBQ meals in an instant! A fine 5-pound chicken, beef brisket, pork belly! Nothing is off limits when you have the power of the Ninja Foodi with you.

The versatility of the Ninja Foodi and its capacity act as multiple appliances allow you to get rid of the steamer, Saute pan, slow cooker, pressure cooker and a myriad of different appliances and use the Ninja Foodi for everything.

The excellent way in which the Ninja Foodi cook, ensure that the temperature inside is able to reach sufficiently high enough levels during pressure cooking to ensure that 99% of harmful microbes are killed during the process. In fact, the Ninja Foodi is even able to kill significantly more resistant microbes as well.

In this book we will discuss the following topics:

- Breakfast
- Mains
- Sides
- Seafood
- Poultry
- Meat
- Vegetables
- Soups And Stews
- Snacks
- Desserts and many more!

INTRODUCTION

The Ninja Foodi may have the most functions among many multicookers sold in the market but it does not mean that it is very difficult to operate. Contrary to popular belief, it is one of the easiest multicooker to operate despite of its bulk and complexity in design (because of the presence of the crisping and pressure lid). This section will enlighten you on how you can use and optimize your Ninja Foodi.

Benefits of Ninja Air Fryer

Fast cooking: It greatly decreases typically long cooking times for all dishes. Cooking time can be reduced 60% to 80% (depending on the ingredient). Faster cooking times mean you can cook real foods from scratch in the time it takes for pizza delivery or to prepare a frozen dinner.

Safe and user-friendly: Ninja Foodi is pre-programmed, and therefore, incidents such as exploding of the cooker do not happen. It has features which are pre-programmed and therefore, all you have to do is to press the correct cooking button.

Saves Energy: It cooks food faster thus reducing cooking significantly. Reduced cooking time translates to energy saving. It can be the only appliance you use therefore making it economical.

Maintaining Nutritional Value: As opposed to most of the existing cooking methods which drain or destroy food's nutrition, the Ninja Air Fryer preserves the nutritional value of the foods being cooked.

It is Convenient: No longer do you have to bother about the size of your kitchen or where you will store the multitude of kitchen appliances needed to concoct one single home cooked meals. Simply place all of your ingredients in your Ninja Air Fryer and allow it do its thing automatically.

BREAKFAST

1. Almond Hash Browns

Preparation Time: 30 minutes

Servings: 6

INGREDIENTS

- 1 ½ lbs. hash browns
- 6 bacon slices; chopped.
- 9 oz. cream cheese
- 1 yellow onion; chopped.
- 1 cup almond milk
- A drizzle of olive oil
- 6 eggs
- 6 spring onions; chopped.
- 2 tbsp. cheddar cheese, shredded
- Salt and black pepper to the taste

DIRECTIONS

1. Set your Foodi on sauté mode, add the oil, heat it up, add the onion and spring onions, stir and cook for 5 minutes.
2. Add hash browns and the bacon, set the Foodi on Air Crisp and cook for 15 minutes, stirring everything halfway
3. Add eggs mixed with cream cheese, milk, salt and pepper, toss and cook everything on Air Crisp for 10 minutes more.
4. Divide between plates, sprinkle the cheese on top and serve for breakfast

2. Quick Apple Oatmeal

Preparation Time: 25 minutes

Servings: 8

INGREDIENTS

- 4 apples, cored and cubed
- ½ cup raisins
- 1/3 cup brown sugar
- 2 cups steel cut oats
- 6 cups water
- 2 tbsp. maple syrup

- 1 tbsp. butter
- 1 tsp. cinnamon powder

DIRECTIONS

1. Put all the ingredients in the Foodi and toss them. Put the pressure lid on, seal and cook on High for 15 minutes, shaking the Foodi halfway
2. Release the pressure naturally for 10 minutes, stir the oatmeal again, divide into bowls and serve

3. Creamy Chili

Preparation Time: 15 minutes

Servings: 4

INGREDIENTS

- 4 eggs; whisked.
- 1 red chili pepper; chopped.
- 2 tbsp. heavy cream
- 2 tbsp. parsley, finely chopped
- Salt and white pepper to the taste

DIRECTIONS

1. In a bowl mix all the ingredients and toss them. Add the reversible rack to the Foodi, add the baking pan and pour the creamy chili mix inside
2. Cook the mix on Baking mode at 400 °F for 10 minutes. Divide the mix between plates and serve

4. Eggplant Breakfast

Preparation Time: 40 minutes

Servings: 2

INGREDIENTS

- 2 eggplants; cubed.
- ¾ cup tomato paste

- 2 cups mozzarella cheese; grated.
- 1 tbsp. avocado oil
- 2 tbsp. cheddar; grated.
- 2 tbsp. fresh basil; chopped.
- 2 tbsp. coconut milk
- ½ tsp. garlic powder
- 2 tsp. cilantro; chopped.
- ½ tsp. Italian seasoning
- Salt and black pepper to the taste

DIRECTIONS

1. Set the Foodi on Sauté mode, add the oil and heat it up. Add the eggplants, salt, pepper, garlic powder and Italian seasoning, toss and cook for 6 minutes
2. Add the coconut milk, tomato paste and all the cheese, set the Foodi on Air Crisp and cook for 10 minutes at 370 °F. Sprinkle the cilantro and the basil on top, divide everything into bowls and serve for breakfast

5. Apple Pudding

Preparation Time: 25 minutes

Servings: 4

INGREDIENTS

- 2 eggs; whisked.
- 1 cup apple, peeled, cored and chopped
- 1 ¼ cups milk
- 2 tbsp. sugar
- ¼ tsp. vanilla extract
- 2 tsp. cinnamon powder
- Cooking spray

DIRECTIONS

1. In a bowl mix all the ingredients except the cooking spray and whisk well. Put the reversible rack in the Foodi machine and add the baking pan inside
2. Grease the pan with the cooking spray and pour the apples mix. Set the Foodi on Baking mode and cook the pudding at 360 °F for 15 minutes. Divide into bowls and serve for breakfast.

6. Artichokes Omelet

Preparation Time: 20 minutes

Servings: 4

INGREDIENTS

- 4 eggs; whisked.
- 4 oz. canned artichokes; drained. and chopped
- 4 garlic cloves; minced.
- 1 tbsp. olive oil
- 1 tsp. soy sauce
- Salt and black pepper to the taste

DIRECTIONS

1. In a bowl mix all the ingredients except the oil and whisk them well.
2. Add the reversible rack in the Foodi, add the baking pan, grease it with the oil and pour the artichokes mix inside
3. Cook the omelet on Baking mode at 350 °F for 10 minutes.
4. Slice the omelet and serve it for breakfast

7. Avocado Mix

Preparation Time: 20 minutes

Servings: 2

INGREDIENTS

- 4 bacon slices; chopped.
- 2 avocados, peeled, pitted and cut into segments
- 1 tbsp. sriracha sauce
- 1 tbsp. lime juice
- A pinch of salt and black pepper

DIRECTIONS

1. Set the Foodi on Sauté mode, heat it up, add the bacon and cook for 4-5 minutes. Add the avocados and all the other ingredients toss a bit, cook for another 5 minutes, divide into bowls and serve

8. Yogurt and Spinach Omelet

Preparation Time: 15 minutes

Servings: 8

INGREDIENTS

- ½ lb. baby spinach
- 8 eggs; whisked.
- 1 ½ cup Greek yogurt
- ½ cup mint; chopped.
- 2 tbsp. olive oil
- Salt and black pepper to the taste

DIRECTIONS

1. In a bowl mix all the ingredients except the oil and whisk well. Add the reversible rack to the Foodi, add the baking pan and pour the eggs mix into the pan
2. Set the Foodi on Baking mode, cook the omelet at 360 °F for 10 minutes, divide between plates and serve for breakfast

9. Mushrooms and Squash Bowls

Preparation Time: 15 minutes

Servings: 4

INGREDIENTS

- 1 red bell pepper, roughly chopped
- 1 yellow squash; cubed.
- 2 green onions, sliced
- 1 cup white mushrooms, sliced
- ½ cup cheddar cheese
- 2 tbsp. olive oil

DIRECTIONS

1. Set the Foodi on Sauté mode, add the oil, heat it, up, add the peppers, mushrooms, green onions and the squash, toss and sauté for 5 minutes. Put the pressure lid on, cook everything on High for 5 more minutes, release the pressure fast for 5 minutes, divide into bowls and serve for breakfast

10. Ninja Toast

Preparation Time: 11 minutes

Servings: 6

INGREDIENTS

- 12 bread slices
- 1 cup butter, soft
- ½ cup maple syrup
- 2 tsp. vanilla extract

DIRECTIONS

1. In a bowl mix the butter with the syrup and vanilla, whisk and brush the bread slices with this mix. Place the slices in the Foodi's basket and cook on Baking mode at 400 °F for 6 minutes. Serve for breakfast

11. Mexican Scramble

Preparation Time: 15 minutes

Servings: 4

INGREDIENTS

- ½ lb. chorizo; chopped.
- 4 eggs; whisked.
- ½ cup corn
- 1 tbsp. parsley; chopped.
- 1 tbsp. cheddar cheese; grated.
- 1 tbsp. olive oil
- Salt and black pepper to the taste

DIRECTIONS

1. Set the Foodi on Sauté mode, add the oil and heat it up. Add the chorizo and the corn, stir and sauté for 5 minutes
2. Add salt, pepper and the eggs, toss, set the Foodi on Air Crisp and cook for another 5 minutes at 360 °F. Add the parsley and the cheese, toss a bit, divide between plates and serve for breakfast

12. Bacon Patties

Preparation Time: 13 minutes

Servings: 4

INGREDIENTS

- 1 puff pastry sheet, rolled and cut into squares
- 8 bacon slices; chopped.
- 4 handful cheddar cheese; grated.
- 4 tsp. mustard

DIRECTIONS

1. Divide the cheese, bacon and mustard on half of the pastry sheet squares, top with the other halves, seal the edges and place all the patties in your Foodi's basket
2. Cook everything on Air Crisp for 10 minutes. Divide the patties between plates and serve for breakfast

13. Potato Frittata
Preparation Time: 26 minutes

Servings: 6

INGREDIENTS

- 1 lb. baby potatoes; chopped.
- 1 oz. cheddar cheese; grated.
- ½ cup heavy cream
- 2 red onions; chopped.
- 8 eggs; whisked.
- 1 tbsp. olive oil
- Salt and black pepper to the taste

DIRECTIONS

1. In a bowl mix all the ingredients except the oil and toss. Drizzle the oil into the Foodi's baking pan and pour the frittata mixture inside
2. Put the reversible rack in the machine, add the baking pan and cook on Baking mode at 350 °F for 20 minutes. Divide the frittata between plates and serve for breakfast

14. Salmon Toast
Preparation Time: 15 minutes

Servings: 4

INGREDIENTS

- 16 oz. smoked salmon, skinless, boneless and cut into strips
- 6 cheddar cheese slices
- 2 spring onions; chopped.
- 6 bread slices
- ¼ cup mayonnaise
- 1 tbsp. lime juice
- 3 tbsp. butter, melted
- 2 tbsp. mustard

DIRECTIONS

1. In a bowl mix salmon with the mayo, mustard, lime juice and spring onions and stir. Grease the bread slices with the butter and spread the salmon mix on each slice
2. Place the slices in the Foodi's basket and cook on Roast at 400 °F for 5 minutes. Divide the toast between plates and serve for breakfast

15. Bread Pudding
Preparation Time: 50 minutes

Servings: 4

INGREDIENTS

- ¾ cup heavy cream
- 4 eggs; whisked.
- 9 cinnamon buns, cut into quarters
- ½ cup cherries, dried
- 1 tbsp. sugar
- ¼ tsp. cloves, ground
- 2 tsp. orange liqueur

DIRECTIONS

1. In a bowl mix all the ingredients and toss. Put the reversible rack in the Foodi, place the baking pan inside and pour the bread pudding inside

2. Set the Foodi on Baking mode and cook the pudding at 325 °F for 40 minutes. Divide into bowls and serve for breakfast

16. Cauliflower Casserole

Preparation Time: 30 minutes

Servings: 4

INGREDIENTS

- 1 cauliflower head, florets separated
- 2 oz. coconut milk
- 2 oz. cheddar cheese; grated.
- 3 eggs
- 2 tsp. parsley; chopped.
- Salt and black pepper to the taste

DIRECTIONS

1. Put the cauliflower in the Foodi's baking pan. In a bowl mix all the other ingredients except the parsley, whisk and pour over the cauliflower
2. Add the reversible rack into the Foodi, add the baking pan and cook everything on Baking mode at 350 °F for 20 minutes. Divide between plates and serve for breakfast

17. Chives Omelet

Preparation Time: 17 minutes

Servings: 4

INGREDIENTS

- 4 eggs; whisked.
- 2 tbsp. cheddar cheese; grated.
- 1 tbsp. cilantro; chopped.
- 4 tbsp. coconut cream
- 2 tbsp. chives; chopped.
- Cooking spray
- Salt and black pepper to the taste

DIRECTIONS

1. In a bowl, mix all the ingredients except the cooking spray and whisk. Add the reversible rack to the Foodi, add the baking pan and grease it with the cooking spray
2. Add the omelet mixture into the pan and cook on Baking mode at 350 °F for 12 minutes. Divide the omelet between plates and serve

18. Tofu and Spinach Bowls

Preparation Time: 15 minutes

Servings: 4

INGREDIENTS

- 12 oz. firm tofu; cubed.
- 8 oz. baby spinach, torn
- 3 carrots; chopped.
- 1 red bell pepper; chopped.
- 2 cup red quinoa, cooked
- ¼ cup soy sauce
- 2 tbsp. olive oil
- 2 tbsp. lime juice

DIRECTIONS

1. Set the Foodi on Sauté mode, add the oil and heat it up. Add the carrots and the bell pepper, stir and sauté for 3 minutes
2. Add the tofu, lime juice, soy sauce, spinach and quinoa, toss, put the pressure lid on and cook on High for 7 minutes. Release the pressure fast for 5 minutes, divide everything into bowls and serve for breakfast.

19. Broccoli Pudding

Preparation Time: 25 minutes

Servings: 4

INGREDIENTS

- 2 cups broccoli florets; chopped.
- ½ cup cheddar cheese, shredded

- ½ cup almonds; chopped.
- ½ cup coconut, shredded
- 3 cups coconut milk

DIRECTIONS

1. Put the reversible rack in the Foodi machine and add the baking pan inside. Mix all the ingredients in the baking pan, set the Foodi on Baking mode and cook at 360 °F for 20 minutes. Divide between plates and serve for breakfast

20. Veggies and Bread Casserole

Preparation Time: 40 minutes

Servings: 6

INGREDIENTS

- 1 lb. white bread; cubed.
- ½ lb. cheddar, shredded
- 1 lb. smoked bacon, cooked and chopped
- ½ lb. Monterey jack, shredded
- 1 red onion; chopped.
- 30 oz. canned tomatoes; chopped.
- 8 eggs; whisked.
- ¼ cup avocado oil
- 2 tbsp. chives; chopped.
- 2 tbsp. chicken stock
- Salt and black pepper to the taste

DIRECTIONS

1. In the Foodi's baking dish, combine all the ingredients: . Add the reversible rack in the machine, add the baking dish and cook the mix on Baking mode at 350 °F for 30 minutes. Divide everything between plates and serve

21. Sausage Coconut Mix

Preparation Time: 30 minutes

Servings: 4

INGREDIENTS

- 4 bacon slices, cooked and crumbled
- 1 lb. breakfast sausage, crumbled
- 2 and ½ cups cheddar cheese, shredded
- 2 eggs
- 2 cups coconut milk
- 3 tbsp. parsley; chopped.
- Cooking spray
- Salt and black pepper to the taste

DIRECTIONS

1. In a bowl mix all the ingredients except the cooking spray and toss. Put the reversible rack in the Foodi, place the baking pan inside and grease it with the cooking spray
2. Add the sausage mix in the pan, spread, set the Foodi on Baking mode and cook at 320 °F for 20 minutes. Serve hot for breakfast

22. Salsa and Cod

Preparation Time: 21 minutes

Servings: 4

INGREDIENTS

- 4 cod fillets, skinless, boneless and cubed
- 1 red onion; chopped.
- 1 green bell pepper; chopped.
- ½ cup salsa
- 1 cup baby spinach
- 1 cup corn
- A drizzle of olive oil
- 4 tbsp. cheddar; grated.

DIRECTIONS

1. Set the Foodi on Sauté mode, add the oil, heat it up, add the onion and sauté for 4 minutes. Add the green bell pepper and the corn, toss and sauté for 4 more minutes
2. Add the fish, salsa and the spinach, put the pressure lid on and cook on High for 8 minutes. Release the pressure fast for 6 minutes, add the cheese, toss, divide

everything between plates and serve for breakfast

23. Turkey & Cauliflower Casserole

Preparation time: 15 minutes

Cooking time: 30 minutes

Servings: 10

INGREDIENTS

- 3 tablespoons olive oil
- 1 large yellow onion
- 48 ounces cauliflower, grated
- 6 organic eggs
- ¼ cup unsweetened almond milk
- Salt and ground black pepper, as required
- 1 pound cooked turkey meat, chopped
- ½ cup Cheddar cheese, shredded

DIRECTIONS

1. Select "Sauté/Sear" setting of Ninja Foodi and place the oil into the pot.
2. Press "Start/Stop" to begin cooking and heat for about 2-3 minutes.
3. Add the onion and cook for about 4-5 minutes.
4. Press "Start/Stop" to stop cooking and stir in the cauliflower.
5. Close the Ninja Foodi with crisping lid and select "Air Crisp".
6. Set the temperature to 350 degrees F for 30 minutes.
7. Press "Start/Stop" to begin cooking.
8. Meanwhile, in a bowl, add the eggs, almond milk, salt and black pepper and beat well.
9. After 15 minutes of cooking, stir the mixture well.
10. Place the egg mixture over cauliflower mixture evenly and top with the turkey meat.
11. Sprinkle with the cheese and immediately, close the Ninja Foodi with crisping lid for about 1-2 minutes.
12. Open the lid and cut into equal-sized wedges.
13. Serve hot.

NUTRITION: Calories: 215, Fats: 11.2g, Net Carbs: 4.2g, Carbs: 8g, Fiber: 3.8g, Sugar: 4g, Proteins: 20.9g, Sodium: 165mg

24. Beef & Spinach Casserole

Preparation time: 15 minutes

Cooking time: 2 hours 35 minutes

Servings: 6

INGREDIENTS

- 1 teaspoon olive oil
- 1 pound grass-fed lean beef
- 1 (8-ouncecan spinach, drained
- 2 medium yellow onions, chopped
- 1 red bell pepper, chopped
- 10 large organic eggs, beaten
- 4 ounces sharp Cheddar cheese, shredded
- ½ cup feta cheese, crumbled

DIRECTIONS

1. Select "Sauté/Sear" setting of Ninja Foodi and place the oil into the pot.
2. Press "Start/Stop" to begin cooking and heat for about 2-3 minutes.
3. Add the beef and cook for about 4-5 minutes.
4. Press "Start/Stop" to stop cooking and drain the grease from the pot.
5. Add the spinach, onions and bell pepper and mix well.
6. Place the beaten eggs on top evenly, followed by the Cheddar cheese and feta cheese.
7. Close the Ninja Foodi with crisping lid and select "Slow Cooker".
8. Set on "Low" for 2½ hours.
9. Press "Start/Stop" to begin cooking.
10. Cut into equal-sized wedges and serve hot.

NUTRITION: Calories: 396, Fats: 24.9g, Net Carbs: 5.1g, Carbs: 7.1g, Fiber: 2g, Sugar: 3.4g, Proteins: 34g, Sodium: 455mg

25. Pork & Salsa Casserole

Preparation time: 15 minutes

Cooking time: 2 hours 40 minutes

Servings: 10

INGREDIENTS

- 1 teaspoon olive oil
- 1 small yellow onion, chopped
- 2 garlic cloves, minced
- 14 ounces ground pork
- Salt and ground black pepper, as required
- 1¼ cups mild salsa
- 12 organic eggs
- 1¼ cups heavy cream
- 1¼ cups Mexican blend cheese, shredded

DIRECTIONS

1. Select "Sauté/Sear" setting of Ninja Foodi and place the oil into the pot.
2. Press "Start/Stop" to begin cooking and heat for about 2-3 minutes.
3. Add the onion and garlic and cook for about 5 minutes.
4. Add the pork and cook for about 4-5 minutes.
5. Add the salsa, salt and black pepper and stir to combine
6. Press "Start/Stop" to stop cooking and transfer the mixture into a bowl.
7. Set aside to cool slightly.
8. In another bowl, add the eggs and cream and beat well.
9. Add the pork mixture and 1 cup of the cheese and stir to combine.
10. Place the mixture in the pot of Ninja Foodi and top with the remaining cheese.
11. Close the Ninja Foodi with crisping lid and select "Slow Cooker".
12. Set on "Low" for 2½ hours.
13. Press "Start/Stop" to begin cooking.
14. Cut into equal-sized wedges and serve hot.

NUTRITION: Calories: 261, Fats: 17.7g, Net Carbs: 3.6g, Carbs: 3.9g, Fiber: 0.3g, Sugar: 2.4g, Proteins: 21.4g, Sodium: 484mg

26. Sausage & Bell Pepper Casserole

Preparation time: 15 minutes

Cooking time: 24 minutes

Servings: 8

INGREDIENTS

- 1 teaspoon olive oil
- 1 pound ground sausage
- 1 green bell pepper, seeded and chopped
- ¼ cup yellow onion, chopped
- 8 organic eggs, beaten
- ½ cup Colby Jack cheese, shredded
- 1 teaspoon fennel seed
- ½ teaspoon garlic salt

DIRECTIONS

1. Select "Sauté/Sear" setting of Ninja Foodi and place the oil into the pot.
2. Press "Start/Stop" to begin cooking and heat for about 2-3 minutes.
3. Add the sausage and cook for about 4-5 minutes.
4. Add the bell pepper and onion and cook for about 4- minutes.
5. Press "Start/Stop" to stop cooking and transfer the sausage mixture into a bowl to cool slightly.
6. Arrange the "Reversible Rack" in the pot of Ninja Foodi.
7. Close the Ninja Foodi with crisping lid and select "Air Crisp".
8. Set the temperature to 390 degrees F for 5 minutes.
9. Press "Start/Stop" to begin preheating.
10. In a baking pan, place the sausage mixture and top with the cheese, followed by the beaten eggs, fennel seed and garlic salt.
11. After preheating, open the lid.
12. Place the pan over the "Reversible Rack".
13. Close the Ninja Foodi with crisping lid and select "Air Crisp".
14. Set the temperature to 390 degrees F for 15 minutes.
15. Press "Start/Stop" to begin cooking.
16. Cut into equal-sized wedges and serve hot.

NUTRITION: Calories: 295, Fats: 23.4g, Net Carbs: 1.9g, Carbs: 2.3g, Fiber: 0.4g, Sugar: 1.3g, Proteins: 18.3g, Sodium: 532mg

NUTRITION: Calories: 383, Fats: 29.4g, Net Carbs: 4.4g, Carbs: 6g, Fiber: 0.6g, Sugar: 1.7g, Proteins: 23.6g, Sodium: 837mg

27. Sausage & Mushroom Casserole

Preparation time: 15 minutes

Cooking time: 23 minutes

Servings: 6

INGREDIENTS

- 1 tablespoon olive oil
- ½ pound spicy ground sausage
- ¾ cup yellow onion, chopped
- 5 fresh mushrooms, sliced
- 8 organic eggs, beaten
- ½ teaspoon garlic salt
- ¾ cup Cheddar cheese, shredded
- ¼ cup sugar-free Alfredo sauce

DIRECTIONS

1. Select "Sauté/Sear" setting of Ninja Foodi and place the oil into the pot.
2. Press "Start/Stop" to begin cooking and heat for about 2-3 minutes.
3. Add the sausage and onions and cook for about 4-5 minutes.
4. Add the mushrooms and cook for about 6-7 minutes.
5. Press "Start/Stop" to stop cooking and drain the grease from pot.
6. Place the beaten eggs, garlic salt, ½ cup of cheese, Alfredo sauce and garlic salt over the sausage mixture and stir to combine.
7. Close the Ninja Foodi with crisping lid and select "Air Crisp".
8. Set the temperature to 390 degrees for 11 minutes.
9. Press "Start/Stop" to begin cooking.
10. After 6 minutes of cooking, stir the sausage mixture well.
11. Cut into equal-sized wedges and serve hot with the topping of remaining cheese.

28. Sausage & Salsa Casserole

Preparation time: 15 minutes

Cooking time: 5 hours 5 minutes

Servings: 8

INGREDIENTS

- 1 teaspoon butter
- 12 ounces gluten-free turkey sausage
- 1 cup salsa
- 1 teaspoon red chili powder
- 1 teaspoon ground cumin
- ½ teaspoon ground coriander
- ½ teaspoon garlic powder
- Salt and ground black pepper, as required
- 10 organic eggs
- 1 cup unsweetened almond milk
- 1 cup Pepper Jack cheese, shredded

DIRECTIONS

1. Select "Sauté/Sear" setting of Ninja Foodi and place the butter into the pot.
2. Press "Start/Stop" to begin cooking and heat for about 2-3 minutes.
3. Add the sausage and cook for about 4-5 minutes.
4. Discard the grease from the pot.
5. Press "Start/Stop" to stop cooking and transfer the mixture into a bowl.
6. Set aside to cool slightly.
7. In a bowl, add the eggs and almond milk and beat well.
8. Add the sausage mixture and cheese and stir to combine.
9. Place the mixture in the pot of Ninja Foodi and top with the remaining cheese.
10. Close the Ninja Foodi with crisping lid and select "Slow Cooker".
11. Set on "High" for 5 hours.
12. Press "Start/Stop" to begin cooking.
13. Cut into equal-sized wedges and serve hot.

NUTRITION: Calories: 372, Fats: 28.1g, Net Carbs: 3.3g, Carbs: 4.1g, Fiber: 0.8g, Sugar: 1.9g, Proteins: 25.9g, Sodium: 857mg

29. Sausage & Veggies Casserole

Preparation time: 15 minutes

Cooking time: 7 hours 3 minutes

Servings: 8

INGREDIENTS

- 2½ cups cauliflower florets
- 12 organic eggs
- ¾ cup unsweetened almond milk
- 1 teaspoon dried oregano, crushed
- ¾ teaspoon paprika
- Salt, as required
- 1 red bell pepper, seeded and chopped finely
- 1 pound gluten-free cooked sausages, cut into slices
- 1½ cups Cheddar cheese, grated

DIRECTIONS

1. In a large pan of boiling water, cook the cauliflower for about 2-3 minutes.
2. Remove from the heat and drain the cauliflower completely.
3. Set aside to cool.
4. In a bowl, add the eggs, almond milk, oregano, paprika and salt and beat until well combined.
5. In the bottom of a greased pot of Ninja Foodie, place the cauliflowers, followed by the bell pepper, sausage slices and Cheddar cheese.
6. Top with the egg mixture evenly.
7. Close the Ninja Foodi with crisping lid and select "Slow Cooker".
8. Set on "Low" for 6-7 hours.
9. Press "Start/Stop" to begin cooking.
10. Cut into equal-sized wedges and serve hot.

NUTRITION: Calories: 389, Fats: 30.1g, Net Carbs: 2.8g, Carbs: 4g, Fiber: 1.2g, Sugar: 2.2g, Proteins: 25.2g, Sodium: 695mg

30. Ham & Cauliflower Casserole

Preparation time: 15 minutes

Cooking time: 7 hours

Servings: 8

INGREDIENTS

- 12 organic eggs
- ½ cup unsweetened almond milk
- Salt and ground black pepper, as required
- 1 head cauliflower, shredded
- 1 small onion, chopped
- 1 pound sugar-free ham, chopped
- 8 ounces Cheddar cheese, shredded

DIRECTIONS

1. In a bowl, add the eggs, almond milk, salt and black pepper and beat well.
2. In the bottom of the greased pot of Ninja Foodie, place one-third of the cauliflower.
3. Top with one-third of onion.
4. Sprinkle with salt and black pepper.
5. Top with one-third of ham pieces and a third of the cheese.
6. Repeat the layers twice.
7. Top with the egg mixture evenly.
8. Close the Ninja Foodi with crisping lid and select "Slow Cooker".
9. Set on "Low" for 6-7 hours.
10. Press "Start/Stop" to begin cooking.
11. Cut into equal-sized wedges and serve hot.

NUTRITION: Calories: 315, Fats: 21.1g, Net Carbs: 4g, Carbs: 5.8g, Fiber: 1.8g, Sugar: 1.8g, Proteins: 25.6g, Sodium: 1000mg

31. Ham & Broccoli Casserole

Preparation time: 15 minutes

Cooking time: 13 minutes

Servings: 6

INGREDIENTS

- 4 organic eggs
- 1 tablespoon unsweetened almond milk
- ¾ teaspoon taco seasoning
- ¼ teaspoon red chili powder
- Salt, as required
- 6 ounces sugar-free ham, cubed
- 1¾ pounds broccoli, cut into small florets
- ¼ cup yellow onion, chopped
- 1 jalapeño pepper, chopped

DIRECTIONS

1. In a heatproof bowl, add the eggs, water, taco seasonings, chili powder and salt and beat until well combined.
2. Add ham, broccoli, onion and jalapeño pepper and stir to combine.
3. In the pot of Ninja Foodi, place 1 cup of water.
4. Arrange the "Reversible Rack" in the pot of Ninja Foodi.
5. With a piece of foil, cover the bowl and place over the "Reversible Rack".
6. Close the Ninja Foodi with the pressure lid and place the pressure valve to "Seal" position.
7. Select "Pressure" and set to "High" for 13 minutes.
8. Press "Start/Stop" to begin cooking.
9. Switch the valve to "Vent" and do a "Quick" release.
10. Open the lid cut the casserole into desired-sized wedges.
11. Serve hot.

NUTRITION: Calories: 138, Fats: 5.9g, Net Carbs: 5g, Carbs: 9g, Fiber: 4g, Sugar: 2.9g, Proteins: 12.2g, Sodium: 519mg

32. Ham & Zucchini Casserole

Preparation time: 15 minutes

Cooking time: 8 hours 7 minutes

Servings: 10

INGREDIENTS

- 2 tablespoons butter
- 1 onion, chopped
- 1 pound zucchini, chopped
- 1 pound sugar-free ham, cubed
- 12 large organic eggs, beaten
- 1 cup heavy whipping cream
- 16 ounces Cheddar cheese, shredded

DIRECTIONS

1. Select "Sauté/Sear" setting of Ninja Foodi and place the butter into the pot.
2. Press "Start/Stop" to begin cooking and heat for about 2-3 minutes.
3. Add the onion and cook for about 4-5 minutes.
4. Add the zucchini and cook for about 1-2 minutes.
5. Meanwhile, in a bowl, add the eggs and cream and beat well.
6. Press "Start/Stop" to stop cooking and stir in the ham, egg mixture and cheese.
7. Close the Ninja Foodi with crisping lid and select "Slow Cooker".
8. Set on "Low" for 8 hours.
9. Press "Start/Stop" to begin cooking.
10. Cut into equal-sized wedges and serve hot.

NUTRITION: Calories: 520, Fats: 39.7g, Net Carbs: 5.4g, Carbs: 7.1g, Fiber: 1.7g, Sugar: 2.5g, Proteins: 34.2g, Sodium: 1200mg

33. Mushroom Casserole

Preparation time: 15 minutes

Cooking time: 6 hours

Servings: 8

INGREDIENTS

- 12 organic eggs
- ½ cup unsweetened almond milk
- Salt and ground black pepper, as required
- 2½ cups fresh baby Bella mushrooms, sliced
- ½ cup sun-dried tomatoes
- 1 tablespoon yellow onion, chopped

- 1 teaspoon garlic, minced
- ½ cup feta cheese, crumbled

DIRECTIONS

1. In a large bowl, add the eggs, almond milk, salt and black and beat until well combined.
2. Add the remaining ingredients except cheese and stir to combine.
3. In the bottom of a greased Ninja Foodie, place the egg mixture and top with the cheese.
4. Close the Ninja Foodi with crisping lid and select "Slow Cooker".
5. Set on "Low" for 4-6 hours.
6. Press "Start/Stop" to begin cooking.
7. Cut into equal-sized wedges and serve hot.

NUTRITION: Calories: 189, Fats: 13.1g, Net Carbs: 3.8g, Carbs: 4.9g, Fiber: 1.1g, Sugar: 1.6g, Proteins: 14.1g, Sodium: 338mg

34. Bacon & Cheese Quiche

Preparation time: 5 minutes

Cooking time: 10 minutes

Servings: 6

INGREDIENTS

- 1 cup cooked bacon, crumbled and divided
- 6 organic eggs
- Salt and ground black pepper, as required
- 1½ cups Gruyere cheese, shredded and divided
- 1 cup cottage cheese
- ½ cup Parmesan cheese, shredded

DIRECTIONS

1. In the pot of Ninja Foodi, place 1 cup of water.
2. Arrange the "Reversible Rack" in the pot of Ninja Foodi.
3. In the bottom of a baking pan, place ½ cup of the bacon.
4. Place the pan over the "Reversible Rack".

5. Close the Ninja Foodi with the crisping lid and select "Broil" for 5 minutes.
6. Press "Start/Stop" to begin preheating.
7. In a blender, add the eggs, 1 cup of gruyere cheese, cottage cheese, Parmesan cheese, salt and black pepper and pulse until smooth.
8. After preheating, open the lid.
9. Place the cheese mixture over the bacon in the pan.
10. Close the Ninja Foodi with the pressure lid and place the pressure valve to "Seal" position.
11. Select "Pressure" and set to "High" for 10 minutes.
12. Press "Start/Stop" to begin cooking.
13. Switch the valve to "Vent" and do a "Quick" release.
14. Open the lid and sprinkle the top of quiche with the remaining cheese and bacon.
15. Now, close the Ninja Foodi with crisping lid and select "Air Crisp".
16. Set the temperature to 330 degrees for 4 minutes.
17. Press "Start/Stop" to begin cooking.
18. Cut into equal-sized wedges and serve hot.

NUTRITION: Calories: 415, Fats: 29.5g, Net Carbs: 2.5g, Carbs: 2.5g, Fiber: 0g, Sugar: 0.6g, Proteins: 133.6g, Sodium: 1100mg

35. Spinach Quiche

Preparation time: 10 minutes

Cooking time: 4 hours

Servings: 4

INGREDIENTS

- 10 ounces frozen chopped spinach, thawed and squeezed
- 4 ounces feta cheese, shredded
- 2 cups unsweetened almond milk
- 4 organic eggs
- ¼ teaspoon red pepper flakes, crushed
- Salt and ground black pepper, as required

DIRECTIONS

1. In the pot of Ninja Foodie, add all the ingredients and mix until well combined.
2. Close the Ninja Foodi with crisping lid and select "Slow Cooker".
3. Set on "Low" for 4 hours.
4. Press "Start/Stop" to begin cooking.
5. Cut into equal-sized wedges and serve hot.

NUTRITION: Calories: 174, Fats: 12.5g, Net Carbs: 3g, Carbs: 5.1g, Fiber: 2.1g, Sugar: 1.8g, Proteins: 12.1g, Sodium: 563mg

36. Coconut Cereal

Preparation time: 10 minutes

Cooking time: 8 hours

Servings: 6

INGREDIENTS

- 1 cup unsweetened coconut, shredded
- 2 cups unsweetened almond milk
- 2 cups water
- 1/3 cup coconut flour, divided
- ½ teaspoon ground cinnamon
- ½ teaspoon organic vanilla extract
- ¼ teaspoon liquid stevia

DIRECTIONS

1. In the pot of Ninja Foodie, add the coconut, almond milk, water, ¼ cup of coconut flour and cinnamon and with a wire whisk, mix until well combined.
2. Close the Ninja Foodi with crisping lid and select "Slow Cooker".
3. Set on "Low" for 8 hours.
4. Press "Start/Stop" to begin cooking.
5. Stir in the remaining coconut flour, vanilla extract and stevia until well combined.
6. Immediately, close the Ninja Foodi with crisping lid for about 2-3 minutes.
7. Serve warm.

NUTRITION: Calories: 65, Fats: 5.7g, Net Carbs: 1.4g, Carbs: 3.3g, Fiber: 1.9g, Sugar: 0.9g, Proteins: o.9g, Sodium: 67mg

37. Nuts Granola

Preparation time: 10 minutes

Cooking time: 1½ hours

Servings: 12

INGREDIENTS

- 1 cup raw pecans
- 1 cup raw almonds
- 1 cup raw walnuts
- 1½ teaspoons ground cinnamon
- ¼ cup Erythritol

DIRECTIONS

1. In the greased pot of Ninja Foodie, add all the ingredients and mix until well combined.
2. Close the Ninja Foodi with crisping lid and select "Slow Cooker".
3. Set on "Low" for 1½-2 hours.
4. Press "Start/Stop" to begin cooking.
5. Transfer the granola onto a large baking sheet and set aside to cool completely before serving.

NUTRITION: Calories: 184, Fats: 17.6g, Net Carbs: 6g, Carbs: 9g, Fiber: 3g, Sugar: 5.8g, Proteins: 5.3g, Sodium: 0mg

38. Nuts & Seeds Granola

Preparation time: 15 minutes

Cooking time: 2 hours

Servings: 12

INGREDIENTS

- 1/3 cup unsalted butter
- 1 teaspoon liquid stevia
- 1 teaspoon organic vanilla extract

- 1½ cups pumpkin seeds
- 1½ cups sunflower seeds
- ½ cup raw pecans, chopped roughly
- ½ cup raw hazelnuts, chopped roughly
- ½ cup raw walnuts, chopped roughly
- ½ cup raw almonds, chopped roughly
- 1 teaspoon ground cinnamon

DIRECTIONS

1. Select "Sauté/Sear" setting of Ninja Foodi and place the butter into the pot.
2. Press "Start/Stop" to begin cooking and heat for about 2-3 minutes.
3. Add the liquid stevia and vanilla extract and stir to combine.
4. Immediately, press "Start/Stop" to stop cooking
5. Now, add the remaining ingredients and stir to combine.
6. Close the Ninja Foodi with crisping lid and select "Slow Cooker".
7. Set on "Low" for 2 hours, stirring after every 30 minutes.
8. Press "Start/Stop" to begin cooking.
9. Transfer the granola onto a large baking sheet and set aside to cool completely before serving.

NUTRITION: Calories: 315, Fats: 29.3g, Net Carbs: 4.2g, Carbs: 7.6g, Fiber: 3.4g, Sugar: 1.1g, Proteins: 8.7g, Sodium: 40mg

39. Chocolaty Granola

Preparation time: 15 minutes

Cooking time: 2 hours

Servings: 20

INGREDIENTS

- 5 cups unsweetened coconut, shredded
- 1 cup almonds, chopped
- 1/3 cups sunflower seeds
- 1/3 cups pumpkin seeds
- ¼ cup cacao nibs
- 2½ ounces coconut oil, melted
- 3 tablespoons Erythritol

- 4 tablespoons cocoa powder unsweetened
- 1 tablespoon lemon zest, grated finely

DIRECTIONS

1. In the pot of Ninja Foodi, add all ingredients and mix well.
2. Close the Ninja Foodi with crisping lid and select "Slow Cooker".
3. Set on "High" for 2 hours.
4. Press "Start/Stop" to begin cooking.
5. Stir the mixture after every 15 minutes.
6. Transfer the granola onto a large baking sheet and set aside to cool completely before serving.

NUTRITION: Calories: 268, Fats: 27.1g, Net Carbs: 2.5g, Carbs: 6.6g, Fiber: 3.5g, Sugar: 2.3g, Proteins: 3.1g, Sodium: 15mg

40. Pumpkin Bread

Preparation time: 15 minutes

Cooking time: 25 minutes

Servings: 4

INGREDIENTS

- ¼ cup coconut flour
- 2 tablespoons stevia blend
- 1 teaspoon organic baking powder
- ¾ teaspoon pumpkin pie spice
- ¼ teaspoon ground cinnamon
- 1/8 teaspoon salt
- ¼ cup canned pumpkin
- 2 large eggs
- 2 tablespoons unsweetened almond milk
- 1 teaspoon organic vanilla extract

DIRECTIONS

1. In a bowl, add the flour, stevia blend, baking powder, spices and salt and mix well.
2. In another large bowl, add the pumpkin, eggs, almond milk, and vanilla extract. Beat until well combined.

3. Add the flour mixture and mix until just combined.
4. Arrange the "Cook & Crisp Basket" in the pot of Ninja Foodi.
5. Close the Ninja Foodi with crisping lid and select "Air Crisp".
6. Set the temperature to 350 degrees F for 5 minutes.
7. Press "Start/Stop" to begin preheating.
8. Place the mixture into a greased parchment paper lined cake pan evenly.
9. After preheating, open the lid.
10. Place the pan into the "Cook & Crisp Basket".
11. Close the Ninja Foodi with crisping lid and select "Air Crisp".
12. Set the temperature to 350 degrees F for 25 minutes.
13. Press "Start/Stop" to begin cooking.
14. Remove the bread pan from pot and place onto a wire rack for about 5-10 minutes.
15. Carefully, remove the bread from pan and place onto a wire rack to cool completely before slicing.
16. Cut the bread into desired-sized slices and serve.

NUTRITION: Calories: 52, Fats: 2.8g, Net Carbs: 2.1g, Carbs: 3g, Fiber: 0.9g, Sugar: 0.9g, Proteins: 3.5g, Sodium: 118mg

41. Zucchini Bread

Preparation time: 15 minutes

Cooking time: 3 hours

Servings: 12

INGREDIENTS

- 1 cup almond flour
- 1/3 cup coconut flour
- 1½ teaspoon organic baking powder
- ½ teaspoon baking soda
- 2 teaspoons ground cinnamon
- ½ teaspoon xanthan gum
- ½ teaspoon salt
- 3 organic eggs
- ¾ cup Erythritol

- 1/3 cup butter, softened
- 2 teaspoons organic vanilla extract
- 2 cups zucchini, shredded
- ½ cup pecans, chopped

DIRECTIONS

1. In a bowl, add the flours, baking powder, baking soda, cinnamon, xanthan gum and salt and mix well.
2. In another large bowl, add the eggs, Erythritol, butter and vanilla extract and beat until well combined.
3. Add the flour mixture and mix until just combined.
4. Fold in the zucchini and pecans.
5. Place the mixture into a silicone bread pan evenly.
6. Arrange a "Reversible Rack" in the pot of Ninja Foodi about ½-inch from the bottom.
7. Place the pan over the "Reversible Rack".
8. Close the Ninja Foodi with crisping lid and select "Slow Cooker".
9. Set on "High" for 2½-3 hours.
10. Press "Start/Stop" to begin cooking.
11. Place the bread pan onto a wire rack for about 5-10 minutes.
12. Carefully, remove the bread from pan and place onto the wire rack to cool completely before slicing.
13. Cut the bread into desired-sized slices and serve.

NUTRITION: Calories: 160, Fats: 14.7g, Net Carbs: 2.3g, Carbs: 4.7g, Fiber: 2.4g, Sugar: 1.1g, Proteins: 4.3g, Sodium: 210mg

42. Zucchini & Coconut Bread

Preparation time: 15 minutes

Cooking time: 3 hours

Servings: 10

INGREDIENTS

- 2½ cups zucchini, shredded
- ½ teaspoon salt
- 1 1/3 cups almond flour

- 2/3 cup coconut, shredded
- ½ cup Erythritol
- ¼ cup unflavored whey protein powder
- 2 teaspoons organic baking powder
- 2 teaspoons ground cinnamon
- ½ teaspoon ground ginger
- ¼ teaspoon ground nutmeg
- 3 large organic eggs
- ¼ cup butter, melted
- ¼ cup water
- ½ teaspoon organic vanilla extract
- ½ cup walnuts, chopped

DIRECTIONS

1. Arrange a large sieve in a sink.
2. Place the zucchini in sieve and sprinkle with salt. Set aside to drain for about 1 hour.
3. With your hands, squeeze out the moisture from zucchini.
4. In a large bowl, add the almond flour, coconut, Erythritol, protein powder, baking powder and spices and mix well.
5. Add the zucchini, eggs, coconut oil, water, and vanilla extract and mix until well combined.
6. Fold in the walnuts.
7. In the bottom of a greased Ninja Foodie, place the mixture.
8. Close the Ninja Foodi with crisping lid and select "Slow Cooker".
9. Set on "Low" for 2½-3 hours.
10. Press "Start/Stop" to begin cooking.
11. Keep the bread inside for about 5-10 minutes.
12. Carefully, remove the bread from pot and place onto a wire rack to cool completely before slicing.
13. Cut the bread into desired-sized slices and serve.

NUTRITION: Calories: 224, Fats: 19.1g, Net Carbs: 3.7g, Carbs: 6.8g, Fiber: 3.1g, Sugar: 1.6g, Proteins: 10g, Sodium: 180mg

43. Carrot Bread

Preparation time: 15 minutes

Cooking time: 3 hours

Servings: 12

INGREDIENTS

- 1 cup almond flour
- 1/3 cup coconut flour
- 1½ teaspoons organic baking powder
- ½ teaspoon baking soda
- ½ teaspoon xanthan gum
- 1 teaspoon ground cinnamon
- ¼ teaspoon ground cloves
- ¼ teaspoon ground nutmeg
- ¼ teaspoon salt
- 1 cup Erythritol
- 1/3 cup coconut oil, softened
- 3 organic eggs
- 1 teaspoon organic vanilla extract
- ½ teaspoon organic almond extract
- 2 cups plus 2 tablespoons carrots, peeled and shredded

DIRECTIONS

1. In a bowl, add the flours, baking powder, baking soda, spices and salt and mix well.
2. In another large bowl, add the Erythritol, coconut oil, eggs and both extracts and beat until well combined.
3. Add the flour mixture and mix until just combined.
4. Fold in the carrots.
5. Place the mixture into a greased 8x4-inch silicone bread pan.
6. Arrange a "Reversible Rack" in the pot of Ninja Foodi.
7. Place the pan over the "Reversible Rack".
8. Close the Ninja Foodi with crisping lid and select "Slow Cooker".
9. Set on "Low" for 3 hours.
10. Press "Start/Stop" to begin cooking.
11. Place the bread pan onto a wire rack for about 5-10 minutes.
12. Carefully, remove the bread from pan and place onto the wire rack to cool completely before slicing.
13. Cut the bread into desired-sized slices and serve.

NUTRITION: Calories: 133, Fats: 11.9g, Net Carbs: 3g, Carbs: 4.8g, Fiber: 1.8g, Sugar: 1.4g, Proteins: 3.6g, Sodium: 178mg

44. Savory Cauliflower Bread

Preparation time: 15 minutes

Cooking time: 4 hours

Servings: 8

INGREDIENTS

- 12 ounces cauliflower florets
- 2 large organic eggs
- 2 cups mozzarella cheese, shredded and divided
- 3 tablespoons coconut flour
- Salt and ground black pepper, as required
- 2 garlic cloves, minced

DIRECTIONS

1. In a food processor, add cauliflower and pulse until rice-like consistency is achieved.
2. Transfer the cauliflower rice into a large bowl.
3. Add 1 cup of the cheese, eggs, coconut flour, salt and black pepper and mix until well combined.
4. In a greased pot of Ninja Foodie, place the cauliflower mixture and press firmly.
5. Sprinkle with garlic and remaining cheese evenly.
6. Close the Ninja Foodi with crisping lid and select "Slow Cooker".
7. Set on "High" for 2-4 hours.
8. Press "Start/Stop" to begin cooking.
9. Keep the bread inside for about 5-10 minutes.
10. Carefully, remove the bread from pot and place onto a platter.
11. Cut the bread into desired-sized slices and serve warm.

NUTRITION: Calories: 72, Fats: 3.3g, Net Carbs: 2.9g, Carbs: 5.9g, Fiber: 3g, Sugar: 1.5g, Proteins: 5.2g, Sodium: 104mg

45. Pecan & Coconut Porridge

Preparation time: 15 minutes

Cooking time: 1 hour

Servings: 4

INGREDIENTS

- 1 cup pecan halves
- ½ cup unsweetened dried coconut shreds
- ¼ cup pumpkin seeds, shelled
- 1 cup water
- 2 teaspoons butter, melted
- 4-6 drops liquid stevia

DIRECTIONS

1. In a food processor, add the pecans, coconut and pumpkin seeds and pulse for about 30 seconds.
2. In the pot of Ninja Foodie, place the pecan mixture and remaining ingredients and stir to combine.
3. Close the Ninja Foodi with crisping lid and select "Slow Cooker".
4. Set on "High" for 1 hour.
5. Press "Start/Stop" to begin cooking.
6. Serve warm.

NUTRITION: Calories: 317, Fats: 31.5g, Net Carbs: 2.9g, Carbs: 7.5g, Fiber: 4.6g, Sugar: 1.8g, Proteins: 5.8g, Sodium: 19mg

46. Pumpkin Porridge

Preparation time: 15 minutes

Cooking time: 5 hours

Servings: 8

INGREDIENTS

- 1 cup unsweetened almond milk, divided
- 2 pounds pumpkin, peeled and cubed into ½-inch size
- 6-8 drops liquid stevia
- ½ teaspoon ground allspice

- 1 tablespoon ground cinnamon
- 1 teaspoon ground nutmeg
- ¼ teaspoon ground cloves

DIRECTIONS

1. In the pot of Ninja Foodie, place ½ cup of almond milk and remaining ingredients and stir to combine.
2. Close the Ninja Foodi with crisping lid and select "Slow Cooker".
3. Set on "Low" for 4-5 hours.
4. Press "Start/Stop" to begin cooking.
5. Stir in the remaining almond milk and with a potato masher, mash the mixture completely.
6. Serve warm.

NUTRITION: Calories: 48, Fats: 0.9g, Net Carbs: 6g, Carbs: 10g, Fiber: 4g, Sugar: 3.8g, Proteins: 1.4g, Sodium: 29mg

47. Breakfast Hasbrown Casserole

Preparation Time: 40 minutes

Servings: 10

INGREDIENTS

- 1 lb. ham; chopped.
- 48 oz. hashbrowns
- ½ cup cheddar cheese, shredded
- 1 yellow onion; chopped.
- ¼ cup milk
- 6 eggs; whisked.
- 3 tbsp. olive oil

DIRECTIONS

1. Set your Foodi on sauté mode, add the oil, heat it up, add the onion, stir and cook for 3-4 minutes.
2. Add hashbrowns and the ham, set the Foodi on Air Crisp and cook for 15 minutes, stirring everything halfway
3. Add eggs mixed with hashbrowns and cook everything on Air Crisp for 10 minutes more. Sprinkle the cheese on top, divide

everything between plates and serve for breakfast

48. Delicious Frittata

Preparation Time: 35 minutes

Servings: 6

INGREDIENTS

- 8 oz. white mushrooms, sliced
- 2 leeks; chopped.
- 12 eggs; whisked.
- ½ cup crème fraiche
- 1 cup cheddar cheese, shredded
- 1 cup water
- 3 tbsp. olive oil
- 2 tbsp. parsley; chopped.
- A pinch of salt and black pepper

DIRECTIONS

1. Set the Foodi on Sauté mode, add the oil and heat it up. Add the leeks, stir and cook for 5 minutes. Add the mushrooms, stir and cook for another 5 minutes
2. In a bowl mix the eggs with the crème fraiche, parsley, salt and pepper and whisk. Add the sautéed mushrooms mix and stir again
3. Add the water to the Foodi, add the reversible rack, add the baking pan inside and pour the eggs mixture inside
4. Set the Foodi on High Pressure and cook everything for 10 minutes. Release the pressure fast for 5 minutes, divide the frittata between plates and serve

49. Mexican Breakfast

Preparation Time: 15 minutes

Servings: 2

INGREDIENTS

- 1 green bell pepper, sliced
- 2 eggs; whisked.
- 1 avocado, peeled, pitted and sliced

- 2 tortillas
- 2 tbsp. cheddar cheese; grated.
- 2 tbsp. salsa
- Salt and black pepper to the taste

DIRECTIONS

1. In a bowl mix all the ingredients except the tortillas and toss them. Put all the ingredients in the Foodi, put the pressure lid on, seal and cook on High for 10 minutes, shaking the Foodi halfway
2. Release the pressure naturally for 10 minutes, divide the bell peppers mix on the tortillas, roll them and serve for breakfast

50. Bacon and Mushrooms

Preparation Time: 17 minutes

Servings: 4

INGREDIENTS

- 10 brown mushrooms, sliced
- ½ cup heavy cream
- ¼ cup cheddar cheese; grated.
- 3 eggs; whisked.
- 1 red onion; chopped.
- 1 tbsp. canola oil
- 2 tbsp. bacon; chopped.
- ½ tsp. thyme, dried
- Salt and black pepper to the taste

DIRECTIONS

1. Set the Foodi on Sauté mode, add the oil and heat it up. Add the bacon, stir and cook for 3 minutes. Add the onion, thyme and the mushrooms, stir and sauté for 4 more minutes
2. Add the eggs mixed with the cream, salt and pepper, set the Foodi on Air Crisp and cook everything for 8 minutes at 370 °F. Sprinkle the cheese all over, toss the mix a bit, divide between plates and serve for breakfast

51. Cheese Peppers Frittata

Preparation Time: 30 minutes

Servings: 6

INGREDIENTS

- 6 oz. jarred roasted red bell peppers; chopped.
- 3 garlic cloves; minced.
- 12 eggs; whisked.
- ½ cup parmesan; grated.
- 2 tbsp. parsley; chopped.
- 2 tbsp. chives; chopped.
- 6 tbsp. ricotta cheese
- A drizzle of olive oil
- Salt and black pepper to the taste

DIRECTIONS

1. In a bowl mix the bell peppers with the eggs, garlic, parsley, salt, pepper, chives and ricotta and whisk. Grease the Foodi's baking pan with the oil and pour the eggs mixture inside
2. Add the reversible rack to the machine, add the baking pan and cook on Baking mode at 300 °F for 20 minutes. Divide between plates and serve

52. Paprika Scrambled Eggs

Preparation Time: 20 minutes

Servings: 4

INGREDIENTS

- 4 eggs; whisked.
- 1 red onion; chopped.
- A drizzle of olive oil
- 2 tsp. sweet paprika
- Salt and black pepper to the taste

DIRECTIONS

1. In a bowl mix the eggs with salt, pepper, the onion and the paprika and whisk. Set

the Foodi on Sauté mode, add the oil, heat it up and add the eggs mix

2. Stir everything well, set the Foodi on Air Crisp and cook the eggs for 10 minutes at 360 °F, shaking the machine halfway. Divide between plates and serve for breakfast

53. Ninja Baked Omelet

Preparation Time: 40 minutes

Servings: 6

INGREDIENTS

- ½ cup red bell pepper; chopped.
- ½ cup green bell pepper; chopped.
- ½ cup chives; chopped.
- 1 cup ham, cooked and chopped
- 1 cup cheddar cheese, shredded
- ½ cup milk
- 8 eggs; whisked.
- A pinch of salt and black pepper
- Cooking spray

DIRECTIONS

1. Put the reversible rack in the Foodi, place the baking pan inside and grease it with cooking spray. In a bowl mix the milk with the eggs, cheese, ham, salt, pepper, bell peppers and the chives and whisk well
2. Pour this into the baking pan, set the Foodi on Bake mode at 315 °F and cook for 30 minutes. Divide the omelet between plates and serve

54. Cheesy Omelet

Preparation Time: 15 minutes

Servings: 2

INGREDIENTS

- 4 eggs; whisked.
- 1 cup cheddar cheese; grated.
- 4 tsp. butter, melted
- 1 tbsp. chives; chopped.
- A pinch of salt and black pepper

DIRECTIONS

1. In a bowl mix half of the butter with all the other ingredients and whisk. Put the reversible rack in the Foodi, add the baking pan inside and grease it with the remaining butter
2. Add the eggs mix in the pan and cook on Baking mode at 370 °F for 10 minutes. Serve for breakfast

55. Bread and Corn Pudding

Preparation Time: 55 minutes

Servings: 6

INGREDIENTS

- 4 bacon slices, cooked and chopped
- 1 ½ cups coconut milk
- 4 eggs; whisked.
- 3 cups bread; cubed.
- 1 tbsp. olive oil
- ½ cup coconut cream
- 2 cups corn
- ½ cup green bell pepper; chopped.
- 1 yellow onion; chopped.
- 3 tbsp. parmesan cheese; grated.
- 1 tsp. thyme; chopped.
- 2 tsp. garlic; grated.
- Salt and black pepper

DIRECTIONS

1. Set the Foodi on Sauté mode, add the oil, heat it up, add the onion and garlic, stir and sauté for 5 minutes. Add the corn, bell peppers, thyme, salt and pepper, toss, cook for 5 more minutes and transfer everything to the Foodi's baking pan
2. Add the eggs mixed with the cream, bread and milk and toss everything
3. Place the reversible rack in the machine, add the baking pan inside, sprinkle the parmesan and the bacon on top and cook on Baking mode at 350 °F for 35 minutes. Divide between plates and serve for breakfast.

56. Blackberries Bowls

Preparation Time: 15 minutes

Servings: 4

INGREDIENTS

- 1 ½ cups corn flakes
- ¼ cup blackberries
- 3 cups milk
- 2 eggs; whisked.
- 4 tbsp. cream cheese, whipped
- 1 tbsp. sugar
- ¼ tsp. nutmeg, ground

DIRECTIONS

1. In a bowl combine all the ingredients: , toss them and pour the whole mixture in the Foodi's baking pan.
2. Add the reversible rack in the machine, add the baking pan and cook the mix on Baking mode at 350 °F for 10 minutes. Divide between plates and serve for breakfast

57. Parmesan Scrambled Eggs

Preparation Time: 17 minutes

Servings: 4

INGREDIENTS

- 3 oz. almond milk
- 2 oz. parmesan cheese; grated.
- 4 eggs; whisked.
- A drizzle olive oil
- A splash of Worcestershire sauce

DIRECTIONS

1. In a bowl mix all the ingredients except the oil and toss well. Set the Foodi on sauté mode, add the oil, heat it up, add the eggs mix, toss, set the machine on Air Crisp and cook for 12 minutes at 360 °F, shaking the pot from time to time. Divide the eggs between plates and serve for breakfast.

58. Pear and Walnuts Oatmeal

Preparation Time: 25 minutes

Servings: 4

INGREDIENTS

- 2 cups pears, peeled and cubed
- ¼ cups sugar
- 1 cup almond milk
- 1 cup old fashioned oats
- ½ cup walnuts; chopped.
- 1 tbsp. butter, soft
- ½ tsp. cinnamon powder

DIRECTIONS

1. Put all the ingredients in the Foodi, toss them, put the pressure lid on and cook on High for 15 minutes. Release the pressure naturally for 10 minutes, divide the oatmeal into bowls and serve for breakfast

59. Tomato Omelet

Preparation Time: 40 minutes

Servings: 2

INGREDIENTS

- 2 eggs; whisked.
- ¼ cup coconut milk
- ½ cup tomatoes; cubed.
- ½ cup cheddar cheese, shredded
- 2 tbsp. spring onions; chopped.
- A pinch of salt and black pepper

DIRECTIONS

1. In a bowl mix all the ingredients: , toss and pour everything into the Foodi's baking pan
2. Place the reversible rack in the machine, add the baking pan and cook the omelet on Baking mode at 360 °F for 30 minutes. Divide the omelet between plates and serve

60. Kale Scramble

Preparation Time: 15 minutes

Servings: 2

INGREDIENTS

- 2 cups kale, torn
- 2 eggs; whisked.
- 1 small shallot; chopped.
- 1 ½ tbsp. mayonnaise
- 1 tsp. olive oil
- A pinch of salt and black pepper

DIRECTIONS

1. Set the Foodi on Sauté mode, add the oil and heat it up. Add the shallot, salt and pepper, stir and cook for 2-3 minutes. Add the kale, toss and cook for 3 more minutes
2. Add the eggs mixed with the mayo, toss everything, set the Foodi on Air Crisp and cook the scramble for 3 minutes at 370 °F. Divide between plates and serve for breakfast

61. Thyme Omelet

Preparation Time: 15 minutes

Servings: 6

INGREDIENTS

- 6 eggs; whisked.
- 1 tsp. thyme, dried
- 2 tbsp. olive oil
- Salt and black pepper to the taste

DIRECTIONS

1. Set the Foodi on Sauté mode, add the oil, heat it, up, add the eggs mixed with thyme, salt and pepper, spread into the Foodi, put the pressure lid on and cook on High for 8 minutes.
2. Release the pressure naturally for 10 minutes, divide between plates and serve for breakfast

62. Chicken Sausage Omelet

Preparation Time: 20 minutes

Servings: 4

INGREDIENTS

- 1 chicken sausage link, sliced
- 4 cherry tomatoes; cubed.
- 4 eggs; whisked.
- 1 tbsp. olive oil
- 1 tbsp. cheddar; grated.
- 1 tbsp. parsley; chopped.
- Salt and black pepper to the taste

DIRECTIONS

1. Put the sausage in the Foodi's basket, set the machine on Roast, cook at 360 °F for 5 minutes and transfer to the machine's baking pan
2. In a bowl mix all the other ingredients: , toss and pour over the sausage. Place the reversible rack in the Foodi, add the baking pan inside and cook everything on Baking mode at 360 °F for 10 minutes. Serve for breakfast.

63. Almond Hash Browns

Preparation Time: 30 minutes

Servings: 6

INGREDIENTS

- 1 ½ lbs. hash browns
- 6 bacon slices; chopped.
- 9 oz. cream cheese
- 1 yellow onion; chopped.
- 1 cup almond milk
- A drizzle of olive oil
- 6 eggs
- 6 spring onions; chopped.
- 2 tbsp. cheddar cheese, shredded
- Salt and black pepper to the taste

DIRECTIONS

1. Set your Foodi on sauté mode, add the oil, heat it up, add the onion and spring onions, stir and cook for 5 minutes.
2. Add hashbrowns and the bacon, set the Foodi on Air Crisp and cook for 15 minutes, stirring everything halfway
3. Add eggs mixed with cream cheese, milk, salt and pepper, toss and cook everything on Air Crisp for 10 minutes more. Divide between plates, sprinkle the cheese on top and serve for breakfast

64. Quick Apple Oatmeal

Preparation Time: 25 minutes

Servings: 8

INGREDIENTS

- 4 apples, cored and cubed
- ½ cup raisins
- 1/3 cup brown sugar
- 2 cups steel cut oats
- 6 cups water
- 2 tbsp. maple syrup
- 1 tbsp. butter
- 1 tsp. cinnamon powder

DIRECTIONS

1. Put all the ingredients in the Foodi and toss them. Put the pressure lid on, seal and cook on High for 15 minutes, shaking the Foodi halfway
2. Release the pressure naturally for 10 minutes, stir the oatmeal again, divide into bowls and serve

65. Creamy Chili

Preparation Time: 15 minutes

Servings: 4

INGREDIENTS

- 4 eggs; whisked.

- 1 red chili pepper; chopped.
- 2 tbsp. heavy cream
- 2 tbsp. parsley, finely chopped
- Salt and white pepper to the taste

DIRECTIONS

1. In a bowl mix all the ingredients and toss them. Add the reversible rack to the Foodi, add the baking pan and pour the creamy chili mix inside
2. Cook the mix on Baking mode at 400 °F for 10 minutes. Divide the mix between plates and serve

66. Eggplant Breakfast

Preparation Time: 40 minutes

Servings: 2

INGREDIENTS

- 2 eggplants; cubed.
- ¾ cup tomato paste
- 2 cups mozzarella cheese; grated.
- 1 tbsp. avocado oil
- 2 tbsp. cheddar; grated.
- 2 tbsp. fresh basil; chopped.
- 2 tbsp. coconut milk
- ½ tsp. garlic powder
- 2 tsp. cilantro; chopped.
- ½ tsp. Italian seasoning
- Salt and black pepper to the taste

DIRECTIONS

1. Set the Foodi on Sauté mode, add the oil and heat it up. Add the eggplants, salt, pepper, garlic powder and Italian seasoning, toss and cook for 6 minutes
2. Add the milk, tomato paste and all the cheese, set the Foodi on Air Crisp and cook for 10 minutes at 370 °F. Sprinkle the cilantro and the basil on top, divide everything into bowls and serve for breakfast

67. Apple Pudding

Preparation Time: 25 minutes

Servings: 4

INGREDIENTS

- 2 eggs; whisked.
- 1 cup apple, peeled, cored and chopped
- 1 ¼ cups milk
- 2 tbsp. sugar
- ¼ tsp. vanilla extract
- 2 tsp. cinnamon powder
- Cooking spray

DIRECTIONS

1. In a bowl mix all the ingredients except the cooking spray and whisk well. Put the reversible rack in the Foodi machine and add the baking pan inside
2. Grease the pan with the cooking spray and pour the apples mix. Set the Foodi on Baking mode and cook the pudding at 360 °F for 15 minutes. Divide into bowls and serve for breakfast.

68. Artichokes Omelet

Preparation Time: 20 minutes

Servings: 4

INGREDIENTS

- 4 eggs; whisked.
- 4 oz. canned artichokes; drained. and chopped
- 4 garlic cloves; minced.
- 1 tbsp. olive oil
- 1 tsp. soy sauce
- Salt and black pepper to the taste

DIRECTIONS

1. In a bowl mix all the ingredients except the oil and whisk them well. Add the reversible rack in the Foodi, add the baking pan, grease it with the oil and pour the artichokes mix inside
2. Cook the omelet on Baking mode at 350 °F for 10 minutes. Slice the omelet and serve it for breakfast

69. Avocado Mix

Preparation Time: 20 minutes

Servings: 2

INGREDIENTS

- 4 bacon slices; chopped.
- 2 avocados, peeled, pitted and cut into segments
- 1 tbsp. sriracha sauce
- 1 tbsp. lime juice
- A pinch of salt and black pepper

DIRECTIONS

1. Set the Foodi on Sauté mode, heat it up, add the bacon and cook for 4-5 minutes. Add the avocados and all the other ingredients: , toss a bit, cook for another 5 minutes, divide into bowls and serve

70. Yogurt and Spinach Omelet

Preparation Time: 15 minutes

Servings: 8

INGREDIENTS

- ½ lb. baby spinach
- 8 eggs; whisked.
- 1 ½ cup Greek yogurt
- ½ cup mint; chopped.
- 2 tbsp. olive oil
- Salt and black pepper to the taste

DIRECTIONS

1. In a bowl mix all the ingredients except the oil and whisk well. Add the reversible rack to the Foodi, add the baking pan and pour the eggs mix into the pan

2. Set the Foodi on Baking mode, cook the omelet at 360 °F for 10 minutes, divide between plates and serve for breakfast

71. Mushrooms and Squash Bowls

Preparation Time: 15 minutes

Servings: 4

INGREDIENTS

- 1 red bell pepper, roughly chopped
- 1 yellow squash; cubed.
- 2 green onions, sliced
- 1 cup white mushrooms, sliced
- ½ cup cheddar cheese
- 2 tbsp. olive oil

DIRECTIONS

1. Set the Foodi on Sauté mode, add the oil, heat it, up, add the peppers, mushrooms, onions and the squash, toss and sauté for 5 minutes.
2. Put the pressure lid on, cook everything on High for 5 more minutes, release the pressure fast for 5 minutes, divide into bowls and serve for breakfast

MAINS

72. Lemony Shrimp Pasta

Preparation time: 13 minutes

Servings: 4

INGREDIENTS

- 1 pound shrimp; peeled and deveined
- 16 ounces favorite pasta; cooked
- 1 cup coconut cream
- 1 tablespoon lemon juice
- 1 teaspoon dill; chopped.
- 2 teaspoons olive oil
- Salt and black pepper to the taste

DIRECTIONS

1. Set the Foodi on sauté mode, add the oil, heat it up, add the shrimp, toss and cook for 3 minutes Add all the other ingredients except the pasta, toss, put the pressure lid on and cook on High for 5 minutes more.
2. Release the pressure fast for 5 minutes, divide the shrimp mix between plates and serve with the pasta.

73. Pork and Kale

Preparation time: 30 minutes

Servings: 6

INGREDIENTS

- 1 pound pork stew meat; cubed
- 1 bunch kale; torn
- 1/4 cup tomato sauce
- 1½ cups brown mushrooms; sliced
- Salt and black pepper to the taste

DIRECTIONS

1. In your Foodi, combine all the ingredients: , toss, put the pressure lid on and cook on High for 20 minutes. Release the pressure

naturally for 10 minutes, divide the mix into bowls and serve.

74. Beef and Brussels Sprouts

Preparation time: 25 minutes

Servings: 4

INGREDIENTS

- 1 pound sirloin steak; cut into strips
- 2 green onions; chopped.
- 2 garlic cloves; minced
- 2 cups Brussels sprouts; shredded
- 1 tablespoon canola oil
- 1 teaspoon soy sauce
- Salt and black pepper to the taste

DIRECTIONS

1. Set the Foodi on Sauté mode, add the oil, heat it up, add the beef strips, toss and brown for 4 minutes.
2. Add all the other ingredients: , toss, put the pressure lid on and cook on High for 10 minutes. Release the pressure for 10 minutes, divide everything into bowls and serve.

75. Chicken Meatballs

Preparation time: 25 minutes

Servings: 4

INGREDIENTS

- 1 pound chicken meat; ground
- 16 ounces tomato sauce
- 1 egg; whisked
- 1/4 cup breadcrumbs
- 1 red onion; chopped.
- 2 garlic cloves; minced
- 1 tablespoon canola oil
- Salt and black pepper to the taste

DIRECTIONS

1. In a bowl, combine the meat with the onion, garlic, the egg, salt, pepper and the bread crumbs, stir and shape medium meatballs out of this mix. Set the Foodi on sauté mode, add the oil, heat it up, add the meatballs and brown them for 5 minutes.
2. Add all the ingredients: , toss, put the pressure lid on and cook on High for 10 minutes. Release the pressure naturally for 10 minutes, divide the mix between plates and serve for lunch.

76. Honey Lamb

Preparation time: 40 minutes

Servings: 4

INGREDIENTS

- 1 pound lamb stew meat; cubed
- 8 bacon slices; cooked and cut into thirds
- 2 red bell pepper; sliced
- 2 tomatoes; sliced
- 1/3 cup bbq sauce
- 2 tablespoons honey

DIRECTIONS

1. In your Ninja Foodi, combine all the ingredients: , toss, put the pressure lid on and cook on High for 30 minutes. Release the pressure naturally for 10 minutes, divide the mix into bowls and serve for lunch.

77. Basil Salmon Cakes

Preparation time: 18 minutes

Servings: 4

INGREDIENTS

- 2/3-pound canned salmon; drained, skinless, boneless and flaked
- 3 green onions; chopped.
- 1 egg; whisked

- 1/2 cup bread crumbs
- 2 tablespoons lime juice
- 1 teaspoon basil; dried
- Cooking spray
- Salt and black pepper to the taste

DIRECTIONS

1. In a bowl, mix all the ingredients except the cooking spray, stir well and shape medium cakes out of this mix.
2. Put the Air Crisp basket in the Foodi, arrange the cakes inside and grease them with the cooking spray.
3. Cook the salmon cakes on Air Crisp for 8 minutes flipping them halfway. Divide the cakes between plates and serve for lunch.

78. Pork and Walnuts

Preparation time: 40 minutes

Servings: 4

INGREDIENTS

- 1½ pounds pork stew meat; cubed
- 1 cup tomato sauce
- 1 garlic clove; minced
- 1 tablespoon olive oil
- 1 tablespoon rosemary; chopped.
- 2 tablespoons walnuts; chopped.
- Salt and black pepper to the taste

DIRECTIONS

1. Set the Foodi on Sauté mode, add the oil, heat it up, add the garlic and the walnuts, toss and cook for 1-2 minutes.
2. Add the meat, stir and brown for 3 minutes more. Add the remaining ingredients: , toss, put the pressure lid on and cook on High for 25 minutes.
3. Release the pressure, divide the mix into bowls and serve for lunch.

79. Shrimp Meatballs and Salsa

Preparation time: 20 minutes

Servings: 2

INGREDIENTS

- 1 egg; whisked
- 1 cup salsa
- 2 cups shrimp; peeled, deveined and chopped.
- 1/2 cup bread crumbs
- 1 tablespoon cilantro; chopped.
- Cooking spray

DIRECTIONS

1. In a bowl, mix all the ingredients except the cooking spray and the salsa, toss and shape small meatballs out of this mix.
2. Put the reversible rack in the Foodi, add the baking pan inside and grease it with cooking spray.
3. Add the salsa to the pan and drop the meatballs inside as well. Set the machine on Baking mode, cook the mix at 370°F for 10 minutes, divide everything into bowls and serve for lunch.

80. Mustard Pork

Preparation time: 45 minutes

Servings: 4

INGREDIENTS

- 1 pound pork stew meat; cubed
- 1 tablespoon butter; melted
- 2 tablespoons mustard
- 2 teaspoons olive oil
- 1/2 teaspoon sweet paprika
- 1 teaspoon rosemary; dried
- Salt and black pepper to the taste

DIRECTIONS

1. Set the Foodi on Sauté mode, add the oil, heat it up, add the meat and brown for 5 minutes. Add the rest of the ingredients: , toss, set the machine on Baking mode and cook at 360°F for 30 minutes.

2. Divide the mix between plates and serve for lunch with a side salad.

81. Paprika Eggplant Salad

Preparation time: 20 minutes

Servings: 4

INGREDIENTS

- 4 eggplants; cubed
- Juice of 1/2 lime
- 3 garlic cloves; minced
- 1/2 cup tomato sauce
- 1 tablespoon olive oil
- 2 teaspoons sweet paprika
- Salt and black pepper to the taste

DIRECTIONS

1. Set the Foodi on Sauté mode, add the oil, heat it up, add the garlic, stir and cook for 1 minutes.
2. Add the rest of the ingredients: , toss, put the pressure lid on and cook on High for 15 minutes. Release the pressure fast for 5 minutes, divide the mix into bowls and serve.

82. Salmon and Rice Stew

Preparation time: 35 minutes

Servings: 4

INGREDIENTS

- 1½ pounds salmon fillet; skinless, boneless and cubed
- 14 ounces veggie stock
- 5 ounces wild rice
- 1 red bell pepper; chopped.
- 1 yellow onion; chopped.
- 1 tablespoon olive oil
- Salt and black pepper to the taste

DIRECTIONS

1. Set the Foodi on Sauté mode, add the oil, heat it up, add the onion and the pepper, stir and sauté for 5 minutes.
2. Add all the other ingredients: , toss, put the pressure lid on and cook on High for 20 minutes. Release the pressure naturally for 10 minutes, divide the stew into bowls and serve.

83. Rosemary Mushroom and Carrot Stew

Preparation time: 30 minutes

Servings: 4

INGREDIENTS

- 1 pound white mushrooms; sliced
- 1/4 cup tomato sauce
- 1 cup spinach; torn
- 2 carrots; sliced
- 1 yellow onion; chopped.
- 1 tablespoon olive oil
- 1/4 teaspoon rosemary; chopped.

DIRECTIONS

1. Set the Foodi on Sauté mode add the oil, heat it up, add the mushrooms and the onion, stir and sauté for 5 minutes.
2. Add all the other ingredients: , toss, put the pressure lid on, cook on High for 15 minutes, release the pressure naturally for 10 minutes.
3. Divide the stew into bowls and serve it for lunch.

84. BBQ Pork

Preparation time: 55 minutes

Servings: 4

INGREDIENTS

- 1 pound pork stew meat; cubed
- 1 red bell pepper; sliced
- 1 cup bbq sauce

- 1 yellow bell pepper; sliced
- 1 tablespoon olive oil
- 1 teaspoon rosemary; chopped.
- Salt and black pepper to the taste

DIRECTIONS

1. Set the Foodi on Sauté mode, add the oil, heat it up, add the meat, rosemary, salt and pepper, toss and brown for 3-4 minutes.
2. Add all the other ingredients: , toss, put the pressure lid on and cook on High for 25 minutes. Release the pressure naturally for 10 minutes, divide the mix into bowls and serve.

85. Pork and Tomatoes

Preparation time: 40 minutes

Servings: 4

INGREDIENTS

- 1 pound pork stew meat; cubed
- 1 cup cherry tomatoes; chopped.
- 1 tablespoon olive oil
- 1 tablespoon balsamic vinegar
- 1 tablespoon rosemary; chopped.
- 2 tablespoons parmesan; grated

DIRECTIONS

1. Set the Foodi on Sauté mode, add the oil, heat it up, add the pork and brown for 3-4 minutes. Add all the ingredients except the parmesan, put the pressure lid on and cook on High for 25 minutes.
2. Release the pressure naturally for 10 minutes, divide the mix between plates, sprinkle the parmesan on top and serve for lunch.

86. Paprika Chicken Bake

Preparation time: 35 minutes

Servings: 4

INGREDIENTS

- 2 chicken breasts; skinless, boneless and cubed
- 1 cup tomato sauce
- 1 tablespoon olive oil
- 2 teaspoons sweet paprika
- Salt and black pepper to the taste

DIRECTIONS

1. Set the Foodi on Sauté mode, add the oil, heat it up, add the chicken and brown for 5 minutes.
2. Add all the other ingredients: , toss, set the machine on Baking mode and cook at 370°F for 20 minutes. Divide the mix between plates and serve for lunch.

87. Zucchini Cakes

Preparation time: 20 minutes

Servings: 4

INGREDIENTS

- 1 pound zucchinis; grated
- 2/3 cup bread crumbs
- 3 ounces cream cheese; soft
- 1 egg; whisked
- 1/2 teaspoon oregano; dried
- A pinch of salt and black pepper
- Cooking spray

DIRECTIONS

1. In a bowl, mix all the ingredients except the cooking spray, stir well and shape medium cakes out of this mix. Put the Air Crisp basket in the Foodi, add the cakes and grease them with cooking spray.
2. Cook the cakes on Air Crisp for 10 minutes, flipping the cakes halfway. Serve the cakes for lunch with a side salad.

88. Chicken Breast

Preparation time: 30 minutes

Servings: 4

INGREDIENTS

- 2 big chicken breasts; skinless, boneless and sliced
- 1/2 cup tomato sauce
- 1 red onion; sliced
- 1 tablespoon Worcestershire sauce
- 1 teaspoon canola oil
- Salt and black pepper to the taste

DIRECTIONS

1. Set the Foodi on Sauté mode, add the oil, heat it up, add the onion, stir and sauté for 5 minutes.
2. Add the rest of the ingredients , toss, put the pressure lid on and cook on High for 15 minutes. Release the pressure naturally for 10 minutes, divide between plates and serve.

89. Cheesy Pasta

Preparation time: 22 minutes

Servings: 4

INGREDIENTS

- 1½ cups spaghetti; cooked
- 1 cup cheddar cheese; shredded
- 1 cup mozzarella cheese; shredded
- 1/2 cup heavy cream
- 1 cup chicken stock
- Salt and black pepper to the taste

DIRECTIONS

1. In your Ninja Foodi, combine all the ingredients, toss, put the pressure lid on and cook on High for 15 minutes. Release the pressure naturally for 10 minutes, divide the spaghetti between plates and serve for lunch.

90. Chicken and Peppers Stew

Preparation time: 25 minutes

Servings: 4

INGREDIENTS

- 2 chicken breasts; skinless; boneless and cubed
- 2 red bell pepper; sliced
- 1 yellow onion, chopped.
- 1 cup tomato puree
- 1 cup cherry tomatoes; halved
- 1/2 cup Italian seasoning
- 1 tablespoon olive oil

DIRECTIONS

1. Set the Foodi on Sauté mode, add the oil, heat it up, add the meat, toss and brown for 3 minutes.
2. Add the onion and the bell peppers, toss and cook for 2-3 minutes more. Add the remaining ingredients: , toss again, put the pressure lid on and cook on High for 10 minutes.
3. Release the pressure naturally for 10 minutes, divide the stew into bowls and serve for lunch.

91. Corn Stew

Preparation time: 25 minutes

Servings: 6

INGREDIENTS

- 30 ounces canned corn; drained
- 1 spring onion; chopped.
- 1 red bell pepper; chopped.
- 2 garlic cloves; minced
- 1 cup tomato puree
- Cooking spray
- 1 teaspoon ginger; grated
- 1/2 teaspoon allspice; ground
- Salt and black pepper to the taste

DIRECTIONS

1. Put the reversible rack in the Foodi, add the baking pan inside and grease it with cooking spray.
2. Add all the ingredients, toss, set the machine on Baking mode and cook at 360°F for 20 minutes. Divide the mix into bowls and serve for lunch.

92. Salmon Tortillas

Preparation time: 15 minutes

Servings: 4

INGREDIENTS

- 6 ounces salmon fillet; skinless, boneless and shredded
- 4 corn tortillas
- 1 cup zucchini; shredded
- 1/3 cup mayonnaise
- 1 cup cheddar cheese; grated
- 2 tablespoons olive oil
- 1 red onion; sliced

DIRECTIONS

1. Set the Foodi on Sauté mode, add the oil, heat it up, add the onion, toss and cook for 2-3 minutes. Add the zucchini and the salmon, toss, set the machine on Air Crisp and cook everything for 6 minutes more.
2. Divide this mix on each corn tortilla, also divide the mayonnaise and the cheese, roll the tortillas and serve them for lunch.

93. Ginger Beef

Preparation time: 40 minutes

Servings: 4

INGREDIENTS

- 1 pound beef stew meat; cubed
- 1/4 cup soy sauce
- 4 ginger slices; minced
- 3 garlic cloves; minced

- 1/2 teaspoon olive oil
- 2 tablespoons sugar

DIRECTIONS

1. Set the Foodi on Sauté mode, add the oil, heat it up, add the meat and brown for 5 minutes.
2. Add all the other ingredients, toss, put the pressure lid on and cook on High for 25 minutes. Release the pressure naturally for 10 minutes, divide the mix into bowls and serve for lunch.

94. Tomato and Peppers Stew

Preparation time: 20 minutes

Servings: 4

INGREDIENTS

- 20 ounces canned tomatoes; roughly cubed
- 1/2 cups veggie stock
- 2 red bell peppers; chopped.
- 1 yellow onion; chopped.
- 2 garlic cloves; minced
- Salt and black pepper to the taste

DIRECTIONS

1. In your Foodi, combine all the ingredients , toss, put the pressure lid on and cook on High for 15 minutes.
2. Release the pressure fast for 5 minutes, divide the mix into bowls and serve for lunch.

95. Mexican Chicken Bowls

Preparation time: 30 minutes

Servings: 4

INGREDIENTS

- 1 pound chicken breasts; skinless, boneless and cut in strips
- 1 red bell pepper; sliced
- 1 green bell pepper; sliced

- 1 yellow onion; chopped.
- 1 cup salsa
- 1 tablespoon lemon juice
- 1/4 teaspoon cumin; ground
- 1/2 teaspoon chili powder
- Cooking spray
- Salt and black pepper to the taste

DIRECTIONS

1. Put the reversible rack in the Foodi, add the baking pan inside and grease with the cooking spray.
2. Add all the ingredients in the pan, toss, set the machine on Baking mode and cook at 370°F for 20 minutes. Divide the mix between plates and serve for lunch.

96. Turkey and Kale Casserole

Preparation time: 35 minutes

Servings: 6

INGREDIENTS

- 2 cups turkey breast; skinless, boneless, cooked and shredded
- 1/2 cup cilantro; chopped.
- 20 kale leaves; chopped.
- 3 cups mozzarella cheese; shredded
- 1/2 cup green onions; chopped.
- 2 cups salsa
- 2 teaspoons chili powder
- Cooking spray

DIRECTIONS

1. Put the reversible rack in the Foodi, add the baking pan inside and grease with cooking spray.
2. Add all the ingredients , toss, set the machine on Baking mode and cook at 350°F for 25 minutes. Divide between plates and serve for lunch

97. Italian Chicken Breast

Preparation time: 30 minutes

Servings: 4

INGREDIENTS

- 2 chicken breasts; boneless, skinless and cubed
- 2 mushrooms; chopped.
- 1 yellow onion; chopped.
- 1/2 cup tomato sauce
- 1 tablespoon butter; melted
- 1 teaspoon soy sauce
- 1 teaspoon Italian seasoning
- 1/2 teaspoon garlic powder
- Salt and black pepper to the taste

DIRECTIONS

1. Set the Foodi on Sauté mode, add the butter, heat it up, add the meat and brown it for 3 minutes. Add the onion and the mushrooms, soy sauce, seasoning, garlic powder, salt and pepper, toss and cook for a couple more minutes.
2. Add the sauce, toss, put the pressure lid on and cook on High for 15 minutes. Release the pressure naturally for 10 minutes, divide everything between plates and serve for lunch.

SIDES

98. Lime Potatoes

Preparation time: 25 minutes

Servings: 4

INGREDIENTS

- 1 pound baby potatoes; halved
- 2 tablespoons lime juice
- 2 teaspoons olive oil

DIRECTIONS

1. In a bowl, mix all the ingredients , toss and put the potatoes in the Foodi's basket. Cook the potatoes on Air Crisp mode for 20 minutes at 390°F, divide between plates and serve.

99. Baby Spinach and Carrots

Preparation time: 25 minutes

Servings: 4

INGREDIENTS

- 1 pound carrots; sliced
- 2 cups baby spinach
- 1 tablespoon lemon juice
- 2 tablespoons olive oil
- 3 tablespoons coconut cream
- Salt and black pepper to the taste

DIRECTIONS

1. In your Foodi, mix all the ingredients except the spinach, cover and cook on High for 12 minutes.
2. Release the pressure naturally for 10 minutes, set the machine on Sauté mode, add the spinach, toss, cook for 3 minutes, divide between plates and serve as a side dish.

100. Creamy Spinach

Preparation time: 9 minutes

Servings: 4

INGREDIENTS

- 14 ounces spinach
- 1 red onion; chopped.
- 1 tablespoon olive oil
- 2 tablespoons milk
- Salt and black pepper to the taste

DIRECTIONS

1. Set the Foodi on Sauté mode, add the oil, heat it up, add the onion and sauté for 2 minutes.
2. Add the remaining ingredients , put the pressure lid on and cook on High 4 minutes. Release the pressure fast for 3 minutes, divide between plates and serve as a side dish.

101. Ginger Sweet Potato Wedges

Preparation time: 30 minutes

Servings: 4

INGREDIENTS

- 2 pounds sweet potatoes; cut into wedges
- 1/4 cup veggie stock
- 1 teaspoon ginger; grated
- 1 teaspoon garlic; minced
- 2 teaspoons lime juice
- Salt and black pepper to the taste

DIRECTIONS

1. Put the reversible rack in the Foodi, add the baking pan inside and mix all the ingredients in it.

2. Set the machine on Baking mode, cook everything at 380°F for 20 minutes. Divide the mix between plates and serve.

102.   Lime Asparagus

Preparation time: 15 minutes

Servings: 4

INGREDIENTS

- 1 bunch asparagus; trimmed
- 2 tablespoons butter; melted
- Juice of 1 lime
- Salt and black pepper to the taste

DIRECTIONS

1. In a bowl, mix all the ingredients , toss, put the asparagus in the Foodi's basket and cook on Air Crisp at 380°F for 10 minutes. Divide between plates and serve.

103.   Sweet Potato Wedges

Preparation time: 15 minutes

Servings: 4

INGREDIENTS

- 2 big sweet potatoes; cut into wedges
- 1 tablespoon rosemary; chopped.
- 2 teaspoons avocado oil
- Salt and black pepper to the taste

DIRECTIONS

1. In a bowl, mix all the ingredients and toss. Put the wedges in your Foodi's basket, set the machine on Air Crisp and cook at 400°F for 10 minutes. Divide between plates and serve as a side dish.

104.   Coriander Zucchinis

Preparation time: 20 minutes

Servings: 4

INGREDIENTS

- 4 zucchinis; sliced
- 1 bunch coriander; chopped.
- 1 yellow onion; chopped.
- 1 tablespoon olive oil
- 1 tablespoon tomato sauce
- Salt and black pepper to the taste

DIRECTIONS

1. Set the Foodi on Sauté mode, add the oil, heat it up, add the onion, stir and sauté for 5 minutes.
2. Add the rest of the ingredients , toss, put the pressure lid on and cook on High for 10 minutes. Release the pressure fast for 5 minutes, divide the mix between plates and serve as a side dish.

105.   Roasted Orange Beets

Preparation time: 25 minutes

Servings: 4

INGREDIENTS

- 1 pound beets; cut into wedges
- 2 tablespoons orange zest; grated
- 2 teaspoons olive oil

DIRECTIONS

1. In a bowl, mix all the ingredients and put the beets in your Foodi's basket. Cook the beets on Air Crisp at 360°F for 20 minutes. Divide between plates and serve.

106.   Turmeric Chickpeas

Preparation time: 40 minutes

Servings: 4

INGREDIENTS

- 2 cups canned chickpeas; drained and rinsed
- 1 cup veggie stock

- 2 spring onion; chopped.
- 2 garlic cloves; minced
- 2 tablespoons olive oil
- 2 teaspoons turmeric powder
- Salt and black pepper to the taste

DIRECTIONS

1. In your Foodi, combine all the ingredients , toss, put the pressure lid on and cook on Low for 30 minutes. Release the pressure naturally for 10 minutes, divide the mix between plates and serve as a side dish.

107. Peas and Walnuts
Preparation time: 30 minutes

Servings: 4

INGREDIENTS

- 1½ pounds peas
- 1/2 pound shallots; chopped.
- 1 tomatoes; cubed
- 1/4 cup walnuts; chopped.
- 2 tablespoons butter; melted
- Salt and black pepper to the taste

DIRECTIONS

1. In your Foodi, combine all the ingredients , toss, put the pressure lid on, cook on High for 20 minutes and release the pressure for 10 minutes. Divide between plates and serve as a side dish.

108. Butternut Squash and Onions
Preparation time: 30 minutes

Servings: 4

INGREDIENTS

- 1/2 cup chicken stock
- 1 red onion; thinly sliced
- 1 big butternut squash; peeled and cubed
- 2 tablespoons butter; melted

DIRECTIONS

1. In your Foodi, combine all the ingredients , toss, put the pressure lid on and cook on High for 20 minutes. Release the pressure naturally for 10 minutes, divide between plates and serve as a side dish.

109. Ginger Mushroom Sauté
Preparation time: 25 minutes

Servings: 4

INGREDIENTS

- 1 pound mushrooms; sliced
- 1 tablespoon ginger; grated
- 2 tablespoons avocado oil
- 4 tablespoons soy sauce
- 4 garlic cloves; minced
- Juice of 1 lemon

DIRECTIONS

1. In your Foodi, combine all the ingredients , toss, put the pressure lid on and cook on High for 15 minutes. Release the pressure naturally for 10 minutes, divide between plates and serve.

110. Cilantro Parsnips
Preparation time: 22 minutes

Servings: 4

INGREDIENTS

- 1 pound parsnips; cut into matchsticks.
- 1/4 cup veggie stock
- 1 tablespoon cilantro; chopped.
- Salt and white pepper to the taste

DIRECTIONS

1. In your Foodi, mix all the ingredients , toss, put the pressure lid on and cook on High for 12 minutes. Release the pressure

naturally for 10 minutes, divide the parsnips mix between plates and serve.

111. Creamy Leeks Sauté

Preparation time: 22 minutes

Servings: 4

INGREDIENTS

- 4 leeks; sliced
- 1 cup coconut cream
- Salt and black pepper to the taste

DIRECTIONS

1. In your Foodi, combine all the ingredients , toss, cover and cook on High for 12 minutes. Release the pressure naturally for 10 minutes, divide the mix between plates and serve.

112. Thyme Celeriac Fries

Preparation time: 30 minutes

Servings: 4

INGREDIENTS

- 1 big celeriac; cut into fries
- 1 tablespoon olive oil
- 2 teaspoons thyme; chopped.
- Salt and black pepper the taste

DIRECTIONS

1. In a bowl, mix all the ingredients and toss well. Put the celery fries in your Foodi's basket and cook at 380°F on Air Crisp for 20 minutes. Divide between plates and serve as a side dish.

113. Garlicky Cauliflower

Preparation time: 25 minutes

Servings: 4

INGREDIENTS

- 1 big cauliflower head; florets separated
- 4 tablespoons butter; melted
- 2 tablespoons garlic; minced
- Salt and black pepper to the taste

DIRECTIONS

1. In a bowl, mix the cauliflower florets with all the other ingredients: , toss and put the florets in your Foodi's basket. Cook on Air Crisp at 390°F for 15 minutes, divide between plates and serve.

114. Cilantro Tomato Mix

Preparation time: 15 minutes

Servings: 4

INGREDIENTS

- 1 pound cherry tomatoes; halved
- 2 tablespoons olive oil
- 1 tablespoon tomato sauce
- 2 tablespoons cilantro; chopped.
- Juice of 1 lime
- Salt and black pepper to the taste

DIRECTIONS

1. In your Foodi, combine all the ingredients: , toss, put the pressure lid on and cook on High for 10 minutes. Release the pressure fast for 5 minutes, divide between plates and serve.

115. Paprika Potatoes

Preparation time: 30 minutes

Servings: 4

INGREDIENTS

- 4 red potatoes; cut into wedges
- 1 tablespoon smoked paprika
- 1 tablespoon olive oil
- Salt and black pepper to the taste

DIRECTIONS

1. In a bowl, mix all the ingredients and toss well. Put the Foodi's basket in the machine, add the potatoes inside, set the Foodi on Air Crisp and cook for 20 minutes at 390°F. Divide between plates and serve as a side dish.

116. Eggplant Side Salad

Preparation time: 15 minutes

Servings: 6

INGREDIENTS

- 1 pound eggplants; roughly cubed
- 1/2 cup tomato sauce
- 1 spring onion; chopped.
- 2 garlic cloves; minced
- Salt and black pepper to the taste

DIRECTIONS

1. In your Foodi, mix all the ingredients , toss, put the pressure lid on and cook on High for 10 minutes. Release the pressure fast for 5 minutes, divide the mix between plates and serve.

117. Buttery Brussels Sprouts

Preparation time: 15 minutes

Servings: 4

INGREDIENTS

- 1 pound Brussels sprouts; halved
- 3 spring onions; chopped.
- 1/2 cup veggie stock
- 2 tablespoons butter; melted
- Salt and black pepper to the taste

DIRECTIONS

1. In your Foodi, combine all the ingredients , toss, put the pressure lid on and cook on High for 10 minutes. Release the pressure

fast for 5 minutes, divide between plates and serve.

118. Creamy Quinoa

Preparation time: 25 minutes

Servings: 4

INGREDIENTS

- 2 cups quinoa
- 1 yellow onion; chopped.
- 4 ounces heavy cream
- 4 cups chicken stock; heated up
- 2 garlic cloves; minced
- 1 tablespoon olive oil
- 2 tablespoons parmesan; grated

DIRECTIONS

1. Set the Foodi on Sauté mode, add the oil, heat it up, add the garlic and the onion, stir and cook for 3-4 minutes.
2. Add the remaining ingredients , toss, put the pressure lid on and cook on High for 12 minutes. Release the pressure naturally for 10 minutes, divide the mix between plates and serve.

119. Creamy Beets

Preparation time: 35 minutes

Servings: 4

INGREDIENTS

- 4 beets; peeled and cubed
- 8 ounces coconut cream
- 2 garlic cloves; minced
- 1 cup veggie stock
- 1 tablespoon olive oil
- Salt and black pepper to the taste

DIRECTIONS

1. Set the Foodi on Sauté mode, add the oil, heat it up, add the garlic and cook for 1 minute.

2. Add the beets and the remaining ingredients , toss, put the pressure lid on and cook on High for 25 minutes. Release the pressure naturally for 10 minutes, divide the mix between plates and serve.

120.   Buttery Artichokes
Preparation time: 25 minutes

Servings: 4

INGREDIENTS

- 4 artichokes; trimmed and cut into quarters
- 3 garlic cloves; minced
- 3 tablespoons butter; melted

DIRECTIONS

1. Put the reversible rack in the Foodi, add the baking pan inside and mix all the ingredients in it. Set the machine on Baking mode, cook at 370°F for 20 minutes, divide between plates and serve.

121.   Minty Spinach Sauté
Preparation time: 12 minutes

Servings: 4

INGREDIENTS

- 1 pound spinach leaves; torn
- 1/4 cup green onions; chopped.
- 1/4 cup mint leaves; chopped.
- 1 tablespoon balsamic vinegar
- 1 teaspoon olive oil
- 1 teaspoon lime juice
- Salt and black pepper to the taste

DIRECTIONS

1. Set the Foodi on Sauté mode, add the oil, heat it up, add the onions, stir and cook for 2 minutes.
2. Add the remaining ingredients , toss, put the pressure lid on and cook on High for 5 minutes. Release the pressure fast for 5 minutes, divide between plates and serve.

122.   Parmesan Brussels Sprouts
Preparation time: 25 minutes

Servings: 4

INGREDIENTS

- 2 pounds Brussels sprouts; halved
- 1 tablespoon olive oil
- 4 tablespoons parmesan; grated
- Salt and black pepper to the taste

DIRECTIONS

1. In your Foodi's basket, mix all the ingredients except the parmesan, toss and cook on Air Crisp at 370°F for 20 minutes. Divide the sprouts between plates, sprinkle the parmesan on top and serve.

123.   Balsamic Red Cabbage
Preparation time: 25 minutes

Servings: 4

INGREDIENTS

- 1 red cabbage head; shredded
- 4 garlic cloves; minced
- 1 tablespoon balsamic vinegar
- 1 tablespoon olive oil
- Salt and black pepper to the taste

DIRECTIONS

1. Set the Foodi on Sauté mode, add the oil, heat it up, add the garlic, stir and cook for 2-3 minutes.
2. Add the remaining ingredients , cover and cook on High for 12 minutes. Release the pressure naturally for 10 minutes, divide the mix between plates and serve.

124.   Cinnamon Squash
Preparation time: 25 minutes

Servings: 4

INGREDIENTS

- 1 butternut squash; peeled and cubed
- 2 garlic cloves; minced
- 1 red onion; julienned
- 1/4 cup veggie stock
- 1/2 teaspoon cinnamon powder
- 1/2 teaspoon ginger; grated
- Cooking spray

DIRECTIONS

1. Put the reversible rack in the Foodi, add the baking pan inside and grease it with cooking spray.
2. Add all the ingredients inside, toss, set the machine on Baking mode and cook at 360°F for 20 minutes. Divide the mix between plates and serve.

125. Red Cabbage

Preparation Time: 30 minutes

Servings: 2

INGREDIENTS

- 1 red cabbage head, shredded
- 1 cup sour cream
- 1 red onion; chopped.
- 4 bacon slices; chopped.
- Salt and black pepper to the taste

DIRECTIONS

1. Set the Foodi on Sauté mode, add the bacon, stir and brown for 3-4 minutes. Add the onion, cabbage, salt and pepper, stir and cook for 4 more minutes
2. Add the sour cream, toss well, put the pressure lid on and cook on High for 12 minutes. Release the pressure naturally for 10 minutes, divide the mix between plates and serve as a side dish.

126. Green Beans Salad

Preparation Time: 30 minutes

Servings: 4

INGREDIENTS

- 1 ½ lbs. green beans, trimmed
- ½ lb. shallots; chopped.
- ¼ cup walnuts; chopped.
- 2 tbsp. olive oil
- Salt and black pepper to the taste

DIRECTIONS

1. In your Foodi's Air Crisp basket, combine all the ingredients . Put the basket in the pot, set it on Air Crisp mode and cook at 360 °F for 20 minutes. Divide between plates and serve as a side dish

127. Roasted Tomato Salad

Preparation Time: 16 minutes

Servings: 2

INGREDIENTS

- 20 oz. cherry tomatoes, cut into quarters
- ½ cup cilantro
- 1 white onion, roughly chopped
- 1 jalapeno pepper; chopped.
- Juice of 1 lime
- 1 tbsp. olive oil
- Salt and black pepper to the taste

DIRECTIONS

1. Set the Foodi on Sauté mode, add the oil, heat it up, add the onion, stir and sauté for 2-3 minutes.
2. Add all the other ingredients , toss, set the machine on Roast mode and cook at 380 °F for 4 minutes. Divide the tomatoes mix between plates and serve

128. Mexican Beans

Preparation Time: 30 minutes

Servings: 4

INGREDIENTS

- 1 cup canned garbanzo beans; drained.
- 1 cup canned cranberry beans; drained.
- 1 cup chicken stock
- 1 bunch parsley; chopped.
- 1 small red onion; chopped.
- 1 garlic clove; minced.
- 2 celery stalks; chopped.
- 5 tbsp. apple cider vinegar
- 4 tbsp. olive oil
- Salt and black pepper to the taste

DIRECTIONS

1. Set the Foodi on Sauté mode, add the oil, heat it up, add the onion and the garlic, stir and sauté for 5 minutes.
2. Add all the other ingredients , toss, put the pressure lid on, cook on High for 15 minutes, release the pressure naturally. Divide between plates and serve as a side dish

129. Potato Mash

Preparation Time: 20 minutes

Servings: 4

INGREDIENTS

- 3 gold potatoes, peeled and cubed
- ½ cup cheddar cheese, shredded
- 1 cup heavy cream
- 1 cup water
- ¼ cup butter, melted
- A pinch of salt and black pepper

DIRECTIONS

1. Put the potatoes and the water in the Foodi, put the pressure lid on, cook on High for 10 minutes and release the pressure naturally for 10 minutes.
2. Drain the potatoes, transfer them to a bowl, mash them, add the butter, the

cheese, cream, salt and pepper, whisk well, divide between plates and serve as a side dish

130. Spiced Squash

Preparation Time: 25 minutes

Servings: 4

INGREDIENTS

- 6 oz. squash; cubed.
- 2 oz. heavy cream
- 1 small yellow onion; chopped.
- 2 garlic cloves; minced.
- 2 tbsp. olive oil
- ½ tsp. cinnamon powder
- ½ tsp. allspice
- ½ tsp. nutmeg, ground
- ½ tsp. ginger; grated.

DIRECTIONS

1. Set the Foodi on Sauté mode, add the oil and heat it up. Add the onion and the garlic, stir and cook for 5 minutes
2. Add all the other ingredients , toss, set the machine on Baking mode and cook everything at 360 °F for 15 minutes. Divide between plates and serve as a side dish.

131. Beans And Tomatoes Mix

Preparation Time: 30 minutes

Servings: 6

INGREDIENTS

- 1 lb. canned red kidney beans; drained..
- ½ lb. cherry tomatoes, cut into quarters.
- 1 yellow onion; chopped.
- 4 garlic cloves; chopped.
- 2 spring onions; minced.
- 1 tsp. olive oil
- 2 tbsp. cilantro; minced.
- 2 tbsp. tomato sauce
- Salt and black pepper to the taste

DIRECTIONS

1. In your Foodi's baking pan, combine all the ingredients except the cilantro and toss
2. Put the reversible rack in the machine, add the baking pan inside, set the Foodi on Baking mode and cook everything for 20 minutes. Add the cilantro, stir, divide between plates and serve.

132. Potatoes and Tomatoes

Preparation Time: 25 minutes

Servings: 6

INGREDIENTS

- 15 oz. potatoes; cubed.
- 6 oz. canned tomatoes; chopped.
- 2 spring onions; chopped.
- 2 tbsp. olive oil
- ½ tsp. nutmeg, ground
- Salt and black pepper to the taste

DIRECTIONS

1. Set the Foodi on Sauté mode, add the oil, heat it up, add the onions, stir and cook for 2-3 minutes.
2. Add the potatoes, nutmeg, tomatoes, salt and pepper, toss, put the pressure lid on and cook on High for 15 minutes. Release the pressure naturally for 10 minutes, divide the mix between plates and serve as a side dish

133. Creamy Cauliflower

Preparation Time: 25 minutes

Servings: 4

INGREDIENTS

- 1 cauliflower head, florets separated
- ½ cup Italian bread crumbs
- ¼ cup raisins
- ½ cup heavy cream
- ½ cup parmesan; grated.

- 1 cup beer
- 1 tbsp. white flour
- 1 tsp. nutmeg, ground
- A pinch of salt and black pepper

DIRECTIONS

1. In the Foodi, combine the beer with the raisins, cauliflower, salt, pepper and the nutmeg, toss, put the pressure lid on and cook on High for 3 minutes
2. Release the pressure fast for 5 minutes, add the cream mixed with the flour, toss everything, set the pot on Sauté mode and cook everything for 5 minutes more
3. In a bowl mix the bread crumbs with the cheese, stir and sprinkle this over the cauliflower mix.
4. Cover the pot, set it on Air Crisp mode and cook at 390 °F for 10 minutes. Divide everything between plates and serve as a side dish

134. Garlic Mushrooms

Preparation Time: 30 minutes

Servings: 4

INGREDIENTS

- 1 lb. brown mushrooms, halved
- 1 tbsp. garlic; minced.
- 1 tbsp. lime juice
- 1 tbsp. chives; chopped.
- 2 tbsp. olive oil
- Salt and black pepper to the taste

DIRECTIONS

1. Set the Foodi on Sauté mode, add the oil and heat it up. Add the garlic and the mushrooms, toss and sauté for 5 minutes
2. Add the lime juice as well, set the machine on Baking mode and cook at 380 °F for 15 minutes. Add the chives, toss, divide everything between plates and serve as a side dish.

135. Sweet Potato and Mayo

Preparation Time: 30 minutes

Servings: 2

INGREDIENTS

- 2 sweet potatoes, peeled and cut into wedges
- 4 tbsp. mayonnaise
- 2 tbsp. olive oil
- ½ tsp. curry powder
- ¼ tsp. coriander, ground
- ½ tsp. cumin, ground
- A pinch of ginger powder
- Salt and black pepper to the taste

DIRECTIONS

1. In your Foodi's Air Crisp basket, mix sweet potato wedges with salt, pepper, coriander, curry powder and the oil and toss well
2. Put the basket in the machine, set it on Air Crisp mode and cook the potatoes at 380 °F for 20 minutes shaking the pot halfway. Transfer the potatoes to a bowl, add rest of the ingredients , toss and serve as a side dish

136. Yummy Eggplant

Preparation Time: 25 minutes

Servings: 4

INGREDIENTS

- 4 eggplants, cut into cubes
- 1 red onion; chopped.
- 1 tbsp. smoked paprika
- 1 tbsp. olive oil
- Salt and black pepper to the taste

DIRECTIONS

1. Set the Foodi on Sauté mode, add the oil and heat it up. Add the eggplants and all the other ingredients , toss, put the

pressure lid on and cook on High for 15 minutes
2. Release the pressure naturally for 10 minutes, divide the mix between plates and serve as a side dish.

137. Buttery Brussels Sprouts

Preparation Time: 30 minutes

Servings: 8

INGREDIENTS

- 3 lbs. Brussels sprouts, trimmed
- 1 lb. bacon; chopped.
- 1 yellow onion; chopped.
- 2 cups heavy cream
- 4 tbsp. butter, melted
- 1 tsp. olive oil
- Salt and black pepper to the taste

DIRECTIONS

1. Put the Brussels sprouts in your Foodi's Air Crisp basket and put the basket in the machine
2. Set it on Air Crisp and cook at 370 °F for 10 minutes. Clean the Foodi and put the sprouts in a bowl. Set the machine on Sauté mode, add the oil and the butter and heat it up
3. Return the Sprouts to the pot, also add the bacon and the onion, stir and cook for 5 more minutes. Add the cream, toss, cook or another 5 minutes, divide between plates and as a side dish.

138. Asian Style Chickpeas

Preparation Time: 30 minutes

Servings: 4

INGREDIENTS

- 30 oz. canned chickpeas; drained.
- 2 tbsp. olive oil
- 2 tsp. garam masala
- ¼ tsp. mustard powder

- ½ tsp. garlic powder
- 1 tsp. sweet paprika
- A pinch of salt and black pepper

DIRECTIONS

1. In a bowl combine all the ingredients and toss them well. Set the Ninja Foodi on Sauté mode, heat it up for 3 minutes and add the chickpeas and sauté them for 6 minutes
2. Transfer them to the Foodi's basket, place the basket in the pot, set it on Air Crisp and cook at 400 °F for 15 minutes. Divide the chickpeas between plates and serve as a side dish

139. Brussels Sprouts

Preparation Time: 25 minutes

Servings: 4

INGREDIENTS

- 1 lb. Brussels sprouts, halved
- 4 bacon strips, cooked and chopped
- 1 tbsp. olive oil
- 2 tsp. garlic powder
- 2 tsp. garlic powder
- A pinch of salt and black pepper

DIRECTIONS

1. In a bowl combine all the ingredients except the bacon and toss. Put the Brussels sprouts in the machine's basket, place the basket inside, set the Foodi on Air Crisp and cook at 390 °F for 20 minutes
2. Divide the Brussels sprouts between plates, sprinkle the bacon on top and serve.

140. Sweet Potato Mash

Preparation Time: 20 minutes

Servings: 4

INGREDIENTS

- 1 ½ lbs. sweet potatoes, peeled and cubed
- 1 cup chicken stock
- 1 tbsp. honey
- 1 tbsp. butter, soft
- Salt and black pepper to the taste

DIRECTIONS

1. In your Foodi, mix the sweet potatoes with the stock, salt and pepper, put the pressure lid on and cook on High for 15 minutes. Release the pressure naturally for 10 minutes
2. Mash the potatoes, add the butter and the honey, whisk well, divide between plates and serve as a side dish.

141. Oregano Potatoes

Preparation Time: 35 minutes

Servings: 2

INGREDIENTS

- 4 gold potatoes, cut into wedges
- 4 garlic cloves; minced.
- ½ cup water
- 2 tbsp. olive oil
- 1 tbsp. oregano; chopped.
- Juice of 1 lemon
- A pinch of salt and black pepper

DIRECTIONS

1. Put the water in the Foodi machine, add the basket and put the potatoes in it. Put the pressure lid on, set the pot on Low and cook for 4 minutes
2. Release the pressure naturally for 10 minutes, drain the potatoes and put them in a bowl. Clean the pot, set it on Sauté mode, add the oil and heat it up
3. Add the potatoes and the rest of the ingredients, toss, set the machine on Roast and cook at 400 °F for 20 minutes. Divide the potatoes between plates and serve.

142. Carrot Puree

Preparation Time: 25 minutes

Servings: 4

INGREDIENTS

- 1 lb. carrots, peeled and halved
- 1 yellow onion; chopped.
- ½ cup chicken stock
- ¼ cup heavy cream
- Salt and black pepper to the taste

DIRECTIONS

1. In your Foodi, combine all the ingredients except the cream, put the pressure lid on and cook on High for 15 minutes. Release the pressure naturally for 10 minutes
2. Mash everything well, add the cream, whisk really well, divide between plates and serve as a side dish.

143. Baked Mushrooms

Preparation Time: 25 minutes

Servings: 4

INGREDIENTS

- 1 lb. white mushrooms, halved
- 1 tbsp. oregano; chopped.
- 2 tbsp. mozzarella cheese; grated.
- 2 tbsp. olive oil
- 1 tbsp. parsley; chopped.
- 1 tbsp. rosemary; chopped.

Salt and black pepper to the taste

DIRECTIONS

1. Set the Foodi on sauté mode, add the oil, heat it up and then combine all the ingredients except the cheese.
2. Sprinkle the cheese on top, set the machine on Baking mode and cook the mushrooms at 380 °F for 15 minutes. Divide the mushrooms between plates and serve as a side dish

144. Roasted Potatoes

Preparation Time: 35 minutes

Servings: 4

INGREDIENTS

- 1 lb. baby potatoes, halved
- ½ cup parsley; chopped.
- ½ cup mayonnaise
- 2 tbsp. tomato paste
- 2 tbsp. olive oil
- 1 tbsp. smoked paprika
- 1 tbsp. garlic powder
- 2 tbsp. white wine vinegar
- 3 tsp. hot paprika
- A pinch of salt and black pepper

DIRECTIONS

1. In a bowl combine the potatoes with the paprika, oil, smoked paprika, garlic powder, salt and pepper and toss. Put the potatoes in the basket and place the basket in the Foodi
2. Set the machine on Air Crisp, cook the potatoes for 25 minutes at 360 °F, transfer them to a bowl, mix with the tomato paste, mayo, vinegar and the parsley, toss and serve as a side dish.

145. Cauliflower Risotto

Preparation Time: 32 minutes

Servings: 4

INGREDIENTS

- 1 cauliflower head, riced
- 15 oz. water chestnuts; drained.
- 1 egg; whisked.
- 1 tbsp. ginger; grated.
- 1 tbsp. lemon juice
- 2 tbsp. olive oil
- 4 tbsp. soy sauce

- 3 garlic cloves; minced.

DIRECTIONS

1. Set the Foodi on Sauté mode, add the oil and heat it up. Add the garlic and the cauliflower rice, toss and cook for 2-3 minutes
2. Add the soy sauce, chestnuts and the ginger, toss, put the pressure lid on and cook on High for 15 minutes.
3. Release the pressure fast for 5 minutes, set the machine on Sauté mode again, add the egg, stir well and cook for 2 more minutes. Divide between plates and serve as a side dish.

146.   Paprika Beets

Preparation Time: 45 minutes

Servings: 4

INGREDIENTS

- 2 lbs. small beets, trimmed and halved
- 1 tbsp. olive oil
- 4 tbsp. sweet paprika

DIRECTIONS

1. In a bowl combine all the ingredients and toss them. Put the beets in your Air Crisp basket and put the basket in the Foodi
2. Set on Air Crisp and cook the beets at 380 °F for 35 minutes. Divide the beets between plates and serve as a side dish.

147.   Creamy Artichokes

Preparation Time: 30 minutes

Servings: 4

INGREDIENTS

- 15 oz. canned artichoke hearts, roughly
- 1 ½ tbsp. thyme; chopped.
- 2 garlic cloves; minced.
- 1 yellow onion; chopped.

- 1 cup heavy cream
- 1 tbsp. olive oil
- 1 tbsp. parmesan; grated.
- Salt and black pepper to the taste

DIRECTIONS

1. Set the Foodi on Sauté mode, add the oil, heat it up, add the onion and the garlic, stir and sauté for 5 minutes. Add all the other ingredients except the thyme and the parmesan, toss, set the machine on Baking mode and cook at 370 °F for 15 minutes
2. Sprinkle the parmesan and the thyme, bake the artichokes mix for 5 more minutes, divide everything between plates and serve.

148.   Broccoli Mash

Preparation Time: 21 minutes

Servings: 4

INGREDIENTS

- 1 broccoli head, florets separated and steamed
- ½ cups veggie stock
- ½ tsp. turmeric powder
- 1 tbsp. olive oil
- 1 tbsp. chives; chopped.
- 1 tbsp. butter, melted
- Salt and black pepper to the taste

DIRECTIONS

1. Set the Foodi on Sauté mode, add the oil, heat it up, add the broccoli florets and cook them for 4 minutes. Add all the other ingredients except the butter and the chives, put the pressure lid on and cook on High for 12 minutes
2. Release the pressure naturally for 10 minutes, mash the broccoli, add the butter and the chives, whisk everything well, divide between plates and serve.

149. Cumin Green Beans

Preparation Time: 20 minutes

Servings: 6

INGREDIENTS

- 1 lb. green beans, trimmed
- 2 garlic cloves; minced.
- 1 tbsp. olive oil
- ½ tsp. cumin seeds
- Salt and black pepper to the taste

DIRECTIONS

1. In a bowl combine all the ingredients and toss well. Put the green beans in the Air Crisp basket and put the basket in the Foodi
2. Set the machine on Air Crisp, cook the green beans at 370 °F for 15 minutes, divide between plates and serve as a side dish.

150. Lemony Carrots

Preparation Time: 25 minutes

Servings: 2

INGREDIENTS

- 1 lb. baby carrots, trimmed
- 2 tsp. olive oil
- 2 tsp. sweet paprika
- Juice of 2 lemons
- Salt and black pepper to the taste

DIRECTIONS

1. In a bowl combine all the ingredients and toss them well. Put the carrots in the Air Crisp basket and place it in the Foodi
2. Set the machine on Air Crisp, cook at 400 °F for 15 minutes, divide between plates and serve as a side dish.

151. Creamy Mushrooms

Preparation Time: 32 minutes

Servings: 4

INGREDIENTS

- 8 oz. mushrooms, sliced
- 4 oz. heavy cream
- 2 garlic cloves; minced.
- 1 yellow onion; chopped.
- 1 tbsp. olive oil
- 2 tbsp. parmesan; grated.
- 1 tbsp. parsley; chopped.

DIRECTIONS

1. Set the Foodi on Sauté mode, add the oil, heat it up, add the onion and the garlic, stir and cook for 2-3 minutes. Add the mushrooms, salt, pepper and the cream, toss, put the pressure lid on and cook on High for 20 minutes
2. Release the pressure naturally for 10 minutes, add the parmesan and the parsley, toss, divide everything between plates and serve

152. Carrot Fries

Preparation Time: 25 minutes

Servings: 4

INGREDIENTS

- 4 mixed carrots cut into sticks
- 2 garlic cloves; minced.
- 2 tbsp. rosemary; chopped.
- 2 tbsp. olive oil
- Salt and black pepper to the taste

DIRECTIONS

1. In a bowl mix all the ingredients and toss them. Put the carrots in the Air Crisp basket and put the basket in the Foodi
2. Set the machine on Air Crisp and cook the fries at 380 °F for 15 minutes. Divide the carrot fries between plates and serve as a side dish.

SEAFOOD

153. Grilled Salmon Burgers

Preparation time: 5-10 min.

Cooking Time: 20 min.

Servings: 2-3

INGREDIENTS

- 1/2 tablespoon Dijon mustard
- 1 ½ tablespoons shallot, finely chopped
- 1 tablespoon cilantro, minced
- ½ pound skinless salmon fillets, cubed
- 1/4 teaspoon salt
- 1 ½ garlic cloves, minced
- ½ tablespoon grated lime zest
- ½ tablespoon soy sauce
- ½ tablespoon honey
- 1/8 teaspoon pepper
- 2 hamburger buns, slice into half

DIRECTIONS

1. In a mixing bowl, combine all the ingredients. Prepare 2 patties from the mixture.
2. Take Ninja Foodi Grill, arrange it over your kitchen platform, and open the top lid.
3. Arrange the grill grate and close the top lid.
4. Press "GRILL" and select the "MED" grill function. Adjust the timer to 10 minutes and then press "START/STOP." Ninja Foodi will start pre-heating.
5. Ninja Foodi is preheated and ready to cook when it starts to beep. After you hear a beep, open the top lid.
6. Arrange the patties over the grill grate.
7. Close the top lid and cook for 5 minutes. Now open the top lid, flip the patties.
8. Close the top lid and cook for 5 more minutes.
9. Serve warm with buns. Add your choice of toppings: lettuce, cheese, tomato, etc.

NUTRITION: Calories: 394 Fat: 20.5g Saturated Fat: 4g Trans Fat: 0g Carbohydrates: 22g Fiber: 3g Sodium: 203mg Protein: 24g

154. Grilled Salmon with Cucumber Sauce

Preparation time: 5-10 min.

Cooking Time: 8 min.

Servings: 4

INGREDIENTS

- ½ tablespoon lime zest, grated
- 1 tablespoon olive oil
- 1/4 teaspoon salt
- 1 tablespoon rice vinegar
- 2 teaspoons sugar
- 1/8 cup lime juice
- 1 cucumber, peeled and chopped
- 1/6 cup cilantro, chopped
- 1 garlic clove, minced
- ½ tablespoon onion, finely chopped
- 1 teaspoon minced ginger root
- 1/4 teaspoon ground coriander
- 1/4 teaspoon ground pepper

Salmon:

- 5 (6 ounces salmon fillets
- 1/2 tablespoon olive oil
- 1/6 cup gingerroot, minced
- 1/4 teaspoon freshly ground pepper
- ½ tablespoon lime juice
- 1/4 teaspoon salt

DIRECTIONS

1. Take food processor or blender, open the lid and inside add the ingredients from the lime zest to ground pepper.
2. Blend to make a smooth mixture.
3. Season the salmon fillets with the ginger, oil, salt, black pepper, and lime juice.

4. Take Ninja Foodi Grill, arrange it over your kitchen platform, and open the top lid.
5. Arrange the grill grate and close the top lid.
6. Press "GRILL" and select the "MED" grill function. Adjust the timer to 8 minutes and then press "START/STOP." Ninja Foodi will start pre-heating.
7. Ninja Foodi is preheated and ready to cook when it starts to beep. After you hear a beep, open the top lid.
8. Arrange the fillets over the grill grate.
9. Close the top lid and cook for 4 minutes. Now open the top lid, flip the fillets.
10. Close the top lid and cook for 4 more minutes.
11. Serve warm with the prepared sauce.

NUTRITION: Calories: 449 Fat: 19g Saturated Fat: 8.5g Trans Fat: 0g Carbohydrates: 18g Fiber: 2g Sodium: 511mg Protein: 32g

155. Shrimp Skewers with Yogurt Sauce

Preparation time: 5-10 min.

Cooking Time: 8 min.

Servings: 4

INGREDIENTS

- 2/3 cup fresh arugula
- 1/3 cup lemon juice
- 1/4 cup yogurt
- 2 teaspoons milk
- 2 tablespoons olive oil
- 1 pound shrimp, peeled and deveined
- 2 green onions, sliced
- 1/2 teaspoon salt
- 1/4 teaspoon ground black pepper
- 1 teaspoon Dijon mustard
- 2 garlic cloves, minced
- 1/2 teaspoon grated lemon zest
- 1 teaspoon cider vinegar
- 1/2 teaspoon sugar
- 12 cherry tomatoes

DIRECTIONS

1. In a mixing bowl, season the shrimp with lemon juice, lemon zest, oil, and garlic. Set aside for 10-15 minutes.
2. Take food processor or blender, open the lid and inside add the arugula, yogurt, milk, green onion, sugar, vinegar, mustard, and ¼ teaspoon salt.
3. Blend to make a smooth mixture.
4. Take the skewers, thread the seasoned shrimp and tomatoes. Thread alternatively. Season the skewers with salt and black pepper.
5. Take Ninja Foodi Grill, arrange it over your kitchen platform, and open the top lid.
6. Arrange the grill grate and close the top lid.
7. Press "GRILL" and select the "MED" grill function. Adjust the timer to 4 minutes and then press "START/STOP." Ninja Foodi will start pre-heating.
8. Ninja Foodi is preheated and ready to cook when it starts to beep. After you hear a beep, open the top lid.
9. Arrange the skewers over the grill grate.
10. Close the top lid and cook for 2 minutes. Now open the top lid, flip the skewers.
11. Close the top lid and cook for 2 more minutes.
12. Serve with the prepared sauce.

NUTRITION: Calories: 334 Fat: 4g Saturated Fat: 0.5g Trans Fat: 0g Carbohydrates: 28g Fiber: 2.5g Sodium: 547mg Protein: 15.5g

156. Crisped Shrimp with Chili Sauce

Preparation time: 5-10 min.

Cooking Time: 15 min.

Servings: 4

INGREDIENTS

- 2 large eggs
- ¼ cup panko bread crumbs
- ¾ cup coconut flakes, unsweetened
- ½ cup all-purpose flour
- 2 teaspoons ground black pepper

- ½ teaspoon sea salt
- 24 peeled, deveined shrimp
- Chili sauce of your choice

DIRECTIONS

1. In a mixing bowl, add the flour, black pepper, and salt. Combine the ingredients to mix well with each other.
2. In another bowl, whisk the eggs. In another bowl, combine the coconut flakes and bread crumbs
3. Coat the shrimps with the flour mixture and then coat with the egg mixture. Lastly, coat with the coconut mixture.
4. Take Ninja Foodi Grill, arrange it over your kitchen platform, and open the top lid.
5. Arrange the Crisping Basket inside the pot. Coat it with some cooking spray.
6. Press "AIR CRISP" and adjust the temperature to 400°F. Adjust the timer to 7 minutes and then press "START/STOP." Ninja Foodi will start pre-heating.
7. Ninja Foodi is preheated and ready to cook when it starts to beep. After you hear a beep, open the top lid.
8. Arrange the shrimps directly inside the basket.
9. Close the top lid and allow it to cook until the timer reads zero. Cook in batches if needed.
10. Serve warm with chili sauce.

NUTRITION: Calories: 356 Fat: 13.5g Saturated Fat: 8g Trans Fat: 0g Carbohydrates: 24.5g Fiber: 4g Sodium: 413mg Protein: 31g

157. Grilled Salmon with Salad Greens

Preparation time: 5-10 min.

Cooking Time: 10 min.

Servings: 2

INGREDIENTS

- 2 teaspoons paprika powder
- Salt and ground black pepper to taste
- 2 salmon fillets

- 2 teaspoons avocado oil
- Lemon wedges for garnish
- Sautéed salad greens to serve (broccoli, kale, spinach, cucumber, etc.

DIRECTIONS

1. Season the salmon with the avocado oil, paprika, salt, and ground black pepper. Refrigerate for 30-60 minutes to marinate.
2. Take Ninja Foodi Grill, arrange it over your kitchen platform, and open the top lid.
3. Arrange the grill grate and close the top lid.
4. Press "GRILL" and select the "MED" grill function. Adjust the timer to 10 minutes and then press "START/STOP." Ninja Foodi will start preheating.
5. Ninja Foodi is preheated and ready to cook when it starts to beep. After you hear a beep, open the top lid.
6. Arrange the salmon fillets over the grill grate.
7. Close the top lid and allow it to cook until the timer reads zero.
8. Serve warm with lemon wedges and salad greens.

NUTRITION: Calories: 272 Fat: 18g Saturated Fat: 3g Trans Fat: 0g Carbohydrates: 9g Fiber: 1g Sodium: 103mg Protein: 28.5g

158. Mexican Tortilla Shrimps

Preparation time: 10 min.

Cooking Time: 10 min.

Servings: 4

INGREDIENTS

- 4 corn tortillas
- 1 teaspoon chili powder
- 1 teaspoon ground cumin
- ¼ teaspoon cayenne pepper
- 1 teaspoon Southwestern seasoning
- 1 pound jumbo shrimp
- Juice of ½ lemon
- 2 cups green cabbage, shredded

- 1 avocado, peeled and sliced

DIRECTIONS

1. In a mixing bowl, add the shrimp, lemon juice, chili powder, cumin, seasoning, and cayenne pepper. Combine the ingredients to mix well with each other.
2. Coat the tortillas with some cooking spray.
3. Take Ninja Foodi Grill, arrange it over your kitchen platform, and open the top lid. Arrange the grill grate and close the top lid.
4. Press "GRILL" and select the "MAX" grill function. Adjust the timer to 1 minute and then press "START/STOP." Ninja Foodi will start pre-heating.
5. Ninja Foodi is preheated and ready to cook when it starts to beep. After you hear a beep, open the top lid. Arrange one tortilla over the grill grate.
6. Close the top lid and allow it to cook until the timer reads zero. Grill other tortillas and set aside.
7. Arrange the shrimps over the grill grate. Adjust the timer to 5 minutes and then press "START/STOP."
8. Close the top lid and allow to cook until the timer reads zero.
9. Add the shrimp mixture over the tortillas, add toppings of your choice, cheese, lemon juice, and serve warm.

NUTRITION: Calories: 241 Fat: 9.5g Saturated Fat: 2g Trans Fat: 0g Carbohydrates: 17.5g Fiber: 6.5g Sodium: 319mg Protein: 26g

159.   Shrimp Potato Kebabs

Preparation time: 5-10 min.

Cooking Time: 20 min.

Servings: 4

INGREDIENTS

- 3 tablespoons canola oil
- 2 tablespoons chopped fresh cilantro
- 1 tablespoon curry powder

- 12 baby potatoes
- 3 cloves garlic, minced
- ¼ teaspoon salt
- 20 peeled and deveined raw shrimp, with tails
- 1 teaspoon lime juice
- ½ cup plain yogurt

DIRECTIONS

1. Add the potatoes in a container. Microwave the potatoes for 2-3 minutes until tender.
2. In a mixing bowl, add the oil, cilantro, garlic, curry powder, and salt. Combine the ingredients to mix well with each other. Set aside 2 tablespoons of the sauce.
3. In the bowl, add the shrimps and potatoes and combine well.
4. Take 4 skewers, thread the shrimps and potatoes. Thread alternatively.
5. Take Ninja Foodi Grill, arrange it over your kitchen platform, and open the top lid. Arrange the grill grate and close the top lid.
6. Press "GRILL" and select the "MED" grill function. Adjust the timer to 5 minutes and then press "START/STOP." Ninja Foodi will start pre-heating.
7. Ninja Foodi is preheated and ready to cook when it starts to beep. After you hear a beep, open the top lid.
8. Arrange the skewers over the grill grate. Close the top lid and allow to cook until the timer reads zero.
9. Combine the yogurt, reserved sauce, and lime juice in a bowl. Serve the shrimps and potatoes with the prepared sauce.

NUTRITION: Calories: 259 Fat: 12.5g Saturated Fat: 3g Trans Fat: 0g Carbohydrates: 16g Fiber: 5g Sodium: 654mg Protein: 20.5g

160.   Rosemary Garlic Salmon

Preparation time: 5-10 min.

Cooking Time: 12 min.

Servings: 2

INGREDIENTS

- 1/4 teaspoon pepper
- 1 garlic clove, minced
- 1/4 teaspoon salt
- 1/4 teaspoon minced fresh rosemary
- 1 teaspoon grated lemon zest
- 2 salmon fillets (6 ounce each

DIRECTIONS

1. In a mixing bowl, add all the ingredients except the salmon. Combine the ingredients to mix well with each other. Add the salmon and combine it well. Set aside for 15 minutes to marinate.
2. Take Ninja Foodi Grill, arrange it over your kitchen platform, and open the top lid.
3. Arrange the grill grate and close the top lid.
4. Press "GRILL" and select the "MED" grill function. Adjust the timer to 6 minutes and then press "START/STOP." Ninja Foodi will start pre-heating.
5. Ninja Foodi is preheated and ready to cook when it starts to beep. After you hear a beep, open the top lid.
6. Arrange the salmon over the grill grate.
7. Close the top lid and cook for 3 minutes. Now open the top lid, flip the salmon.
8. Close the top lid and cook for 3 more minutes.
9. Serve warm.

NUTRITION: Calories: 253 Fat: 7.5g Saturated Fat: 3g Trans Fat: 0g Carbohydrates: 22.5g Fiber: 3g Sodium: 374mg Protein: 36.5g

161. Shrimp Lettuce Salad

Preparation time: 10 min.

Cooking Time: 5 min.

Servings: 4

INGREDIENTS

- 3 garlic cloves, minced
- Sea salt and ground black pepper to taste

- 1 pound jumbo shrimps
- Juice of ½ lemon
- 2 heads romaine lettuce, chopped
- ¾ cup Caesar dressing
- ½ cup grated Parmesan cheese

DIRECTIONS

1. In a mixing bowl, add the shrimps with lemon juice, garlic, salt, and black pepper. Combine the ingredients to mix well with each other.
2. Take Ninja Foodi Grill, arrange it over your kitchen platform, and open the top lid.
3. Arrange the grill grate and close the top lid.
4. Press "GRILL" and select the "MAX" grill function. Adjust the timer to 5 minutes and then press "START/STOP." Ninja Foodi will start pre-heating.
5. Ninja Foodi is preheated and ready to cook when it starts to beep. After you hear a beep, open the top lid.
6. Arrange the shrimps over the grill grate.
7. Close the top lid and allow to cook until the timer reads zero. Combine the romaine lettuce with the Caesar dressing.
8. Serve the shrimps warm with the Caesar mixture and cheese on top.

NUTRITION: Calories: 286 Fat: 11.5g Saturated Fat: 3.5g Trans Fat: 0g Carbohydrates: 18.5g Fiber: 2g Sodium: 712mg Protein: 29.5g

162. Vegetable Salmon Meal

Preparation time: 5-10 min.

Cooking Time: 10 min.

Servings: 2

INGREDIENTS

- 1/4 cup yellow pepper, julienned
- 1/4 cup green pepper, julienned
- 1/2 teaspoon lemon-pepper seasoning
- 1/2 cup carrots, shredded
- 2 (6 ounce eachsalmon fillets
- 2 teaspoons lemon juice

- 1/4 teaspoon salt
- 1/2 teaspoon parsley flakes, dried
- 1/8 teaspoon black pepper

- 1 teaspoon paprika
- ½ teaspoon black pepper

DIRECTIONS

1. Season the salmon fillets with lemon pepper seasoning; place them in two square foil sheets. Add the remaining ingredients and close the foil to make pockets.
2. Take Ninja Foodi Grill, arrange it over your kitchen platform, and open the top lid.
3. Arrange the grill grate and close the top lid.
4. Press "GRILL" and select the "MED" grill function. Adjust the timer to 10 minutes and then press "START/STOP." Ninja Foodi will start pre-heating.
5. Ninja Foodi is preheated and ready to cook when it starts to beep. After you hear a beep, open the top lid.
6. Ninja Foodi is preheated and ready to cook when it starts to beep. After you hear a beep, open the top lid.
7. Arrange the pockets over the grill grate.
8. Close the top lid and cook for 5 minutes. Now open the top lid, flip the pockets.
9. Close the top lid and cook for 5 more minutes. Serve warm.

NUTRITION: Calories: 346 Fat: 5.5g Saturated Fat: 1g Trans Fat: 0g Carbohydrates: 18g Fiber: 4g Sodium: 249mg Protein: 35g

163. Mustard Crisped Cod

Preparation time: 5-10 min.

Cooking Time: 10 min.

Servings: 4

INGREDIENTS

- 1 large egg
- 1 teaspoon Dijon mustard
- ½ cup bread crumbs
- 1 pound cod fillets
- ¼ cup all-purpose flour
- 1 tablespoon dried parsley

DIRECTIONS

1. Take the fish fillets; slice into 1-inch-wide strips.
2. In a mixing bowl, whisk the eggs. Add the mustard and combine it well. Add the flour in another bowl.
3. In another bowl, add the bread crumbs, dried parsley, paprika, and black pepper Combine well.
4. Coat the strips with the flour first. Then coat with the egg mixture and coat with the crumbs.
5. Take Ninja Foodi Grill, arrange it over your kitchen platform, and open the top lid.
6. Arrange the Crisping Basket inside the pot. Spray it with some cooking oil.
7. Press "AIR CRISP" and adjust the temperature to 390°F. Adjust the timer to 10 minutes and then press "START/STOP." Ninja Foodi will start preheating.
8. Ninja Foodi is preheated and ready to cook when it starts to beep. After you hear a beep, open the top lid.
9. Arrange the strips directly inside the basket. Close the top lid and allow to cook until the timer reads zero. Serve warm.

NUTRITION: Calories: 206 Fat: 4g Saturated Fat: 1g Trans Fat: 0g Carbohydrates: 17g Fiber: 1.5g Sodium: 214mg Protein: 24g

164. Butter Spiced Grilled Salmon

Preparation time: 5-10 min.

Cooking Time: 10 min.

Servings: 4

INGREDIENTS

- 2 teaspoons cayenne pepper
- 2 pounds salmon fillets
- 2 teaspoons salt
- 6 tablespoons butter, melted
- 1 ¼ teaspoon onion salt

- 2 tablespoons lemon pepper
- 1 teaspoon white pepper, ground
- 1 teaspoon black pepper, ground
- 3 tablespoons smoked paprika
- 1 teaspoon dry basil
- 1 teaspoon ancho chili powder
- 1 teaspoon dry oregano
- Lemon wedges and dill sprigs

DIRECTIONS

1. Season the salmon fillets with butter. In a mixing bowl, add other ingredients . Combine well.
2. Coat the salmon with the bowl mixture.
3. Take Ninja Foodi Grill, arrange it over your kitchen platform, and open the top lid.
4. Arrange the grill grate and close the top lid.
5. Press "GRILL" and select the "MED" grill function. Adjust the timer to 10 minutes and then press "START/STOP." Ninja Foodi will start preheating.
6. Ninja Foodi is preheated and ready to cook when it starts to beep. After you hear a beep, open the top lid.
7. Arrange the salmon fillets over the grill grate.
8. Close the top lid and cook for 5 minutes. Now open the top lid, flip the fillets.
9. Close the top lid and cook for 5 more minutes. Serve warm.

NUTRITION: Calories: 362 Fat: 7.5g Saturated Fat: 2g Trans Fat: 0g Carbohydrates: 17g Fiber: 1g Sodium: 342mg Protein: 26.5g

165. Spiced Grilled Shrimps

Preparation time: 5-10 min.

Cooking Time: 6 min.

Servings: 2

INGREDIENTS

- 1 teaspoon garlic salt
- ½ teaspoon black pepper
- 1 tablespoon paprika
- 1 tablespoon garlic powder

- 2 tablespoons olive oil
- 1 pound jumbo shrimps, peeled and deveined
- 2 tablespoons brown sugar

DIRECTIONS

1. In a mixing bowl, add all the ingredients . Combine the ingredients to mix well with each other.
2. Refrigerate for 30-60 minutes to marinate.
3. Take Ninja Foodi Grill, arrange it over your kitchen platform, and open the top lid.
4. Arrange the grill grate and close the top lid.
5. Press "GRILL" and select the "MED" grill function. Adjust the timer to 6 minutes and then press "START/STOP." Ninja Foodi will start preheating.
6. Ninja Foodi is preheated and ready to cook when it starts to beep. After you hear a beep, open the top lid.
7. Arrange the shrimps over the grill grate.
8. Close the top lid and cook for 3 minutes. Now open the top lid, flip the shrimps.
9. Close the top lid and cook for 3 more minutes. Serve warm.

NUTRITION: Calories: 368 Fat: 27.5g Saturated Fat: 3g Trans Fat: 0g Carbohydrates: 23g Fiber: 7.5g Sodium: 182mg Protein: 6g

166. Baked Parmesan Fish

Preparation time: 5-10 min.

Cooking Time: 13 min.

Servings: 2-3

INGREDIENTS

- 1/4 teaspoons salt
- 3/4 cup breadcrumbs
- 1/4 cup Parmesan cheese, grated
- 1/4 teaspoon ground dried thyme
- 1/4 cup butter, melted
- 1 pound haddock fillets
- 3/4 cup milk

DIRECTIONS

1. Coat the fish fillets in milk; season with salt. Set aside.
2. In a mixing bowl, add the breadcrumbs, parmesan cheese, and thyme. Combine well.
3. Coat the fillets in the breadcrumb mixture.
4. Take Ninja Foodi Grill, arrange it over your kitchen platform, and open the top lid.
5. Press "BAKE" and adjust the temperature to 325°F. Adjust the timer to 13 minutes and then press "START/STOP." Ninja Foodi will start preheating.
6. Ninja Foodi is preheated and ready to cook when it starts to beep. After you hear a beep, open the top lid.
7. Arrange the fish fillets directly inside the pot.
8. Close the top lid and allow it to cook until the timer reads zero. Flip the fillets after 8 minutes and then cook for the remaining time. Serve warm.

NUTRITION: Calories: 483 Fat: 27g Saturated Fat: 12g Trans Fat: 0g Carbohydrates: 16.5g Fiber: 2g Sodium: 1056mg Protein: 44.5g

167. Fish Greens Bowl

Preparation time: 5-10 min.

Cooking Time: 6 min.

Servings: 4

INGREDIENTS

- 6 tablespoons extra-virgin olive oil
- 1 ½ pounds tuna, cut into four strips
- 2 tablespoons rice wine vinegar
- ¼ teaspoon sea salt
- ½ teaspoon ground black pepper
- 2 tablespoons sesame oil
- 1 (10-ouncebag baby greens
- ½ English cucumber, sliced

DIRECTIONS

1. In a mixing bowl, add the rice vinegar, ¼ teaspoon of salt, and ½ teaspoon of pepper. Combine the ingredients to mix well with each other.
2. Add the oil and combine again.
3. Season the fish with salt and pepper, and drizzle with the sesame oil.
4. Take Ninja Foodi Grill, arrange it over your kitchen platform, and open the top lid.
5. Arrange the grill grate and close the top lid.
6. Press "GRILL" and select the "MAX" grill function. Adjust the timer to 6 minutes and then press "START/STOP." Ninja Foodi will start pre-heating.
7. Ninja Foodi is preheated and ready to cook when it starts to beep. After you hear a beep, open the top lid.
8. Arrange the fish over the grill grate.
9. Close the top lid and allow to cook until the timer reads zero.
10. Serve warm with the baby greens, veggies, and vinaigrette on top.

NUTRITION: Calories: 418 Fat: 28g Saturated Fat: 4.5g Trans Fat: 0g Carbohydrates: 6.5g Fiber: 2g Sodium: 208mg Protein: 35g

168. BBQ Roasted Shrimps

Preparation time: 5-10 min.

Cooking Time: 7 min.

Servings: 2

INGREDIENTS

- 3 tablespoons minced chipotles in adobo sauce
- ¼ teaspoon salt
- 1/4 cup barbecue sauce
- Juice of 1/2 orange
- ½-pound large shrimps

DIRECTIONS

1. In a mixing bowl, add all the ingredients. Combine the ingredients to mix well with each other.
2. Set aside to marinate for 15 minutes.
3. Take Ninja Foodi Grill, arrange it over your kitchen platform, and open the top lid. Lightly grease cooking pot with some oil or cooking spray.
4. Press "ROAST" and adjust the temperature to 400°F. Adjust the timer to 7 minutes and then press "START/STOP." Ninja Foodi will start pre-heating.
5. Ninja Foodi is preheated and ready to cook when it starts to beep. After you hear a beep, open the top lid.
6. Arrange the shrimps directly inside the pot.
7. Close the top lid and allow it to cook until the timer reads zero.
8. Serve warm.

NUTRITION: Calories: 173 Fat: 2g Saturated Fat: 0.5g Trans Fat: 0g Carbohydrates: 21g Fiber: 2g Sodium: 1143mg Protein: 17.5g

169. Arugula Shrimp

Preparation time: 5-10 min.

Cooking Time: 12 min.

Servings: 4

INGREDIENTS

- 1/2 cup parsley, minced
- 1/3 cup pistachios, shelled
- 2 tablespoons lemon juice
- 3/4 cup arugula
- 1 garlic clove, peeled
- 1/2 cup olive oil
- 1/4 teaspoon lemon zest, grated
- 1 ½ pound uncooked shrimp, peeled and deveined
- 1/4 teaspoon salt
- 1/8 teaspoon ground black pepper
- 1/4 cup Parmesan cheese, shredded

DIRECTIONS

1. Take food processor or blender, open the lid and inside add the ingredients from the parsley to lemon zest.
2. Blend to make a smooth mixture. Add the salt, pepper, Parmesan cheese, and blend again.
3. Add the shrimps and combine them well. Refrigerate for 1 hour to marinate.
4. Take the skewers, thread the shrimps. Thread alternatively.
5. Take Ninja Foodi Grill, arrange it over your kitchen platform, and open the top lid.
6. Arrange the grill grate and close the top lid.
7. Press "GRILL" and select the "MED" grill function. Adjust the timer to 6 minutes and then press "START/STOP." Ninja Foodi will start pre-heating.
8. Ninja Foodi is preheated and ready to cook when it starts to beep. After you hear a beep, open the top lid.
9. Arrange the skewers over the grill grate.
10. Close the top lid and cook for 3 minutes. Now open the top lid, flip the skewers.
11. Close the top lid and cook for 3 more minutes.
12. Serve warm.

NUTRITION: Calories: 302 Fat: 16g Saturated Fat: 2g Trans Fat: 0g Carbohydrates: 6g Fiber: 1.5g Sodium: 401mg Protein: 33.5g

170. Crisped Fish Nuggets

Preparation time: 5-10 min.

Cooking Time: 20 min.

Servings: 3-4

INGREDIENTS

- ½ cup all-purpose flour
- 1 tablespoon parmesan cheese
- 2 tablespoons coconut oil
- 2 cloves of garlic, chopped
- 3 white fish fillets, cut into cubes

DIRECTIONS

1. In a mixing bowl, mix the combine all the ingredients except the fish. Add the fillets and combine them well.
2. Refrigerate for 1-2 hours to marinate.
3. Take Ninja Foodi Grill, arrange it over your kitchen platform, and open the top lid.
4. Arrange the Crisping Basket inside the pot.
5. Press "AIR CRISP" and adjust the temperature to 390°F. Adjust the timer to 20 minutes and then press "START/STOP." Ninja Foodi will start pre-heating.
6. Ninja Foodi is preheated and ready to cook when it starts to beep. After you hear a beep, open the top lid.
7. Arrange the fish fillets directly inside the basket.
8. Close the top lid and allow to cook until the timer reads zero.
9. Serve warm.

NUTRITION: Calories: 203 Fat: 14.5g Saturated Fat: 5g Trans Fat: 0g Carbohydrates: 9g Fiber: 2g Sodium: 286mg Protein: 11g

171. Garlic Roasted Salmon

Preparation time: 5-10 min.

Cooking Time: 8 min.

Servings: 4

INGREDIENTS

- 1 tablespoon olive oil
- 1 teaspoon dried basil
- 1 pound salmon fillet
- 2 cloves of garlic, minced
- 1 teaspoon ground black pepper
- 1/2 teaspoon salt
- 1 tablespoon parsley, chopped
- 1 tablespoon lemon juice

DIRECTIONS

1. In a mixing bowl, add all the ingredients except the salmon. Combine the ingredients to mix well with each other.

2. Add the salmon fillets and combine them well. Refrigerate for 1 hour to marinate.
3. Take Ninja Foodi Grill, arrange it over your kitchen platform, and open the top lid. Lightly grease cooking pot with some oil or cooking spray.
4. Press "ROAST" and adjust the temperature to 400°F. Adjust the timer to 8 minutes and then press "START/STOP." Ninja Foodi will start pre-heating.
5. Arrange the salmon fillets over the grill grate. Drizzle 1 tablespoon olive oil on top and add the leftover marinade on top.
6. Close the top lid and allow to cook until the timer reads zero.
7. Serve warm.

NUTRITION: Calories: 411 Fat: 21g Saturated Fat: 4g Trans Fat: 0g Carbohydrates: 5g Fiber: 1g Sodium: 624mg Protein: 45g

172. Grilled Soy Cod

Preparation time: 5-10 min.

Cooking Time: 15 min.

Servings: 4

INGREDIENTS

- 3 tablespoons brown sugar
- 1 teaspoon sesame oil
- 1 pound baby bok choy, halved lengthwise
- 2 tablespoons soy sauce
- 1 tablespoon white wine or mirin
- 4 (6-ouncecod fillets
- ¼ cup miso paste
- ¼ teaspoon red pepper flakes

DIRECTIONS

1. Take a zip-lock bag, add the cod, miso, brown sugar, ¾ teaspoon of sesame oil, and white wine.
2. Add the fillets and shake well. Refrigerate for 30 minutes.
3. Take Ninja Foodi Grill, arrange it over your kitchen platform, and open the top lid.
4. Arrange the grill grate and close the top lid.

5. Press "GRILL" and select the "MAX" grill function. Adjust the timer to 8 minutes and then press "START/STOP." Ninja Foodi will start pre-heating.
6. Ninja Foodi is preheated and ready to cook when it starts to beep. After you hear a beep, open the top lid.
7. Arrange the fillets over the grill grate.
8. Close the top lid and allow to cook until the timer reads zero.
9. Set aside the cooked fillets.
10. Press "GRILL" and select the "MAX" grill function. Adjust the timer to 9 minutes and then press "START/STOP." Ninja Foodi will start pre-heating.
11. Ninja Foodi is preheated and ready to cook when it starts to beep. After you hear a beep, open the top lid.
12. Arrange the bok choy over the grill grate.
13. Close the top lid and allow to cook until the timer reads zero.
14. Serve the grilled fish with the bok choy.

NUTRITION: Calories: 231 Fat: 4g Saturated Fat: 0.5g Trans Fat: 0g Carbohydrates: 15g Fiber: 2g Sodium: 1142mg Protein: 33g

173.   Farfalle Tuna Casserole with Cheese

Preparation Time: 60 Minutes

Servings: 4

INGREDIENTS

- 6 ounces farfalle
- 1 (12-ouncecan full cream milk; divided
- 2 (5- to 6-ouncecans tuna, drained
- 1 medium onion; chopped
- 1 large carrot; chopped
- 1 cup vegetable broth
- 2 cups shredded Monterey Jack cheese
- 1 cup chopped green beans
- 2½ cups panko bread crumbs
- 3 tablespoons butter, melted
- 1 tablespoon olive oil
- 1 teaspoon salt
- 2 teaspoons corn starch

DIRECTIONS

1. On the Foodi, Choose Sear/Sauté and adjust to Medium. Press Start to preheat the pot.
2. Heat the oil until shimmering and sauté the onion and carrots for 3 minutes, stirring, until softened.
3. Add the farfalle, ¾ cup of milk, broth, and salt to the pot. Stir to combine and submerge the farfalle in the liquid with a spoon.
4. Seal the pressure lid, choose pressure; adjust the pressure to Low and the cook time to 5 minutes; press Start. After cooking, do a quick pressure release and carefully open the pressure lid.
5. Choose Sear/Sauté and adjust to Less for low heat. Press Start. Pour the remaining milk on the farfalle.
6. In a medium bowl, mix the cheese and cornstarch evenly and add the cheese mixture by large handfuls to the sauce while stirring until the cheese melts and the sauce thickens. Add the tuna and green beans, gently stir. Heat for 2 minutes.
7. In another bowl, mix the crumbs and melted butter well. Spread the crumbs over the casserole. Close the crisping lid and press Broil. Adjust the cook time to 5 minutes; press Start. When ready, the topping should be crisp and brown. If not, broil for 2 more minutes. Serve immediately.

174.   Tuna Salad with Potatoes and Asparagus

Preparation Time: 60 minutes

Servings: 4

INGREDIENTS

- 1½ pounds potatoes, quartered
- 8 ounces asparagus, cut into three
- 2 cans tuna, drained
- ½ cup pimento stuffed green olives
- ½ cup coarsely chopped roasted red peppers

- 1 cup water
- 2 tablespoons chopped fresh parsley
- 2 tablespoons red wine vinegar; divided
- 3 tablespoons olive oil
- ¼ teaspoon freshly ground black pepper
- 1 teaspoon salt; divided, plus more as needed

DIRECTIONS

1. Pour the water into the inner pot and set the reversible rack. Place the potatoes on the rack. Lock the pressure lid into place and set to Seal. Choose Pressure; adjust the pressure to High and the cook time to 4 minutes. Press Start/Stop.
2. After pressure cooking, perform a quick pressure release and carefully open the pressure lid. Take out the rack, empty the water in the pot, and return the pot to the base.
3. Arrange the potatoes and asparagus on the Crisping Basket. Drizzle the half of olive oil on them, and season with salt.
4. Place the basket in the pot. Close the crisping lid; choose Air Crisp, adjust the temperature to 375°F, and the cook time to 12 minutes. Press Start.
5. After 8 minutes, open the lid, and check the veggies. The asparagus will have started browning and crisping. Gently toss with the potatoes and close the lid. Continue cooking for the remaining 4 minutes.
6. Take out the basket, pour the asparagus and potatoes into a salad bowl. Sprinkle with 1 tablespoon of red wine vinegar and mix to coat.
7. In a bowl, pour the remaining oil, remaining vinegar, salt, and pepper. Whisk to combine.
8. To the potatoes and asparagus, add the roasted red peppers, olives, parsley, and tuna. Drizzle the dressing over the salad and mix to coat. Adjust the seasoning and serve immediately.

175. Cod on Lentils

Preparation Time: 65 Minutes

Servings: 4

INGREDIENTS

- 4 cod fillets
- 1 lemon, juiced
- 1 yellow bell pepper; diced
- 1 red bell pepper; diced
- 4 cups vegetable broth
- 1 cup panko breadcrumbs
- ¼ cup minced fresh cilantro
- 2 cups lentils, soaked
- 1 tablespoon olive oil
- 4 tablespoons melted butter
- 1 teaspoon lemon zest
- 1 teaspoon salt

DIRECTIONS

1. Choose Sear/Sauté on the pot and set to Medium High. Choose Start/Stop to preheat the pot. Combine the oil, lentils, yellow and red bell peppers in the preheated pot and cook for 1 minute. Mix in the vegetable broth.
2. Seal the pressure lid, choose Pressure, set to High, and set the time to 6 minutes. Choose Start/Stop.
3. In a small bowl, combine the breadcrumbs, butter, cilantro, lemon zest, lemon juice, and salt. Spoon the breadcrumb mixture evenly on the cod fillet.
4. When cooking ended, perform a quick pressure release, and carefully open the pressure lid.
5. Fix the reversible rack in the pot, which will be over the lentils. Lay the cod fillets on the rack.
6. Close the crisping lid. Choose Air Crisp, set the temperature to 350°F, and set the time to 12 minutes; press Start/Stop.
7. When ready, share the lentils into four serving plates, and top with salmon.

176. Haddock with Sanfaina

Preparation Time: 40 Minutes

Servings: 4

INGREDIENTS

- 4 haddock fillets
- 1 (14.5-ouncecan diced tomatoes, drained
- ½ small onion; sliced
- 1 small jalapeño pepper, seeded and minced
- 2 large garlic cloves, minced
- 1 eggplant; cubed
- 1 bell pepper; chopped
- 1 bay leaf
- ⅓ cup sliced green olives
- ¼ cup chopped fresh chervil; divided
- 3 tablespoons olive oil
- 3 tablespoons capers; divided
- ½ teaspoon dried basil
- ¼ teaspoon salt

DIRECTIONS

1. Season the fish on both sides with salt, place in the refrigerator, and make the sauce. Press Sear/Sauté and set to Medium. Press Start. Melt the butter until no longer foaming. Add onion, eggplant, bell pepper, jalapeño, and garlic; sauté for 5 minutes.
2. Stir in the tomatoes, bay leaf, basil, olives, half of the chervil, and half of the capers. Remove the fish from the refrigerator and lay on the vegetables in the pot.
3. Seal the pressure lid, choose Pressure; adjust the pressure to Low and the cook time to 3 minutes; press Start. After cooking, do a quick pressure release and carefully open the lid. Remove and discard the bay leaf.
4. Transfer the fish to a serving platter and spoon the sauce over. Sprinkle with the remaining chervil and capers. Serve.

177. Succotash with Basil Crusted Fish

Preparation Time: 65 Minutes

Servings: 4

INGREDIENTS

- 4 firm white fish fillets; at least 1 inch thick
- 1 large tomato, seeded and chopped
- ½ small onion; chopped
- 1 bay leaf
- 1 garlic clove, minced
- 1 medium red chili, seeded and chopped
- ¼ cup mayonnaise
- 1 ½ cups breadcrumbs
- ¼ cup chicken stock
- ¼ cup chopped fresh basil
- 1 cup frozen corn
- 1 cup frozen mixed beans
- 1 cup butternut squash; cubed
- 1 tablespoon olive oil
- 1 tablespoon Dijon-style mustard
- ¼ teaspoon cayenne pepper
- ½ teaspoon Worcestershire sauce
- 1 teaspoon salt; divided
- Cooking spray

DIRECTIONS

1. Press Sear/Sauté and adjust to Medium. Press Start to preheat the pot. Heat the oil and sauté the onion, garlic, and red chili pepper in the oil for 4 minutes or until the vegetables are soft.
2. Stir in the corn, squash, mixed beans, bay leaf, cayenne, chicken stock, Worcestershire sauce, and ½ teaspoon salt. Seal the pressure lid, choose Pressure; adjust the pressure to High and the cook time to 5 minutes. Press Start.
3. Season the fish fillets with the remaining salt. In a small bowl, mix the mayonnaise and mustard. Pour the breadcrumbs and basil into another bowl.
4. Use a brush to spread the mayonnaise mixture on all sides of the fish and dredge each piece in the basil breadcrumbs to be properly coated.
5. Once the succotash is ready, perform a quick pressure release and carefully open the pressure lid. Stir in the tomato and remove the bay leaf.
6. Set the reversible rack in the upper position of the pot, line with aluminum foil, and carefully lay the fish in the rack. Oil the top of the fish with cooking spray.
7. Close the crisping lid and Choose Bake/Roast; adjust the temperature to

375°F and the cook time to 8 minutes. Press Start.

8. After 4 minutes, open the lid. Use tongs to turn them over and oil the other side with cooking spray. Close the lid and continue cooking. Serve the fillets with the succotash.

178. Crab Cakes

Preparation Time: 55 Minutes

Servings: 4

INGREDIENTS

- ½ cup cooked crab meat
- ¼ cup breadcrumbs
- ¼ cup chopped celery
- ¼ cup chopped red pepper
- ¼ cup chopped red onion
- Zest of ½ lemon
- 3 tablespoon mayonnaise
- 1 tablespoon chopped basil
- 2 tablespoon chopped parsley
- Old Bay seasoning, as desired
- Cooking spray

DIRECTIONS

1. Place all ingredients in a large bowl and mix well until thoroughly incorporated. Make 4 large crab cakes from the mixture and place on a lined sheet. Refrigerate for 30 minutes, to set.
2. Spay the air basket with cooking spray and arrange the crab cakes in it.
3. Close the crisping lid and cook for 7 minutes on each side on Air Crisp at 390 F.

179. Cajun Salmon with Lemon

Preparation Time: 10 Minutes

Servings: 1

INGREDIENTS

- 1 salmon fillet
- Juice of ½ lemon
- 2 lemon wedges
- 1 tablespoon Cajun seasoning
- 1 tablespoon chopped parsley; for garnishing
- ¼ teaspoon brown sugar

DIRECTIONS

1. Meanwhile, combine the sugar and lemon and coat the salmon with this mixture thoroughly. Coat the salmon with the Cajun seasoning as well.
2. Place a parchment paper into the Ninja Foodi, close the crisping lid and cook the salmon for 7 minutes on Air Crisp mode at 350 F. If you use a thicker fillet, cook no more than 6 minutes. Serve with lemon wedges and chopped parsley.

180. Mackerel en Papillote with Vegetables

Preparation Time: 25 min + 2 h for marinating

Servings: 6

INGREDIENTS

1. 3 large whole mackerel, cut into 2 pieces
2. 1 pound asparagus, trimmed
3. 1 carrot, cut into sticks
4. 1 celery stalk, cut into sticks
5. 3 cloves garlic, minced
6. 2 lemons, cut into wedges
7. 6 medium tomatoes, quartered
8. 1 large brown onion; sliced thinly
9. 1 Orange Bell pepper, seeded and cut into sticks
10. ½ cup butter; at room temperature
11. 1 ½ cups water
12. 2 ½ tablespoon Pernod
13. Salt and black pepper to taste

DIRECTIONS

1. Cut out 6 pieces of parchment paper a little longer and wider than a piece of fish with kitchen scissors. Then, cut out 6 pieces of foil slightly longer than the parchment papers.

2. Lay the foil wraps on a flat surface and place each parchment paper on each aluminium foil.
3. In a bowl, add tomatoes, onions, garlic, bell pepper, pernod, butter, asparagus, carrot, celery, salt, and pepper. Use a spoon to mix them.
4. Place each fish piece on the layer of parchment and foil wraps. Spoon the vegetable mixture on each fish. Then, wrap the fish and place the fish packets in the refrigerator to marinate for 2 hours. Remove the fish to a flat surface.
5. Open the Ninja Foodi, pour the water in, and fit the reversible rack at the bottom of the pot. Put the packets on the trivet.
6. Seal the lid and select Steam mode on High pressure for 3 minutes. Press Start/Stop to start cooking.
7. Once the timer has ended, do a quick pressure release, and open the lid.
8. Remove the trivet with the fish packets onto a flat surface. Carefully open the foil and using a spatula. Return the packets to the pot, on top of the rack.
9. Close the crisping lid and cook on Air Crisp for 3 minutes at 300 F. Then, remove to serving plates. Serve with lemon wedges.

181.   Alaskan Cod with Fennel and Beans

Preparation Time: 25 Minutes

Servings: 4

INGREDIENTS

- 2 (18 oz) Alaskan cod, cut into 4 pieces each
- 2 cloves garlic, minced
- 2 small onions; chopped
- 1 head fennel, quartered
- ½ cup olive brine
- 1 cup Pinto beans, soaked, drained and rinsed
- 1 cup green olives, pitted and crushed
- ½ cup basil leaves
- ½ cup tomato puree
- 3 cups chicken broth
- 4 tablespoon olive oil
- Salt and black pepper to taste

- Lemon slices to garnish

DIRECTIONS

1. Heat the olive oil and add the garlic and onion. Stir-fry on Sear/Sauté mode until the onion softens. Pour in chicken broth and tomato puree. Let simmer for about 3 minutes.
2. Add fennel, olives, beans, salt, and pepper. Seal the lid and select Steam mode on High pressure for 10 minutes. Press Start/Stop to start cooking.
3. Once the timer has stopped, do a quick pressure release, and open the lid.
4. Transfer the beans to a plate with a slotted spoon. Adjust broth's taste with salt and pepper and add the cod pieces to the cooker.
5. Close the lid again, secure the pressure valve, and select Steam mode on Low pressure for 3 minutes. Press Start/Stop.
6. Once the timer has ended, do a quick pressure release, and open the lid. Remove the cod into soup plates, top with the beans and basil leaves, and spoon the broth over them. Serve with a side of crusted bread.

182.   Black Mussels

Preparation Time: 45 Minutes

Servings: 4

INGREDIENTS

- 1 ½ lb. black mussels, cleaned and de-bearded
- 1 white onion; chopped finely
- 10 tomatoes, skin removed and chopped
- 3 large chilies, seeded and chopped
- 3 cloves garlic, peeled and crushed
- 1 cup dry white wine
- 3 cups vegetable broth
- ⅓ cup fresh basil leaves
- 1 cup fresh parsley leaves
- 4 tablespoon tomato paste
- 3 tablespoon olive oil

DIRECTIONS

1. Heat the olive oil on Sear/Sauté mode, and stir-fry the onion, until soft. Add the chilies and garlic, and cook for 2 minutes, stirring frequently. Stir in the tomatoes and tomato paste, and cook for 2 more minutes. Then, pour in the wine and vegetable broth. Let simmer for 5 minutes.
2. Add the mussels, close the lid, secure the pressure valve, and press Steam mode on High pressure for 3 minutes. Press Start/Stop to start cooking.
3. Once the timer has ended, do a natural pressure release for 15 minutes, then a quick pressure release, and open the lid.
4. Remove and discard any unopened mussels. Then, add half of the basil and parsley, and stir. Close the crisping lid and cook on Broil mode for 5 minutes.
5. Dish the mussels with sauce in serving bowls and garnish it with the remaining basil and parsley. Serve with a side of crusted bread.

183. Potato Chowder with Peppery Prawns

Preparation Time: 80 Minutes

Servings: 4

INGREDIENTS

- 4 slices serrano ham; chopped
- 16 ounces frozen corn
- 16 prawns, peeled and deveined
- 1 onion; chopped
- 2 Yukon Gold potatoes; chopped
- ¾ cup heavy cream
- 2 cups vegetable broth
- 2 tablespoons olive oil
- 4 tablespoons minced garlic; divided
- 1 teaspoon dried rosemary
- 1 teaspoon salt; divided
- 1 teaspoon freshly ground black pepper; divided
- ½ teaspoon red chili flakes

DIRECTIONS

1. Choose Sear/Sauté on the pot and set to Medium High. Choose Start/Stop to preheat the pot. Add 1 tablespoon of the olive oil and cook the serrano ham, 2 tablespoons of garlic, and onion, stirring occasionally; for 5 minutes. Fetch out one-third of the serrano ham into a bowl for garnishing.
2. Add the potatoes, corn, vegetable broth, rosemary, half of the salt, and half of the black pepper to the pot.
3. Seal the pressure lid, hit Pressure and set to High. Set the time to 10 minutes, and press Start.
4. In a bowl, toss the prawns in the remaining garlic, salt, black pepper, the remaining olive oil, and the red chili flakes. When done cooking, do a quick pressure release and carefully open the pressure lid.
5. Stir in the heavy cream and fix the reversible rack in the pot over the chowder.
6. Spread the prawn in the rack. Close the crisping lid. Choose Broil and set the time to 8 minutes. Choose Start/Stop. When the timer has ended, remove the rack from the pot.
7. Ladle the corn chowder into serving bowls and top with the prawns. Garnish with the reserved ham and serve immediately.

184. Seared Scallops with Butter Caper Sauce

Preparation Time: 18 Minutes

Servings: 6

INGREDIENTS

- 2 lb. sea scallops, foot removed
- 1 cup dry white wine
- 10 tablespoon butter, unsalted
- 4 tablespoon olive oil
- 4 tablespoon capers, drained
- 3 teaspoon lemon zest

DIRECTIONS

1. Melt the butter to caramel brown on Sear/Sauté. Use a soup spook to fetch the butter out into a bowl. Next, heat the oil in the pot, once heated add the scallops and sear them on both sides to golden brown which is about 5 minutes. Remove to a plate and set aside.
2. Pour the white wine in the pot to deglaze the bottom while using a spoon to scrape the bottom of the pot of any scallop bits.
3. Add the capers, butter, and lemon zest. Use a spoon to stir the mixture once gently.
4. After 40 seconds, spoon the sauce with capers over the scallops. Serve with a side of braised asparagus.

185. Italian Flounder

Preparation Time: 70 Minutes

Servings: 4

INGREDIENTS

- 4 flounder fillets
- 3 slices prosciutto; chopped
- 2 (6-ouncebags baby kale
- ½ small red onion; chopped
- ½ cup whipping cream
- 1 cup panko breadcrumbs
- 2 tablespoons chopped fresh parsley
- 3 tablespoons unsalted butter, melted and divided
- ¼ teaspoon fresh ground black pepper
- ½ teaspoon salt; divided

DIRECTIONS

1. On the Foodi, choose Sear/Sauté and adjust to Medium. Press Start to preheat the inner pot. Add the prosciutto and cook until crispy, about 6 minutes. Stir in the red onions and cook for about 2 minutes or until the onions start to soften. Sprinkle with half of the salt.
2. Fetch the kale into the pot and cook, stirring frequently until wilted and most of the liquid has evaporated, about 4-5 minutes. Mix in the whipping cream.
3. Lay the flounder fillets over the kale in a single layer. Brush 1 tablespoon of the melted butter over the fillets and sprinkle with the remaining salt and black pepper.
4. Close the crisping lid and choose Bake/Roast. Adjust the temperature to 300°F and the cook time to 3 minutes. Press Start.
5. Combine the remaining butter, the parsley and breadcrumbs in a bowl.
6. When done cooking, open the crisping lid. Spoon the breadcrumbs mixture on the fillets.
7. Close the crisping lid and Choose Bake/Roast. Adjust the temperature to 400°F and the cook time to 6 minutes. Press Start.
8. After about 4 minutes, open the lid and check the fish. The breadcrumbs should be golden brown and crisp. If not, close the lid and continue to cook for an additional two minutes.

186. Oyster Stew

Preparation Time: 12 Minutes

Servings: 4

INGREDIENTS

- 3 (10 ozjars shucked oysters in liqueur
- 3 Shallots, minced
- 3 cloves garlic, minced
- 2 cups chopped celery
- 2 cups bone broth
- 2 cups heavy cream
- 3 tablespoon olive oil
- 3 tablespoon chopped parsley
- Salt and white pepper to taste

DIRECTIONS

1. Add oil, garlic, shallot, and celery. Stir-fry them for 2 minutes on Sear/Sauté mode, and add the heavy cream, broth, and oysters. Stir once or twice.

2. Close the lid, secure the pressure valve, and select Steam mode on High pressure for 3 minutes. Press Start/Stop. Once the timer has stopped, do a quick pressure release, and open the lid.

3. Season with salt and white pepper. Close the crisping lid and cook for 5 minutes on Broil mode. Stir and dish the oyster stew into serving bowls. Garnish with parsley and top with some croutons.

187. Monk Fish with Greens

Preparation Time: 22 Minutes

Servings: 4

INGREDIENTS

- 4 (8 oz) monk fish fillets, cut in 2 pieces each
- ½ lb. baby bok choy, stems removed and chopped largely
- 2 cloves garlic; sliced
- 1 lemon, zested and juiced
- ½ cup chopped green beans
- 1 cup kale leaves
- 2 tablespoon olive oil
- Lemon wedges to serve
- Salt and white pepper to taste

DIRECTIONS

1. Pour in the coconut oil, garlic, red chili, and green beans. Stir fry for 5 minutes on Sear/Sauté mode. Add the kale leaves, and cook them to wilt, about 3 minutes.

2. Meanwhile, place the fish on a plate and season with salt, white pepper, and lemon zest. After, remove the green beans and kale into a plate and set aside.

3. Back to the pot, add the olive oil and fish. Brown the fillets on each side for about 2 minutes and then add the bok choy in.

4. Pour the lemon juice over the fish and gently stir. Cook for 2 minutes and then press Start/Stop to stop cooking.

5. Spoon the fish with bok choy over the green beans and kale. Serve with a side of

lemon wedges and there, you have a complete meal.

188. Paprika and Garlic Salmon

Preparation Time: 10 Minutes

Servings: 4

INGREDIENTS

- 4 (5 oz salmon fillets
- 2 cloves garlic, minced
- 1 lime, juiced
- 1 cup water
- 2 tablespoon chopped parsley
- 2 tablespoon hot water
- 1 tablespoon maple syrup
- 2 tablespoon olive oil
- 2 teaspoon cumin powder
- 1 ½ teaspoon paprika
- Salt and black pepper to taste

DIRECTIONS

1. In a bowl, add cumin, paprika, parsley, olive oil, hot water, maple syrup, garlic, and lime juice. Mix with a whisk. Set aside.

2. Open the Ninja Foodi and pour the water in. Then, fit the rack. Season the salmon with pepper and salt; and place them on the rack.

3. Close the lid, secure the pressure valve, and select Steam mode on High pressure for 3 minutes. Press Start/Stop. Once the timer has ended, do a quick pressure release, and open the pot.

4. Close the crisping lid and cook on Air Crisp mode for 3 minutes at 300 F. Use a set of tongs to transfer the salmon to a serving plate and drizzle the lime sauce all over it. Serve with steamed swiss chard.

189. Tuna Patties

Preparation Time: 50 Minutes

Servings: 2

INGREDIENTS

- 5 oz. of canned tuna
- 1 small onion; diced
- 2 eggs
- ¼ cup flour
- ½ cup milk
- 1 teaspoon lime juice
- 1 teaspoon paprika
- 1 teaspoon chili powder, optional
- ½ teaspoon salt

DIRECTIONS

1. Place all ingredients in a bowl, and mix to combine. Make two large patties, or a few smaller ones, out of the mixture. Place them on a lined sheet and refrigerate for 30 minutes.
2. Close the crisping lid and cook the patties for about 6 minutes on each side on Roast mode at 350 F.

190. White Wine Mussels

Preparation Time: 15 Minutes

Servings: 5

INGREDIENTS

- 2 pounds mussels, cleaned and debearded
- 1 cup white wine
- ½ cup water
- 1 teaspoon garlic powder
- Juice from 1 lemon

DIRECTIONS

1. In the Foodi, mix garlic powder, water and wine. Put the mussels into the steamer basket, rounded-side should be placed facing upwards to fit as many as possible.
2. Insert reversible rack in the Foodi and lower steamer basket onto the reversible rack.
3. Seal lid and cook on Low pressure for 1 minute. When ready, release the pressure quickly.
4. Remove unopened mussels. Coat the mussels with the wine mixture. Serve with a

side of French fries or slices of toasted bread.

191. Creamy Crab Soup

Preparation Time: 45 Minutes

Servings: 4

INGREDIENTS

- 2 lb. Crabmeat Lumps
- 2 celery stalk; diced
- 1 white onion; chopped
- ¾ cup heavy cream
- ½ cup Half and Half cream
- 1 ½ cup chicken broth
- ¾ cup Muscadet
- 6 tablespoon butter
- 6 tablespoon flour
- 3 teaspoon Worcestershire sauce
- 3 teaspoon old bay Seasoning
- 2 teaspoon Hot sauce
- 3 teaspoon minced garlic
- Salt to taste
- Lemon juice to serve
- Chopped dill to serve

DIRECTIONS

1. Melt the butter on Sear/Sauté mode, and mix in the all-purpose flour, in a fast motion to make a rue. Add celery, onion, and garlic.
2. Stir and cook until soft and crispy; for 3 minutes. While stirring, gradually add the half and half cream, heavy cream, and broth.
3. Let simmer for 2 minutes. Add Worcestershire sauce, old bay seasoning, Muscadet, and hot sauce. Stir and let simmer for 15 minutes. Add the crabmeat and mix it well into the sauce.
4. Close the crisping lid and cook on Broil mode for 10 minutes to soften the meat.
5. Dish into serving bowls, garnish with dill and drizzle squirts of lemon juice over. Serve with a side of garlic crusted bread.

192. Paella Señorito

Preparation Time: 25 Minutes

Servings: 5

INGREDIENTS

- 1 pound frozen shrimp, peeled and deveined
- 2 garlic cloves, minced
- 1 onion; chopped
- 1 lemon, cut into wedges
- 1 red bell pepper; diced
- 2 cups fish broth
- ¼ cup olive oil
- 1 cup bomba rice
- ¼ cup frozen green peas
- 1 teaspoon paprika
- 1 teaspoon turmeric
- salt and ground white pepper to taste
- chopped fresh parsley

DIRECTIONS

1. Warm oil on Sear/Sauté. Add in bell pepper and onions and cook for 5 minutes until fragrant. Mix in garlic and cook for one more minute until soft.
2. Add paprika, ground white pepper, salt and turmeric to the vegetables and cook for 1 minute.
3. Stir in fish broth and rice. Add shrimp in the rice mixture. Seal the pressure lid, choose Pressure, set to High, and set the timer to 5 minutes; press Start. When ready, release the pressure quickly.
4. Stir in green peas and let sit for 5 minutes until green peas are heated through. Serve warm garnished with parsley and lemon wedges.

193. Cod Cornflakes Nuggets

Preparation Time: 25 Minutes

Servings: 4

INGREDIENTS

- 1 ¼ lb. cod fillets, cut into chunks
- 1 egg
- 1 cup cornflakes
- ½ cup flour
- 1 tablespoon olive oil
- 1 tablespoon water
- Salt and pepper, to taste

DIRECTIONS

1. Add the oil and cornflakes in a food processor, and process until crumbed. Season the fish chunks with salt and pepper.
2. Beat the egg along with 1 tablespoon water. Dredge the chunks in flour first, then dip in the egg, and coat with cornflakes. Arrange on a lined sheet. Close the crisping lid and cook at 350 F for 15 minutes on Air Crisp mode.

194. Mediterranean Cod

Preparation Time: 20 Minutes

Servings: 4

INGREDIENTS

- 4 fillets cod
- 1 bunch fresh thyme sprigs
- 1 pound cherry tomatoes, halved
- 1 clove garlic, pressed
- 1 cup white rice
- 2 cups water
- 1 cup Kalamata olives
- 2 tablespoon pickled capers
- 1 tablespoon olive oil; divided
- 1 teaspoon olive oil
- 1 pinch ground black pepper
- 3 pinches salt

DIRECTIONS

1. Line a parchment paper to the steamer basket of your Foodi. Place about half the tomatoes in a single layer on the paper.

Sprinkle with thyme, reserving some for garnish. Arrange cod fillets on the top of tomatoes. Sprinkle with a little bit of olive oil.

2. Spread the garlic, pepper, salt, and remaining tomatoes over the fish. In the pot, mix rice and water. Lay a trivet over the rice and water. Lower steamer basket onto the trivet.

3. Seal the pressure lid, choose Pressure, set to High, and set the timer to 7 minutes. Press Start. When ready, release the pressure quickly.

4. Remove the steamer basket and trivet from the pot. Use a fork to fluff rice. Plate the fish fillets and apply a garnish of olives, reserved thyme, pepper, remaining olive oil, and capers. Serve with rice.

195. Steamed Sea Bass with Turnips

Preparation Time: 15 Minutes

Servings: 4

INGREDIENTS

- 4 sea bass fillets
- 4 sprigs thyme
- 1 lemon; sliced
- 2 turnips; sliced
- 1 white onion; sliced into thin rings
- 1½ cups water
- 2 teaspoon olive oil
- 2 pinches salt
- 1 pinch ground black pepper

DIRECTIONS

1. Add water to the Foodi. Set a reversible rack into the pot. Line a parchment paper to the bottom of steamer basket. Place lemon slices in a single layer on the reversible rack.

2. Arrange fillets on the top of the lemons, cover with onion and thyme sprigs and top with turnip slices.

3. Drizzle pepper, salt, and olive oil over the mixture. Put steamer basket onto the

reversible rack. Seal lid and cook on Low for 8 minutes; press Start.

4. When ready, release pressure quickly. Serve over the delicate onion rings and thinly sliced turnips.

196. Coconut Shrimp

Preparation Time: 30 Minutes

Servings: 2

INGREDIENTS

- 8 large shrimp
- ½ cup orange jam
- ½ cup shredded coconut
- ½ cup breadcrumbs
- 8 oz. coconut milk
- 1 tablespoon honey
- ½ teaspoon cayenne pepper
- ¼ teaspoon hot sauce
- 1 teaspoon mustard
- ¼ teaspoon salt
- ¼ teaspoon pepper

DIRECTIONS

1. Combine the breadcrumbs, cayenne pepper, shredded coconut, salt, and pepper in a small bowl. Dip the shrimp in the coconut milk, first, and then in the coconut crumbs.

2. Arrange in the lined Ninja Foodi basket, close the crisping lid and cook for 20 minutes on Air Crisp mode at 350 F.

3. Meanwhile whisk the jam, honey, hot sauce, and mustard. Serve the shrimp with the sauce.

197. Fish Finger Sandwich

Preparation Time: 20 Minutes

Servings: 4

INGREDIENTS

- 4 cod fillets
- 2 oz. breadcrumbs

- 10 capers
- 4 bread rolls
- 4 lettuce leaves
- 2 tablespoon flour
- 4 tablespoon pesto sauce
- Salt and pepper, to taste

DIRECTIONS

1. Season the fillets with some salt and pepper, and coat them with the flour, and then dip in the breadcrumbs.
2. You should get at the layer of breadcrumbs, that's why we don't use eggs for this recipe. Arrange the fillets onto a baking mat.
3. Close the crisping lid and cook for about 10 to 15 minutes on Air Crisp mode at 370 F. Cut the bread rolls in half.
4. Place a lettuce leaf on top of the bottom halves; place the fillets over. Spread a tablespoon of pesto sauce on top of each fillet; top with the remaining halves.

198.   Parmesan Tilapia

Preparation Time: 15 Minutes

Servings: 4

INGREDIENTS

- ¾ cup grated Parmesan cheese
- 4 tilapia fillets
- 1 tablespoon olive oil
- 1 tablespoon chopped parsley
- ¼ teaspoon garlic powder
- 2 teaspoon paprika
- ¼ teaspoon salt

DIRECTIONS

1. Mix parsley, Parmesan, garlic, salt, and paprika, in a shallow bowl. Brush the olive oil over the fillets, and then coat them with the Parmesan mixture.
2. Place the tilapia onto a lined baking sheet, and then into the Ninja Foodi.
3. Close the crisping lid and cook for about 4 to 5 minutes on all sides on Air Crisp mode at 350 F.

199.   Cod Parcel

Preparation time: 15 minutes

Cooking time: 8 minutes

Servings: 2

INGREDIENTS

- 2 (4-ouncecod fillets
- ½ teaspoon garlic powder
- Salt and ground black pepper, as required
- 2 fresh dill sprigs
- 4 lemon slices
- 2 tablespoons butter

DIRECTIONS

1. Arrange 2 large parchment squares onto a smooth surface.
2. Place 1 fillet in the center of each parchment square and sprinkle with garlic powder, salt and black pepper.
3. Top each fillet with 1 dill sprig, 2 lemon slices and 1 tablespoon of butter.
4. Fold each parchment paper around the fillets to seal.
5. In the pot of Ninja Foodi, place 1 cup of water.
6. Arrange the "Reversible Rack" in the pot of Ninja Foodi.
7. Place the fish parcels over the "Reversible Rack".
8. Close the Ninja Foodi with the pressure lid and place the pressure valve to "Seal" position.
9. Select "Pressure" and set to "High for 8 minutes.
10. Press "Start/Stop" to begin cooking.
11. Switch the valve to "Vent" and do a "Quick" release.
12. Transfer fish parcels onto serving plates.
13. Carefully, unwrap the parcels and serve.

NUTRITION: Calories: 197, Fats: 12.6g, Net Carbs: 0.8g, Carbs: 1g, Fiber: 0.2g, Sugar: 0.2g, Proteins: 20.6g, Sodium: 231mg

200.   Cheesy Snapper

Preparation time: 15 minutes

Cooking time: 1½ hours

Servings: 6

INGREDIENTS

- 6 tablespoons butter
- 3 tablespoons almond flour
- ½ tablespoon dry mustard
- ¼ tablespoon ground nutmeg
- 1 teaspoon salt
- 1¼ cups unsweetened almond milk
- 1½ teaspoons fresh lemon juice
- 1 cup Cheddar cheese, shredded
- 3 pounds frozen snapper fillets, thawed

DIRECTIONS

1. In a medium pan, melt butter over medium heat and cook flour, mustard, nutmeg and salt and cook for about 2 minutes, stirring continuously.
2. Slowly, add the milk, stirring continuously until smooth.
3. Add the lemon juice and cheese and cook until cheese is melted, stirring continuously.
4. Remove from the heat.
5. In the pot of Ninja Foodi, place the fish fillets and top with cheese sauce evenly.
6. Close the Ninja Foodi with crisping lid and select "Slow Cooker".
7. Set on "High" for 1½ hours.
8. Press "Start/Stop" to begin cooking.
9. Serve hot.

NUTRITION: Calories: 509, Fats: 28.4g, Net Carbs: 1.1g, Carbs: 1.9g, Fiber: 0.8g, Sugar: 0.4g, Proteins: 65.4g, Sodium: 759mg

201.   Crispy Hake

Preparation time: 15 minutes

Cooking time: 12 minutes

Servings: 4

INGREDIENTS

- 1 egg
- 4 ounces pork rinds, crushed
- 2 tablespoons olive oil
- 4 (6-ounceshake fillets
- 1 lemon, cut into wedges

DIRECTIONS

1. Arrange the greased "Cook & Crisp Basket" in the pot of Ninja Foodi.
2. Close the Ninja Foodi with crisping lid and select "Air Crisp".
3. Set the temperature to 350 degrees F for 5 minutes.
4. Press "Start/Stop" to begin preheating.
5. In a shallow bowl, beat the egg.
6. In another bowl, add the pork rinds, and oil and mix until a crumbly mixture forms.
7. Dip fish fillets into the egg and then, coat with the pork rinds mixture.
8. After preheating, open the lid.
9. Arrange the haddock fillets in the prepared "Cook & Crisp Basket" in a single layer.
10. Close the Ninja Foodi with crisping lid and select "Air Crisp".
11. Set the temperature to 350 degrees F for 12 minutes.
12. Press "Start/Stop" to begin cooking.
13. Garnish with lemon wedges and serve hot.

NUTRITION: Calories: 347, Fats: 19.4g, Net Carbs: 1.5g, Carbs: 1.6g, Fiber: 0.1g, Sugar: 0.2g, Proteins: 43.7g, Sodium: 778mg

202.   Sardine in Tomato Gravy

Preparation time: 15 minutes

Cooking time: 8 hours

Servings: 8

INGREDIENTS

- 2 tablespoons olive oil
- 2 pounds fresh sardines, cubed

- 4 plum tomatoes, chopped finely
- 1 large onion, sliced
- 2 garlic cloves, minced
- 1 cup tomato puree
- Salt and ground black pepper, as required

DIRECTIONS

1. In the pot of Ninja Foodi, spread the oil evenly.
2. Place sardine over oil and top with the remaining all ingredients .
3. Close the Ninja Foodi with crisping lid and select "Slow Cooker".
4. Set on "Low" for 8 hours.
5. Press "Start/Stop" to begin cooking.
6. Serve hot.

NUTRITION: Calories: 301, Fats: 16.7g, Net Carbs: 6g, Carbs: 8g, Fiber: 2g, Sugar: 4.8g, Proteins: 29.4g, Sodium: 610mg

203. Garlicky Tuna

Preparation time: 15 minutes

Cooking time: 4¼ hours

Servings: 2

INGREDIENTS

- 2 tablespoons olive oil
- 4-5 garlic cloves, chopped finely
- 1 small jalapeño pepper, chopped finely
- ½ fresh red chili, chopped finely
- Salt and ground black pepper, as required
- ¾ pound fresh tuna, cut into 1-inch cubes

DIRECTIONS

1. In the pot of Ninja Foodi, add all the ingredients except for tuna and stir to combine.
2. Close the Ninja Foodi with crisping lid and select "Slow Cooker".
3. Set on "Low" for 4 hours.
4. Press "Start/Stop" to begin cooking.
5. Add the tuna cubes and stir to combine.

6. Close the Ninja Foodi with crisping lid and select "Slow Cooker".
7. Set on "High" for 15 minutes.
8. Press "Start/Stop" to begin cooking.
9. Serve hot.

NUTRITION: Calories: 450, Fats: 27.8g, Net Carbs: 2.5g, Carbs: 2.9g, Fiber: 0.4g, Sugar: 0.3g, Proteins: 45.7g, Sodium: 164mg

204. Sesame Seed Coated Tuna

Preparation time: 15 minutes

Cooking time: 6 minutes

Servings: 2

INGREDIENTS

- 1 organic egg white
- ¼ cup white sesame seeds
- 1 tablespoon black sesame seeds
- Salt and ground black pepper, as required
- 2 (6-ouncestuna steaks

DIRECTIONS

1. Arrange the greased "Cook & Crisp Basket" in the pot of Ninja Foodi.
2. Close the Ninja Foodi with crisping lid and select "Air Crisp".
3. Set the temperature to 400 degrees F for 5 minutes.
4. Press "Start/Stop" to begin preheating.
5. In a shallow bowl, beat the egg white.
6. In another bowl, mix together the sesame seeds, salt, and black pepper.
7. Dip the tuna steaks into egg white and then, coat with the sesame seeds mixture.
8. After preheating, open the lid.
9. Place the fish fillets into the "Cook & Crisp Basket" in a single layer.
10. Close the Ninja Foodi with crisping lid and select "Air Crisp".
11. Set the temperature to 400 degrees F for 6 minutes.
12. Press "Start/Stop" to begin cooking.
13. Flip the fish fillets once halfway through.
14. Serve hot.

NUTRITION: Calories: 425, Fats: 19.7g, Net Carbs: 2.2g, Carbs: 4.3g, Fiber: 2.1g, Sugar: 02g, Proteins: 55.9g, Sodium: 181mg

205. Creamy Tuna Cakes

Preparation time: 15 minutes

Cooking time: 15 minutes

Servings: 4

INGREDIENTS

- 2 (6-ouncescans tuna, drained
- 1½ tablespoons mayonnaise
- 1½ tablespoon almond flour
- 1 tablespoon fresh lemon juice
- 1 teaspoon dried dill
- 1 teaspoon garlic powder
- ½ teaspoon onion powder
- Pinch of salt and ground black pepper

DIRECTIONS

1. Arrange the greased "Cook & Crisp Basket" in the pot of Ninja Foodi.
2. Close the Ninja Foodi with crisping lid and select "Air Crisp".
3. Set the temperature to 400 degrees F for 5 minutes.
4. Press "Start/Stop" to begin preheating.
5. In a large bowl, mix together the tuna, mayonnaise, flour, lemon juice, dill, and spices.
6. Make 4 equal-sized patties from the mixture.
7. Place the tuna cakes into the "Cook & Crisp Basket" in a single layer.
8. Close the Ninja Foodi with crisping lid and select "Air Crisp".
9. Set the temperature to 400 degrees F for 15 minutes.
10. Press "Start/Stop" to begin cooking.
11. Flip the tuna cakes once after 10 minutes.
12. Serve hot.

NUTRITION: Calories: 214, Fats: 12.1g, Net Carbs: 1g, Carbs: 1.4g, Fiber: 0.4g, Sugar: 0.5g, Proteins: 1322.8g, Sodium: 117mg

206. Mahi-Mahi with Tomatoes

Preparation time: 15 minutes

Cooking time: 15 minutes

Servings: 6

INGREDIENTS

- 3 tablespoons butter
- 1 (28-ouncecan sugar-free diced tomatoes
- 1 yellow onion, sliced
- 2 tablespoons fresh lemon juice
- 1 teaspoon dried oregano
- Salt and ground black pepper, as required
- 6 (4-ouncemahi-mahi fillets

DIRECTIONS

1. Select "Sauté/Sear" setting of Ninja Foodi and place the butter into the pot.
2. Press "Start/Stop" to begin cooking and heat for about 2-3 minutes.
3. Add all the ingredients except fish fillets and cook for about 8-10 minutes.
4. Press "Start/Stop" to stop cooking and place the fish fillets over sauce.
5. With a spoon, place some sauce over fillets.
6. Close the Ninja Foodi with the pressure lid and place the pressure valve to "Seal" position.
7. Select "Pressure" and set to "High for 5 minutes.
8. Press "Start/Stop" to begin cooking.
9. Switch the valve to "Vent" and do a "Quick" release.
10. Serve hot with the topping of sauce.

NUTRITION: Calories: 174, Fats: 6.1g, Net Carbs: 5g, Carbs: 7.1g, Fiber: 2.1g, Sugar: 4.4g, Proteins: 22.6g, Sodium: 172mg

207. Parmesan Shrimp

Preparation time: 20 minutes

Cooking time: 20 minutes

Servings: 4

INGREDIENTS

- 2/3 cup Parmesan cheese, grated
- 4 garlic cloves, minced
- 2 tablespoons olive oil
- 1 teaspoon dried basil
- ½ teaspoon dried oregano
- 1 teaspoon onion powder
- ½ teaspoon red pepper flakes, crushed
- Ground black pepper, as required
- 2 pounds shrimp, peeled and deveined
- 1-2 tablespoons fresh lemon juice

DIRECTIONS

1. Arrange the greased "Cook & Crisp Basket" in the pot of Ninja Foodi.
2. Close the Ninja Foodi with crisping lid and select "Air Crisp".
3. Set the temperature to 350 degrees F for 5 minutes.
4. Press "Start/Stop" to begin preheating.
5. In a large bowl, add the Parmesan cheese, garlic, oil, herbs, and spices and mix well
6. Add the shrimp and toss to coat well.
7. After preheating, open the lid.
8. Place half of the shrimp into the "Cook & Crisp Basket" in a single layer.
9. Close the Ninja Foodi with crisping lid and select "Air Crisp".
10. Set the temperature to 320 degrees F for 10 minutes.
11. Press "Start/Stop" to begin cooking.
12. Transfer the shrimp onto a platter.
13. Repeat with the remaining shrimp.
14. Drizzle with lemon juice and serve immediately.

NUTRITION:

Calories: 386, Fats: 14.2g, Net Carbs: 5g, Carbs: 5.3g, Fiber: 0.3g, Sugar: 0.4g, Proteins: 57.3g, Sodium: 670mg

208. Buttered Shrimp

Preparation time: 15 minutes

Cooking time: 50 minutes

Servings: 6

INGREDIENTS

- 8 garlic cloves, chopped
- ¼ cup fresh cilantro, chopped
- 1/3 cup unsalted butter
- ½ teaspoon lemon pepper
- ¼ teaspoon cayenne pepper
- Ground black pepper, as required
- 2 pounds extra-large shrimp, peeled and deveined

DIRECTIONS

1. In the pot of Ninja Foodi, add all the ingredients except for shrimp and stir to combine.
2. Close the Ninja Foodi with crisping lid and select "Slow Cooker".
3. Set on "High" for 30 minutes.
4. Press "Start/Stop" to begin cooking.
5. Add the shrimp and stir to combine.
6. Close the Ninja Foodi with crisping lid and select "Slow Cooker".
7. Set on "High" for 20 minutes.
8. Press "Start/Stop" to begin cooking.
9. Serve hot.

NUTRITION: Calories: 415, Fats: 19.3g, Net Carbs: 5.4g, Carbs: 5.7g, Fiber: 0.3g, Sugar: 0.1g, Proteins: 52.3g, Sodium: 664mg

209. Spicy Shrimp

Preparation time: 15 minutes

Cooking time: 5 minutes

Servings: 3

INGREDIENTS

- 1 pound tiger shrimp
- 3 tablespoons olive oil
- 1 teaspoon old bay seasoning
- ½ teaspoon cayenne pepper
- ½ teaspoon smoked paprika
- Salt, as required

DIRECTIONS

1. Arrange the greased "Cook & Crisp Basket" in the pot of Ninja Foodi.
2. Close the Ninja Foodi with crisping lid and select "Air Crisp".
3. Set the temperature to 390 degrees F for 5 minutes.
4. Press "Start/Stop" to begin preheating.
5. In a large bowl, add all the ingredients and stir to combine.
6. After preheating, open the lid.
7. Place the shrimp into the "Cook & Crisp Basket".
8. Close the Ninja Foodi with crisping lid and select "Air Crisp".
9. Set the temperature to 390 degrees F for 5 minutes.
10. Press "Start/Stop" to begin cooking.
11. Serve hot.

NUTRITION: Calories: 272, Fats: 15.7g, Net Carbs: 0.2g, Carbs: 0.4g, Fiber: 0.2g, Sugar: 0.1g, Proteins: 31.7g, Sodium: 603mg

210.   Shrimp with Tomatoes

Preparation time: 15 minutes

Cooking time: 7¼ hours

Servings: 4

INGREDIENTS

- 1 (14-ouncecan sugar-free peeled tomatoes, chopped finely
- 4 ounces canned sugar-free tomato paste
- 2 garlic cloves, minced
- 2 tablespoons fresh parsley, chopped
- Salt and ground black pepper, as required
- 1 teaspoon lemon pepper
- 2 pounds cooked shrimp, peeled and deveined

DIRECTIONS

1. In the pot of Ninja Foodi, add all the ingredients except for shrimp and stir to combine.

2. Close the Ninja Foodi with crisping lid and select "Slow Cooker".
3. Set on "Low" for 6-7 hours.
4. Press "Start/Stop" to begin cooking.
5. Add the shrimp and stir to combine.
6. Close the Ninja Foodi with crisping lid and select "Slow Cooker".
7. Set on "High" for 15 minutes.
8. Press "Start/Stop" to begin cooking.
9. Serve hot.

NUTRITION: Calories: 210, Fats: 2.8g, Net Carbs: 7g, Carbs: 9g, Fiber: 2g, Sugar: 4.1g, Proteins: 36g, Sodium: 419mg

211.   Shrimp with Bell Peppers

Preparation time: 20 minutes

Cooking time: 3½ hours

Servings: 8

INGREDIENTS

- 1½ cups red bell pepper, seeded and sliced
- 1½ cups green bell pepper, seeded and sliced
- 2 cups tomatoes, chopped finely
- 1 garlic clove, minced
- ½ teaspoon dried thyme, crushed
- ½ teaspoon dried basil, crushed
- ¼ teaspoon cayenne pepper
- 1 teaspoon lemon pepper
- ¼ teaspoon red pepper flakes, crushed
- Salt and ground black pepper, as required
- ¼ cup homemade chicken broth
- 2 pounds large shrimp, peeled and deveined

DIRECTIONS

1. In the pot of Ninja Foodi, add all the ingredients except for shrimp and stir to combine.
2. Close the Ninja Foodi with crisping lid and select "Slow Cooker".
3. Set on "High" for 3 hours.
4. Press "Start/Stop" to begin cooking.
5. Add the shrimp and stir to combine.

6. Close the Ninja Foodi with crisping lid and select "Slow Cooker".
7. Set on "High" for 30 minutes.
8. Press "Start/Stop" to begin cooking.
9. Serve hot.

NUTRITION: Calories: 108, Fats: 0.2g, Net Carbs: 4.3g, Carbs: 5.7g, Fiber: 1.2g, Sugar: 2g, Proteins: 22.2g, Sodium: 188mg

212. Curried Shrimp

Preparation time: 15 minutes

Cooking time: 4 minutes

Servings: 3

INGREDIENTS

- 1 pound shrimp, peeled and deveined
- 1 tablespoon garlic, minced
- 1 teaspoon curry powder
- Salt and ground black pepper, as required
- 8 ounces unsweetened coconut milk

DIRECTIONS

1. In a bowl, add all ingredients and mix until well combined.
2. In a baking pan, place the shrimp mixture.
3. In the pot of Ninja Foodi, place 2 cups of water.
4. Arrange the "Reversible Rack" in the pot of Ninja Foodi.
5. Place the pan over the "Reversible Rack".
6. Close the Ninja Foodi with the pressure lid and place the pressure valve to "Seal" position.
7. Select "Pressure" and set to "Low" for 4 minutes.
8. Press "Start/Stop" to begin cooking.
9. Switch the valve to "Vent" and do a "Quick" release.
10. stir the curry well and serve hot.

NUTRITION: Calories: 360, Fats: 20.7g, Net Carbs: 5g, Carbs: 7g, Fiber: 2g, Sugar: 2.6g, Proteins: 34.6g, Sodium: 432mg

213. Shrimp & Cauliflower Curry

Preparation time: 20 minutes

Cooking time: 2 hours

Servings: 6

INGREDIENTS

- 3 cups tomatoes, chopped finely
- 1½ cups small cauliflower florets
- 1 celery stalk, chopped
- 1 small yellow onion, chopped
- 1 cup unsweetened coconut milk
- 2 tablespoon curry powder
- Salt and ground black pepper, as required
- 1½ pounds shrimp, peeled and deveined

DIRECTIONS

1. In the pot of Ninja Foodi, add all the ingredients except for shrimp and stir to combine.
2. Close the Ninja Foodi with crisping lid and select "Slow Cooker".
3. Set on "High" for 80 minutes.
4. Press "Start/Stop" to begin cooking.
5. Add the shrimp and stir to combine.
6. Close the Ninja Foodi with crisping lid and select "Slow Cooker".
7. Set on "High" for 40 minutes.
8. Press "Start/Stop" to begin cooking.
9. Serve hot.

NUTRITION: Calories: 229, Fats: 7.9g, Net Carbs: 6.3g, Carbs: 9g, Fiber: 2.7g, Sugar: 4g, Proteins: 28g, Sodium: 323mg

214. Shrimp Scampi

Preparation time: 20 minutes

Cooking time: 7 minutes

Servings: 3

INGREDIENTS

- 4 tablespoons salted butter

- 1 tablespoon fresh lemon juice
- 1 tablespoon garlic, minced
- 2 teaspoons red pepper flakes, crushed
- 1 pound shrimp, peeled and deveined
- 2 tablespoons fresh basil, chopped
- 1 tablespoon fresh chives, chopped
- 2 tablespoons homemade chicken broth

DIRECTIONS

1. Arrange a 7-inch round baking pan in the "Cook & Crisp Basket".
2. Now, arrange the "Cook & Crisp Basket" in the pot of Ninja Foodi.
3. Close the Ninja Foodi with crisping lid and select "Air Crisp".
4. Set the temperature to 325 degrees F for 5 minutes.
5. Press "Start/Stop" to begin preheating.
6. After preheating, open the lid and carefully remove the pan from Ninja Foodi.
7. In the heated pan, place butter, lemon juice, garlic, and red pepper flakes and mix well.
8. Place the pan in the "Cook & Crisp Basket".
9. Close the Ninja Foodi with crisping lid and select "Air Crisp".
10. Set the temperature to 325 degrees F for 7 minutes.
11. Press "Start/Stop" to begin cooking.
12. After 2 minutes of cooking, stir in the shrimp, basil, chives and broth.
13. Place the pan onto a wire rack for about 1 minute.
14. Stir the mixture and serve hot.

NUTRITION: Calories: 327, Fats: 18.3g, Net Carbs: 3.5g, Carbs: 4.2g, Fiber: 0.5g, Sugar: 0.3g, Proteins: 35.3g, Sodium: 512mg

215. Shrimp Kabobs

Preparation time: 15 minutes

Cooking time: 8 minutes

Servings: 2

INGREDIENTS

- ¾ pound shrimp, peeled and deveined
- 2 tablespoons fresh lemon juice
- 1 teaspoon garlic, minced
- ½ teaspoon paprika
- ½ teaspoon ground cumin
- Salt and ground black pepper, as required
- 1 tablespoon fresh cilantro, chopped

DIRECTIONS

1. Arrange the greased "Cook & Crisp Basket" in the pot of Ninja Foodi.
2. Close the Ninja Foodi with crisping lid and select "Air Crisp".
3. Set the temperature to 350 degrees F for 5 minutes.
4. Press "Start/Stop" to begin preheating.
5. In a bowl, mix together the lemon juice, garlic, and spices.
6. Add the shrimp and mix well.
7. Thread the shrimp onto presoaked wooden skewers.
8. After preheating, open the lid.
9. Place the shrimp skewers into the "Cook & Crisp Basket".
10. Close the Ninja Foodi with crisping lid and select "Air Crisp".
11. Set the temperature to 390 degrees F for 8 minutes.
12. Press "Start/Stop" to begin cooking.
13. Flip the shrimp kabobs once halfway through.
14. Transfer the shrimp kabobs onto serving plates.
15. Garnish with fresh cilantro and serve immediately.

NUTRITION: Calories: 212, Fats: 3.2g, Net Carbs: 3.5g, Carbs: 3.9g, Fiber: 0.4g, Sugar: 0.4g, Proteins: 39.1g, Sodium: 497mg

216. Shrimp Wraps

Preparation time: 20 minutes

Cooking time: 3 minutes

Servings: 8

INGREDIENTS

- 1 pound fresh shrimp, peeled and deveined
- 1 cup radishes, trimmed and julienned
- 1 cup carrot, peeled and shredded
- Salt and ground black pepper, as required
- 8 large butter lettuce leaves

DIRECTIONS

1. In the pot of Ninja Foodi, place the shrimp and enough water to cover.
2. Close the Ninja Foodi with the pressure lid and place the pressure valve to "Seal" position.
3. Select "Pressure" and set to "High for 3 minutes.
4. Press "Start/Stop" to begin cooking.
5. Switch the valve to "Vent" and do a "Quick" release.
6. With tongs, transfer the shrimp into a bowl.
7. Set aside to cool slightly.
8. Add the cucumber, carrot, salt and black pepper and toss to coat well.
9. Arrange 1 lettuce leaf onto each serving plate.
10. Place the shrimp mixture in each leaf evenly and serve immediately.

NUTRITION: Calories: 76, Fats: 1g, Net Carbs: 2.3g, Carbs: 2.9g, Fiber: 0.6g, Sugar: 1g, Proteins: 13.1g, Sodium: 173mg

217. Creamy Lobster Tails

Preparation time: 20 minutes

Cooking time: 3 minutes

Servings: 3

INGREDIENTS

- 1 teaspoon old bay seasoning
- 2 pounds fresh lobster tails
- 1 scallion, chopped
- ½ cup mayonnaise
- 2 tablespoons unsalted butter, melted
- 2 tablespoons fresh lemon juice, divided

DIRECTIONS

1. In the pot of Ninja Foodi, place 1½ cups of water and 1-2 pinches of old bay seasoning.
2. Arrange the "Reversible Rack" in the pot of Ninja Foodi.
3. Arrange the lobster tail over the "Reversible Rack", shell side down, meat side up.
4. Drizzle the lobster tails with 1 tablespoon of lemon juice.
5. Close the Ninja Foodi with the pressure lid and place the pressure valve to "Seal" position.
6. Select "Pressure" and set to "Low" for 3 minutes.
7. Press "Start/Stop" to begin cooking.
8. Switch the valve to "Vent" and do a "Quick" release.
9. Transfer the tails into the bowl of ice bath for about 1 minute.
10. With kitchen shears, cut the underbelly of the tail down the center.
11. Remove the meat and chop it up into large chunks.
12. In a large bowl, add the lobster meat, scallions, mayonnaise, butter, seasoning and lemon juice and mix well.
13. Refrigerate for at least 15 minutes before serving.

NUTRITION: Calories: 582, Fats: 36.9g, Net Carbs: 0.4g, Carbs: 0.6g, Fiber: 0.2g, Sugar: 0.3g, Proteins: 57.7g, Sodium: 1900mg

218. Buttered Crab Legs

Preparation time: 20 minutes

Cooking time: 4 minutes

Servings: 2

INGREDIENTS

- 1½ pounds frozen crab legs
- Salt, as required
- 2 tablespoons butter, melted

DIRECTIONS

1. In the pot of Ninja Foodi, place 1 cup of water and 1 teaspoon of salt.
2. Arrange the "Reversible Rack" in the pot of Ninja Foodi.
3. Place the crab legs over the "Reversible Rack "and sprinkle with salt.
4. Close the Ninja Foodi with the pressure lid and place the pressure valve to "Seal" position.
5. Select "Pressure" and set to "High" for 4 minutes.
6. Press "Start/Stop" to begin cooking.
7. Switch the valve to "Vent" and do a "Quick" release.
8. Transfer crab legs onto a serving platter.
9. Drizzle with butter and serve.

NUTRITION: Calories: 445, Fats: 16.7g, Net Carbs: 0g, Carbs: 0g, Fiber: 0g, Sugar: 0g, Proteins: 65.4g, Sodium: 2000mg

219.   Rosemary Scallops

Preparation time: 15 minutes

Cooking time: 7 minutes

Servings: 6

INGREDIENTS

- ½ cup butter
- 4 garlic cloves, minced
- 1 tablespoon fresh rosemary, chopped
- 1 tablespoon fresh thyme, chopped
- 2 pounds sea scallops
- Salt and ground black pepper, as required

DIRECTIONS

1. Select "Sauté/Sear" setting of Ninja Foodi and place the butter into the pot.
2. Press "Start/Stop" to begin cooking and heat for about 2-3 minutes.
3. Add the garlic and rosemary and cook, uncovered for about 1 minute.
4. Stir in the scallops, salt and black pepper and cook for about 2 minutes.

5. Press "Start/Stop" to stop cooking.
6. Close the Ninja Foodi with crisping lid and select "Air Crisp".
7. Set the temperature to 350 degrees F for 3 minutes.
8. Press "Start/Stop" to begin cooking.
9. Serve hot.

NUTRITION: Calories: 275, Fats: 16.6g, Net Carbs: 4.4g, Carbs: 4.9g, Fiber: 0.4g, Sugar: 0g, Proteins: 25.7g, Sodium: 353mg

220.   Scallops in Capers Sauce

Preparation time: 15 minutes

Cooking time: 6 minutes

Servings: 3

INGREDIENTS

- 12 (1-ouncesea scallops, cleaned and patted very dry
- Salt and ground black pepper, as required
- ¼ cup olive oil
- 2 tablespoons fresh parsley, finely chopped
- 2 teaspoons capers, finely chopped
- 1 teaspoon fresh lemon zest, finely grated
- ½ teaspoon garlic, finely chopped

DIRECTIONS

1. Arrange the greased "Cook & Crisp Basket" in the pot of Ninja Foodi.
2. Close the Ninja Foodi with crisping lid and select "Air Crisp".
3. Set the temperature to 400 degrees F for 5 minutes.
4. Press "Start/Stop" to begin preheating.
5. Season each scallop with salt and black pepper evenly.
6. After preheating, open the lid.
7. Place the scallops into the "Cook & Crisp Basket" in a single layer.
8. Close the Ninja Foodi with crisping lid and select "Air Crisp".
9. Set the temperature to 400 degrees F for 6 minutes.
10. Press "Start/Stop" to begin cooking.

11. Meanwhile, for sauce: in a bowl, mix the remaining ingredients .
12. Press "Start/Stop" to stop cooking and open the lid
13. Transfer the scallops onto serving plates.
14. Top with the sauce and serve immediately.

NUTRITION: Calories: 246, Fats: 17.7g, Net Carbs: 3g, Carbs: 3.2g, Fiber: 0.2g, Sugar: 0.1g, Proteins: 19.2g, Sodium: 291mg

221. Scallops with Spinach

Preparation time: 15 minutes

Cooking time: 10 minutes

Servings: 3

INGREDIENTS

- 1 (10-ouncepackage frozen spinach, thawed and drained
- 12 sea scallops
- Olive oil cooking spray
- Salt and ground black pepper, as required
- ¾ cup heavy whipping cream
- 1 tablespoon sugar-free tomato paste
- 1 teaspoon garlic, minced
- 1 tablespoon fresh basil, chopped

DIRECTIONS

1. Arrange the greased "Cook & Crisp Basket" in the pot of Ninja Foodi.
2. Close the Ninja Foodi with crisping lid and select "Air Crisp".
3. Set the temperature to 350 degrees F for 5 minutes.
4. Press "Start/Stop" to begin preheating.
5. In the bottom of a 7-inch heatproof pan, place the spinach.
6. Spray each scallop with cooking spray and then, sprinkle with a little salt and black pepper.
7. Arrange scallops on top of the spinach in a single layer.
8. In a bowl, add the cream, tomato paste, garlic, basil, salt and black pepper and mix well.

9. Place the cream mixture over the spinach and scallops evenly.
10. Close the Ninja Foodi with crisping lid and select "Air Crisp".
11. Set the temperature to 350 degrees F for 10 minutes.
12. Press "Start/Stop" to begin cooking.
13. Meanwhile, for sauce: in a bowl, mix the remaining ingredients .
14. Serve hot.

NUTRITION: Calories: 237, Fats: 12.4g, Net Carbs: 6.3g, Carbs: 8g, Fiber: 2.3g, Sugar: 1.1g, Proteins: 23.8g, Sodium: 207mg

222. Creamy Mussels

Preparation time: 25 minutes

Cooking time: 2 hours 20 minutes

Servings: 6

INGREDIENTS

- 1 cup homemade chicken broth
- 1 tablespoon red boat fish sauce
- 1 small yellow onion, chopped
- 2 garlic cloves, grated
- 1 lemongrass stalk, smashed
- 1 small Serrano pepper, chopped
- 2 pounds fresh mussels, scrubbed and debearded
- 1½ cups unsweetened coconut milk
- ¼ cup fresh cilantro leaves
- 1 teaspoon fresh lime zest, grated
- 1 tablespoon fresh lime juice

DIRECTIONS

1. In the pot of Ninja Foodi, add the broth, fish sauce, onion, garlic, lemongrass and serrano and stir to combine.
2. Close the Ninja Foodi with crisping lid and select "Slow Cooker".
3. Set on "High" for 2 hours.
4. Press "Start/Stop" to begin cooking.
5. Add the mussels and coconut milk and stir to combine.

6. Close the Ninja Foodi with crisping lid and select "Slow Cooker".
7. Set on "High" for 20 minutes.
8. Press "Start/Stop" to begin cooking.
9. Stir in the cilantro, lime zest and juice and serve.

NUTRITION: Calories: 232, Fats: 11.7g, Net Carbs: 7g, Carbs: 8g, Fiber: 1g, Sugar: 2.1g, Proteins: 20g, Sodium: 712mg

223. Herbed Seafood Stew

Preparation time: 25 minutes

Cooking time: 4¾ hours

Servings: 8

INGREDIENTS

- 1 celery stalk, chopped
- 1 yellow onion, chopped
- 3 garlic cloves, chopped
- 1 cup fresh cilantro leaves, chopped
- 1 cup tomatoes, chopped finely
- 4 cups homemade chicken broth
- 2 tablespoons fresh lemon juice
- 2 tablespoons olive oil
- 3 teaspoons mixed dried herbs (rosemary, thyme, marjoram
- Salt and ground black pepper, as required
- 1 pound cod fillets, cubed
- 1 pound shrimp, peeled and deveined
- 1 pound scallops
- ¾ cup crabmeat

DIRECTIONS

1. In the pot of Ninja Foodi, add all ingredients except seafood and mix well.
2. Close the Ninja Foodi with crisping lid and select "Slow Cooker".
3. Set on "High" for 4 hours.
4. Press "Start/Stop" to begin cooking.
5. Add the seafood and stir to combine.

6. Now, set on "Low" for 45 minutes.
7. Press "Start/Stop" to begin cooking.
8. Serve hot.

NUTRITION: Calories: 216, Fats: 5.6g, Net Carbs: 4.9g, Carbs: 5.7g, Fiber: 1.3g, Sugar: 1.2g, Proteins: 34.4g, Sodium: 322mg

224. Seafood & Tomato Stew

Preparation time: 20 minutes

Cooking time: 4 hours 50 minutes

Servings: 8

INGREDIENTS

- 2 tablespoons olive oil
- 1 pound tomatoes, chopped
- 1 large yellow onion, chopped finely
- 2 garlic cloves, minced
- 2 teaspoons curry powder
- 6 sprigs fresh parsley
- Salt and ground black pepper, as required
- 1½ cups homemade chicken broth
- 1½ pounds salmon, cut into cubes
- 1½ pounds shrimp, peeled and deveined

DIRECTIONS

1. In the pot of Ninja Foodi, add all ingredients except seafood and mix well.
2. Close the Ninja Foodi with crisping lid and select "Slow Cooker".
3. Set on "High" for 4 hours.
4. Press "Start/Stop" to begin cooking.
5. Add the seafood and stir to combine.
6. Now, set on "Low" for 50 minutes.
7. Press "Start/Stop" to begin cooking.
8. Serve hot.

NUTRITION: Calories: 265, Fats: 10.4g, Net Carbs: 4.3g, Carbs: 5.5g, Fiber: 1.2g, Sugar: 2.1g, Proteins: 37g, Sodium: 281mg

POULTRY

225. Chicken and Broccoli Platter

Preparation Time: 10 minutes

Cooking time: 15 minutes

Servings: 4

INGREDIENTS

- 1 tablespoon olive oil
- 1 tablespoon butter
- 2 large chicken breasts, boneless
- ½ cup onion, chopped
- 14 ounces chicken broth
- ½ teaspoon salt
- ½ teaspoon pepper
- 1/8 teaspoon red pepper flakes
- 1 tablespoon parsley
- 1 tablespoon arrowroot
- 2 tablespoons water
- 4 ounces light cream cheese, cubed
- 1 cup cheddar cheese, shredded
- 3 cups steamed broccoli, chopped

DIRECTIONS

1. Season the chicken breast with pepper and salt
2. Set your Ninja Foodi to Saute mode and add butter and vegetable oil
3. Allow it to melt and transfer the seasoned chicken to the pot. Allow it to brown
4. Remove the chicken and add the onions to the pot, Saute them for 5 minutes
5. Add chicken broth, pepper, red pepper and salt, parsley. Add the browned breast
6. Lock up the lid and cook for about 5 minutes at high pressure
7. Once done, quick release the pressure. Remove the chicken and shred it up into small portions
8. Take a bowl and add 2 tablespoons of water and dissolve cornstarch \
9. Select the simmer mode and add the mixture to the Ninja Foodi
10. Toss in the cubed and shredded cheese. Stir completely until everything is melted
11. Toss in the diced chicken again and the steamed broccoli and cook for 5 minutes
12. Once done, sever with white rice and shredded cheese as garnish

226. Complex Garlic and Lemon Chicken

Preparation Time: 10 minutes

Cooking time: 30 minutes

Servings: 6

INGREDIENTS

- 1-2 pounds chicken breast
- 1 teaspoon salt
- 1 onion, diced
- 1 tablespoon ghee
- 5 garlic cloves, minced
- ½ cup organic chicken broth
- 1 teaspoon dried parsley
- 1 large lemon juice
- 3-4 teaspoon arrowroot flour

DIRECTIONS

1. Set your Ninja Foodi to Saute mode. Add diced up onion and cooking fat
2. Allow the onions to cook for 5 -10 minutes
3. Add the rest of the ingredients except arrowroot flour
4. Lock up the lid and set the pot to poultry mode. Cook until the timer runs out
5. Allow the pressure to release naturally
6. Once done, remove ¼ cup of the sauce from the pot and add arrowroot to make a slurry
7. Add the slurry to the pot to make the gravy thick. Keep stirring well. Serve!

227. Chicken Puttanesca

Preparation Time: 10 minutes

Cooking time: 50 minutes

Servings: 6

INGREDIENTS

- 6 chicken thigh, skin on
- 2 tablespoons extra virgin olive oil
- 2 garlic cloves, crushed
- Salt and pepper to taste
- ½ teaspoon red chili flakes
- 14 and ½ ounces tomatoes, chopped
- 6 ounces black olives, pitted
- 1 tablespoon capers
- 1 tablespoon fresh basil, chopped
- ¾ cup of water

DIRECTIONS

1. Set your Ninja Foodi to Saute mode and add oil, allow the oil to heat up
2. Add chicken pieces and Saute for 5 minutes until browned, transfer the browned chicken to a platter
3. Add chopped tomatoes, olives, water, capers, garlic, chopped basil, salt, pepper, red chili flakes and stir well, bring the mix to a simmer. Add the chicken pieces to your pot
4. Lock up the lid and cook on HIGH pressure for 12 minutes
5. Release the pressure naturally. Serve with a side of veggies if wanted, enjoy!

228. Awesome Ligurian Chicken

Preparation Time: 10 minutes

Cooking time: 15 minutes

Servings: 4

INGREDIENTS

- 2 garlic cloves, chopped
- 3 sprigs fresh rosemary
- 2 sprigs fresh sage
- ½ bunch parsley
- 3 lemon, juiced

- 4 tablespoons extra virgin olive oil
- 1 teaspoon salt
- ¼ teaspoon pepper
- 1 and ½ cup of water
- 1 whole chicken, cut into parts
- 3 and ½ ounces black gourmet salt-cured olives
- 1 fresh lemon

DIRECTIONS

1. 1.Take a bowl and add chopped up garlic, parsley, sage, and rosemary
2. 2.Pour lemon juice, olive oil to a bowl and season with salt and pepper
3. 3.Remove the chicken skin and from the chicken pieces and carefully transfer them to a dish
4. 4.Pour the marinade on top of the chicken pieces and allow them to chill for 2-4 hours
5. 5.Set your Ninja Foodi to Saute mode and add olive oil, allow it to heat up. Add chicken and browned on all sides
6. 6.Measure out the marinade and add to the pot (it should cover the chicken, add a bit of water if needed). Lock up the lid and cook on HIGH pressure for 10 minutes
7. 7.Release the pressure naturally. The chicken out and transfer to a platter
8. 8.Cover with a foil and allow them to coolSet your pot in Saute mode and reduce the liquid to ¼
9. 9.Add the chicken pieces again to the pot and allow them to warm
10. 10.Sprinkle a bit of olive, lemon slices, and rosemary. Enjoy!

229. Garlic and Lemon Chicken Dish

Preparation Time: 10 minutes

Cooking time: 30 minutes

Servings: 4

INGREDIENTS

- 2-3 pounds chicken breast
- 1 teaspoon salt
- 1 onion, diced

- 1 tablespoon ghee
- 5 garlic cloves, minced
- ½ cup organic chicken broth
- 1 teaspoon dried parsley
- 1 large lemon, juiced
- 3-4 teaspoon arrowroot flour

DIRECTIONS

1. Set your pot to Saute mode. Add diced up onion and cooking fat
2. Allow the onions to cook for 5 -10 minutes
3. Add the rest of the ingredients except arrowroot flour
4. Lock up the lid and set the pot to poultry mode. Cook until the timer runs out
5. Allow the pressure to release naturally
6. Once done, remove ¼ cup of the sauce from the pot and add arrowroot to make a slurry
7. Add the slurry to the pot to make the gravy thick. Keep stirring well. Serve!

230.   The Hungarian Chicken Meal

Preparation Time: 10 minutes

Cooking time: 8 hours

Servings: 6

INGREDIENTS

- 1 tablespoon extra-virgin olive oil
- 2 pounds boneless chicken thigh
- ½ cup chicken broth
- Juice and zest of 1 lemon
- 2 teaspoon garlic, minced
- 2 teaspoon paprika
- ½ teaspoon salt
- 1 cup cashew cream
- 1 tablespoon parsley, chopped

DIRECTIONS

1. Lightly grease the inner pot of your Ninja Foodi with olive oil. Add chicken thigh to Ninja Foodi
2. Take a bowl and add broth, lemon juice, garlic, paprika, zest, and salt

3. Mix and pour the mixture over chicken. Cook on LOW for 7-8 hours
4. Remove heat and stir in cashew cream. Serve with a topping of parsley. Enjoy!

231.   Lime and Cilantro Chicken Meal

Preparation Time: 10 minutes

Cooking time: 2 hours 45 minutes

Servings: 4

INGREDIENTS

- 2 small limes
- ¼ cup cilantro, chopped
- ½ tablespoon fresh garlic, minced
- 1 teaspoon salt
- ½ teaspoon pepper
- 4 pounds chicken drumsticks

DIRECTIONS

1. Juice the lime and add them to your Ninja Foodi
2. Add ¼ cup of chopped cilantro, 1 teaspoon of salt, ½ a tablespoon of freshly minced garlic
3. Add the chicken drumsticks to the Ninja Foodi and coat them well
4. Cover and cook on SLOW COOK MODE (HIGH)for 2 and a ½ hour
5. Pre-heat your oven to a temperature of 500 degrees F. Line up a cookie sheet with foil
6. Transfer the cooker drumstick from the cooker to the foil using tongs
7. Bake for 10 minutes until they are nicely browned, making sure to turn them halfway through
8. Serve with the cooking juices. Enjoy!

232.   The Original Mexican Chicken Cacciatore

Preparation Time: 10 minutes

Cooking time: 33 minutes

Servings: 4

INGREDIENTS

- Extra virgin olive oil'
- 3 shallots, chopped
- 4 garlic cloves, crushed
- 1 green bell pepper, sliced
- ½ cup organic chicken broth
- 10 ounces mushrooms, sliced
- 5-6 skinless chicken breasts
- 2 cans (14.5 ounces) organic crushed tomatoes
- 2 tablespoons organic tomato paste
- 1 can (14.5 ounces) black olives, pitted
- Fresh parsley
- Salt and pepper to taste

DIRECTIONS

1. Add oil to your pot and set the Ninja Foodi to Saute mode
2. Add shallots, bell pepper and cook for 2 minutes
3. Add broth and bring to a boil for 23 minutes. Add garlic and mushrooms
4. Gently place the chicken on the top of the whole mixture
5. Cover the chicken with tomato paste and crushed tomatoes
6. Lock up the lid and cook on HIGH pressure for 8 minutes
7. Release the pressure naturally over 10 minutes and stir in parsley, olive oil, pepper, salt, and red pepper flakes. Serve!

233. Magnificent Chicken Curry Soup

Preparation Time: 10 minutes

Cooking time: 30 minutes

Servings: 4

INGREDIENTS

- 1 and ½ cups unsweetened coconut milk
- 1 pound chicken thigh, skinless
- 3-4 garlic cloves, crushed
- ½ an onion, finely diced
- 2-inch knob ginger, minced
- 1 cup mushrooms, sliced
- 4 ounces baby spinach
- ½ teaspoon of cayenne pepper
- ½ teaspoon turmeric
- 1 teaspoon salt
- 1 teaspoon Garam Masala
- ¼ cup cilantro, chopped

DIRECTIONS

1. Add the listed ingredients to Ninja Foodi
2. Lock lid and cook on HIGH pressure for 10 minutes. Naturally, release pressure over 10 minutes
3. Remove meat and shred it, return the shredded meat to the pot
4. Set your pot to Saute mode and stir for a minute
5. Serve and enjoy!. Enjoy!

234. Summer Time Chicken Salad

Preparation Time: 10 minutes

Cooking time: 10 minutes

Servings: 4

INGREDIENTS

- 8 boneless chicken thighs
- Kosher salt
- 1 tablespoon of ghee
- 1 small onion, chopped
- 2 medium carrots, chopped
- ½ a pound of cremini mushrooms
- 3 garlic cloves, peeled and crushed
- 2 cups of 14-ounce cherry tomatoes
- ½ a cup of 2 ounces of pitted green olives
- ¼ teaspoon of freshly cracked black pepper
- ½ a cup of thinly sliced basil leaves
- ¼ a cup of coarsely chopped Italian parsley

DIRECTIONS

1. Season the chicken thigh with ¾ teaspoon of kosher salt and keep it in your fridge for about 2 days

2. Set your Ninja Foodi to Saute mode and add ghee and allow it to melt
3. Once the Ghee is simmering, add carrots, onions, mushrooms and ½ a teaspoon of salt
4. Saute the veggies until they are tender (should be around 3-5 minutes
5. Drop the tomato paste and garlic to your pot and cook for 30 seconds
6. Add seasoned chicken to the pot alongside olives and cherry tomatoes
7. Give everything a stir
8. Lock up the lid and cook for 7-10 minutes at HIGH pressure
9. Once done, allow the pressure to quick release
10. Stir in fresh herbs and enjoy!

235.   Ham and Stuffed Turkey Rolls

Preparation Time: 10 minutes

Cooking time: 20 minutes

Servings: 4

INGREDIENTS

- 4 tablespoons fresh sage leaves
- 8 ham slices
- 8 (6 ouncesturkey cutlets
- Salt and pepper to taste
- 2 tablespoons butter, melted

DIRECTIONS

1. Season turkey cutlets with salt and pepper
2. Roll turkey cutlets and wrap each of them with ham slices tightly
3. Coat each roll with butter and gently place sage leaves evenly over each cutlet
4. Transfer to Ninja Foodi
5. Lock lid and select Bake/Roast mode and bake for 10 minutes at 360 degrees F
6. Open lid and flip, lock lid and bake for 10 minutes more. Enjoy!

236.   High-Quality Belizean Chicken Stew

Preparation Time: 10 minutes

Cooking time: 20 minutes

Servings: 4

INGREDIENTS

- 4 whole chicken
- 1 tablespoon coconut oil
- 2 tablespoons achiote seasoning
- 2 tablespoons white vinegar
- 3 tablespoons Worcestershire sauce
- 1 cup yellow onion, sliced
- 3 garlic cloves, sliced
- 1 teaspoon ground cumin
- 1 teaspoon dried oregano
- ½ teaspoon black pepper
- 2 cups chicken stock

DIRECTIONS

1. Take a large sized bowl and add achiote paste, vinegar, Worcestershire sauce, oregano, cumin and pepper. Mix well and add chicken pieces and rub the marinade all over them
2. Allow the chicken to sit overnight. Set your pot to Saute mode and add coconut oil
3. Once the oil is hot, add the chicken pieces to the pot and brown them in batches (each batch for 2 minutes). Remove the seared chicken and transfer them to a plate
4. Add onions, garlic to the pot and Saute for 2-3 minutes . Add chicken pieces back to the pot
5. Pour chicken broth to the bowl with marinade and stir well. Add the mixture to the pot
6. Seal up the lid and cook for about 20 minutes at high pressure
7. Once done, release the pressure naturally . Season with a bit of salt and serve!

237.   The Great Poblano Chicken Curry

Preparation Time: 10 minutes

Cooking time: 15 minutes

Servings: 4

INGREDIENTS

- 1 cup onion, diced
- 3 poblano peppers, chopped
- 5 garlic cloves,1 cup cauliflower, diced
- 1 and ½ pounds large chicken breast chunks
- ¼ cup cilantro, chopped
- 1 teaspoon ground coriander
- 1 teaspoon ground cumin
- 1-2 teaspoons salt
- 2 and ½ cups of water
- 2 ounces cream cheese

DIRECTIONS

1. Add everything to your Ninja Foodi except cheese and lock up the lid
2. Cook on HIGH pressure for 15 minutes. Release the pressure naturally over 10 minutes
3. Remove the chicken with tongs and place it on the side
4. Use an immersion blender to blend the soup and veggies. Set your pot to Saute mode
5. Once the broth is hot add cream cheese (Cut in chunks). Whisk well
6. Shred the chicken and transfer it back to the pot. Serve and enjoy!

238. Hearty Chicken Yum

Preparation Time: 30 minutes

Cooking time: 40 minutes

Servings: 4

INGREDIENTS

- 2 tablespoons fresh boneless chicken thigh
- 3 tablespoons homemade ketchup
- 1 and ½ teaspoon salt
- 2 teaspoons garlic powder
- ¼ cup ghee
- ½ teaspoon ground black pepper
- 3 tablespoons organic tamari
- ¼ cup stevia

DIRECTIONS

1. Add the listed ingredients to your Ninja Foodi and give it a nice stir
2. Lock up the lid and cook for about 18 minutes under HIGH pressure
3. Quick release the pressure. Open the lid and transfer the chicken to a bowl
4. Shred it u using a fork
5. Set your pot to Saute mode and allow the liquid to be reduced for 5 minutes
6. Pour the sauce over your chicken Yum and serve with vegetables. Enjoy!

239. The Turkey Pizza Casserole

Preparation Time: 10 minutes

Cooking time: 10 minutes

Servings: 4

INGREDIENTS

- 2 cups tomatoes, crushed
- 1 pound ground turkey
- 1 pack pepperoni
- ½ cup mozzarella cheese
- ½ cup oregano cheese
- ½ teaspoon salt
- 2 garlic cloves, minced
- ½ teaspoon pepper
- ½ teaspoon onion powder

DIRECTIONS:

1. Take a medium sized bowl and add crushed tomatoes, seasoning
2. Pour ¼ of crushed tomatoes to your Ninja Foodi
3. Layer ¼ of ground turkey, pepperoni and cheese on top
4. Keep repeating until the ingredients are used up
5. Lock up the lid and cook on HIGH pressure for 6 minutes
6. Remove and allow it to cool for about 15 minutes. Cut it up and serve. Enjoy!

240. Heartfelt Chicken Curry Soup

Preparation Time: 10 minutes

Cooking time: 10 minutes

Servings: 4

INGREDIENTS

- 1 teaspoon Garam Masala
- ½ teaspoon cayenne
- ½ teaspoon ground turmeric
- 1 teaspoon salt
- 4 ounces baby spinach
- 1 cup mushrooms, sliced
- 1 (2-inch pieceginger, finely chopped
- 3-4 garlic cloves, crushed
- ½ onion, diced
- 1 and ½ cups unsweetened coconut milk
- 1 pound boneless, skinless chicken thighs
- ¼ cup chopped fresh cilantro

DIRECTIONS

1. Add chicken, coconut milk, onion, garlic, ginger, mushrooms, spinach, salt, turmeric, cayenne, garam masala and cilantro to the inner pot of your Ninja Foodi
2. Lock lid and cook on HIGH pressure for 10 minutes
3. Release pressure naturally over 10 minutes. Use tongs to transfer chicken to a plate, shred it
4. Stir chicken back to the soup and stir. Enjoy!

241. Your's Truly Lime Chicken Chili

Preparation Time: 10 minutes

Cooking time: 23 minutes

Servings: 6

INGREDIENTS

- ¼ cup cooking wine (Keto-Friendly
- ½ cup organic chicken broth
- 1 onion, diced

- 1 teaspoon salt
- ½ teaspoon paprika
- 5 garlic cloves, minced
- 1 tablespoon lime juice
- ¼ cup butter
- 2 pounds chicken thighs
- 1 teaspoon dried parsley
- 3 green chilies, chopped

DIRECTIONS

1. Set your Ninja-Foodi to Sauté mode and add onion and garlic
2. Sauté for 3 minutes, add remaining ingredients
3. Lock lid and cook on Medium-HIGH pressure for 20 minutes
4. Release pressure naturally over 10 minutes. Serve and enjoy!

242. Hungry Man's Indian Chicken Keema

Preparation Time: 10 minutes

Cooking time: 10 minutes

Servings: 6

INGREDIENTS

- 1 tablespoon coconut oil
- 1 teaspoon cumin seeds
- ½ teaspoon turmeric
- 1 tablespoon garlic, grated
- 1 tablespoon ginger, grated
- 1 large onion, diced
- 2 tomatoes, diced
- 2 teaspoons mild red chili powder
- 1 teaspoon Garam masala
- 1 teaspoon salt
- 2 tablespoons coriander powder
- 1 pound ground chicken
- ½ cup cilantro

DIRECTIONS

1. Set your Ninja Foodi to Saute mode and add cumin seeds

2. Toast for 30 seconds. Add turmeric powder and give it a nice mix
3. Add garlic, ginger and mix well again. Add onion and Saute for 2 minutes
4. Add tomatoes, Garam Masala, red chili powder, coriander, salt and mix well
5. Add ground chicken and keep Sautéing it while breaking it up with a spatula
6. Add ½ a cup of water . Lock up the lid and cook on HIGH pressure for 4 minutes
7. Release the pressure naturally over 10 minutes
8. Garnish with a bit of cilantro and serve . Enjoy!

243.   The Borderline Crack Chicken

Preparation Time: 10 minutes

Cooking time: 25 minutes

Servings: 4

INGREDIENTS

- 4 ounces cheddar cheese
- 3 tablespoons arrowroot
- 1 cup of water
- 8 ounces cream cheese
- 1 pack ranch seasoning
- 2 pounds boneless chicken breast
- 6-8 cooked bacon

DIRECTIONS

1. Add chicken to your Ninja Foodi. Add cream cheese
2. Sprinkle ranch seasoning over chicken add water
3. Lock lid and cook for 25 minutes on HIGH pressure. Quick release pressure
4. Take the chicken out and shred into pieces
5. Set your pot to SAUTE mode and add a mixture of arrowroot and water
6. Add cheese and shredded chicken. Stir and bacon. Enjoy!

244.   The Decisive Red Curry Chicken

Preparation Time: 10 minutes

Cooking time: 10 minutes

Servings: 6

INGREDIENTS

- 1 tablespoon of olive oil
- 2-4 tablespoon of red curry paste
- 1 and a ½ pound of thin chicken breast
- 1-2 tablespoon of fish sauce
- 1 tablespoon of stevia
- 1 jalapeno chili
- 1 cup yellow onion, sliced
- 1 cup red pepper, sliced
- 1 cup yellow pepper, sliced
- 1 cup orange pepper, sliced
- A handful of Thai basil leaves

DIRECTIONS

1. Set your Ninja Foodi to Saute mode and add oil, allow the oil to heat up
2. Add 2 tablespoon of red curry paste. Saute for 30 seconds
3. Add chicken and mix it well with the curry paste. Add coconut milk
4. Lock up the lid and cook on HIGH pressure for 2 minutes
5. Release the pressure naturally over 10 minutes. Open and stir in fish sauce and stevia
6. Add onion, red, yellow, orange peppers and stir well
7. Set your Ninja Foodi to Saute mode and bring the curry to a gentle boil. Serve and enjoy!

245.   Spinach and Chicken Curry

Preparation Time: 10 minutes

Cooking time: 12 minutes

Servings: 4

INGREDIENTS

- 10 ounce of Spinach
- 1 pound of chicken thigh cut up into 2-3 pieces

- 1 tablespoon of oil
- ½ a teaspoon of cumin seeds
- 1-inch ginger chopped up
- 6 pieces of cloves
- 2 medium onions cut up into pieces

Spices

- ¼ teaspoon of turmeric
- ½ a teaspoon of red chili powder
- 2 teaspoon of coriander
- 1 teaspoon of salt

DIRECTIONS:

1. Set your Ninja Foodi to Saute mode and add oil, allow the oil to heat up
2. Add cumin seeds, garlic, and ginger and cook for 30 seconds
3. Stir in garlic and the cut onions and Saute them for 1 minute more
4. Add spices and give it a nice stir. Add spinach with the chicken pieces on top of the spinach
5. Lock up the lid and allow them to cook at HIGH pressure for 8 minutes
6. Once done, do a quick release and open up the lid. Remove the chicken pieces from the pot and keep them on the side
7. Take an immersion blender and blend the whole mixture until you have a creamy texture
8. Cut up your chicken in small portions and add them back to the curry
9. Set the pot to Saute mode once more and give the whole curry a quick boil (without lid).Enjoy!

246.   Cheese Dredged Lemon Chicken

Preparation Time: 10 minutes

Cooking time: 8 minutes

Servings: 4

INGREDIENTS

- 1 tablespoon olive oil
- 3 chicken breast, boneless and skinless

- 1 cup spicy salsa
- ½ cup feta cheese, crumbled
- ½ teaspoon ground cumin
- ½ teaspoon red chili powder
- ¼ cup fresh lime juice

DIRECTIONS

1. Add olive oil to Instant Pot and set your pot to Saute mode
2. Add chicken breast to the pot and brown both sides. Transfer chicken to a plate
3. Add cumin, chili powder, lime juice, salsa to pot. Stir and return chicken
4. Lock lid and cook on HIGH pressure for 8 minutes. Quick release pressure
5. Transfer chicken breast and sauté to plate. Sprinkle crumbled cheese. Serve and enjoy!

247.   Best Chicken Wings

Preparation Time: 10 minutes

Cooking time: 25 minutes

Servings: 4

INGREDIENTS

- 24 chicken wing segments
- 2 tablespoons toasted sesame oil
- 2 tablespoons Asian-Chile-Garlic sauce
- 2 tablespoons stevia
- 2 garlic cloves, minced
- 1 tablespoon toasted sesame seeds

DIRECTIONS

1. Add 1 cup water to Foodie's inner pot, place reversible rack in the pot in lower portions, place chicken wings in the rack. Place lid into place and seal the valve
2. Select pressure mode to HIGH and cook for 10 minutes
3. Make the glaze by taking a large bowl and whisking in sesame oil, Chile-Garlic sauce, honey and garlic
4. Once the chicken is cooked, quick release the pressure and remove pressure lid

5. Remove rack from the pot and empty remaining water. Return inner pot to the base
6. Cover with crisping lid and select Air Crisp mode, adjust the temperature to 375 degrees F, pre-heat for 3 minutes
7. While the Foodi pre-heats, add wings to the sauce and toss well to coat it
8. Transfer wings to the basket, leaving any excess sauce in the bowl
9. Place the basket in Foodi and close with Crisping mode, select Air Crisp mode and let it cook for 8 minutes, gently toss the wings and let it cook for 8 minutes more
10. Once done, drizzle any sauce and sprinkle sesame seeds. Enjoy!

248.   Simple and Juicy Chicken Stock

Preparation Time: 10 minutes

Cooking time: 2hours

Servings: 4

INGREDIENTS

- 2 pounds meaty chicken bones
- ¼ teaspoon salt
- 3 and ½ cups of water

DIRECTIONS

1. Place chicken parts in Foodi and season with salt
2. Add water, place the pressure cooker lid and seal the valve, cook on HIGH pressure for 90 minutes. Release the pressure naturally over 10 minutes
3. Line a colander with cheesecloth and place it over a large bowl, pour chicken parts and stock into the colander and strain out the chicken and bones
4. Let the stock cool and let it peel off any layer of fat that might accumulate on the surface
5. Use as needed!

249.   Keto-Friendly Chicken Tortilla

Preparation Time: 15 minutes

Cooking time: 15 minutes

Servings: 4

INGREDIENTS

- 1 tablespoon avocado oil
- 1 pound pastured organic boneless chicken breasts
- ½ cup of orange juice
- 2 teaspoons gluten-free Worcestershire sauce
- 1 teaspoon garlic powder
- 1 teaspoon salt
- ½ teaspoon chili powder
- ½ teaspoon paprika

DIRECTIONS

1. Set your Ninja Foodi to Sauté mode and add oil, let the oil heat up
2. Add chicken on top, take a bowl and add remaining ingredients mix well
3. Pour the mixture over chicken. Lock lid and cook on HIGH pressure for 15 minutes
4. Release pressure naturally over 10 minutes
5. Shred the chicken and serve over salad green shells such as cabbage or lettuce. Enjoy!

250.   Honey Garlic Chicken and Okra

Preparation Time: 25 Minutes

Servings: 4

INGREDIENTS

- 4 boneless; skinless chicken breasts; sliced
- 4 spring onions, thinly sliced
- 6 garlic cloves, grated
- ⅓ cup honey
- 1 cup rice, rinsed
- ¼ cup tomato puree
- ½ cup soy sauce
- 2 cups water
- 2 cups frozen okra
- 1 tablespoon cornstarch
- 2 tablespoon rice vinegar

- 1 tablespoon olive oil
- 1 tablespoon water
- 2 teaspoon toasted sesame seeds
- ½ teaspoon salt

DIRECTIONS

1. In the inner pot of the Foodi, mix garlic, tomato puree, vinegar, soy sauce, ginger, honey, and oil; toss in chicken to coat. In an ovenproof bowl, mix water, salt and rice. Set the reversible rack on top of chicken. Lower the bowl onto the reversible rack.
2. Seal the pressure lid, choose Pressure, set to High, and set the timer to 10 minutes; press Start. Release pressure naturally for 5 minutes, release the remaining pressure quickly.
3. Use a fork to fluff the rice. Lay okra onto the rice. Allow the okra steam in the residual heat for 3 minutes. Take the trivet and bowl from the pot. Set the chicken to a plate.
4. Press Sear/Sauté. In a small bowl, mix 1 tablespoon of water and cornstarch until smooth; stir into the sauce and cook for 3 to 4 minutes until thickened.
5. Divide the rice, chicken, and okra between 4 bowls. Drizzle sauce over each portion; garnish with spring onions and sesame seeds.

251.   Sticky Drumsticks

Preparation Time: 50 Minutes

Servings: 4

INGREDIENTS

- 1 lb. drumsticks
- 2 tablespoon honey
- 2 teaspoon dijon mustard
- Cooking spray
- Salt and pepper to taste

DIRECTIONS

1. Combine the honey, mustard, salt, and pepper in a large bowl. Add in the chicken

and toss to coat. Cover and put in the fridge for 30 minutes.
2. Preheat your Foodi to 380 degrees F. Grease the Foodi basket with cooking spray. Arrange the drumsticks on the basket. Cook for 20 minutes on Air Crisp mode. After 10 minutes, shake the drumsticks.

252.   Saucy Chicken Breasts

Preparation Time: 45 Minutes

Servings: 4

INGREDIENTS

- 4 chicken breasts, boneless and skinless
- ½ cup chicken broth
- ½ cup chives; sliced
- 1 tablespoon cornstarch
- 1 tablespoon water
- 2 tablespoon olive oil
- 2 tablespoon soy sauce
- 2 tablespoon tomato paste
- 2 tablespoon honey
- 2 tablespoon minced garlic
- salt and ground black pepper to taste

DIRECTIONS

1. Season the chicken with pepper and salt. Warm oil on Sear/Sauté. Add in chicken and cook for 5 minutes until lightly browned.
2. In a small bowl, mix garlic, soy sauce, honey, and tomato paste; pour the mixture over the chicken. Stir in ½ cup broth. Seal the pressure lid, choose Pressure, set to High, and set the timer to 12 minutes. Press Start.
3. When ready, release the pressure quickly. Set the chicken to a bowl. Mix water and cornstarch to create a slurry; briskly stir the mixture into the sauce that is remaining in the pan for 2 minutes until thickened. Serve the chicken with the sauce and chives.

253.   Chicken with Tomatoes and Capers

Preparation Time: 45 Minutes

Servings: 4

INGREDIENTS

- 4 chicken legs
- 1 onion; diced
- 2 garlic cloves; minced
- ⅓ cup red wine
- 2 cups diced tomatoes
- ⅓ cup capers
- ¼ cup fresh basil
- 2 pickles; chopped
- 2 tablespoon olive oil
- sea salt and fresh ground black pepper to taste

DIRECTIONS

1. Sprinkle pepper and salt over the chicken. Warm oil on Sear/Sauté. Add in onion and cook for 3 minutes until fragrant; add in garlic and cook for 30 seconds until softened.
2. Mix the chicken with vegetables and cook for 6 to 7 minutes until lightly browned.
3. Add red wine to the pan to deglaze, scrape the pan's bottom to get rid of any browned bits of food; stir in tomatoes. Seal the pressure lid, choose Pressure, set to High, and set the timer to 12 minutes; press Start.
4. When ready, release the pressure quickly. To the chicken mixture, add basil, capers and pickles. Serve the chicken in plates covered with the tomato sauce mixture.

254. Chicken Thighs with Cabbage
Preparation Time: 35 Minutes

Servings: 4

INGREDIENTS

- 1 pound green cabbage, shredded
- 4 slices pancetta; diced
- 4 chicken thighs, boneless skinless
- 1 cup chicken broth
- 1 tablespoon Dijon mustard
- 1 tablespoon lard
- Fresh parsley; chopped
- salt and ground black pepper to taste

DIRECTIONS

1. Warm lard on Sear/Sauté. Fry pancetta for 5 minutes until crisp. Set aside. Season chicken with pepper and salt. Sear in Foodi for 2 minutes each side until browned. In a bowl, mix mustard and chicken broth.
2. In your Foodi, add pancetta and chicken broth mixture. Seal the pressure lid, choose Pressure, set to High, and set the timer to 6 minutes. Press Start. When ready, release the pressure quickly.
3. Open the lid, mix in green cabbage, seal again, and cook on High Pressure for 2 minutes. When ready, release the pressure quickly. Serve with sprinkled parsley.

255. Turkey Casserole
Preparation Time: 45 Minutes

Servings: 5

INGREDIENTS

- 1 pound turkey breast; cubed
- 2 (14 ouncescans fire-roasted tomatoes
- ½ sweet onion; diced
- 3 cloves garlic; minced
- 1 jalapeno pepper; minced
- 2 bell peppers; cut into thick strips
- 1½ cups water
- 1 cup salsa
- 1 tablespoon olive oil
- 5 tablespoon fresh oregano; chopped
- 2 teaspoon ancho chili powder
- 2 teaspoon chili powder
- 1 teaspoon ground cumin
- Sea salt to taste

DIRECTIONS

1. Warm the oil on Sear/Sauté. Add in garlic, onion and jalapeño and cook for 5 minutes until fragrant. Stir turkey into the pot; cook for 5-6 minutes until browned.

2. Add in salsa, tomatoes, bell peppers, and water; apply a seasoning of sea salt, ancho chili powder, cumin, and chili powder. Seal the pressure lid, choose Pressure, set to High, and set the timer to 10 minutes on High. When ready, release the pressure quickly. Top with oregano and serve.

256. Chicken with Black Beans

Preparation Time: 25 Minutes

Servings: 4

INGREDIENTS

- 4 boneless; skinless chicken drumsticks
- 2 green onions, thinly sliced
- 3 garlic cloves, grated
- 2 cups canned black beans
- ½ cup soy sauce
- ½ cup chicken broth
- 1 (1 inchpiece fresh ginger, grated
- 1 tablespoon sriracha
- 1 tablespoon sesame oil
- 1 tablespoon cornstarch
- 1 tablespoon water
- 2 tablespoon toasted sesame seeds; divided
- 3 tablespoon honey
- 2 tablespoon tomato paste

DIRECTIONS

1. In your Foodi, mix the soy sauce, honey, ginger, tomato paste, chicken broth, sriracha, and garlic. Stir well until smooth; toss in the chicken to coat.
2. Seal the pressure lid, choose Pressure, set to High, and set the timer to 3 minutes. Press Start. Release the pressure immediately.
3. Open the lid and Press Sear/Sauté. In a small bowl, mix water and cornstarch until no lumps remain; stir into the sauce and cook for 5 minutes until thickened.
4. Stir sesame oil and 1½ tablespoon sesame seeds through the chicken mixture; garnish with extra sesame seeds and green onions. Serve with black beans.

257. Greek Style Turkey Meatballs

Preparation Time: 30 Minutes

Servings: 6

INGREDIENTS

- 1 pound ground turkey
- 1 carrot; minced
- ½ celery stalk; minced
- 1 onion; minced and divided
- 1 egg, lightly beaten
- 3 cups tomato puree
- 2 cups water
- ½ cup plain bread crumbs
- ⅓ cup feta cheese, crumbled
- 1 tablespoon olive oil
- 2 teaspoon salt; divided
- ½ teaspoon dried oregano
- ¼ teaspoon ground black pepper

DIRECTIONS

1. In a mixing bowl, thoroughly combine half the onion, oregano, ground turkey, salt, bread crumbs, pepper, and egg and stir until everything is well incorporated.
2. Heat oil on Sear/Sauté, and cook celery, remaining onion, and carrot for 5 minutes until soft. Pour in water, and tomato puree. Adjust the seasonings as necessary.
3. Roll the mixture into meatballs, and drop into the sauce. Seal the pressure lid, choose Pressure, set to High, and set the timer to 5 minutes. Press Start. Allow the cooker to cool and release pressure naturally for 20 minutes. Serve topped with feta cheese.

258. Basil Cheddar Stuffed Chicken

Preparation Time: 25 Minutes

Servings: 4

INGREDIENTS

- 2 large chicken breasts, skinless
- 4 cherry tomatoes, halved
- 4 slices cheddar cheese

- A handful of fresh basil leaves
- 2 tablespoon olive oil
- Salt and pepper to taste

DIRECTIONS

1. With a sharp knife; cut a slit into the side of each chicken breast. Put 2 slices of cheese, 3-4 basil leaves, and 4 cherry tomato halves into each slit. Use toothpicks to keep the chicken breasts closed.
2. Season the meat with salt and pepper, and brush with some olive oil. Grease the Foodi basket with the remaining olive oil and place the chicken breasts in the basket; close the crisping lid and cook for 12 minutes at 370 F.
3. After 6 minutes, turn the breasts over. Once ready, leave to sit the chicken breasts, then slice each one in half and serve with salad.

259. Chicken Burgers with Avocado

Preparation Time: 15 Minutes

Servings: 8

INGREDIENTS

- 1 lb. ground chicken
- 1 tomato; sliced
- 1 red onion; chopped
- 1 Avocado; sliced
- ½ cup mayonnaise
- 1 egg, beaten
- 4 buns, halved
- 1 small red potato, shredded
- A pinch of ground chili
- A pinch of ground cumin
- Fresh cilantro; chopped
- Salt and pepper to taste
- Cooking spray

DIRECTIONS

1. Mix the chicken, onion, egg, potato, cumin, chili, cilantro, salt, and pepper in a large bowl with your hands until you have an even burger mixture.

2. Shape the mixture into 8 patties. Grease your Foodi basket with cooking spray.
3. Arrange the burgers onto the basket. Close the crisping lid and cook for 10 minutes, at 360 F. After 5 minutes, shake the patties.
4. To assemble your burgers, spread mayonnaise on the bottom of each half of the buns, top with a chicken patty, then put over a tomato slice. Cover with the other half of the buns and arrange on a serving platter to serve.

260. Honey Glazed Chicken Kabobs

Preparation Time: 20 Minutes

Servings: 4

INGREDIENTS

- 4 chicken breasts; skinless and cubed
- Juice from 1 Lime
- 4 tablespoon honey.
- ½ teaspoon ground paprika
- Salt and pepper to taste

DIRECTIONS

1. In a large bowl, combine the honey, soy sauce, lime juice, paprika, salt, and pepper. Add in the chicken cubes and toss to coat.
2. Load 8 small skewers with honey-glazed chicken. Lay the kabobs into the Foodi basket, close the crisping lid and cook for 15 minutes at 360 F. After 8 minutes, turn the kabobs over. Drizzle the remaining honey sauce and serve with sautéed veggies.

261. Herby Chicken with Asparagus Sauce

Preparation Time: 1 hr

Servings: 4

INGREDIENTS

- 1 (3 ½ poundsYoung Whole Chicken
- 8 ounces asparagus, trimmed and chopped
- 1 onion; chopped

- 1 cup chicken stock
- 4 fresh thyme; minced
- 3 fresh rosemary; minced
- 4 garlic cloves; minced
- 2 lemons, zested and quartered
- 1 fresh thyme sprig
- 1 tablespoon flour
- 1 tablespoon soy sauce
- 2 tablespoon olive oil
- 1 teaspoon olive oil
- Cooking spray
- salt and freshly ground black pepper to taste
- Chopped parsley to garnish

DIRECTIONS

1. Rub all sides of the chicken with garlic, rosemary, black pepper, lemon zest; minced thyme, and salt. Into the chicken cavity, insert lemon wedges.
2. Warm oil on Sear/Sauté. Add in onion and asparagus, and cook for 5 minutes until softened. Mix in chicken stock, 1 thyme sprig, black pepper, soy sauce, and salt.
3. Into the inner pot, set trivet over asparagus mixture. On top of the trivet, place your chicken with breast-side up.
4. Seal the pressure lid, choose Pressure, set to High, and set the timer to 20 minutes. Press Start. Once ready, do a quick release. Remove the chicken to a serving platter.
5. In the inner pot, sprinkle flour over asparagus mixture and blend the sauce with an immersion blender until desired consistency. Top the chicken with asparagus sauce and garnish with parsley.

262. Chicken Fajitas with Avocado

Preparation Time: 30 Minutes

Servings: 4

INGREDIENTS

- 4 chicken breasts, boneless and skinless
- 1 (24 ouncescan diced tomatoes
- 3 bell peppers, julienned
- 1 shallot; chopped

- 4 garlic cloves; minced
- 4 flour tortillas
- 1 avocado; sliced
- 1 taco seasoning
- 2 tablespoon cilantro; chopped
- 1 tablespoon olive oil
- Juice of 1 lemon
- salt and pepper to taste

DIRECTIONS

1. In a bowl, mix taco seasoning and chicken until evenly coated. Warm oil on Sear/Sauté. Sear chicken for 2 minutes per side until browned. To the chicken, add tomatoes, shallot, lemon juice, garlic, and bell peppers; season with pepper and salt.
2. Seal the pressure lid, choose Pressure, set to High, and set the timer to 4 minutes. Press Start. When ready, release the pressure quickly.
3. Move the bell peppers and chicken to tortillas. Add avocado slices and serve.

263. Chicken Tenders with Rice and Broccoli

Preparation Time: 60 Minutes

Servings: 3

INGREDIENTS

- 1 pound chicken tenderloins
- 1 can condensed cream chicken soup
- 1 package instant long grain rice
- 1 cup chopped broccoli
- 2 cups water
- 1 tablespoon minced garlic

DIRECTIONS

1. Place the chicken quarters in the Foodi. Season with salt, pepper and a tablespoon of oil and cook for 30 minutes on Roast mode at 390 F. Meanwhile, in a bowl, mix rice, water; minced garlic, soup, and broccoli. Combine the mixture very well.

Remove the chicken from the Foodi and place it on a platter to drain.

2. Spread the rice mixture on the bottom of the dish and place the chicken on top of the rice. Close the crisping lid and cook for 30 minutes on Roast mode at 390 F.

264. Tuscany Turkey Soup

Preparation Time: 40 Minutes

Servings: 4

INGREDIENTS

- 1 pound hot turkey sausage
- 4 Italian bread slices
- 3 celery stalks; chopped
- 3 garlic cloves; chopped
- 1 (15-ozcan cannellini beans, rinsed
- 9 ounces refrigerated tortellini
- 1 Parmesan cheese rind
- 1 red onion; chopped
- ½ cup dry white wine
- 4 cups chicken broth
- 2 cups chopped spinach
- ½ cup grated Parmesan cheese
- 2 tablespoon melted butter
- 2 tablespoon olive oil
- ½ teaspoon fennel seeds
- 1 teaspoon salt
- Cooking spray

DIRECTIONS

1. On the Foodi, choose Sear/Sauté and adjust to Medium. Press Start to preheat the inner pot. Heat olive oil and cook the sausage for 4 minutes, while stirring occasionally until golden brown.

2. Stir in the celery, garlic, and onion, season with the salt and cook for 2 to 3 minutes, stirring occasionally. Pour in the wine and bring the mixture to a boil until the wine reduces by half. Scrape the bottom of the pot to let off any browned bits. Add the chicken stock, fennel seeds, tortellini, Parmesan rind, cannellini beans, and spinach.

3. Lock the pressure lid into place and to seal. Select Pressure; adjust the pressure to High and the cook time to 5 minutes; press Start. Brush the butter on the bread slices, and sprinkle with half of the cheese. Once the timer is over, perform a natural pressure release for 5 minutes.

4. Grease the reversible rack with cooking spray and fix in the upper position of the pot. Lay the bread slices on the rack.

5. Close the crisping lid and Choose Broil. Adjust the cook time to 5 minutes; press Start.

6. When the bread has browned and crisp, transfer from the rack to a cutting board and let cool for a couple of minutes. Cut the slices into cubes.

7. Ladle the soup into bowls and sprinkle with the remaining cheese. Share the croutons among the bowls and serve.

265. Asian Chicken

Preparation Time: 35 Minutes

Servings: 4

INGREDIENTS

- 1 lb. chicken; cut in stripes
- 1 large onion
- 3 green peppers; cut in stripes
- 2 tomatoes; cubed
- 1 pinch fresh and chopped coriander
- 1 pinch ginger
- 1 tablespoon mustard
- 1 tablespoon cumin powder
- 2 tablespoon oil
- Salt and black pepper

DIRECTIONS

1. Heat the oil in a deep pan. Add in the mustard, onion, ginger, cumin and green chili peppers. Sauté the mixture for 2-3 minutes. Then, add the tomatoes, coriander, and salt and keep stirring.

2. Coat the chicken with oil, salt, and pepper and cook for 25 minutes on Air Crisp mode

at 380 F. Remove from the Foodi and pour the sauce over and around.

266. Tom Yum Wings

Preparation Time: 4 hours 20 Minutes

Servings: 2

INGREDIENTS

- 8 chicken wings
- 2 tablespoon cornstarch
- 2 tablespoon tom yum paste
- 1 tablespoon water
- 2 tablespoon potato starch
- ½ teaspoon baking powder

DIRECTIONS

1. Combine the tom yum paste and water, in a small bowl. Place the wings in a large bowl, add the tom yum mixture and coat well.
2. Cover the bowl and refrigerate for 4 hours. Preheat the Foodi to 370 degrees F.
3. Combine the baking powder, cornstarch, and potato starch. Dip each wing in the starch mixture.
4. Place on a lined baking dish in the Foodi and cook for 7 minutes on Air Crisp mode. Flip over and cook for 5 to 7 minutes more.

267. Buttered Turkey

Preparation Time: 25 Minutes

Servings: 6

INGREDIENTS

- 6 turkey breasts, boneless and skinless
- 1 stick butter, melted
- 2 cups panko breadcrumbs
- ½ teaspoon cayenne pepper
- ½ teaspoon black pepper
- 1 teaspoon salt

DIRECTIONS

1. In a bowl, combine the panko breadcrumbs, half of the black pepper, the cayenne pepper, and half of the salt.
2. In another bowl, combine the melted butter with salt and pepper. Brush the butter mixture over the turkey breast.
3. Coat the turkey with the panko mixture. Arrange on a lined Foodi basket. Close the crisping lid and cook for 15 minutes at 390 F on Air Crisp mode, flipping the meat after 8 minutes.

268. Greek Chicken with Potatoes

Preparation Time: 40 Minutes

Servings: 4

INGREDIENTS

- 4 potatoes, peeled and quartered
- 4 boneless skinless chicken drumsticks
- 2 lemons, zested and juiced
- 1 cucumber, thinly sliced
- 2 Serrano peppers, stemmed, cored, and chopped
- 1 cup packed watercress
- ½ cup cherry tomatoes, quartered
- ¼ cup Kalamata olives, pitted
- ¼ cup hummus
- ¼ cup feta cheese, crumbled
- 4 cups water
- 3 tablespoon finely chopped parsley
- 1 tablespoon olive oil
- 2 teaspoon fresh oregano
- ¼ teaspoon freshly ground black pepper
- Lemon wedges; for serving
- Salt to taste

DIRECTIONS

1. In the cooker, add water and potatoes. Set trivet over them. In a baking bowl, mix lemon juice, olive oil, black pepper, oregano, zest, salt, and red pepper flakes. Add chicken drumsticks in the marinade and stir to coat.

2. Set the bowl with chicken on the trivet in the inner pot. Seal the lid, select Pressure and set the time to 15 minutes on High pressure. Press Start.

3. When ready, do a quick pressure release. Take out the bowl with chicken and the trivet from the pot. Drain potatoes and add parsley and salt.

4. Split the potatoes among four serving plates and top with watercress, cucumber slices, hummus, cherry tomatoes, chicken, olives, and feta cheese. Each bowl should be garnished with a lemon wedge.

269. Chicken Wings

Preparation Time: 25 Minutes

Servings: 4

INGREDIENTS

- 8 chicken wings
- 1 tablespoon onion powder
- 1 tablespoon garlic powder
- 1 tablespoon ranch salad mix
- 1 tablespoon cayenne pepper
- ½ teaspoon paprika
- Cooking spray

DIRECTIONS

1. Combine the paprika, ranch salad mix, onion powder, garlic powder, and cayenne pepper in a bowl. Pour the seasoning all over the chicken and oil with cooking spray.

2. Place in the Foodi basket, close the crisping lid and cook for 15 minutes at 380 F. After half of the cooking time, shake the wings. Oil the chicken again with cooking spray and continue cooking until the wings are crispy. Serve hot.

270. Crumbed Sage Chicken Scallopini

Preparation Time: 12 Minutes

Servings: 4

INGREDIENTS

- 4 chicken breasts; skinless and boneless
- 2 oz. flour
- 3 oz. breadcrumbs
- 2 eggs, beaten
- 2 tablespoon grated Parmesan cheese
- 1 tablespoon fresh; chopped sage
- Cooking spray

DIRECTIONS

1. Place some plastic wrap underneath and on top of the chicken breasts. Using a rolling pin beat the meat until it becomes fragile.

2. In a small bowl, combine the Parmesan, sage, and breadcrumbs. Dip the chicken in the egg first, and then in the sage mixture.

3. Spray with cooking oil and arrange the meat in the Foodi. Cook for 7 minutes on Air Crisp mode at 370 F.

271. Rosemary Lemon Chicken

Preparation Time: 60 Minutes

Servings: 2

INGREDIENTS

- 2 chicken breasts
- 2 rosemary sprigs
- ½ lemon; cut into wedges
- 1 tablespoon oyster sauce
- 3 tablespoon brown sugar
- 1 tablespoon soy sauce
- ½ tablespoon olive oil
- 1 teaspoon minced ginger

DIRECTIONS

1. Place the ginger, soy sauce, and olive oil, in a bowl. Add the chicken and coat well. Cover the bowl and refrigerate for 30 minutes. Transfer the marinated chicken to the Foodi basket.

2. Close the crisping lid and cook for about 6 minutes on Air Crisp mode at 370 F.

3. Mix the oyster sauce, rosemary and brown sugar in a small bowl. Pour the sauce over

the chicken. Arrange the lemon wedges in the dish. Return to the Foodi and cook for 13 more minutes on Air Crisp mode.

272. Sweet Garlicky Chicken Wings

Preparation Time: 20 Minutes

Servings: 4

INGREDIENTS

- 16 chicken wings
- 4 garlic cloves; minced
- ¾ cup potato starch
- ¼ cup butter
- ¼ cup honey
- ½ teaspoon salt

DIRECTIONS

1. Rinse and pat dry the wings, and place them in a bowl. Add the starch to the bowl, and mix to coat the chicken.
2. Place the chicken in a baking dish that has been previously coated lightly with cooking oil. Close the crisping lid and cook for 5 minutes on Air Crisp mode at 370 F.
3. Meanwhile, whisk the rest of the ingredients together in a bowl. Pour the sauce over the wings and cook for another 10 minutes.

273. Spicy Chicken Wings.

Preparation Time: 25 Minutes

Servings: 2

INGREDIENTS

- 10 chicken wings
- ½ tablespoon honey
- 2 tablespoon hot chili sauce
- ½ tablespoon lime juice
- ½ teaspoon kosher salt
- ½ teaspoon black pepper

DIRECTIONS

1. Mix the lime juice, honey, and chili sauce. Toss the mixture over the chicken wings.
2. Put the wings in the fryer's basket, close the crisping lid and cook for 25 minutes on Air Crisp mode at 350 F. Shake the basket every 5 minutes.

274. Chicken with Prunes

Preparation Time: 55 Minutes

Servings: 6

INGREDIENTS

- 1 whole chicken, 3 lb
- ¼ cup packed brown sugar
- ½ cup pitted prunes
- 2 bay leaves
- 3 minced cloves of garlic
- 2 tablespoon olive oil
- 2 tablespoon capers
- 1 tablespoon dried oregano
- 1 tablespoon chopped fresh parsley
- 2 tablespoon red wine vinegar
- Salt and black pepper to taste

DIRECTIONS

1. In a big and deep bowl, mix the prunes, olives, capers, garlic, olive oil, bay leaves, oregano, vinegar, salt, and pepper.
2. Spread the mixture on the bottom of a baking tray, and place the chicken.
3. Preheat the Foodi to 360° F. Sprinkle a little bit of brown sugar on top of the chicken, close the crisping lid and cook for 45-55 minutes on Air Crisp mode. When ready, garnish with fresh parsley.

275. Cordon Bleu Chicken

Preparation Time: 40 Minutes

Servings: 4

INGREDIENTS

- 4 skinless and boneless chicken breasts
- 4 slices Swiss cheese
- 4 slices ham
- 1 cup heavy whipping cream
- ½ cup dry white wine
- 3 tablespoon all-purpose flour
- 4 tablespoon butter
- 1 teaspoon chicken bouillon granules
- 1 teaspoon paprika

DIRECTIONS

1. Pound the chicken breasts and put a slice of ham and then a slice of swiss cheese on each of the breasts. Fold the edges over the filling and secure the sides with toothpicks.
2. In a medium bowl, combine the paprika and the flour and coat the chicken pieces. Close the crisping lid and fry the chicken for 20 minutes on Air Crisp mode at 380 F.
3. Meanwhile, in a large skillet over medium heat, melt the butter and add the bouillon and the wine. Reduce the heat to low.
4. Add in the heavy cream and let simmer for 20-25 minutes. When the chicken is done, remove to a serving platter and drizzle with the sauce; serve hot.

276. Chicken Stroganoff with Fetucini

Preparation Time: 35 Minutes

Servings: 4

INGREDIENTS

- 2 large boneless skinless chicken breasts
- 8 ounces fettucini
- ½ cup sliced onion
- ½ cup dry white wine
- 1 cup sautéed mushrooms
- ¼ cup heavy cream
- 1 ½ cups water
- 2 cups chicken stock
- 2 tablespoon butter
- 1 tablespoon flour
- 2 tablespoon chopped fresh dill to garnish

- ½ teaspoon Worcestershire sauce
- 1½ teaspoon salt

DIRECTIONS

1. Season the chicken on both sides with salt and set aside. Choose Sear/Sauté and adjust to Medium. Press Start to preheat the pot. Melt the butter and sauté the onion until brown, about 3 minutes.
2. Mix in the flour to make a roux, about 2 minutes and gradually pour in the dry white wine while stirring and scraping the bottom of the pot to release any browned bits. Allow the white wine to simmer and to reduce by two-thirds.
3. Pour in the water, chicken stock, 1 tablespoon of salt, and fettucini. Mix and arrange the chicken on top of the fettucini.
4. Lock the pressure lid to Seal. Choose Pressure; adjust the pressure to High and the cook time to 5 minutes; press Start. When done pressure-cooking, perform a quick pressure release.
5. Transfer the chicken breasts to a cutting board to cool slightly, and then cut into bite-size chunks. Return the chicken to the pot and stir in the Worcestershire sauce and mushrooms. Add the heavy cream and cook until the mixture stops simmering. Ladle the stroganoff into bowls and garnish with dill.

277. Greek Chicken

Preparation Time: 45 Minutes

Servings: 6

INGREDIENTS

- 1 whole chicken (3 lb); cut in pieces
- ½ cup olive oil
- 3 garlic cloves; minced
- Juice from 1 lemon
- ½ cup white wine
- 1 tablespoon chopped fresh oregano
- 1 tablespoon fresh thyme
- 1 tablespoon fresh rosemary
- Salt and black pepper, to taste

DIRECTIONS

1. In a large bowl, combine the garlic, rosemary, thyme, olive oil, lemon juice, oregano, salt, and pepper. Mix all ingredients very well and spread the mixture into the Foodi basket.
2. Stir in the chicken. Sprinkle with wine and cook for 45 minutes on Air Crisp mode at 380 F.

278. Buttermilk Chicken Thighs

Preparation Time: 4 hours 40 Minutes

Servings: 6

INGREDIENTS

- 1 ½ lb. chicken thighs
- 2 cups buttermilk
- 2 cups flour
- 1 tablespoon paprika
- 1 tablespoon baking powder
- 2 teaspoon black pepper
- 1 teaspoon cayenne pepper
- 3 teaspoon salt divided

DIRECTIONS

1. Rinse and pat dry the chicken thighs. Place the chicken thighs in a bowl. Add cayenne pepper, 2 teaspoon salt, black pepper, and buttermilk, and stir to coat well.
2. Refrigerate for 4 hours. Preheat the Foodi to 350 degrees F. In another bowl, mix the flour, paprika, 1 teaspoon salt, and baking powder.
3. Dredge half of the chicken thighs, one at a time, in the flour, and then place on a lined dish. Close the crisping lid and cook for 18 minutes on Air Crisp mode, flipping once halfway through. Repeat with the other batch.

279. Korean Barbecued Satay

Preparation Time: 4h 15 Minutes

Servings: 4

INGREDIENTS

- 1 lb. boneless; skinless chicken tenders
- ½ cup pineapple juice
- ½ cup soy sauce
- ⅓ cup sesame oil
- 4 scallions; chopped
- 1 pinch black pepper
- 4 cloves garlic; chopped
- 2 teaspoon sesame seeds, toasted
- 1 teaspoon fresh ginger, grated

DIRECTIONS

1. Skew each tender and trim any excess fat. Mix the other in one large bowl.
2. Add the skewered chicken and place in the fridge for 4 to 24 hours.
3. Preheat the Foodi to 370 degrees F. Using a paper towel, pat the chicken dry. Fry for 10 minutes on Air Crisp mode.

280. Thyme Turkey Nuggets

Preparation Time: 20 Minutes

Servings: 2

INGREDIENTS

- 8 oz. turkey breast, boneless and skinless
- 1 cup breadcrumbs
- 1 egg, beaten
- 1 tablespoon dried thyme
- ½ teaspoon dried parsley
- Salt and pepper, to taste

DIRECTIONS

1. Mince the turkey in a food processor. Transfer to a bowl. Stir in the thyme and parsley, and season with salt and pepper.
2. Take a nugget-sized piece of the turkey mixture and shape it into a ball, or another form. Dip it in the breadcrumbs, then egg, then in the breadcrumbs again. Place the nuggets onto a prepared baking dish. Close the crisping lid and cook for 10 minutes on Air Crisp mode at 350 F.

281.   Turkey and Brown Rice Salad with Peanuts

Preparation Time: 60 Minutes

Servings: 4

INGREDIENTS

- 1 pound turkey tenderloins
- 3 celery stalks, thinly sliced
- 1 apple, cored and cubed
- 1 cup brown rice
- ½ cup peanuts, toasted
- 4 cups water
- A pinch of sugar
- 3 tablespoon apple cider vinegar
- ⅛ teaspoon freshly ground black pepper
- ¼ teaspoon celery seeds
- 2¼ teaspoon salt
- 3 teaspoon peanut oil; divided

DIRECTIONS

1. Pour the water into the inner pot. Stir in the brown rice and 1 teaspoon of salt. Lock the pressure lid into the Seal position. Choose Pressure; adjust the pressure to High and the cook time to 10 minutes. Press Start.
2. Season the turkey on both sides with salt; set aside. After cooking the brown rice, perform a natural pressure release for 10 minutes. Carefully open the lid and spoon the rice into a large bowl to cool completely.
3. Put the turkey in the Crisping Basket and brush with 2 teaspoons of peanut oil. Fix in the basket. Close the crisping lid and Choose Bake/Roast; adjust the temperature to 375°F and the cook time to 12 minutes; press Start.
4. Pour the remaining peanut oil and the vinegar into a jar with a tight-fitting lid. Add the black pepper, celery seeds, salt, and sugar.
5. Close the jar and shake until the ingredients properly combined. When the turkey is ready, transfer to a plate to cool for several

minutes. Cut it into bite-size chunks and add to the rice along with the peanuts, celery, and apple.
6. Pour half the dressing over the salad and toss gently to coat, adding more dressing as desired. Proceed to serve the salad.

282.   Sweet & Spicy Chicken Breasts

Preparation time: 15 minutes

Cooking time: 16 minutes

Servings: 6

INGREDIENTS

- 2½ pounds grass-fed frozen boneless chicken breasts
- 1 tablespoon fresh oregano, minced
- 1 teaspoon fresh lemon zest, grated
- 1 tablespoon smoked paprika
- 1 tablespoon cayenne pepper
- 1 teaspoon ground ginger
- 1 teaspoon garlic powder
- Salt, as required
- ¼ cup olive oil
- 2 tablespoons fresh lemon juice
- 1 tablespoon yacon syrup

DIRECTIONS

1. In the pot of Ninja Foodi, place ½ cup of water.
2. Arrange the greased "Cook & Crisp Basket" in the pot of Ninja Foodi.
3. Place the chicken breasts into the "Cook & Crisp Basket".
4. Close the Ninja Foodi with pressure lid and place the pressure valve to "Seal" position.
5. Select "Pressure" and set to "High" for 4 minutes.
6. Press "Start/Stop" to begin cooking.
7. Switch the valve to "Vent" and do a "Quick" release.
8. Meanwhile, in a large bowl, add the remaining ingredients and mix well.
9. With tongs, transfer the chicken breasts into the bowl of the oil mixture and toss to coat well.

10. Return chicken breasts into the basket.
11. Now, close the Ninja Foodi with crisping lid and select "Air Crisp".
12. Set the temperature to 400 degrees F for 12 minutes.
13. Press "Start/Stop" to begin cooking.
14. After 8 minutes, coat the chicken breasts with the remaining oil mixture.
15. Serve hot.

NUTRITION: Calories: 448, Fats: 22.8g, Net Carbs: 2.3g, Carbs: 3.4g, Fiber: 1.1g, Sugar: 1.1g, Proteins: 55.2g, Sodium: 193mg

283. Braised Chicken Breasts

Preparation time: 10 minutes

Cooking time: 4 hours

Servings: 4

INGREDIENTS

- ½ teaspoon dried parsley
- ¼ teaspoon garlic powder
- ¼ teaspoon onion powder
- ¼ teaspoon paprika
- Salt and ground black pepper, as required
- 4 (5-ouncegrass-fed boneless, skinless chicken breasts
- ¼ cup homemade chicken broth
- 1 tablespoon butter

DIRECTIONS

1. In a small bowl, mix together the parsley, spices, salt and black pepper.
2. Rub both sides of the chicken breasts with spice mixture.
3. In the pot of Ninja Foodi, add the broth and butter and mix well.
4. Place the chicken breasts in the broth mixture.
5. Close the Ninja Foodi with crisping lid and select "Slow Cooker".
6. Set on "Low" for 3-4 hours.
7. Press "Start/Stop" to begin cooking.
8. Serve hot.

NUTRITION: Calories: 297, Fats: 13.4g, Net Carbs: 0.3g, Carbs: 0.4g, Fiber: 0.1g, Sugar: 0.1g, Proteins: 41.2g, Sodium: 186

284. Mustard Chicken Breasts

Preparation time: 15 minutes

Cooking time: 32 minutes

Servings: 2

INGREDIENTS

- 2 (8-ouncegrass-fed frozen chicken breasts
- Salt and ground black pepper, as required
- 2 tablespoons Dijon mustard
- 2 tablespoons yacon syrup
- 1 tablespoon fresh parsley, chopped

DIRECTIONS

1. In the pot of Ninja Foodi, place 1 cup of water.
2. Arrange the "Reversible Rack" in the pot of Ninja Foodi.
3. Place the chicken breasts over the "Reversible Rack".
4. Close the Ninja Foodi with the pressure lid and place the pressure valve to "Seal" position.
5. Select "Pressure" and set to "High" for 22 minutes.
6. Press "Start/Stop" to begin cooking.
7. Switch the valve to "Vent" and do a "Natural" release.
8. Meanwhile, in a bowl, place the mustard and yacon syrup and mix well.
9. Coat the chicken breasts with mustard mixture evenly.
10. Now, close the Ninja Foodi with crisping lid and select "Broil" for 10 minutes.
11. Press "Start/Stop" to begin cooking.
12. Serve hot with the garnishing of parsley.

NUTRITION: Calories: 467, Fats: 17.5g, Net Carbs: 6g, Carbs: 7g, Fiber: 1g, Sugar: 3.7g, Proteins: 66.4g, Sodium: 458mg

285.   Parmesan Crusted Chicken Breasts

Preparation time: 0 minutes

Cooking time: 0 minutes

Servings: 4

INGREDIENTS

- 1 organic egg
- 1 cup pork rinds, crushed
- ½ cup Parmesan cheese, shredded
- 1 tablespoon Italian seasonings
- 1 teaspoon garlic powder
- Salt and ground black pepper, as required
- 1 pound grass-fed chicken breasts

DIRECTIONS

1. In a shallow bowl, beat the egg.
2. In another shallow bowl, mix together the pork rinds, Parmesan cheese, Italian seasoning, garlic powder, salt and black powder.
3. Dip each chicken breast into whipped egg then, coat with Parmesan mixture.
4. In the pot of Ninja Foodi, place 1 cup of water.
5. Arrange the "Reversible Rack" in the pot of Ninja Foodi.
6. Place the chicken breasts over the "Reversible Rack".
7. Close the Ninja Foodi with the pressure lid and place the pressure valve to "Seal" position.
8. Select "Pressure" and set to "High" for 10 minutes.
9. Press "Start/Stop" to begin cooking.
10. Switch the valve to "Vent" and do a "Quick" release.
11. Now, close the Ninja Foodi with crisping lid and select "Air Crisp".
12. Set the temperature to 390 degrees F for 15 minutes.
13. Press "Start/Stop" to begin cooking.
14. Serve hot.

NUTRITION: Calories: 247, Fats: 10.7g, Net Carbs: 1.2g, Carbs: 1.3g, Fiber: 0.1g, Sugar: 0.6g, Proteins: 34.6g, Sodium: 403mg

286.   Crispy Chicken Breasts

Preparation time: 15 minutes

Cooking time: 40 minutes

Servings: 3

INGREDIENTS

- ¼ cup almond flour
- 1 large organic egg, beaten
- ¼ cup fresh cilantro, chopped
- 1 cup pork rinds, crushed
- 3 (5-ouncegrass-fed boneless, skinless chicken breasts

DIRECTIONS

1. Arrange a grease wire rack into a baking pan. Set aside.
2. In a shallow, dish place the flour.
3. In a second shallows dish, mix together the egg and cilantro.
4. In a third shallow dish, place pork rinds.
5. Coat the chicken breasts with flour, then dip into eggs and finally coat with pork rinds.
6. Arrange the chicken thighs into the prepared baking pan.
7. Arrange the "Reversible Rack" in the pot of Ninja Foodi.
8. Close the Ninja Foodi with crisping lid and select "Bake/Roast".
9. Set the temperature to 375 degrees F for 5 minutes.
10. Press "Start/Stop" to begin preheating.
11. After preheating, open the lid.
12. Place the pan over the "Reversible Rack".
13. Close the Ninja Foodi with crisping lid and select "Bake/Roast".
14. Set the temperature to 375 degrees F for 40 minutes.
15. Press "Start/Stop" to begin cooking.
16. Serve hot.

NUTRITION: Calories: 416, Fats: 21.1g, Net Carbs: 0.9g, Carbs: 1.9g, Fiber: 1g, Sugar: 0.5g, Proteins: 50.2g, Sodium: 358mg

287.   Brie Stuffed Chicken Breasts

Preparation time: 15 minutes

Cooking time: 20 minutes

Servings: 4

INGREDIENTS

- 2 (8-ouncegrass-fed skinless, boneless chicken fillets
- Salt and ground black pepper, as required
- 4 brie cheese slices
- 1 tablespoon fresh chive, minced
- 4 bacon slices

DIRECTIONS

1. Cut each chicken fillet in 2 equal-sized pieces.
2. Carefully, make a slit in each chicken piece horizontally about ¼-inch from the edge.
3. Open each chicken piece and season with the salt and black pepper.
4. Place 1 cheese slice in the open area of each chicken piece and sprinkle with chives.
5. Close the chicken pieces and wrap each one with a bacon slice.
6. Secure with toothpicks.
7. In the pot of Ninja Foodi, place 1 cup of water.
8. Arrange the "Cook & Crisp Basket" in the pot of Ninja Foodi.
9. Place rolled chicken breasts into the "Cook & Crisp Basket".
10. Close the Ninja Foodi with the pressure lid and place the pressure valve to "Seal" position.
11. Select "Pressure" and set to "High" for 5 minutes.
12. Press "Start/Stop" to begin cooking.
13. Switch the valve to "Vent" and do a "Quick" release.
14. Now, close the Ninja Foodi with crisping lid and Select "Air Crisp".
15. Set the temperature to 355 degrees F for 15 minutes.
16. Press "Start/Stop" to begin cooking.
17. Place the rolled chicken breasts onto a cutting board.
18. Cut into desired-sized slices and serve.

NUTRITION: Calories: 271, Fats: 13.4g, Net Carbs: 0.8g, Carbs: 1.2g, Fiber: 0.4g, Sugar: 0.1g, Proteins: 35.2g, Sodium: 602mg

288.   Bacon Wrapped Chicken Breasts

Preparation time: 20 minutes

Cooking time: 20 minutes

Servings: 4

INGREDIENTS

- 1 tablespoon Erythritol
- 8 Fresh basil leaves
- 2 tablespoons red boat fish sauce
- 2 tablespoons water
- 2 (8-ouncegrass-fed boneless chicken breasts, cut each breast in half horizontally
- Salt and ground black pepper, as required
- 8 bacon strips
- 1 tablespoon yacon syrup

DIRECTIONS

1. In a small heavy-bottomed pan, add Erythritol over medium-low heat and cook for about 2-3 minutes or until caramelized, stirring continuously.
2. Stir in the basil, fish sauce and water.
3. Remove from heat and transfer into a large bowl.
4. Sprinkle the chicken with salt and black pepper.
5. Add the chicken pieces in basil mixture and coat generously.
6. Refrigerate to marinate for about 4-6 hours.
7. Wrap each chicken piece with 2 bacon strips.
8. Coat each piece with yacon syrup slightly.

9. Arrange the greased "Cook & Crisp Basket" in the pot of Ninja Foodi.
10. Close the Ninja Foodi with crisping lid and select "Air Crisp".
11. Set the temperature to 365 degrees F for 5 minutes.
12. Press "Start/Stop" to begin preheating.
13. After preheating, open the lid.
14. Place the chicken breasts into the "Cook & Crisp Basket".
15. Close the Ninja Foodi with crisping lid and select "Air Crisp".
16. Set the temperature to 365 degrees F for 20 minutes.
17. Press "Start/Stop" to begin cooking.
18. Serve hot.

NUTRITION: Calories: 540, Fats: 32.4g, Net Carbs: 2.4g, Carbs: 2.4g, Fiber: 0g, Sugar: 0.9g, Proteins: 56.1g, Sodium: 2017mg

289. Bacon & Cheese Stuffed Chicken Breasts

Preparation time: 20 minutes

Cooking time: 28 minutes

Servings: 0

INGREDIENTS

- 6 ounces cream cheese, softened
- 6 cooked bacon slices, chopped
- 1½ cups mozzarella cheese, shredded
- 4 scallion, sliced
- Ground black pepper, as required
- 1½ cups pork rinds, crushed
- 2 organic eggs
- ½ teaspoon Italian seasoning
- ¼ teaspoon onion powder
- ¼ teaspoon garlic powder
- 4 (5-ouncegrass-fed chicken breasts, pounded into ¼-inch thickness
- Salt, as required
- Olive oi cooking spray

DIRECTIONS

1. Select "Sauté/Sear" setting of Ninja Foodi and place the bacon into the pot.
2. Press "Start/Stop" to begin and cook for about 6-8 minutes.
3. Press "Start/Stop" to stop cooking and with a slotted spoon transfer the bacon into a bowl.
4. Drain all the grease from the pot.
5. In a bowl, add the cooked bacon, cream cheese, mozzarella cheese, scallion and black pepper and mix well.
6. Ina shallow bowl, add the eggs, Italian seasoning, onion powder and garlic powder and beat well.
7. In another shallow bowl, place the pork rinds.
8. Season the chicken breast with salt and black pepper.
9. Spread cheese mixture onto each chicken breast.
10. Roll up each chicken breast and secure with toothpicks.
11. Dip each rolled chicken breast into egg mixture then coat with the pork rinds.
12. Arrange the greased "Cook & Crisp Basket" in the pot of Ninja Foodi.
13. Close the Ninja Foodi with crisping lid and select "Air Crisp".
14. Set the temperature to 375 degrees F for 5 minutes.
15. Press "Start/Stop" to begin preheating.
16. After preheating, open the lid.
17. Place the chicken breasts into the "Cook & Crisp Basket" and spray with the cooking spray.
18. Close the Ninja Foodi with crisping lid and select "Air Crisp".
19. Set the temperature to 375 degrees F for 20 minutes.
20. Press "Start/Stop" to begin cooking.
21. Serve hot.

NUTRITION: Calories: 753, Fats: 48g, Net Carbs: 2.8g, Carbs: 3.3g, Fiber: 0.5g, Sugar: 0.8g, Proteins: 72.1g, Sodium: 1195mg

290. Cream Cheese Stuffed Chicken Breasts

Preparation time: 15 minutes

Cooking time: 8 hours

Servings: 4

INGREDIENTS

- ¾ cup cream cheese, softened
- 2 tablespoon fresh chives, chopped
- 4 (6-ouncegrass-fed boneless, skinless chicken breast halves, pounded into ½-inch thickness
- Pinch of ground black pepper
- 8 bacon strips

DIRECTIONS

1. In a bowl, add the cream cheese, chives and black pepper and mix well.
2. Season the chicken breasts with a pinch of black pepper.
3. Place the cream cheese mixture in the center of each chicken breast.
4. Wrap each chicken piece with 2 bacon strips.
5. Grease the pot of Ninja Foodi lightly.
6. In the pot of Ninja Foodi, place the chicken breasts.
7. Close the Ninja Foodi with crisping lid and select "Slow Cooker".
8. Set on "Low" for 6-8 hours.
9. Press "Start/Stop" to begin cooking.
10. Serve hot.

NUTRITION: Calories: 787, Fats: 51.8g, Net Carbs: 2g, Carbs: 2.1g, Fiber: 0.1g, Sugar: 0.1g, Proteins: 73.8g, Sodium: 1603mg

291. Sausage Stuffed Chicken Breast

Preparation time: 15 minutes

Cooking time: 15 minutes

Servings: 4

INGREDIENTS

- 4 (4-ouncegrass-fed skinless, boneless chicken breasts
- 4 sausages, casing removed

DIRECTIONS

1. With a rolling pin, roll each chicken breast for about 1 minute.
2. Place 1 sausage over each chicken breast.
3. Roll each breast around the sausage and secure with toothpicks.
4. Arrange the greased "Cook & Crisp Basket" in the pot of Ninja Foodi.
5. Close the Ninja Foodi with crisping lid and select "Air Crisp".
6. Set the temperature to 375 degrees F for 5 minutes.
7. Press "Start/Stop" to begin preheating.
8. After preheating, open the lid.
9. Place the chicken breasts into the "Cook & Crisp Basket".
10. Close the Ninja Foodi with crisping lid and select "Air Crisp".
11. Set the temperature to 375 degrees F for 15 minutes.
12. Press "Start/Stop" to begin cooking.
13. Serve hot.

NUTRITION: Calories: 310, Fats: 16.3g, Net Carbs: 0g, Carbs: 0g, Fiber: 0g, Sugar: 0g, Proteins: 38.3g, Sodium: 307mg

292. Spinach Stuffed Chicken Breasts

Preparation time: 15 minutes

Cooking time: 30 minutes

Servings: 2

INGREDIENTS

- 1 tablespoon olive oil
- 1¾ ounces fresh spinach
- ¼ cup ricotta cheese, shredded
- 2 (4-ouncegrass-fed skinless, boneless chicken breasts
- Salt and ground black pepper, as required

- 2 tablespoons cheddar cheese, grated
- ¼ teaspoon paprika

DIRECTIONS

1. Select "Sauté/Sear" setting of Ninja Foodi and place the oil into the pot.
2. Press "Start/Stop" to begin cooking and heat for about 2-3 minutes.
3. Add the spinach and cook for about 3-4 minutes.
4. Stir in the ricotta and cook for about 40-60 seconds.
5. Press "Start/Stop" to stop cooking and transfer the spinach mixture into a bowl.
6. Set aside to cool.
7. Cut slits into the chicken breasts about ¼-inch apart but not all the way through.
8. Stuff each chicken breast with the spinach mixture.
9. Sprinkle each chicken breast with salt and black pepper and then with cheddar cheese and paprika.
10. Arrange the greased "Cook & Crisp Basket" in the pot of Ninja Foodi.
11. Close the Ninja Foodi with crisping lid and select "Air Crisp".
12. Set the temperature to 390 degrees F for 5 minutes.
13. Press "Start/Stop" to begin preheating.
14. After preheating, open the lid.
15. Place the chicken breasts into the "Cook & Crisp Basket".
16. Close the Ninja Foodi with crisping lid and select "Air Crisp".
17. Set the temperature to 390 degrees F for 25 minutes.
18. Press "Start/Stop" to begin cooking.
19. Serve hot.

NUTRITION: Calories: 353, Fats: 20.3g, Net Carbs: 2g, Carbs: 2.7g, Fiber: 0.7g, Sugar: 0.3g, Proteins: 38.9g, Sodium: 277mg

293. Veggies Stuffed Chicken Breasts

Preparation time: 20 minutes

Cooking time: 40 minutes

Servings: 6

INGREDIENTS

- 6 (5-ouncegrass-fed boneless, skinless chicken breast s
- 2 cups fresh baby spinach, chopped
- 4 tablespoons roasted red peppers, chopped
- 3 cups mozzarella cheese, shredded and divided
- 2 tablespoon olive oil
- 2 cups homemade chicken broth
- 6 ounces tomato sauce

DIRECTIONS

1. With a rolling pin, roll each chicken breast for about 1 minute.
2. In a bowl, add the spinach, roasted red peppers and 2 cups of mozzarella cheese and mix well.
3. Place the spinach mixture over each chicken breast evenly.
4. Roll each breast around the spinach mixture and secure with toothpicks.
5. Season each chicken breast with salt and black pepper.
6. Select "Sauté/Sear" setting of Ninja Foodi and place the oil into the pot.
7. Press "Start/Stop" to begin cooking and heat for about 2-3 minutes.
8. Add the chicken breasts and cook for about 5 minutes, flipping once halfway through.
9. Press "Start/Stop" to stop cooking and transfer the chicken breasts into a bowl.
10. In the pot of Ninja Foodi, place the chicken broth.
11. Arrange the "Reversible Rack" in the pot of Ninja Foodi.
12. Place the chicken breasts over the "Reversible Rack".
13. Close the Ninja Foodi with crisping lid and select "Bake/Roast".
14. Set the temperature to 350 degrees F for 35 minutes.
15. Press "Start/Stop" to begin cooking.

16. After 25 minutes of cooking, top each chicken breast with tomato sauce and remaining mozzarella.
17. Serve hot.

NUTRITION: Calories: 252, Fats: 10.4g, Net Carbs: 2.2g, Carbs: 2.9g, Fiber: 0.7g, Sugar: 1.7g, Proteins: 35.1g, Sodium: 554mg

294. Crispy Chicken Cutlets

Preparation time: 15 minutes

Cooking time: 30 minutes

Servings: 4

INGREDIENTS

- ¾ cup almond flour
- 2 large organic eggs
- 1½ cups pork rinds, crushed
- ¼ cup Parmesan cheese, grated
- 1 tablespoon mustard powder
- Salt and ground black pepper, as required
- 4 (6-ounces(¼-inch thickgrass-fed skinless, boneless chicken cutlets
- 1 lemon, cut into slices

DIRECTIONS

1. In a shallow bowl, add the flour.
2. In a second bowl, crack the eggs and beat well.
3. In a third bowl, mix together the pork rinds, cheese, mustard powder, salt, and black pepper.
4. Season the chicken with salt, and black pepper.
5. Coat the chicken with flour, then dip into beaten eggs and finally coat with the pork rinds mixture.
6. Arrange the greased "Cook & Crisp Basket" in the pot of Ninja Foodi
7. Close the Ninja Foodi with crisping lid and select "Air Crisp".
8. Set the temperature to 355 degrees F for 5 minutes.
9. Press "Start/Stop" to begin preheating.
10. After preheating, open the lid.

11. Place the chicken cutlets into the "Cook & Crisp Basket".
12. Close the Ninja Foodi with crisping lid and select "Air Crisp".
13. Set the temperature to 355 degrees F for 30 minutes.
14. Press "Start/Stop" to begin cooking.
15. Serve hot with the topping of lemon slices.

NUTRITION:

Calories: 598, Fats: 32.8g, Net Carbs: 2.5g, Carbs: 5.3g, Fiber: 2.8g, Sugar: 1.2g, Proteins: 63.1g, Sodium: 466mg

295. Crispy Chicken Tenders

Preparation time: 25 minutes

Cooking time: 12 minutes

Servings: 4

INGREDIENTS

- 1 cup almond flour
- 3 organic eggs, beaten
- 1 cup pork rinds, crushed
- 1 pound grass-fed chicken tenders
- Kosher salt, as required

DIRECTIONS

1. In 3 different shallow bowls, place the flour, eggs and pork rinds respectively.
2. Coat the chicken tenders with the flour, then dip into eggs and finally, coat with pork rinds evenly.
3. Arrange the greased "Reversible Rack" in the pot of Ninja Foodi.
4. Close the Ninja Foodi with crisping lid and select "Bake/Roast".
5. Set the temperature to 360 degrees F for 5 minutes.
6. Press "Start/Stop" to begin preheating.
7. After preheating, open the lid.
8. Place the chicken tenders over the "Reversible Rack" without overlapping.
9. Close the Ninja Foodi with crisping lid and select "Bake/Roast".

10. Set the temperature to 360 degrees F for 12 minutes.
11. Press "Start/Stop" to begin cooking.
12. Serve hot with the sprinkling of salt.

NUTRITION: Calories: 371, Fats: 21.8g, Net Carbs: 2.3g, Carbs: 5.3g, Fiber: 3g, Sugar: 1.3g, Proteins: 32.4g, Sodium: 461mg

296.   Spiced Pulled Chicken

Preparation time: 15 minutes

Cooking time: 8 hours

Servings: 4

INGREDIENTS

- 1 pound grass-fed skinless, boneless chicken breasts
- 1½ teaspoons ground cumin
- 3 teaspoons chili powder
- 1½ cups homemade chicken broth

DIRECTIONS

1. In the pot of Ninja Foodi, add all ingredients and mix well.
2. Close the Ninja Foodi with crisping lid and select "Slow Cooker".
3. Set on "Low" for 8 hours.
4. Press "Start/Stop" to begin cooking.
5. Transfer the breasts into a large bowl.
6. With a fork, shred the breasts and serve.

NUTRITION: Calories: 156, Fats: 4.6g, Net Carbs: 1g, Carbs: 1.8g, Fiber: 0.8g, Sugar: 0.2g, Proteins: 26.4g, Sodium: 88mg

297.   Sweet Pulled Chicken

Preparation time: 15 minutes

Cooking time: 4 hours

Servings: 8

INGREDIENTS

- ¼ cup low-sodium soy sauce
- ¼ cup sugar-free blackberry jam
- ¼ cup yacon syrup
- ½ teaspoon red pepper flakes, crushed
- 5 (8-ouncegrass-fed boneless, skinless chicken breasts

DIRECTIONS

1. Grease the pot of Ninja Foodi generously.
2. In a bowl, add all the ingredients except the chicken breasts and mix well.
3. In the prepared pot, place the chicken breasts and top with the yacon syrup mixture.
4. Close the Ninja Foodi with crisping lid and select "Slow Cooker".
5. Set on "High" for 4 hours.
6. Press "Start/Stop" to begin cooking.
7. With 2 forks, shred the meat and stir with sauce well.
8. Serve hot.

NUTRITION: Calories: 287, Fats: 10.5g, Net Carbs: 5.3g, Carbs: 5.3g, Fiber: 0g, Sugar: 1.8g, Proteins: 41.5g, Sodium: 564mg

298.   Butter Chicken

Preparation time: 15 minutes

Cooking time: 9 minutes

Servings: 8

INGREDIENTS

- ½ cup butter, cubed and divided
- 1 large yellow onion, chopped finely
- 6 garlic cloves, minced
- 2 tablespoons fresh ginger, minced
- 3 pounds grass-fed boneless, skinless chicken breasts, cubed
- 1 cup homemade tomato sauce
- 3 tablespoons homemade tomato paste
- 1½ tablespoons garam masala
- 1 teaspoon ground turmeric
- 1 teaspoon kosher salt

- 2/3 cup homemade chicken broth
- 2/3 cup heavy cream
- ¼ cup fresh cilantro, chopped

DIRECTIONS

1. Select "Sauté/Sear" setting of Ninja Foodi and place 2 tablespoons of the butter into the pot.
2. Press "Start/Stop" to begin cooking and heat for about 5 minutes.
3. Add the onion, garlic and ginger and cook for about 2 minutes.
4. Press "Start/Stop" to stop cooking and stir in the remaining ingredients except the cream and cilantro.
5. Close the Ninja Foodi with pressure lid and place the pressure valve to "Seal" position.
6. Select "Pressure" and set to "High" for 5 minutes.
7. Press "Start/Stop" to begin cooking.
8. Switch the valve to "Vent" and do a "Quick" release.
9. Now, select "Sauté/Sear" setting of Ninja Foodi and Press "Start/Stop" to begin cooking.
10. Stir in the remaining butter and heavy cream and cook for 2 minutes.
11. Press "Start/Stop" to stop cooking and serve hot with the garnishing of cilantro.

NUTRITION: Calories: 438, Fats: 26.1g, Net Carbs: 5.4g, Carbs: 6.8g, Fiber: 1.4g, Sugar: 3g, Proteins: 42.9g, Sodium: 723mg

299. Creamy Tomato Chicken

Preparation time: 15 minutes

Cooking time: 6 hours

Servings: 4

INGREDIENTS

- ¾ cup homemade chicken broth
- 1 cup sour cream
- 1½ cups fresh tomatoes, chopped finely
- 1 jalapeño pepper, chopped finely
- 2 tablespoons fresh rosemary, chopped

- Salt and ground black pepper, as required
- 6 (4-ouncegrass-fed boneless, skinless chicken breasts

DIRECTIONS

1. In the pot of Ninja Foodi, add all the ingredients and stir to combine.
2. Close the Ninja Foodi with crisping lid and select "Slow Cooker".
3. Set on "Low" for 6 hours.
4. Press "Start/Stop" to begin cooking.
5. Serve hot.

NUTRITION: Calories: 418, Fats: 20.9g, Net Carbs: 3g, Carbs: 3.5g, Fiber: 0.5g, Sugar: 1.3g, Proteins: 51.4g, Sodium: 291mg

300. Chicken Kabobs

Preparation time: 20 minutes

Cooking time: 14 minutes

Servings: 3

INGREDIENTS

- 4 scallions, chopped
- 1 tablespoon fresh ginger, finely grated
- 4 garlic cloves, minced
- 2 tablespoons fresh lime juice
- 2 tablespoons low-sodium soy sauce
- 1 tablespoon olive oil
- 2 teaspoons Erythritol
- Pinch of black pepper
- 1 pound grass-fed chicken tenders

DIRECTIONS

1. In a large baking dish, mix together the scallion, ginger, garlic, pineapple juice, soy sauce, oil, sesame seeds, and black pepper.
2. Thread chicken tenders onto the pre-soaked wooden skewers.
3. Add the skewers into the baking dish and coat with marinade evenly.
4. Cover and refrigerate for about 2 hours or overnight.

5. Arrange the greased "Cook & Crisp Basket" in the pot of Ninja Foodi.
6. Close the Ninja Foodi with crisping lid and select "Air Crisp".
7. Set the temperature to 390 degrees F for 5 minutes.
8. Press "Start/Stop" to begin preheating.
9. After preheating, open the lid.
10. Place the half of the skewers into the "Cook & Crisp Basket".
11. Close the Ninja Foodi with crisping lid and select "Air Crisp".
12. Set the temperature to 390 degrees F for 7 minutes.
13. Press "Start/Stop" to begin cooking.
14. Repeat with the remaining skewers.
15. Serve hot.

NUTRITION: Calories: 344, Fats: 15.9g, Net Carbs: 3.1g, Carbs: 3.7g, Fiber: 0.6g, Sugar: 1.2g, Proteins: 45g, Sodium: 721mg

301. Chicken & Veggie Kabobs

Preparation time: 20 minutes

Cooking time: 18 minutes

Servings: 6

INGREDIENTS

- 6 (4-ouncesgrass-fed boneless, skinless chicken thigh fillets, trimmed and cut into cubes
- 1 tablespoon jerk seasoning
- 3 large zucchini, sliced
- 12 ounces white mushrooms, stems removed
- Salt and ground black pepper, as required
- 1 tablespoon sugar-free jerk sauce

DIRECTIONS

1. In a bowl, mix together the chicken cubes and jerk seasoning.
2. Cover the bowl and refrigerate overnight.
3. Sprinkle the zucchini slices, and mushrooms with salt and black pepper.

4. Thread the chicken and vegetables onto greased metal skewers.
5. Arrange the greased "Cook & Crisp Basket" in the pot of Ninja Foodi.
6. Close the Ninja Foodi with crisping lid and select "Air Crisp".
7. Set the temperature of Ninja Foodi to 370 degrees F for 5 minutes.
8. Press "Start/Stop" to begin preheating.
9. After preheating, open the lid.
10. Place the half of the skewers into the "Cook & Crisp Basket".
11. Close the Ninja Foodi with crisping lid and select "Air Crisp".
12. Set the temperature to 370 degrees F for 9 minutes.
13. Press "Start/Stop" to begin cooking.
14. Flip and coat the kabobs with jerk sauce once halfway through.
15. Repeat with the remaining skewers.
16. Serve hot.

NUTRITION: Calories: 259, Fats: 8.9g, Net Carbs: 6.4g, Carbs: 8.8g, Fiber: 2.4g, Sugar: 5.1g, Proteins: 36.5g, Sodium: 148mg

302. Chicken Burgers

Preparation time: 20 minutes

Cooking time: 30 minutes

Servings: 4

INGREDIENTS

- 6 (4-ouncegrass-fed boneless, skinless chicken breasts
- 1 teaspoon mustard powder
- ½ teaspoon paprika
- 1 teaspoon Worcestershire sauce
- 1 cup almond flour
- 1 small organic egg
- ½ cup pork rinds, crushed finely
- ¼ teaspoon dried parsley
- ¼ teaspoon dried tarragon
- ¼ teaspoon dried oregano
- 1 teaspoon dried garlic
- 1 teaspoon chicken seasoning
- ½ teaspoon cayenne pepper

- Salt and ground black pepper, as required

DIRECTIONS

1. In a food processor, add the chicken breasts and pulse until minced.
2. Add the mustard, paprika, Worcester sauce, salt, and black pepper and pulse until well combined.
3. Make 4 equal-sized patties from the mixture.
4. In a shallow bowl, place the flour.
5. In a second bowl, crack the egg and beat well.
6. In a third bowl, mix well pork rinds, dried herbs, and spices.
7. Coat each chicken patty with flour, then dip into egg and finally, coat with pork rinds mixture.
8. Arrange the greased "Cook & Crisp Basket" in the pot of Ninja Foodi.
9. Close the Ninja Foodi with crisping lid and select "Air Crisp".
10. Set the temperature to 355 degrees F for 5 minutes.
11. Press "Start/Stop" to begin preheating.
12. After preheating, open the lid.
13. Place the chicken patties into the "Cook & Crisp Basket" in a single layer.
14. Close the Ninja Foodi with crisping lid and select "Air Crisp".
15. Set the temperature to 355 degrees F for 30 minutes.
16. Press "Start/Stop" to begin cooking.
17. Flip the patties once halfway through.
18. Serve hot.

NUTRITION: Calories: 547, Fats: 30.3g, Net Carbs: 2.9g, Carbs: 6.2g, Fiber: 3.3g, Sugar: 1.4g, Proteins: 53.3g, Sodium: 264mg

303. Chicken Soup

Preparation time: 15 minutes

Cooking time: 6 hours

Servings: 6

INGREDIENTS

- 2 tablespoons unsalted butter, melted
- 4 cups grass-fed cooked chicken, chopped
- 8 cups fresh spinach, chopped
- 1 large carrot, peeled and chopped
- 1 small onion, chopped finely
- ½ tablespoon garlic, minced
- Salt and ground black pepper, as required
- 6 cups homemade chicken broth

DIRECTIONS

1. In the pot of Ninja Foodi, add all ingredients and mix well.
2. Close the Ninja Foodi with crisping lid and select "Slow Cooker".
3. Set on "Low" for 6 hours.
4. Press "Start/Stop" to begin cooking.
5. Serve hot.

NUTRITION: Calories: 210, Fats: 6.8g, Net Carbs: 3.5g, Carbs: 5g, Fiber: 1.5g, Sugar: 1.3g, Proteins: 30.5g, Sodium: 197mg

304. Chicken & Carrot Stew

Preparation time: 0 minutes

Cooking time: 6 hours

Servings: 6

INGREDIENTS

- 4 (5-ouncegrass-fed boneless chicken breast, cubed
- 3 cups carrots, peeled and cubed
- 2 celery stalks, chopped
- 1 medium yellow onion, chopped
- 2 garlic cloves, minced
- Salt and ground black pepper, as required
- ½ teaspoon dried thyme
- 2 cups homemade chicken broth
- 2 tablespoons olive oil

DIRECTIONS

1. In the pot of Ninja Foodi, add all ingredients except the oil and mix well.
2. Close the Ninja Foodi with crisping lid and select "Slow Cooker".
3. Set on "Low" for 6 hours.
4. Press "Start/Stop" to begin cooking.
5. Stir in oil and serve hot.

NUTRITION: Calories: 193, Fats: 9.4g, Net Carbs: 6g, Carbs: 8g, Fiber: 2g, Sugar: 3g, Proteins: 18.3g, Sodium: 374mg

305.   Teriyaki Chicken with Broccoli
Preparation time: 15 minutes

Cooking time: 14 minutes

Servings: 3

INGREDIENTS

- 3 (5-ouncegrass-fed boneless, skinless chicken breasts
- 1 head broccoli, cut in 2-inch florets
- 1 tablespoon olive oil
- Salt and ground black pepper, as required
- ¼ cup sugar-free teriyaki sauce

DIRECTIONS

1. In the pot of Ninja Foodi, place 1 cup of water.
2. Arrange the "Reversible Rack" in the pot of Ninja Foodi.
3. Arrange the chicken breasts over the rack.
4. Close the Ninja Foodi with pressure lid and place the pressure valve to "Seal" position.
5. Select "Pressure" and set to "High" for 2 minutes.
6. Press "Start/Stop" to begin cooking.
7. Meanwhile, in a bowl, add the broccoli, oil salt and black pepper and toss to coat well.
8. Switch the valve to "Vent" and do a "Natural" release for about 10 minutes. Then do a "Quick" release.
9. Coat the chicken breasts with teriyaki sauce generously.

10. Arrange the broccoli florets around the chicken breasts.
11. Now, close the Ninja Foodi with crisping lid and select "Broil" for12 minutes.
12. Press "Start/Stop" to begin cooking.
13. Serve the chicken breasts alongside the broccoli.

NUTRITION: Calories: 360, Fats: 15.5g, Net Carbs: 6.8g, Carbs: 9g, Fiber: 2.2g, Sugar: 4.8g, Proteins: 44.8g, Sodium: 1120mg

306.   Chicken with Cauliflower
Preparation time: 15 minutes

Cooking time: 5 hours

Servings: 4

INGREDIENTS

- 1 pound grass-fed skinless, boneless chicken thighs, cubed
- 1½ cups homemade chicken broth
- 1 small white onion, chopped
- 2 garlic cloves, minced
- 2 cups cauliflower florets
- Salt and ground black pepper, as required

DIRECTIONS

1. In the pot of Ninja Foodi, add all ingredients and mix well.
2. Close the Ninja Foodi with crisping lid and select "Slow Cooker".
3. Set on "Low" for 5 hours.
4. Press "Start/Stop" to begin cooking.
5. Serve hot.

NUTRITION: Calories: 169, Fats: 4.1g, Net Carbs: 3.5g, Carbs: 5.2g, Fiber: 1.7g, Sugar: 2g, Proteins: 27.3g, Sodium: 83mg

307.   Chicken with Mushrooms
Preparation time: 15 minutes

Cooking time: 8 hours 10 minutes

Servings: 6

INGREDIENTS

- 1 tablespoon olive oil
- 6 grass-fed skinless, boneless chicken breasts
- 4 cups fresh button mushrooms, sliced
- 1 cup homemade chicken broth
- Salt and ground black pepper, as required

DIRECTIONS

1. Select "Sauté/Sear" setting of Ninja Foodi and place the oil into the pot.
2. Press "Start/Stop" to begin cooking and heat for about 2-3 minutes.
3. Add the chicken and cook, uncovered for about 5 minutes per side.
4. Press "Start/Stop" to stop cooking and stir in the remaining ingredients .
5. Close the Ninja Foodi with crisping lid and select "Slow Cooker".
6. Set on "Low" for 7-8 hours.
7. Press "Start/Stop" to begin cooking.
8. Serve hot.

NUTRITION: Calories: 249, Fats: 8.8g, Net Carbs: 1.2g, Carbs: 1.7g, Fiber: 0.5g, Sugar: 0.9g, Proteins: 40.3g, Sodium: 218mg

308. Chicken with Mushrooms & Spinach

Preparation time: 15 minutes

Cooking time: 5 hours

Servings: 5

INGREDIENTS

- 1½ pounds grass-fed boneless chicken breasts, cut into thin strips
- 1½ cup fresh button mushrooms, sliced
- 2 cups fresh spinach, chopped
- 1 yellow onion, sliced thinly
- 1 cup homemade chicken broth
- Pinch of cayenne pepper
- Sea Salt and ground black pepper, as required

DIRECTIONS

1. In the pot of Ninja Foodi, add all ingredients and mix well.
2. Close the Ninja Foodi with crisping lid and select "Slow Cooker".
3. Set on "Low" for 5 hours.
4. Press "Start/Stop" to begin cooking.
5. Serve hot.

NUTRITION: Calories: 282, Fats: 10.5g, Net Carbs: 2.5g, Carbs: 3.4g, Fiber: 0.9g, Sugar: 1.5g, Proteins: 41.6g, Sodium: 281mg

309. Chicken with Asparagus & Zucchini

Preparation time: 20 minutes

Cooking time: 8 hours 40 minutes

Servings: 8

INGREDIENTS

- 2 pounds grass-fed skinless, boneless chicken breast tenders
- 1 large onion, chopped
- 2 cups asparagus, trimmed and cut into 2-inch pieces
- 1 tablespoon fresh thyme, chopped
- 1 teaspoon garlic powder
- Salt and ground black pepper, as required
- 4 medium zucchinis, spiralized with blade C
- 1 cup sour cream
- 1 cup Cheddar cheese, shredded

DIRECTIONS

1. In the pot of Ninja Foodi, add the chicken, onion, asparagus, thyme, garlic powder, salt and black pepper and mix well.
2. Close the Ninja Foodi with crisping lid and select "Slow Cooker".
3. Set on "Low" for 8 hours.
4. Press "Start/Stop" to begin cooking.
5. Place the zucchini noodles over the chicken mixture and top with cheese and cream.
6. Close the Ninja Foodi with crisping lid and select "Slow Cooker".
7. Set on "Low" for 30-40 minutes.

8. Press "Start/Stop" to begin cooking.
9. Stir the mixture well and serve hot.

NUTRITION: Calories: 292, Fats: 15g, Net Carbs: 5.9g, Carbs: 8.2g, Fiber: 2.3g, Sugar: 3.4g, Proteins: 32g, Sodium: 155mg

310. Turkey Wings

Preparation time: 10 minutes

Cooking time: 26 minutes

Servings: 4

INGREDIENTS

- 2 pounds turkey wings
- 4 tablespoons chicken rub
- 3 tablespoons olive oil

DIRECTIONS

1. In a large bowl, add the turkey wings, chicken rub and oil and mix well.
2. Arrange the greased "Cook & Crisp Basket" in the pot of Ninja Foodi.
3. Close the Ninja Foodi with crisping lid and select "Air Crisp".
4. Set the temperature to 380 degrees F for 5 minutes.
5. Press "Start/Stop" to begin preheating.
6. After preheating, open the lid.
7. Place the turkey wings into the "Cook & Crisp Basket".
8. Close the Ninja Foodi with crisping lid and select "Air Crisp".
9. Set the temperature to 380 degrees F for 26 minutes.
10. Press "Start/Stop" to begin cooking.
11. Flip the turkey wings once halfway through.

12. Serve hot.

NUTRITION: Calories: 204, Fats: 15.5g, Net Carbs: 3g, Carbs: 3g, Fiber: 0g, Sugar: 0g, Proteins: 11.5g, Sodium: 465mg

311. Herbed Turkey Legs

Preparation time: 10 minutes

Cooking time: 12 hours

Servings: 3

INGREDIENTS

- 3 turkey legs
- 2 tablespoons fresh herbs, chopped
- 1 tablespoon coconut oil, melted
- 1 teaspoon paprika
- ½ teaspoon garlic salt
- 1 teaspoon seasoning salt

DIRECTIONS

1. In a large bowl, add all the ingredients and mix well.
2. Arrange the greased "Reversible Rack" in the pot of Ninja Foodi.
3. Arrange the turkey legs over the "Reversible Rack".
4. Close the Ninja Foodi with crisping lid and select "Slow Cooker".
5. Set on "Low" for 12 hours.
6. Press "Start/Stop" to begin cooking.
7. Serve hot.

NUTRITION: Calories: 325, Fats: 14.7g, Net Carbs: 0.6g, Carbs: 1.2g, Fiber: 0.6g, Sugar: 0.2g, Proteins: 47.8g, Sodium: 776mg

MEAT

312. Delicious Braised Pork Neck Bones

Preparation Time: 40 minutes

Servings: 6

INGREDIENTS

- 3 lbs. Pork Neck Bones
- 4 tbsp. Olive Oil
- 1 White Onion, sliced
- 1/2 cup Red Wine
- 2 cloves Garlic, smashed
- 1 tbsp. Tomato Paste
- 1 tsp. dried Thyme
- 1 cup Beef Broth
- Salt and Black Pepper to taste

DIRECTIONS

1. Open the lid and select Sear/Sauté mode. Warm the olive oil
2. Meanwhile season the pork neck bones with salt and pepper. After, place them in the oil to brown on all sides. Work in batches.
3. Each batch should cook in about 5 minutes. Then, remove them onto a plate.
4. Add the onion and season with salt to taste. Stir with a spoon and cook the onions until soft, for a few minutes. Then, add garlic, thyme, pepper, and tomato paste. Cook them for 2 minutes, constant stirring to prevent the tomato paste from burning
5. Next, pour the red wine into the pot to deglaze the bottom. Add the pork neck bones back to the pot and pour the beef broth over it
6. Close the lid, secure the pressure valve, and select Pressure mode on High pressure for 10 minutes. Press Start/Stop to start cooking.
7. Once the timer has ended, let the pot sit for 10 minutes before doing a quick pressure release. Close the crisping lid and cook on Broil mode for 5 minutes, until nice and tender.
8. Dish the pork neck into a serving bowl and serve with the red wine sauce spooned over and a right amount of broccoli mash

313. Oregano Meatballs

Preparation Time: 30 minutes

Servings: 6

INGREDIENTS

- 1 lb. pork meat; minced.
- 1 cup tomato puree
- ½ tbsp. lime peel; grated.
- 1 tbsp. oregano; chopped.
- 1 tbsp. bread crumbs
- 2 tbsp. parmesan; grated.
- Salt and black pepper to the taste

DIRECTIONS

1. In a bowl mix all the Ingredients except the tomato puree, stir well and shape medium meatballs out of this mix. Set the Foodi on Sauté mode, add the meatballs and brown them for 3 minutes
2. Add the tomato puree, toss a bit, put the pressure lid on and cook on High for 15 minutes. Release the pressure naturally for 10 minutes, divide the meatballs into bowls and serve as an appetizer

314. Paprika Pork Chops

Preparation Time: 25 minutes

Servings: 6

INGREDIENTS

- 4 medium pork chops
- 2 garlic cloves; minced.

- ¼ cup olive oil
- 1 tbsp. sweet paprika
- Salt and black pepper to the taste

DIRECTIONS

1. In a bowl mix the all the ingredients and toss. Put the pork chops in the Foodi's basket, set the machine on Air Crisp and cook at 400 °F for 15 minutes. Divide the chops between plates and serve.

315. Pork Shoulder Chops With Carrots

Preparation Time: 70 minutes

Servings: 4 to 6

INGREDIENTS

- 3 lb. bone in pork shoulder chops, each 1/2 to 3/4 inch thick
- 6 medium carrots
- 1/3 cup maple syrup
- 1/3 cup chicken broth
- 3 medium garlic cloves
- 1 tbsp. bacon fat
- 1/3 cup soy sauce
- 1/2 tsp. ground black pepper

DIRECTIONS

1. Melt the bacon fat in a Ninja Foodi Multi-cooker, turned to the browning function. Add about half the chops and brown well, turning once, about 5 minutes. Transfer these to a large bowl and brown the remaining chops
2. Stir the carrots and garlic into the pot; cook for 1 minute, constantly stirring. Pour in the soy sauce, maple syrup and broth, stirring to dissolve the maple syrup and to get up any browned bits on the bottom of the pot. Stir in the pepper. Return the shoulder chops and their juices to the pot. Stir to coat them in the sauce
3. High pressure for 40 minutes. Lock the lid on the Ninja Foodi Multi-cooker and then cook for 40 minutes

4. To get 40 minutes' cook time, press *Pressure* button and use the Time Adjustment button to adjust the cook time to 40 minutes.
5. Pressure Release. Let the pressure to come down naturally for at least 14 to 16 minutes, then quick release any pressure left in the pot
6. Finish the dish. Close crisping lid and select Broil, set time to 7 minutes.
7. Transfer the chops, carrots and garlic cloves to a large serving bowl. Skim the fat off the sauce and ladle it over the.

316. Cinnamon Pork

Preparation Time: 30 minutes

Servings: 4

INGREDIENTS

- 1 lb. pork stew meat; cubed.
- 1 yellow onion; chopped.
- 1 garlic clove; minced.
- 2 tbsp. olive oil
- 3 tbsp. parsley; chopped.
- 1 tsp. cinnamon powder
- Salt and black pepper to the taste

DIRECTIONS

1. Set the Foodi on Sauté mode, add the oil and heat it up. Add the onion, stir and sauté for 5 minutes. Add the meat, garlic, cinnamon, salt and pepper, toss and sauté for 4-5 minutes more
2. Add the parsley, put the pressure lid on and cook on High for 12 minutes more. Release pre pressure naturally for 10 minutes, divide everything into bowls and serve

317. Chinese Pork

Preparation Time: 90 minutes

Servings: 8

INGREDIENTS

- 3 lbs. pork shoulder roast
- 4 garlic cloves; minced.
- ¼ cup ketchup
- ¼ cup soy sauce
- ½ cup chicken stock
- ½ cup hoisin sauce
- ½ cup honey
- 1 tsp. Chinese five spice powder
- 4 tsp. ginger; grated.

DIRECTIONS

1. Combine all the ingredients in the Foodi machine, put the pressure lid on and cook on High for 1 hour and 20 minutes. Release the pressure naturally for 10 minutes, divide everything between plates and serve

318. Honey Mustard Pork Tenderloin Recipe

Preparation Time: 30 minutes

Servings: 4

INGREDIENTS

- 2 lbs. Pork Tenderloin
- 1 tbsp. Worcestershire Sauce
- 1/2 tbsp. Cornstarch
- 1/2 cup Chicken Broth
- 1/4 cup Balsamic Vinegar
- 1 clove Garlic, minced
- 2 tbsps. Olive Oil
- 1/4 cup Honey
- 1 tsp. Sage Powder
- 1 tbsp. Dijon Mustard
- 4 tbsp. Water
- Salt and Black Pepper to taste
- Brussels sprouts, sautéed

DIRECTIONS

1. Put the pork on a clean flat surface and pat dry using paper towels. Season with salt and pepper. Select Sear/Sauté mode.

2. Heat the oil and brown the pork on both sides, for about 4 minutes in total. Remove the pork onto a plate and set aside

3. Add in honey, chicken broth, balsamic vinegar, garlic, Worcestershire sauce, mustard, and sage powder. Stir the INGREDIENTS and return the pork to the pot

4. Close the lid, secure the pressure valve, and select Pressure mode on High for 15 minutes. Once the timer has ended, do a quick pressure release. Remove the pork with tongs onto a plate and wrap it in aluminum foil

5. Next, mix the cornstarch with water and pour it into the pot. Select Sear/Sauté mode, stir the mixture and cook until it thickens. Then, turn the pot off after the desired thickness is achieved.

6. Unwrap the pork and use a knife to slice it with 3 to 4-inch thickness. Arrange the slices on a serving platter and spoon the sauce all over it. Serve with a syrupy sautéed Brussels sprouts.

319. BBQ Pork with Ginger Coconut and Sweet Potatoes

Preparation Time: 40 minutes

Servings: 4

INGREDIENTS

- 4 frozen uncooked boneless pork chops 8-ounces each
- 3 sweet potatoes, peeled, cut in 1-inch cubes
- 1/2 cup unsweetened coconut milk
- 1 tsp. Chinese five spice powder
- 1/2 stick 1/4 cup butter
- 1 tbsp. fresh ginger, peeled, minced
- 1/4 cup hoisin sauce
- 1/3 cup honey
- 1 ½ tbsp. soy sauce
- 1 tsp. kosher salt
- 1/2 tsp. white pepper

DIRECTIONS

1. Place sweet potatoes and coconut milk into the pot. Place reversible rack inside pot over sweet potatoes, making sure rack is in the higher position.
2. Place pork chops on rack. Assemble pressure lid, making sure the PRESSURE RELEASE valve is in the SEAL position. Select PRESSURE and set to HIGH. Set time to 4 minutes. Select START/STOP to begin.
3. While pork chops and sweet potatoes are cooking, whisk together hoisin sauce, honey, soy sauce, and Chinese five spice powder.
4. When pressure cooking is complete, quick release the pressure by moving the PRESSURE RELEASE valve to the VENT position. Carefully remove lid when unit has finished releasing pressure
5. Remove rack with pork from pot. Mash sweet potatoes with butter, ginger, and salt, using a mashing utensil that won't scratch the nonstick surface of the pot
6. Place rack with pork back in pot and brush top of pork generously with 1/2 of sauce mixture.
7. Close crisping lid. Select BROIL and set time to 15 minutes. Select START/STOP to begin. After 5 minutes, open lid, flip pork chops, then brush them with remaining sauce.
8. Close lid to resume cooking. Check after 10 minutes and remove if desired doneness is achieved. If not, cook up to 5 more minutes, checking frequently. When cooking is complete, remove pork from rack and allow to rest for 5 minutes before serving with mashed potatoes

320. Special Biscuits

Preparation Time: 40 minutes

Servings: 6

INGREDIENTS

- 12 oz. pork sausage, crumbled
- 16 oz. biscuit dough
- ½ cup cheddar cheese, shredded
- 3 cups milk
- ¼ cup white flour
- 2 tbsp. butter
- A pinch of salt and black pepper

DIRECTIONS

1. Set the Foodi on Sauté mode, heat it up, add the sausage, salt and pepper, stir and cook for 5 minutes. Add the butter, milk and the flour, whisk well and cook for 7 minutes.
2. Meanwhile, separate each biscuit and fill each with the cheddar cheese. Put the reversible rack in the Foodi, place the biscuits in on the rack and lower it into the gravy
3. Set the machine on Baking mode and cook the biscuits at 325 °F for 15 minutes. Divide the biscuits between plates, drizzle the gravy all over and serve as a side

321. Pork Loin and Apples

Preparation Time: 43 minutes

Servings: 8

INGREDIENTS

- 1 3 lb. boneless pork loin roast
- 1 large red onion, halved and thinly sliced
- 2 medium tart green apples, such as Granny Smith, peeled, cored and thinly sliced
- 1/2 cup moderately sweet white wine, such as Riesling
- 2 tbsp. unsalted butter
- 1/4 cup chicken broth
- 4 fresh thyme sprigs
- 2 bay leaves
- 1/2 tsp. salt
- 1/2 tsp. ground black pepper

DIRECTIONS

1. Melt the butter in the Ninja Foodi Multi-cooker, set on the *Sauté* function. Add the pork loin and brown it on all sides,

turning occasionally, about 8 minutes in all. Transfer to a large plate.

2. Add the onion to the pot; cook, often stirring, until softened, about 3 minutes. Stir in the apple, thyme and bay leaves. Pour in the wine and scrape up any browned bits on the bottom of the pot

3. Pour in the broth; stir in the salt and pepper. Nestle the pork loin into this apple mixture; pour any juices from the plate into the pot.

4. High pressure for 30 minutes. Lock the lid on the Ninja Foodi Multi-cooker and then cook for 30 minutes.

5. To get 30 minutes' cook time, press *Pressure* button and adjust the time

6. Pressure Release. Use the quick release method to bring the pot's pressure to normal

7. Finish the dish. Close crisping lid and select Broil, set time to 7 minutes.

8. Transfer the pork to a cutting board; let stand for 5 minutes while you dish the sauce into serving bowls or onto a serving platter. Slice the loin into 1/2-inch-thick rounds and lay these over the sauce.

322.   Pork Meatballs

Preparation Time: 25 minutes

Servings: 12

INGREDIENTS

- 1 lb. pork meat, ground
- 2 garlic cloves; minced.
- ½ cup bread crumbs
- 2 cups sweet and sour sauce
- ½ cup pineapple; chopped.
- 1 cup scallions; chopped.
- 1 egg; whisked.
- 1 tbsp. ginger; grated.
- 1 tbsp. mustard
- 2 tbsp. soy sauce
- 1 tsp. coriander, ground
- Juice of 1 lime

DIRECTIONS

1. In a bowl combine all the ingredients except the sauce, stir well and shape medium meatballs out of this mix

2. Put the meatballs in your Foodi, add the sweet and sour sauce, toss gently, put the pressure lid on and cook the meatballs on High for 15 minutes. Release the pressure naturally for 10 minutes, divide the meatballs into bowls and serve

323.   Simple Spare Ribs with Wine

Preparation Time: 75 minutes

Servings: 4

INGREDIENTS

- 1 lb. pork spare ribs, cut into pieces
- 1 tbsp. corn starch
- 1 tbsp. olive oil
- 1 – 2 tsp. water
- Green onions as garnish
- 1 tsp. fish sauce optional
- Black Bean Marinade:
- 3 cloves garlic, minced
- 1 tsp. sesame oil
- 1 tsp. sugar
- 1 tbsp. ginger, grated
- 1 tbsp. black bean sauce
- 1 tbsp. light soy sauce
- A pinch of white pepper

DIRECTIONS

1. Marinate the pork spare ribs with Black Bean Marinade in an oven-safe bowl. Then, sit it in the fridge for 25 minutes.

2. First, mix 1 tbsp. of olive oil into the marinated spare ribs. Then, add 1 tbsp. of cornstarch and mix well. Finally, add 1 – 2 tsp. of water into the spare ribs and mix well

3. Add 1 cup of water into the Ninja Foodi Multi-cooker. Place steam rack in the Ninja Foodi Multi-cooker. Then, put the bowl of spare ribs on the rack

4. High pressure for 15 minutes. Lock the lid on the Ninja Foodi Multi-cooker and then cook for 15 minutes.

5. To get 15 minutes' cook time, press *Pressure* Button and then adjust the time

6. Pressure Release. Let the pressure to come down naturally for at least 15 minutes, then quick release any pressure left in the pot.

7. Finish the dish. Close crisping lid. Select *Air Crisp*, set temperature to 375°F and set time to 10 minutes. Check after 5 minutes, cooking for an additional 5 minutes if dish needs more browning

8. Taste and add one tsp. of fish sauce and green onions as garnish if you like. Serve immediately.

324. Yummy Pork Chops

Preparation Time: 35 minutes

Servings: 6

INGREDIENTS

- 1 lb. pork chops
- 3 cups chicken stock
- 1 garlic clove; minced.
- 1 ½ cups heavy cream
- 2 yellow onions; chopped.
- 1 tbsp. olive oil
- 2 tbsp. sweet paprika
- 2 tbsp. dill; chopped.
- Salt and black pepper to the taste

DIRECTIONS

1. Put the pork chops in your Foodi's basket, season with salt, pepper, garlic and the paprika, rub, set the machine on Air Crisp and cook at 380 °F for 10 minutes. Transfer the pork chops to the Foodi's baking pan, add all the other INGREDIENTS and toss

2. Place the baking pan in the machine, set it on Baking mode and cook at 370 °F for 15 minutes more. Divide everything between plates and serve hot

325. Delicious Pulled Pork Sandwiches

Preparation Time: 60 minutes

Servings: 8

INGREDIENTS

- 2 ½ – 3 lb. uncooked boneless pork shoulder, cut in 1-inch cubes
- 1 can 6-ounces tomato paste
- 2 tbsp. barbecue seasoning
- 1 cup apple cider vinegar
- 1 tbsp. garlic powder
- 2 tsp. kosher salt
- Coleslaw and Potato rolls for

DIRECTIONS

1. Add pork, spices, and vinegar to the pot. Assemble pressure lid, making sure the pressure release valve is in the SEAL position. Select PRESSURE and set to HIGH. Set time to 35 minutes. Select START/STOP to begin

2. When pressure cooking is complete, quick release the pressure by turning the pressure release valve to VENT position. Carefully remove lid when unit has finished releasing pressure.

3. Select SEAR/SAUTÉ and set to MEDIUM-HIGH. Select START/STOP to begin

4. Add tomato paste and stir to incorporate. Allow pork to simmer for 10 minutes, or until the liquid has reduced by half, as shown above, stirring occasionally with a wooden spoon or silicone tongs to shred the pork.

5. Serve pulled pork on potato rolls topped with coleslaw.

326. Garlic Pork Chops

Preparation Time: 30 minutes

Servings: 4

INGREDIENTS

- 4 pork chops

- 4 garlic cloves; minced.
- 2 tbsp. rosemary; chopped.
- 2 tbsp. olive oil
- Salt and black pepper to the taste

DIRECTIONS

1. In a bowl mix all the ingredients and toss them well. Put the reversible rack in the Foodi and add the basket inside
2. Add the pork chops to the basket, set the machine on Air Crisp and cook at 400 °F for 20 minutes. Serve with a side salad.

327.   Buttery Pork Steaks

Preparation Time: 24 minutes

Servings: 4

INGREDIENTS

- 4 pork steaks
- 2 tbsp. butter, melted
- 1 tbsp. smoked paprika
- Salt and black pepper to the taste

DIRECTIONS

1. In a bowl mix all the ingredients and toss them. Put the steaks in the Foodi's basket, set the machine on Air Crisp and cook at 390 °F for 7 minutes on each side. Divide the steaks between plates and serve

328.   Garlic Pork

Preparation Time: 35 minutes

Servings: 4

INGREDIENTS:

- 1 ½ lbs. pork stew meat; cubed.
- 1 tbsp. smoked paprika
- 3 tbsp. olive oil
- 3 tbsp. garlic; minced.
- Salt and black pepper to the taste

DIRECTIONS:

1. In the Foodi's baking pan, combine all the ingredients and toss. Put the reversible rack in the machine, add the baking pan inside, set the pot on Roast mode and cook at 390 °F for 25 minutes. Divide everything between plates and serve with a side salad

329.   Pork Chops

Preparation Time: 25 minutes

Servings: 4

INGREDIENTS

- 2 lbs. pork chops, boneless
- 1 green cabbage head, shredded
- 2 cups chicken stock
- A pinch of salt and black pepper
- 2 tbsp. butter, melted

DIRECTIONS

1. Put all the ingredients in the Foodi machine, put the pressure lid on and cook on High for 15 minutes. Release the pressure naturally for 10 minutes, divide everything between plates and serve

330.   Rosemary Sausage and Onion

Preparation Time: 35 minutes

Servings: 4

INGREDIENTS:

- 6 pork sausage links, halved
- 2 yellow onion, sliced
- 2 garlic cloves; minced.
- 1 tbsp. rosemary; chopped.
- 1 tbsp. olive oil
- 1 tbsp. sweet paprika
- Salt and black pepper to the taste

DIRECTIONS

1. In your Foodi's baking pan, combine all the ingredients and toss. Put the reversible rack in the Foodi, add the baking pan, set the machine on Baking mode and cook at 370 °F for 25 minutes. Divide between plates and serve

331. Pork Carnitas

Preparation Time: 55 minutes

Servings: 4

INGREDIENTS

- 2 lbs. pork butt; cubed.
- 1 yellow onion; chopped.
- 6 garlic cloves; minced.
- ½ cup chicken stock
- Juice of 1 orange
- A pinch of salt and black pepper
- ½ tsp. oregano, dried

½ tsp. cumin, ground

DIRECTIONS

1. Put all the ingredients in the Ninja Foodi machine, put the pressure lid on and cook on High for 20 minutes.
2. Release the pressure fast for 4 minutes, set the machine on Sauté mode and cook everything for 15 minutes more. Set the Foodi on Broil mode, cook everything for 8 more minutes. Divide everything into bowls and serve

332. Ninja Pulled Pork

Preparation Time: 2 hour 5 minutes

Servings: 10

INGREDIENTS

- 1 4- to 4½ lb. bone in skinless pork shoulder, preferably pork butt

- Up to 1 ½ cups light-colored beer, preferably a pale ale or amber lager
- 1/2 tsp. garlic powder
- 1/2 tsp. ground cloves
- 1/2 tsp. ground cinnamon
- 2 tbsp. smoked paprika
- 2 tbsp. packed dark brown sugar
- 1 tbsp. ground cumin
- 1/2 tbsp. dry mustard
- 1 tsp. ground coriander
- 1 tsp. dried thyme
- 1 tsp. onion powder
- 1 tsp. salt
- 2 tsp. ground black pepper

DIRECTIONS

1. Mix the smoked paprika, brown sugar, cumin, pepper, mustard, coriander, thyme, onion powder, salt, garlic powder, cloves and cinnamon in a small bowl. Massage the mixture all over the pork.
2. Set the pork in the Ninja Foodi Multi-cooker. Pour 1cup beer into the electric cooker without knocking the spices off the meat
3. High pressure for 80 minutes. Lock the lid on the Ninja Foodi Multi-cooker and then cook for 80 minutes.
4. To get 80 minutes' cook time, press *Pressure* button and use the Time Adjustment button to adjust the cook time to 80 minutes.
5. Pressure Release. Let its pressure fall to normal naturally, 25 to 35 minutes
6. Finish the dish. Close crisping lid and select Broil, set time to 7 minutes
7. Transfer the meat to a large cutting board. Let stand for 5 minutes. Use a spoon to skim as much fat off the sauce in the pot as possible
8. Set the *Sauté* function. Bring the sauce to a simmer, stirring occasionally; continue boiling the sauce, often stirring, until reduced by half, 7 to 10 minutes.
9. Use two forks to shred the meat off the bones; discard the bones and any attached cartilage. Pull any large chunks of meat apart with the forks and stir the meat back

into the simmering sauce to reheat. Serve and Enjoy!

333. Amazing Pork Chops with Applesauce

Preparation Time: 50 minutes

Servings: 4

INGREDIENTS

- 2 to 4 pork loin chops we used center cut, bone-on
- 2 gala apples, thinly sliced
- 1 tsp. cinnamon powder
- 1 tbsp. honey
- 1/2 cup unsalted homemade chicken stock or water
- 1 tbsp. grapeseed oil or olive oil
- 1 small onion, sliced
- 3 cloves garlic, roughly minced
- 2 tbsp. light soy sauce
- 1 tbsp. butter
- Kosher salt and ground black pepper to taste
- 2 pieces whole cloves optional
- 1 ½ tbsp. cornstarch mixed with 2 tbsp. water optional

DIRECTIONS

1. Make a few small cut around the sides of the pork chops so they will stay flat and brown evenly
2. Season the pork chops with a generous amount of kosher salt and ground black pepper.
3. Heat up your Ninja Foodi Multi-cooker. Add grapeseed oil into the pot. Add the seasoned pork chops into the pot, then let it brown for roughly 2 – 3 minutes on each side. Remove and set aside.
4. Add the sliced onions and stir. Add a pinch of kosher salt and ground black pepper to season if you like. Cook the onions for roughly 1 minute until softened. Then, add garlic and stir for 30 seconds until fragrance

5. Add in the thinly sliced gala apples, whole cloves optional and cinnamon powder, then give it a quick stir. Add the honey and partially deglaze the bottom of the pot with a wooden spoon
6. Add chicken stock and light soy sauce, then fully deglaze the bottom of the pot with a wooden spoon. Taste the seasoning and add more salt and pepper if desired
7. Place the pork chops back with all the meat juice into the pot
8. High pressure for 10 minutes. Lock the lid on the Ninja Foodi Multi-cooker and then cook for 10 minutes.
9. To get 10 minutes' cook time, press *Pressure* button and use the Time Adjustment button to adjust the cook time to 10 minutes
10. Pressure Release. Let it fully natural release roughly 10 minutes. Open the lid carefully.
11. Finish the dish. Close crisping lid. Select *Air Crisp*, set temperature to 375°F and set time to 10 minutes. Check after 10 minutes, cooking for an additional 5 minutes if dish needs more browning
12. Remove the pork chops and set aside. Turn the Multi-cooker to the Sauté setting. Remove the cloves and taste the seasoning one more time.
13. Add more salt and pepper if desired. Add butter and stir until it has fully dissolved into the sauce
14. Mix the cornstarch with water and mix it into the applesauce one third at a time until desired thickness.
15. Drizzle the applesauce over the pork chops and serve immediately with side dishes!

334. Peppers and Pork Stew

Preparation Time: 30 minutes

Servings: 4

INGREDIENTS

- 1 large yellow or white onion, chopped.
- 1 large green bell pepper, stemmed, cored and cut into 1/4-inch-thick strips

- 1 lb. boneless center-cut pork loin chops, cut into 1/4-inch-thick strips
- 1 large red bell pepper, stemmed, cored and cut into 1/4-inch-thick strips
- 1 14-ounce can diced tomatoes, drained about 1 3/4 cups
- 2 tsp. minced, seeded fresh jalapeño chile
- 2 tsp. dried oregano
- 2 tbsp. olive oil
- 2 tsp. minced garlic
- 2 ½ cups canned hominy drained and rinsed
- 1 cup chicken broth

DIRECTIONS

1. Heat the oil in a Ninja Foodi Multi-cooker, turned to the Sauté function. Add the onion and both bell peppers; cook, often stirring, until the onion softens, about 4 minutes.
2. Add the garlic, jalapeño and oregano; stir well until aromatic, less than 20 seconds. Add the hominy, tomatoes, broth and pork; stir over the heat for 1 minute
3. High pressure for 12 minutes. Lock the lid on the Ninja Foodi Multi-cooker and then cook for 12 minutes.
4. To get 12 minutes' cook time, press *Pressure* button and use the Time Adjustment button to adjust the cook time to 12 minutes.
5. Pressure Release. Use the quick release method to bring the pot's pressure back to normal. Unlock and open the cooker. Stir well before serving

335.   Smoked Pork

Preparation Time: 40 minutes

Servings: 6

INGREDIENTS

- 2 and ½ lbs. pork loin, boneless and cubed
- ¾ cup beef stock
- 1 tbsp. smoked paprika
- 2 tbsp. olive oil
- ½ tbsp. garlic powder
- 1 tsp. oregano, dried

- 1 tsp. basil, dried
- Salt and black pepper to the taste

DIRECTIONS

1. In your Foodi's baking pan, combine all the ingredients and toss. Put the reversible rack in the machine, add the baking pan, set the pot on Roast mode and cook at 370 °F for 30 minutes. Divide everything between plates and serve

336.   Premium Pork Chili Colorado

Preparation Time: 5 minutes

Cooking time: 8 hours

Servings: 6

INGREDIENTS

- 3 pounds pork shoulder, cut into 1-inch cubes
- 1 teaspoon garlic powder
- 1 onion, chopped
- 1 teaspoon chipotle chili powder
- 1 tablespoon chili powder
- 1 teaspoon of sea salt

DIRECTIONS

1. Add listed ingredients to Ninja Foodi
2. Lock lid and cook on SLOW COOK Mode (LOW for 8-10 hours. Serve and enjoy!

337.   Advanced Smothered Pork Chops

Preparation Time: 5 minutes

Cooking time: 28 minutes

Servings: 6

INGREDIENTS

- 6 ounce of boneless pork loin chops
- 1 tablespoon of paprika
- 1 teaspoon of garlic powder
- 1 teaspoon of onion powder

- 1 teaspoon of black pepper
- 1 teaspoon of salt
- ¼ teaspoon of cayenne pepper
- 2 tablespoon of coconut oil
- ½ of a sliced medium onion
- 6-ounce baby Bella mushrooms, sliced
- 1 tablespoon of butter
- ½ a cup of whip cream
- ¼ teaspoon of xanthan gum
- 1 tablespoon parsley, chopped

DIRECTIONS

- Take a small bowl and add garlic powder, paprika, onion powder, black pepper, salt, and cayenne pepper. Rinse the pork chops and pat them dry
- Sprinkle both sides with 1 teaspoon of the mixture making sure to rub the seasoning all over the meat. Reserve the remaining spice
- Set your Ninja Foodi to Saute mode and add coconut oil, allow the oil to heat up
- Brown the chops 3 minutes per sides. Remove and cancel the Saute mode
- Add sliced onion to the base of your pot alongside mushrooms
- Top with the browned pork chops. Lock up the lid and cook on HIGH pressure for 25 minutes
- Release the pressure naturally over 10 minutes, remove the pork chops and keep them on a plate. Set your pot to Saute mode and whisk in remaining spices mix, heavy cream, and butter
- Sprinkle ¼ teaspoon of xanthan gum and stir. Simmer for 3-5 minutes and remove the heat
- Add a bit more xanthan gum if you require a heavier gravy
- Top the pork chops with the gravy and sprinkle parsley. Serve!

338.   The Big Deal Bone-y Pork Chops

Preparation Time: 10 minutes

Cooking time: 13 minutes

Servings: 4

INGREDIENTS

- 4 and ¾ thick bone-in pork chops
- Salt and pepper as needed
- 1 cup baby carrots
- 1 onion, chopped
- 1 cup of mixed vegetables
- 3 tablespoons Worcestershire sauce

DIRECTIONS

1. Take a bowl and add pork chops, season with pepper and salt
2. Take a skillet and place it over medium heat, add 2 teaspoons of butter and melt it
3. Toss the pork chops and brown them. Each side should take about 3-5 minutes
4. Set your Ninja Foodi to Saute mode and add 2 tablespoons of butter, add carrots and Saute them. Pour broth and Worcestershire
5. Add pork chops and lock up the lid. Cook on HIGH pressure for 13 minutes
6. Release the pressure naturally over 10 minutes. Enjoy!

339.   Coconut and Ginger Pork Dish

Preparation Time: 5 minutes

Cooking time: 45 minutes

Servings: 6

INGREDIENTS

- 1 tablespoon avocado oil
- ¾ pound pork butt
- 1 teaspoon ground coriander
- 1 teaspoon ground cumin
- 1 teaspoon salt
- 1 teaspoon pepper
- 2-inch piece ginger, peeled and chopped
- 1 onion, peeled and cut
- ½ a can coconut milk
- Lime wedges, garnish

DIRECTIONS

1. Take a bowl and add coriander, salt, pepper, and cumin
2. Use your finger to rub the seasoning all over the roast
3. Coat the bottom of your Ninja Foodi with 1 tablespoon of avocado oil
4. Add the meat to the pot. Surround it with onions, ginger, garlic and a half can of coconut milk
5. Lock up the lid and cook on HIGH pressure for 45 minutes. Serve in bowls and garnish with lime
6. Enjoy!

340. Bacon Kale And Winning Delight

Preparation Time: 5 minutes

Cooking time: 6 hours

Servings: 6

INGREDIENTS

- 2 tablespoons bacon fat
- 2 pounds kale, rinsed and chopped
- 2 bacon slices, cooked and chopped
- 2 teaspoons garlic, minced
- 2 cups vegetable broth
- Salt and pepper to taste

DIRECTIONS

1. Grease inner pot of your Ninja Foodi with bacon fat
2. Add kale, garlic, bacon, and broth to insert and toss to coat
3. Cover and cook on SLOW COOK Mode (LOW for 6 hours
4. Season with salt and pepper. Serve and enjoy!

341. Rosemary Pork Roast

Preparation Time: 5 minutes

Cooking time: 8 hours

Servings: 6

INGREDIENTS

- 3 pounds pork shoulder roast
- 1 cup bone broth
- 6 sprigs fresh rosemary
- 4 sprigs basil leaves
- 1 tablespoon chives, chopped
- ¼ teaspoon ground black pepper

DIRECTIONS

1. Add listed ingredients to Ninja Foodi
2. Lock lid and cook on SLOW COOK Mode (LOWfor 8-10 hours. Serve and enjoy!
3. Nutrition Values (Per Serving
4. Calories: 248
5. Fat: 8g
6. Carbohydrates: 0.7g
7. Protein: 39g

342. Apple And Sauerkraut Loin

Preparation Time: 5 minutes

Cooking time: 50 minutes

Servings: 6

INGREDIENTS

- 2-3 pounds pork loin roast
- ½ teaspoon salt
- ½ teaspoon fresh ground pepper
- 2 large onion, chopped
- 3 garlic cloves, chopped
- 2-3 cups chicken bone broth
- 4-6 cups sauerkraut, rinsed and drained
- 3 apples, peeled and cored

DIRECTIONS

1. Season the roast with pepper and salt. Set your pot to Saute mode and add ghee
2. Add roast and brown on all sides. Remove the roast and keep it on the side
3. Add garlic, onion, and broth and Scrap brown bits from the Ninja Foodi

4. Return the roast to your Ninja Foodi to lock up the lid. Cook on HIGH pressure for 45 minutes
5. Perform quick release. Add sauerkraut, apple to the cooker
6. Lock up the lid and cook on HIGH pressure for 5 minutes longer
7. Quick release the pressure. Slice the roast and serve with the sauce. Enjoy!

343. Bacon And Brussels Platter

Preparation Time: 10 minutes

Cooking time: 5 minutes

Servings: 4

INGREDIENTS

- 5 bacon slices, chopped
- 6 cups Brussels sprouts, chopped
- ¼ teaspoon salt
- Pepper as needed
- 2 tablespoons water
- 2 tablespoons balsamic vinegar

DIRECTIONS

1. Set your Ninja Foodi to Saute mode and add chopped bacon, Saute until crispy
2. Add chopped Brussels sprouts and stir well to coat it
3. Add water and sprinkle a bit of salt
4. Lock up the lid and cook on HIGH pressure for 4-6 minutes
5. Release the pressure naturally
6. Set your pot to Saute mode and Saute the Brussels for a while longer
7. Transfer to serving the dish
8. Drizzle balsamic vinegar on top and enjoy!

344. Healthy Oxtail Ragout

Preparation Time: 5 minutes

Cooking time: 35 minutes

Servings: 6

INGREDIENTS

- 2 tablespoons butter
- 1 large onion, diced
- 2 carrots, diced
- 1 and ½ cups beef bone broth
- 1 can tomatoes
- 2 bay leaves
- 1-2 teaspoons thyme
- ½ teaspoon rosemary
- ½ teaspoon salt
- 3 peppercorns
- 3 oxtails, joins separated
- 2 teaspoons red wine vinegar

DIRECTIONS

1. Set your Ninja Foodi to Saute mode and add onions, butter, celery, and carrots and Saute for 2 minutes. Add beef bone broth, thyme, bay leaves, salt, rosemary, peppercorns, and stir
2. Add oxtails. Lock up the lid and cook on HIGH pressure for 30 minutes
3. Release the pressure naturally. Skim any excess fat
4. Discard the peppercorn and bay leaves and add red wine vinegar. Serve and enjoy!

345. Lemon And Pork Chops Artichokes

Preparation Time: 10 minutes

Cooking time: 24 minutes

Servings: 4

INGREDIENTS

- 2 tablespoons clarified butter
- 2 pieces 2-inch thick bone-in pork chops
- 3 ounces pancetta, diced
- 2 teaspoons ground black pepper
- 1 medium shallot, minced
- 4 lemon zest strips, 2-inch size
- 1 teaspoon dried rosemary
- 2 teaspoons garlic, minced
- 1 box (9 ouncesbox frozen artichoke heart, quarters

- ¼ cup chicken broth

DIRECTIONS

1. Set your pot to Saute mode and add pancetta, cook for 5 minutes
2. Transfer the browned pancetta to a plate and season your chops with pepper
3. Add the chops to your pot and cook for 4 minutes
4. Transfer the chops to a plate and keep repeating until they all of them are browned
5. Add shallots to the pot and cook for 1 minute
6. Add lemon zest, garlic, rosemary, and garlic, and stir until aromatic
7. After a while, stir in broth and artichokes. Return the pancetta back to the cooker
8. return the chops to your pot
9. Lock up the lid and let it cook for about 24 minutes at high pressure
10. Release pressure quickly. Unlock and transfer the chops to a carving board
11. Slice up the eye of your meat off the bone and slice the meat into strips

Divide in serving bowls and sauce ladled up

346. Simple Pressure Cooked Lamb Meat

Preparation Time: 5 minutes \ Cooking time: 55 minutes

Servings: 4

INGREDIENTS

- 2 tablespoons butter
- ½ teaspoon turmeric powder
- 1 pound ground lamb meat
- 1 cup onions, chopped
- 1 teaspoon salt
- 1 tablespoon garlic, minced
- ½ teaspoon ground coriander
- ½ teaspoon cayenne pepper
- 1 tablespoon ginger, minced
- ½ teaspoon cumin powder

DIRECTIONS

1. Set your Ninja Foodi to Saute mode and add garlic, ginger, and onions
2. Saute for 3 minutes and add ground meat, spices
3. Lock lid and cook on HIGH pressure for 20 minutes
4. Release pressure naturally over 10 minutes.Serve and enjoy!

347. Sassy Evergreen Pork Chops

Preparation Time: 10 minutes

Cooking time: 4 hours

Servings: 4

INGREDIENTS

- 6-8 boneless pork chops
- ¼ cup arrowroot flour
- 2 teaspoons dry mustard
- 1 teaspoon garlic powder
- 1 and ½ cups beef stock
- Cooking fat
- Salt and pepper to taste

DIRECTIONS

1. Take a bowl and add flour, garlic powder, black pepper, dry mustard and salt
2. Coat the pork chop with the mixture and keep any extra flour on the side
3. Take a skillet and place it over medium-high heat. Add cooking fat and allow the fat to melt
4. Brown the chops for 1-2 minutes per side and transfer to your Ninja Foodi
5. Add beef stock to the flour mixture and mix well
6. Pour the beef stock mix to the chops and place lid
7. Cook on SLOW COOK MODE (HIGH for 3 hours. Enjoy!

348. The Pork "Loin" With Pear

Preparation Time: 5 minutes

Cooking time: 12 minutes

Servings: 4

INGREDIENTS

- 2 tablespoons clarified butter
- 4 pieces ½ inch thick bone-in pork loin
- ½ teaspoon salt
- ½ teaspoon pepper
- 2 medium yellow onion, peeled and cut up into 8 wedges
- 2 large Bosc pears, peeled and cored, cut into 4 wedges
- ½ cup unsweetened pear, cider
- ½ teaspoon ground allspice
- Dash of hot pepper

DIRECTIONS

1. Set your Ninja Foodi to Saute mode and add 1 tablespoon of butter, allow the butter to melt
2. Add chops and Saute for 4 minutes
3. Transfer the chops to a plate and cook the remaining and brown them
4. Add onion and pears in the pot and allow them to Saute for 3 minutes more until the pears are slightly browned. Pour cider and stir in allspice, pepper sauce
5. Nestle the chops back. Lock up the lid and cook on HIGH pressure for 10 minutes
6. Perform quick release. Serve over rice!

349.   Creative Garlic And Butter Pork

Preparation Time: 5 minutes + marinate time

Cooking time: 40 minutes

Servings: 4

INGREDIENTS

- 1 tablespoon coconut butter
- 1 tablespoon coconut oil
- 2 teaspoons garlic cloves, grated
- 2 teaspoons parsley
- Salt and pepper to taste

- 4 pork chops, sliced into strips

DIRECTIONS

1. Add listed INGREDIENTS to Pork Strips and mix well
2. Marinate for 1 hour. Transfer pork to Ninja Foodi
3. Lock Crisping Lid and Air Crisp for 10 minutes at 400 degrees F. Serve and enjoy!

350.   Elegant Lamb Spare Ribs

Preparation Time: 4-5 hours\ Cooking time: 20 minutes

Servings: 4

INGREDIENTS

- ingredients for the Lamb
- 2.5 pounds of pastured lamb spare ribs
- 2 teaspoons of kosher salt
- 1 tablespoon of curry powder
- ingredients

For the sauce

- 1 t tablespoon of coconut oil
- 1 large sized coarsely chopped onion
- ½ a pound of minced garlic
- 1 tablespoon of curry powder
- 1 tablespoon of kosher salt
- Juice from about 1 lemon
- 1 and a 1/4th cup of divided cilantro
- 4 thinly sliced scallion

DIRECTIONS

1. Take a bowl and add spare ribs
2. Season with 2 teaspoons of salt, 1 teaspoon of curry powder and mix well making sure that the ribs are coated fully. Cover it up and allow them to chill for 4 hours
3. Cover it up and let them freeze for at least 4 hours
4. Set your Ninja Foodi to Saute mode and add coconut oil and allow it to heat up
5. Add spare ribs and allow them to brown. Once done, transfer them to another plate

6. Take a blender and add tomatoes and onion and blend them well to a paste
7. Add the minced garlic to your Ninja Foodi (still in Saute mode
8. Keep stirring the garlic while carefully pouring the prepared paste
9. Add curry powder, chopped up cilantro, salt, and lemon juice
10. Allow the whole mixture to come to a boil. Add spare ribs and stir until it is coated well
11. Lock up the lid and cook for 20 minutes at HIGH pressure
12. Allow the pressure to release naturally once done.Scoop out the grease and season with some salt. Enjoy!

351. Cool Lamb Tajine

Preparation Time: 5 minutes

Cooking time: 50 minutes

Servings: 6

INGREDIENTS

- 2 and a /13 pound of lamb shoulder
- 1 teaspoon of cinnamon powder
- 1 teaspoon of ginger powder
- 1 teaspoon of turmeric powder
- 2 cloves of crushed garlic
- 3 tablespoon of olive oil
- 10 ounce of prunes pitted and soaked
- 1 cup of vegetable stock
- 2 medium roughly sliced onion
- 1 piece of bay leaf
- 1 stick of cinnamon
- 1 teaspoon of pepper
- 1 and a ½ teaspoon of salt
- 3 and a ½ ounce of almonds
- 1 tablespoon of sesame seeds

DIRECTIONS

1. Take a bowl and add ground cinnamon, ginger, turmeric, garlic and 2 spoons of olive oil
2. Make a paste. Cover the lamb with the paste

3. Take a bowl and add dried prunes with boiling water and cover, keep it on the side
4. Set your Ninja Foodi to Saute mode and add olive oil. Add onion and cook for 3 minutes
5. Transfer the onion to a bowl and keep it on the side
6. Add meat and brown all sides for about 10 minutes. Deglaze using vegetable stock
7. Add onions, cinnamon stick, bay leaf.Lock up the lid and cook on HIGH pressure for 35 minutes
8. Release the pressure naturally. Add rinsed and drained prunes and set the pot to Saute mode
9. Reduce the liquid by simmer for 5 minutes
10. Discard the bay leaf and sprinkle toasted almonds alongside sesame seeds. Enjoy

352. Pork and Cauliflower Dish

Preparation Time: 10 minutes

Cooking time: 65 minutes

Servings: 4

INGREDIENTS

- 1 onion, chopped
- 4 cloves garlic, crushed and minced
- 4 cups cauliflower, chopped
- 2 ribs celery
- Salt and pepper to taste
- 3-pound pork roast
- 8 ounces mushrooms, sliced
- 2 tablespoons coconut oil
- 2 tablespoons ghee

DIRECTIONS

1. Add onion, garlic, cauliflower, celery to Ninja Foodi
2. Put pork roast on top. Season with salt and pepper
3. Add 2 cups of water. Lock lid and cook on HIGH pressure 60 minutes
4. Quick release pressure. Transfer roast to baking pan

5. Add pan to oven and bake for 5 minutes at 400 degrees F
6. Prepare gravy by transfer the remaining contents from the pot to a blender
7. Blend until smooth. Set your pot to Saute mode and add coconut oil and ghee
8. Add mushrooms and blended mixture. Cook for 5 minutes
9. Serve pot roast with mushroom gravy and enjoy!

Nutrition Values: Per Serving Calories: 697 Fat: 56g Carbohydrates: 8g Protein: 81g

353.   Lime and Ginger Low Carb Pork

Preparation Time: 10 minutes

Cooking time:4-7 hours

Servings: 4

INGREDIENTS

- 1 tablespoon avocado oil
- 2 and ½ pounds pork loin
- Salt and pepper to taste
- 1 teaspoon stevia drops
- ¼ cup tamari
- 1 tablespoon Worcestershire sauce
- Juice of 1 lime
- 2 garlic cloves, minced
- 1 tablespoon fresh ginger
- Fresh cilantro

DIRECTIONS

1. Set your Ninja Foodi to Saute mode and add oil, let the oil heat up
2. Season pork with salt and pepper and add to the pot
3. Take a bowl and whisk in remaining INGREDIENTS except for cilantro and pour it over pork
4. Lock lid and cook on SLOW COOK mode. Cook for 4-7 hours on HIGH pressure
5. Naturally, release pressure over 10 minutes. Garnish with cilantro. Serve and enjoy!

354.   Generous Indian Lamb Shanks

Preparation Time: 5 minutes

Cooking time: 45 minutes

Servings: 5

INGREDIENTS

- 3 pounds lamb shanks
- Salt as needed
- Fresh ground pepper as needed
- 2 tablespoons ghee
- 2 onion, chopped
- 2 celery, chopped
- 1 large onion, chopped
- 1 tablespoon tomato paste
- 3 garlic cloves, peeled and mashed
- 1 cup bone broth
- 1 teaspoon red boat fish sauce
- 1 tablespoon vinegar

DIRECTIONS

1. Season the shanks with pepper and salt
2. Set your pot to Saute mode and add ghee, allow the ghee to melt and heat up
3. Add shanks and cook for 8-10 minutes until a nice brown texture appears
4. In the meantime, chop the vegetables
5. Once you have a nice brown texture on your lamb, remove it from the Instant Pot and keep it on the side. Add vegetables and season with salt and pepper
6. Add a tablespoon of ghee and mix
7. Add vegetables, garlic clove, tomato paste and give it a nice stir
8. Add shanks and pour broth, vinegar, fish sauce. Sprinkle a bit of pepper and lock up the lid
9. Cook on HIGH pressure for 45 minutes. Release the pressure naturally over 10 minutes
10. Serve the shanks and enjoy!

355.   Greek Lamb Gyros

Preparation Time: 5 minutes \ Cooking time: 25 minutes

Servings: 4

INGREDIENTS

- 8 garlic cloves
- 1 and ½ teaspoon salt
- 2 teaspoons dried oregano
- 1 and ½ cups of water
- 2 pounds lamb meat, ground
- 2 teaspoons rosemary
- ½ teaspoon pepper
- 1 small onion, chopped
- 2 teaspoons ground marjoram

DIRECTIONS

1. Add onion, garlic, marjoram, rosemary, salt and pepper to food processor and process
2. Add ground lamb meat and process again. Press meat mixture into pan
3. Transfer loaf to Ninja Foodi and "BAKE/ROAST" for 25 minutes at 375 degrees f
4. Serve and enjoy!

356. Pork Dish with Coconut Added In

Preparation Time: 10 minutes

Cooking time: 4 hours

Servings: 4

INGREDIENTS

- 2 tablespoons coconut oil
- 4 pounds boneless pork shoulder, cut into 2-inch pieces
- Salt and pepper to taste
- 1 large onion, chopped
- 3 tablespoons garlic cloves, minced
- 3 tablespoons fresh ginger, minced
- 1 tablespoon curry powder
- 1 tablespoon ground cumin
- ½ teaspoon ground turmeric
- 1 cup unsweetened coconut milk
- Chopped cilantro, green onions for garnish

DIRECTIONS

1. Take a large sized skillet and add coconut oil
2. Allow it to heat up and add pork in batches, brown them and season with a bit of salt and pepper. Transfer to a Ninja Foodi
3. Making sure that there are 2 tablespoons of the worth of fat in the skillet, add onion, garlic, ginger, cumin, curry, turmeric and cook over low heat for 5 minutes
4. Add the mix to your Ninja Foodi and place the lid
5. Cook on SLOW COOK MODE (LOWfor 4 hours
6. Serve with a garnish of cilantro and scallions. Enjoy!

357. Tastiest Pork Cheek Stew

Preparation Time: 10 minutes

Cooking time: 45 minutes

Servings: 4

INGREDIENTS

- 4 pounds of pork cheeks
- 2 tablespoons avocado oil
- 1 and ½ cups of chicken broth
- 8 ounces cremini mushrooms
- 1 large leek, cut into ½ inch chunks
- 1 small onion, diced
- 6 garlic cloves, peeled
- 1 teaspoon salt
- Juice of ½ lemon

DIRECTIONS

1. Set your Ninja Foodi to Saute mode and add oil
2. Cut up the cheeks into 2 x 3 inch even pieces and add them to the Pot
3. Sear them until nicely browned
4. Pour broth over the browned cheeks alongside mushroom, onion, leek, garlic, sea salt
5. Lock up the lid and cook on HIGH pressure for 45 minutes

6. Release the pressure naturally and shred the meat. Stir the meat well with the sauce and serve!

358. Veal And Rosemary Stew

Preparation Time: 10 minutes

Cooking time: 20 minutes

Servings: 4

INGREDIENTS

- 2 sprigs rosemary
- 1 tablespoon olive oil
- 1 tablespoon butter
- 8 ounces shallots
- 2 carrots, chopped
- 2 stalks celery, chopped
- 2 tablespoons almond flour
- 3 pounds veal
- Water as needed
- 2 teaspoon salt

DIRECTIONS

1. Set the Ninja Foodi to Saute mode and add olive oil, allow the oil to heat up
2. Add butter and chopped rosemary and stir. Add celery, shallots, carrots and Saute for a while
3. Shove the veggies on the side and add the meat cubes, brown them slightly and pour just enough stock to gently cover them
4. Lock up the lid and cook on 20 minutes on HIGH pressure
5. Release the pressure naturally over 10 minutes
6. Open and set the pot to Saute mode, allow it to simmer. Enjoy!

359. Keto – Suitable Steamed Pork

Preparation Time: 5 minutes

Cooking time: 45 minutes

Servings: 4

INGREDIENTS

- 2 boneless pork chops
- 2 tablespoons fresh orange juice
- 2 cups of water
- ¼ teaspoon ground cloves
- ¼ teaspoon ground coriander
- ¼ teaspoon cinnamon, ground
- 1 pinch cayenne pepper

DIRECTIONS

1. Add listed ingredients to Ziploc bag and let them marinate for 2 hours
2. Place a reversible rack inside the pot and attach Crisping Lid
3. Pour water into a pot and place marinated meat on the rack
4. Lock lid and STEAM for 45 minutes
5. Serve and enjoy!

360. Refined Carrot and Bacon Soup

Preparation Time: 10 minutes

Cooking time: 4 minutes

Servings: 4

INGREDIENTS

- 2 pounds carrots, peeled
- 4 cups broth
- ½ cup yellow onion, chopped
- ½ pack bacon cut into ¼ inch pieces
- ½ cup apple cider vinegar
- ½ cup white vinegar

DIRECTIONS

1. Set your Ninja Foodi to Saute mode and add butter, allow the butter to melt and add bacon and onion, Saute for a while. Slice 1 -2 heirloom carrots thinly and add them to a small bowl
2. Add vinegar to cover them, allow them to pickle
3. Chop the remaining carrots into inch long pieces

4. Add chopped carrots and broth to your Instant Pot
5. Lock up the lid and cook on HIGH pressure for 4 minutes. Perform a natural release
6. Use an immersion blender break down the carrots until you have a smooth mix
7. Stir in onions and bacon, salt and apple cider vinegar. Serve and enjoy!

361. Lovely Pulled Pork Ragu

Preparation Time: 10 minutes

Cooking time: 45 minutes

Servings: 4

INGREDIENTS

- 18 ounce of pork tenderloin
- 1 teaspoon of kosher salt
- Black pepper as needed
- 1 teaspoon of olive oil
- 5 cloves of garlic
- 1 can of 28-ounce tomatoes, crushed
- 1 small sized jar of roasted red peppers
- 2 sprigs of thyme
- 2 pieces of bay leaves
- 1 tablespoon fresh parsley, chopped

DIRECTIONS

1. Set your Ninja Foodi to Saute mode. Season the pork with pepper and salt
2. Add oil to your pot and allow the oil to heat up. Add garlic and Saute for 1 and a ½ minute
3. Remove with a slotted spoon. Add pork and brown for 2 minutes on both sides
4. Add the remaining ingredients and garlic (make sure to reserve half of the kale for later use
5. Lock up the lid and cook on HIGH pressure for 45 minutes
6. Naturally, release the pressure over 10 minutes and discard the bay leaves
7. Shred the pork using a fork and garnish with parsley. Enjoy!

362. The Calabacita Squash meal

Preparation Time: 10 minutes

Cooking time: 90 minutes

Servings: 4

INGREDIENTS

- 1 pork tenderloin
- 1 tablespoon of chili powder
- 1 tablespoon of ground cumin
- 1 tablespoon of garlic powder
- 1 and a ½ teaspoon of salt
- 1 tablespoon of butter/ghee
- 14 ounce of tomatoes, diced
- 6 Calabacita squash, deseeded

For the chipotle cream sauce

- 1/3 cup of canola-oil free mayo
- 3 tablespoon of fresh lime juice
- 1 and a ½ a teaspoon of chipotle/ chili powder

DIRECTIONS

1. Prepare the tenderloin by dusting it with half of the chili powder, garlic, cumin and salt
2. Set your Ninja Foodi to Saute mode and add butter, allow the butter to melt
3. Add seasoned pork and sear all sides for 3-4 minutes until browned
4. Add 4-6 cups of water and lock up the lid
5. Cook on MEAT mode at default settings and release the pressure naturally over 10 minutes
6. Transfer the pork to a large mixing bowl and shred it into small pieces
7. Add canned tomatoes and remaining spice to the bowl. Stir well
8. Spread the deseeded squash into a large rimmed baking sheet with the cut side facing up
9. Stuff the squash with the pork mixture and bake for 45 minutes at 350 degrees Fahrenheit

10. Prepare the sauce by mixing the sauce ingredients
11. Pour the sauce on top of the pork and garnish with cilantro. Serve and enjoy!

363. Pork Cutlets with Blueberry Sauce

Preparation time: 10 minutes

Cooking time: 20 minutes

Servings: 5

INGREDIENTS

- 12 ounces ground pork
- ⅓ cup lemon juice
- 1/3 cup blueberries
- 1 tablespoon Erythritol
- 1 teaspoon cilantro
- ½ teaspoon thyme
- 1 egg
- 1 tablespoon ground ginger
- 1 tablespoon olive oil
- 1 tablespoon coconut flour
- 1 teaspoon paprika

DIRECTIONS

1. Combine the ground pork with the cilantro, thyme, paprika, and egg and stir well until smooth. Make medium cutlets from the ground meat mixture.
2. Set the pressure cooker to "Sauté" mode. Pour the olive oil into the pressure cooker and add the pork cutlets. Cook the cutlets for 10 minutes until golden brown on both sides.
3. Put the blueberries in the blender and blend until smooth. Add the Erythritol, ground ginger, coconut flour, and lemon juice. Blend the mixture and cook for 1 minute. When the cutlets are cooked, pour the blueberry sauce into the pressure cooker. Close the lid and cook the dish on "Sauté" mode for 10 minutes.
4. Remove the pork cutlets from the pressure cooker, sprinkle them with the plum sauce and serve.

NUTRITION: Calories 161, Fat 6.7, Fiber 1.6, Carbs 4.5, Protein 19.7

364. Spicy Boiled Sausages

Preparation time: 15 minutes

Cooking time: 18 minutes

Servings: 9

INGREDIENTS

- 5 ounces sausage casings
- 1 tablespoon minced garlic
- 1 tablespoon cayenne pepper
- 1 teaspoon chili powder
- ½ teaspoon ground black pepper
- 1 teaspoon salt
- 6 ounces ground pork
- 6 ounces ground beef
- 1 tablespoon olive oil
- 1 cup of water
- 1 teaspoon turmeric

DIRECTIONS

1. Combine the ground pork and ground beef together in a mixing bowl. Sprinkle the mixture with the garlic, cayenne pepper, ground black pepper, salt, and turmeric. Mix well using your hands. Fill the sausage cases with the ground meat mixture. Set the pressure cooker to "Sauté" mode. Pour water into the pressure cooker and preheat it for 5 minutes. Transfer the sausages to the pressure cooker and close the lid. Cook the sausages for 10 minutes. Preheat the oven to 365 F. When the cooking time ends, remove the boiled sausages from the pressure cooker and sprinkle them with the olive oil. Transfer the sausages to the oven and cook for 8 minutes. When the sausages are golden brown, remove them from the oven and let them rest before serving.

NUTRITION: Calories 158, Fat 11.5, Fiber 1, Carbs 2.94, Protein 12

365. Meat Trio with Gravy

Preparation time: 10 minutes

Cooking time: 25 minutes

Servings: 8

INGREDIENTS

- 8 ounces beef
- 7 ounces pork
- 8 ounces lamb
- 1 cup red wine
- ¼ cup lemon juice
- 1 tablespoon Erythritol
- 1 tablespoon ground black pepper
- 1 teaspoon oregano
- 1 tablespoon butter
- 1 tablespoon fresh rosemary
- 1 cup chicken stock
- 1 tablespoon tomato paste
- 1 tablespoon minced garlic

DIRECTIONS

1. Chop the pork, beef, and lamb into medium-sized pieces. Combine the meat mixture and red wine together and let it marinate for 10 minutes. Remove the meat mixture from the red wine and sprinkle it with Erythritol, ground black pepper, oregano, rosemary, and garlic and stir well. Set the pressure cooker to "Sauté" mode. Add the butter to the pressure cooker and melt it. Add the meat mixture into the pressure cooker and sauté it for 10 minutes. Add chicken stock and stir. Close the pressure cooker lid and cook the dish on "Sauté" mode for 15 minutes. When the time ends meat is tender, remove the dish from the pressure cooker and let it rest before serving. Serve the dish with the gravy.

NUTRITION: Calories 188, Fat 6.4, Fiber 0.6, Carbs 2.7, Protein 23.5

366. Italian Beef

Preparation time: 25 minutes

Cooking time: 35 minutes

Servings: 4

INGREDIENTS

- 2 bell peppers
- 1 tablespoon cayenne pepper
- ¼ cup garlic
- 1 pound beef
- 1 tablespoon butter
- 1 cup chicken stock
- 1 onion
- 1 cup Italian greens
- 1 teaspoon salt
- 1 teaspoon Erythritol
- ⅓ cup tomato paste
- 1 tablespoon oregano

DIRECTIONS

1. Peel the garlic and slice it. Remove the seeds from the bell peppers and dice them. Combine the sliced garlic with the chopped bell pepper. Sprinkle the mixture with the salt, Erythritol, greens, tomato paste, and oregano and stir well. Place the beef in the tomato mixture and coat well. Let the beef marinate for 10 minutes. Set the pressure cooker to "Pressure" mode. Place the beef into the pressure cooker and add the chicken stock and butter. Sprinkle the meat with the cayenne pepper. Close the pressure cooker lid and cook for 35 minutes. When the cooking time ends, remove the beef from the pressure cooker and slice it into the serving pieces.

NUTRITION: Calories 307, Fat 10.7, Fiber 3.3, Carbs 15.7, Protein 37.3

367. Salisbury Steak

Preparation time: 15 minutes

Cooking time: 10 minutes

Servings: 5

INGREDIENTS

- ½ cup onion soup mix
- 1 pound ground beef
- 2 eggs
- 1 cup of water
- 1 tablespoon mustard
- 1 teaspoon salt
- 1 teaspoon ground white pepper
- 1 tablespoon olive oil
- 1 teaspoon tomato paste

DIRECTIONS

1. Beat the eggs in a mixing bowl and whisk them. Add the mustard, salt, and ground white pepper. and stir well until smooth. Put the ground beef in the egg mixture and Combine well. Make medium sized balls from the meat mixture and flatten them. Set the pressure cooker to "Sauté" mode. Pour the olive oil into the pressure cooker and preheat it at the sauté mode. Add the steaks and sauté the dish for 2 minutes on each side. Combine the tomato paste and onion soup together and stir well. Pour the soup mixture into the pressure cooker and close the lid. Cook the dish on "Pressure" mode for 5 minutes. When the cooking time ends, remove the dish from the pressure cooker and serve with the gravy from the pressure cooker.

NUTRITION: Calories 323, Fat 21.9, Fiber 0, Carbs 2.92, Protein 27

368.   Pork Chili

Preparation time: 15 minutes

Cooking time: 45 minutes

Servings: 8

INGREDIENTS

- 1 cup black soybeans
- 10 ounces ground pork

- 1 teaspoon tomato paste
- 1 cup chicken stock
- 1 tablespoon butter
- 1 teaspoon cilantro
- 1 teaspoon oregano
- 1 cup bok choy, chopped
- ¼ cup green beans
- 3 cups of water
- 2 carrots
- 3 red onions
- 1 tablespoon salt

DIRECTIONS

1. Combine the ground pork with the tomato paste, butter, cilantro, oregano, and salt. and stir well. Set the pressure cooker to "Sauté" mode. Place the ground pork mixture into the pressure cooker and sauté it for 2 minutes, stirring frequently.
2. Add the green beans and water. Peel the carrots and red onions. Chop the vegetables and add them into the pressure cooker. Sprinkle the stew mixture with the bok choy, and stir it well.
3. Close the pressure cooker lid and cook the dish on "Pressure" mode for 40 minutes. When the cooking time ends, open the pressure cooker lid and mix the chili well. Transfer the chili to serving bowls.

NUTRITION: Calories 194, Fat 7.5, Fiber 3.7, Carbs 13.1, Protein 18.7

369.   Marinated Pork Steak

Preparation time: 20 minutes

Cooking time: 25 minutes

Servings: 6

INGREDIENTS

- ¼ cup beer
- ¼ cup olive oil
- 1 teaspoon cayenne pepper
- 1 teaspoon cilantro
- 1 teaspoon oregano

- 1 tablespoon salt
- 1 teaspoon ground black pepper
- 1 pound pork tenderloin
- 1 onion

DIRECTIONS

1. Combine the cayenne pepper, olive oil, cilantro, oregano, salt, and ground black pepper together in a mixing bowl. Peel the onion and grind it. Add the onion in the spice mixture and mix it well until smooth.
2. Add beer and stir well. Dip the pork tenderloin in the beer mixture and let it marinate for at least 10 minutes. Set the pressure cooker to "Pressure" mode.
3. Transfer the marinated meat into the pressure cooker. Cook for 25 minutes. When the cooking time ends, release the remaining pressure and open the pressure cooker. Remove the cooked meat from the pressure cooker and serve.

NUTRITION: Calories 219, Fat 13.3, Fiber 1, Carbs 3.35, Protein 21

370. Lemon Beef Steak

Preparation time: 15 minutes

Cooking time: 20 minutes

Servings: 4

INGREDIENTS

- ¼ cup lemon
- 1 pound beef steak
- 3 tablespoons lemon zest
- 1 tablespoon olive oil
- 3 tablespoons sesame oil
- 1 teaspoon apple cider vinegar
- 1 tablespoon white pepper
- ½ teaspoon paprika
- 1 tablespoon fresh cilantro

DIRECTIONS

1. Squeeze the juice from the lemon and combine it with the lemon zest. Add the

sesame oil, apple cider vinegar, white pepper, paprika, and cilantro and stir well. Rub the beef steak with the spice mixture and let it rest for 5 minutes. Pour the olive oil into the pressure cooker and preheat it at the sauté mode. Set the pressure cooker to "Sauté" mode. Place the beef steak into the pressure cooker and sauté it for 2 minutes on each side. Close the pressure cooker lid and cook the dish for 15 minutes at the "Pressure" mode. When the dish is cooked, release the pressure and open the pressure cooker lid. Transfer the steak to serving plates.

NUTRITION: Calories 295, Fat 20.7, Fiber 1, Carbs 3.38, Protein 23

371. Corned Beef

Preparation time: 10 minutes

Cooking time: 68 minutes

Servings: 10

INGREDIENTS

- 3 pounds beef brisket
- 1 teaspoon oregano
- 1 teaspoon cilantro
- 1 teaspoon paprika
- 1 teaspoon basil
- 1 teaspoon cayenne pepper
- 1 tablespoon mustard seeds
- 1 tablespoon minced garlic
- 2 cups of water

DIRECTIONS

1. Combine the oregano, cilantro, paprika, basil, cayenne pepper, mustard seeds, and garlic together in a mixing bowl and stir well. Set the pressure cooker to "Pressure" mode. Pour the water into the pressure cooker and add the beef brisket. Sprinkle the meat with the spice mixture. Close the pressure cooker lid and cook for 68 minutes. When the cooking time ends, release the remaining pressure and open

the pressure cooker lid. Transfer the corned beef to a cutting board and let it rest. Cut into slices and serve.

NUTRITION: Calories 187, Fat 8, Fiber 0, Carbs 0.71, Protein 28

372. Semi-sweet Pork Stew

Preparation time: 15 minutes

Cooking time: 40 minutes

Servings: 8

INGREDIENTS

- 5 tablespoon liquid stevia
- 14 ounces of pork tenderloin
- 3 carrots
- 1 teaspoon cayenne pepper
- 8 ounces cauliflower
- 2 white onions
- 1 teaspoon ground black pepper
- 1 tablespoon olive oil
- 1 teaspoon cilantro
- 1 cup green beans
- ½ lime
- 3 cups chicken stock

DIRECTIONS

1. Chop the pork tenderloin roughly and sprinkle it with the cayenne pepper, ground black pepper, and cilantro and stir well. Peel the onions and carrots. Chop the onions, carrots, and lime. Place the chopped meat and the vegetables into the pressure cooker. Chop the cauliflower into the medium pieces and add them into the pressure cooker. Add green beans and chicken stock. and stir well. Set the pressure cooker to "Pressure" mode. Close the pressure cooker lid and cook for 40 minutes. When the cooking time ends, open the pressure cooker lid and transfer the stew to serving bowls. Sprinkle it with the stevia and serve.

NUTRITION: Calories 124, Fat 3.8, Fiber 2.6, Carbs 8.3, Protein 14.6

373. Pork Chimichangas

Preparation time: 15 minutes

Cooking time: 30 minutes

Servings: 6

INGREDIENTS

- 6 ounces almond flour tortillas
- 1 tablespoon olive oil
- 1 pound pork
- 1 teaspoon garlic powder
- ½ teaspoon chili powder
- 4 tablespoons tomato paste
- 5 tablespoon butter
- ½ teaspoon ground cumin
- 1 teaspoon salt
- 1 teaspoon ground black pepper
- 1 teaspoon cilantro

DIRECTIONS

1. Ground the pork and combine it with the garlic powder and chili powder. Sprinkle the mixture with the salt, ground black pepper, and cilantro and stir well.
2. Add tomato paste and stir it. Set the pressure cooker to "Sauté" mode. Place the butter into the pressure cooker and melt it. Add the ground pork mixture and sauté for 10 minutes. Stir it frequently using a spoon.
3. Close the pressure cooker lid and cook the dish on "Pressure" mode for 15 minutes. When the cooking time ends, remove the dish from the pressure cooker and let it rest briefly. Spread the tortillas with the ground meat mixture and wrap them. Pour the olive oil into the pressure cooker.
4. Add the wrapped tortillas and heat for 3 minutes on each side. Remove the dish from the pressure cooker and let it rest briefly and serve.

NUTRITION: Calories 294, Fat 17.7, Fiber 1, Carbs 18.89, Protein 16

374.   Stuffed Meatloaf

Preparation time: 15 minutes

Cooking time: 30 minutes

Servings: 12

INGREDIENTS

- 2 pounds ground beef
- 5 eggs, boiled
- 1 red bell pepper
- 1 white onion
- 4 tablespoons chives
- 1 tablespoon starch
- 1 teaspoon ground black pepper
- 1 teaspoon salt
- 2 eggs
- 1 teaspoon butter
- 1 teaspoon olive oil
- 1 tablespoon coconut flour
- 1 teaspoon ground rosemary

DIRECTIONS

1. Peel the eggs. Peel the onion and remove the seeds from the red bell pepper. Chop the onion and the red bell pepper. Add chives and mix well. Combine the ground beef with the ground black pepper, starch, salt, butter, coconut flour, and ground rosemary together in a mixing bowl and stir well.
2. After this, beat the eggs in the mixture and stir until smooth. Separate the meat into two parts. Pour the olive oil and place the one part of the ground meat into the pressure cooker. Spread the ground meat with the onion mixture and place the eggs in the middle.
3. Cover the eggs with the remaining ground meat and shape into a loaf. Close the pressure cooker lid and cook the dish on "Pressure" mode for 30 minutes. When the dish is cooked, release the pressure and open the pressure cooker lid. Remove the meatloaf from the pressure cooker carefully and let it rest. Cut into slices and serve.

NUTRITION: Calories 165, Fat 5.7, Fiber 0.9, Carbs 3.4, Protein 23.9

375.   Stuffed Lettuce

Preparation time: 10 minutes

Cooking time: 10 minutes

Servings: 8

INGREDIENTS

- 10 ounces lettuce leaves
- ½ cup tomato paste
- 7 ounces Parmesan
- 1-pound ground beef
- 4 ounces ground pork
- 2 cups of water
- 1 teaspoon salt
- 1 teaspoon ground black pepper
- 1 teaspoon turmeric
- 1 tablespoon butter
- 1 teaspoon oregano
- ⅓ cup cream

DIRECTIONS

1. Grate the Parmesan and place it in a mixing bowl. Add the tomato paste, ground pork, ground beef, salt, ground black pepper, turmeric, butter, and oregano and stir well.
2. Set the pressure cooker to "Pressure" mode. Place the ground beef mixture into the pressure cooker. Combine the water and cream together in a mixing bowl and stir. Pour the cream mixture into the pressure cooker.
3. Close the lid and cook for 15 minutes. When the cooking time ends, release the remaining pressure and open the pressure cooker lid. Stuff the lettuce leaves with the ground meat mixture.

NUTRITION: Calories 245, Fat 11.5, Fiber 1.1, Carbs 5.8, Protein 29.9

376.   Mexican Meatballs

Preparation time: 10 minutes

Cooking time: 8 minutes

Servings: 6

INGREDIENTS

- 1 tablespoon Erythritol
- 1 tablespoon water
- 1 pound ground pork
- ½ cup tomato juice
- 1 teaspoon oregano
- 1 tablespoon olive oil
- 1 chile pepper
- 1 cup chicken stock
- 1 tablespoon coconut flour
- 1 teaspoon flax meal
- 1 tablespoon fresh thyme
- 1 teaspoon ground coriander
- 1 tablespoon onion powder

DIRECTIONS

1. Combine the oregano, coconut flour, flax meal, thyme, ground coriander, onion powder, and ground pork together in a mixing bowl. Chop the chile pepper and add it to the ground pork mixture. Mix well until smooth. Preheat the pressure cooker at the "Sauté" mode. Pour the olive oil into the pressure cooker. Make medium-sized meatballs from the ground pork mixture and place them into the pressure cooker. Sauté the meatballs for 2 minutes on each side until golden brown. Remove the meatballs from the pressure cooker. Put Erythritol and water into the pressure cooker and stir well. Add the meatballs and cook for 2 minutes. Remove the meatballs from the pressure cooker and serve.

NUTRITION: Calories 151, Fat 5.6, Fiber 1.4, Carbs 3.9, Protein 20.7

377. Pork Enchiladas

Preparation time: 15 minutes

Cooking time: 15 minutes

Servings: 8

INGREDIENTS

- 7 ounces almond flour tortillas
- 1 pound pork tenderloin
- 1 teaspoon ground black pepper
- 1 cup cream
- ½ red chili
- 3 tablespoons ancho chile sauce
- 1 large onion
- 1 teaspoon garlic powder
- 7 ounces Cheddar cheese
- 1 teaspoon paprika

DIRECTIONS

1. Sprinkle the pork tenderloin with the ground black pepper and paprika. Set the pressure cooker to "Pressure" mode. Place the pork into the pressure cooker.
2. Add cream and close the lid. Cook for 14 minutes. Preheat the oven to 365 F and put the tortillas inside. Cook the tortillas for 4 minutes. Remove them from the oven set aside. Grate the Cheddar cheese and peel the onion. Dice the onion.
3. When the meat is cooked, remove it from the pressure cooker and let it rest briefly. Shred the meat using a fork. Combine the shredded meat with the chili sauce and mix well. Spread the tortillas with the shredded meat and sprinkle them with the diced onion. Sprinkle the tortillas with the grated cheese and garlic powder. Wrap the tortillas and serve.

NUTRITION: Calories 263, Fat 12.6, Fiber 1, Carbs 21.81, Protein 16

378. Soy Sauce Pork Strips

Preparation time: 20 minutes

Cooking time: 15 minutes

Servings: 6

INGREDIENTS

- 1 cup of soy sauce
- 1 tablespoon Erythritol

- 1 tablespoon sesame seeds
- 1 teaspoon cumin seeds
- 1 tablespoon onion powder
- ⅓ teaspoon miso paste
- 10 ounces of pork fillet
- 1 tablespoon olive oil
- ½ cup of water

DIRECTIONS

1. Combine the soy sauce Erythritol, sesame seeds, cumin seeds, onion powder, olive oil and water in a mixing bowl. Stir well until the sugar is dissolved. Cut the pork fillet into strips and place the pork in the soy sauce mixture. Mix well and let the pork marinate for 10 minutes. Preheat the pressure cooker at the "Sauté" mode for 2 minutes. Add the pork strips and marinade to the pressure cooker and close the lid. Cook the dish on "Pressure" mode for 13 minutes. When the cooking time ends, release the remaining pressure and open the pressure cooker lid. Transfer the pork strips to serving plates.

NUTRITION: Calories 167, Fat 9.2, Fiber 0.7, Carbs 6.7, Protein 16.3

379. Glazed Beef Meatballs with Sesame Seeds

Preparation time: 15 minutes

Cooking time: 10 minutes

Servings: 6

INGREDIENTS

- 1 teaspoon water
- 2 tablespoons Erythritol
- 1 tablespoon butter
- 1 teaspoon ground black pepper
- 2 tablespoons sesame seeds
- 12 ounces ground beef
- 1 egg
- 1 teaspoon salt

DIRECTIONS

1. Beat the egg in a mixing bowl. Add the ground black pepper, sesame seeds, salt, and semolina and mix well.
2. Add the ground beef and combine. Make small meatballs from the ground beef mixture. Set the pressure cooker to "Sauté" mode.
3. Add the butter into the pressure cooker and melt it. Put the ground pork meatballs into the pressure cooker and sauté the meatballs for 5 minutes on both sides.
4. Add water to the pressure cooker. Sprinkle the meatballs with Erythritol and close the pressure cooker lid. Cook the dish on "Pressure" mode for 5 minutes.
5. When the cooking time ends, release the remaining pressure and open the pressure cooker lid. Transfer the cooked meatballs to a serving plate.

NUTRITION: Calories 151, Fat 7.7, Fiber 0.4, Carbs 1, Protein 18.7

380. Lasagna

Preparation time: 15 minutes

Cooking time: 25 minutes

Servings: 8

INGREDIENTS

- 7 ounces eggplants, sliced
- 10 ounces Parmesan cheese
- 6 ounces Mozzarella cheese
- 1 teaspoon salt
- 1 teaspoon paprika
- 1 cup cream
- ½ cup chicken stock
- 1 onion
- 1 teaspoon minced garlic
- 10 ounces ground beef
- 1 cup tomato paste
- 1 tablespoon chives

DIRECTIONS

1. Grate the Parmesan and Mozzarella cheeses. Combine the salt, paprika, and chives together in a mixing bowl. Add the garlic and tomato paste and stir well.

2. Add ground beef and combine well. Spread the lasagna noodles with the ground beef mixture. Peel the onion. Dice it. Place the eggplants into the pressure cooker one by one. Sprinkle them with the diced onion and grated cheese. Pour the cream into the pressure cooker and close the lid. Cook the dish on "Sauté" mode for 25 minutes. When the lasagna is cooked, remove it from the pressure cooker and let it rest briefly before serving.

NUTRITION: Calories 300, Fat 15.5, Fiber 2.6, Carbs 12.2, Protein 30.3

381. Beef Bulgogi

Preparation time: 10 minutes

Cooking time: 35 minutes

Servings: 10

INGREDIENTS

- 3 pounds beef
- 1 onion
- 1 tablespoon chives
- 2 carrot
- ½ tablespoon sesame seeds
- 1 teaspoon olive oil
- ½ cup of soy sauce
- 4 tablespoon of rice wine
- ¼ cup chicken stock
- 1 teaspoon fresh ginger
- 1 teaspoon Erythritol
- 1 teaspoon minced garlic

DIRECTIONS

1. Peel the onion and dice it. Peel the carrots and grate them. Set the pressure cooker to "Sauté" mode. Put the grated carrot and diced onion into the pressure cooker. Add

olive oil, soy sauce, chives, rice wine, chicken stock, fresh ginger, Erythritol, and minced garlic and stir well. Add the ground beef and combine well. Close the pressure cooker lid and cook for 35 minutes. When the cooking time ends, remove the bulgogi from the pressure cooker and stir again. Place the bulgogi in a serving dish, sprinkle with the sesame seeds and serve

NUTRITION: Calories 248, Fat 11.5, Fiber 2, Carbs 7.68, Protein 30

382. Rack of Lamb

Preparation time: 15 minutes

Cooking time: 25 minutes

Servings: 6

INGREDIENTS

- 13 ounces lamb rack
- 1 cup red wine
- 1 tablespoon Erythritol
- 1 teaspoon ground black pepper
- 1 teaspoon cilantro
- 1 cup chicken stock
- 1 onion
- 3 tablespoons butter
- 1 tablespoon olive oil
- 1 teaspoon curry
- 1 teaspoon fresh rosemary

DIRECTIONS

1. Combine the red wine, Erythritol, ground black pepper, cilantro, chicken stock, curry, and rosemary together in a mixing bowl and stir. Peel the onion and chop it. Add the chopped onion in the mixture and stir again. Place the lamb rack in the red wine mixture and let it marinate for at least 10 minutes. Set the pressure cooker to "Pressure" mode. Add the butter into the pressure cooker and melt it. Add the marinated lamb rack and sprinkle it with the curry. Close the lid and cook for 25 minutes. When the cooking time ends,

remove the lamb from the pressure cooker and let it rest before serving.

NUTRITION: Calories 208, Fat 13.9, Fiber 1, Carbs 5.49, Protein 14

383. Lamb Espetadas

Preparation time: 15 minutes

Cooking time: 25 minutes

Servings: 5

INGREDIENTS

- 2 onions
- 1 pound lamb
- 1 tablespoon paprika
- 1 tablespoon olive oil
- 1 teaspoon oregano
- 1 tablespoon cilantro
- ½ teaspoon bay leaf
- 1 tablespoon of sea salt
- ¼ chili
- ¼ cup red wine
- 1 teaspoon apple cider vinegar
- 1 teaspoon black-eyed peas

DIRECTIONS

1. Chop the lamb roughly. Sprinkle the chopped lamb with the oregano, cilantro, sea salt, chili, red wine, apple cider vinegar, and black-eyed peas in a mixing bowl and stir well.
2. Let the mixture sit for 5 minutes. Peel the onions and blend well using a blender. Take the chopped meat and put it on the wooden skewers. Spread the meat with the blended onion. Preheat the pressure cooker on "Sauté" mode for 3 minutes.
3. Place the lamb skewers into the pressure cooker and sprinkle the meat with the olive oil. Close the lid and cook for 25 minutes. When the dish is cooked, remove the food from the pressure cooker and let it rest briefly before serving.

NUTRITION: calories 281, fat 18.2, fiber 1, carbs 5.24, protein 23

384. Lamb Cutlets

Preparation time: 10 minutes

Cooking time: 12 minutes

Servings: 5

INGREDIENTS

- 14 ounces ground lamb
- 2 white onions
- 1 teaspoon ground black pepper
- 1 egg
- 1 tablespoon salt
- 1 teaspoon cilantro
- ½ teaspoon ground rosemary
- 1 cup fresh basil
- 1 teaspoon olive oil
- 1 teaspoon minced garlic
- ¼ teaspoon sage
- 1 teaspoon paprika

DIRECTIONS

1. Combine the ground lamb, ground black pepper, egg, salt, cilantro, ground rosemary, minced garlic, and paprika in a mixing bowl and stir well. Peel the onions and dice them.
2. Add the onion to the ground lamb mixture and stir well. Chop the basil and combine it with the sage. Set the pressure cooker to "Sauté" mode. Pour the olive oil into the pressure cooker and add basil mixture. Sauté the mixture for 2 minutes, stirring frequently.
3. Remove the basil mixture from the pressure cooker. Make medium-sized cutlets from the lamb mixture and put them into the pressure cooker. Cook the cutlets for 10 minutes or until golden brown on both sides. Remove the lamb cutlets from the pressure cooker, let them rest briefly and serve.

NUTRITION: Calories 237, Fat 12.9, Fiber 2, Carbs 11.65, Protein 19

385. Lamb with Thyme

Preparation time: 10 minutes

Cooking time: 45 minutes

Servings: 8

INGREDIENTS

- 1 cup fresh thyme
- 1 tablespoon olive oil
- 2 pounds lamb
- 1 teaspoon oregano
- 1 tablespoon ground black pepper
- 1 teaspoon paprika
- ¼ cup of rice wine
- 1 teaspoon Erythritol
- 4 tablespoons butter
- ¼ cup chicken stock
- 1 tablespoon turmeric

DIRECTIONS

1. Chop the fresh thyme and combine it with the oregano, ground black pepper, paprika, rice wine, Erythritol, chicken stock, and turmeric. Mix up the mixture. Sprinkle the lamb with the spice mixture and stir it carefully.
2. After this, transfer the lamb mixture in the pressure cooker and add olive oil. Close the pressure cooker lid and cook the dish at the meat mode for 45 minutes. When the meat is cooked – remove it from the pressure cooker. Chill the lamb little and slice it. Enjoy!

NUTRITION: Calories 313, Fat 16.5, Fiber 2.8, Carbs 8.7, Protein 32.7

386. Asian Lamb

Preparation time: 10 minutes

Cooking time: 45 minutes

Servings: 5

INGREDIENTS

- 1 cup of soy sauce
- 1 tablespoon tahini
- 3 tablespoons olive oil
- 8 ounces lamb
- 1 onion
- ⅓ cup garlic clove
- 1 teaspoon Erythritol
- 1 teaspoon starch
- 1 teaspoon salt
- 1 tablespoon black olives
- 1 tablespoon coriander
- 1 teaspoon sage

DIRECTIONS

1. Combine the soy sauce and tahini together in a mixing bowl and mix well. Set the pressure cooker to "Sauté" mode. Pour the olive oil into the pressure cooker.
2. Add the garlic and sauté the mixture for 2 minutes. Add the brown Erythritol, starch, salt, black olives, coriander, and sage. Stir the mixture and sauté it for 30 seconds. Pour the soy sauce mixture into the pressure cooker.
3. Peel the onion and dice it. Add the diced onion and lamb into the pressure cooker and close the lid. Cook the dish on "Sauté" mode for 40 minutes. When the dish is cooked, remove the food from the pressure cooker and let it rest briefly before serving.

NUTRITION: Calories 229, Fat 13.6, Fiber 1.5, Carbs 10.4, Protein 17.3

387. Spinach-stuffed Rack of Lamb

Preparation time: 15 minutes

Cooking time: 30 minutes

Servings: 5

INGREDIENTS

- 3 cups fresh spinach

- 1 tablespoon minced garlic
- 1 pound lamb rack
- 1 tablespoon curry paste
- ½ cup chicken stock
- 1 tablespoon olive oil
- 1 teaspoon butter
- 1 teaspoon salt
- 1 teaspoon fresh ginger
- 3 tablespoons cream

DIRECTIONS

1. Wash the spinach, dry it well and chop it. Transfer the spinach to a blender and puree. Put the blended spinach in a mixing bowl and add garlic, curry paste, and fresh ginger and stir well. Rub the lamb rack with the salt, olive oil, and butter. Make the small cuts in the lamb rack and stuff it with the spinach mixture.
2. Set the pressure cooker to "Pressure" mode. Place the stuffed lamb rack into the pressure cooker and add chicken stock. Close the lid and cook for 30 minutes. When the cooking time ends, remove the lamb from the pressure cooker and let it rest briefly before slicing into.

NUTRITION: Calories 213, Fat 13.6, Fiber 1, Carbs 3.17, Protein 20

388.   Lamb and Avocado Salad

Preparation time: 10 minutes

Cooking time: 35 minutes

Servings: 7

INGREDIENTS

- 1 avocado, pitted
- 1 cucumber
- 8 ounces lamb fillet
- 3 cups of water
- 1 teaspoon salt
- 1 teaspoon cayenne pepper
- 3 tablespoons olive oil
- 1 garlic clove

- 1 teaspoon basil
- 1 tablespoon sesame oil
- 1 cup lettuce

DIRECTIONS

1. Set the pressure cooker to "Sauté" mode. Place the lamb fillet into the pressure cooker and add water. Sprinkle the mixture with the salt. Peel the garlic clove and add it to the lamb mixture.
2. Close the lid and cook for 35 minutes. Meanwhile, slice the cucumbers and peel and chop the avocado. Combine the ingredients in a mixing bowl. Chop the lettuce roughly and add it to the mixing bowl. Sprinkle the mixture with the cayenne pepper, olive oil, basil, and sesame oil and toss well.
3. When the meat is cooked, remove it from the pressure cooker and let it rest briefly. Chop the meat roughly and add it to a mixing bowl. Mix up the salad carefully and transfer it to a serving bowl. Serve the dish warm.

NUTRITION: Calories 203, Fat 17.5, Fiber 2, Carbs 3.47, Protein 9

389.   Garlic Lamb Stew

Preparation time: 15 minutes

Cooking time: 35 minutes

Servings: 8

INGREDIENTS

- 1 cup garlic
- 1 tablespoon garlic powder
- 1 teaspoon cilantro
- 3 carrots
- 1 cup asparagus, chopped
- 4 cups chickens stock
- ½ cup half and half
- 2 onions
- 1 pound lamb
- 1 cup parsley
- 1 tablespoon salt

- 1 tablespoon olive oil

DIRECTIONS

1. Peel the garlic and slice it. Combine the sliced garlic with the garlic powder and stir well. Add the cilantro and olive oil and stir. Peel the carrots and onions.
2. Chop the vegetables roughly. Set the pressure cooker to "Sauté" mode. Place the chopped vegetable and the garlic mixture into the pressure cooker. Chop the parsley and add it into the pressure cooker too.
3. Chop the lamb and add it into the pressure cooker. Add the asparagus, water, half and half, and salt and stir well. Close the pressure cooker lid and cook for 35 minutes. When the stew is cooked, release the pressure and open the pressure cooker lid. Ladle the stew into serving bowls.

NUTRITION: Calories 195, Fat 7.9, Fiber 2.2, Carbs 13, Protein 18.7

390. Soft Lamb Shoulder

Preparation time: 10 minutes

Cooking time: 25 minutes

Servings: 6

INGREDIENTS

- 1 cup sour cream
- 1 tablespoon ground black pepper
- 1 tablespoon garlic powder
- 1 tablespoon onion powder
- 1 teaspoon basil
- 9 ounces lamb shoulder
- 1 teaspoon chives
- 3 tablespoons butter

DIRECTIONS

1. Combine the sour cream, ground black pepper, garlic powder, onion powder, basil, chives, and butter together in a mixing bowl and stir well until smooth. Put the lamb sub in the sour cream mixture and mix well. Let the meat marinate for 3 hours.
2. Preheat the pressure cooker at the "Pressure" mode and place the lamb mixture inside. Close the pressure cooker lid and cook for 25 minutes. When the cooking time ends, release the remaining pressure and open the pressure cooker lid. Place the lamb on the serving plate and cut into portions.

NUTRITION: Calories 224, Fat 17, Fiber 1 Carbs 5.58, Protein 12

VEGAN/VEGETARIAN

391. All-Time Mixed Vegetable Curry

Preparation Time: 10 minutes

Cooking time: 3 minutes

Servings: 6

INGREDIENTS

- 3 cups leeks, sliced
- 6 cups rainbow chard, stems and leaves, chopped
- 1 cup celery, chopped
- 2 tablespoons garlic, minced
- 1 teaspoon dried oregano
- 1 teaspoon salt
- 2 teaspoons fresh ground black pepper
- 3 cups chicken broth
- 2 cups yellow summer squash, sliced into 1/ inch slices
- ¼ cup fresh parsley, chopped
- ¾ cup heavy whip cream
- 4-6 tablespoons parmesan cheese, grated

DIRECTIONS

1. Add leeks, chard, celery, 1 tablespoon garlic, oregano, salt, pepper and broth to your Ninja Foodi
2. Lock lid and cook on HIGH pressure for 3 minutes. Quick release pressure
3. Open the lid and add more broth, set your pot to Saute mode and adjust heat to HIGH
4. Add yellow squash, parsley and remaining 1 tablespoon garlic
5. Let it cook for 2-3 minutes until the squash is soft. Stir in cream and sprinkle parmesan
6. Serve and enjoy!

392. Worthy Caramelized Onion

Preparation Time: 10 minutes

Cooking time: 30-35 minutes

Servings: 6

INGREDIENTS

- 2 tablespoons unsalted butter
- 3 large onions sliced
- 2 tablespoons water
- 1 teaspoon salt

DIRECTIONS

1. Set your Ninja Foodi to Sauté mode and add set temperature to medium heat, pre-heat the inner pot for 5 minutes. Add butter and let it melt, add onions, water, and stir
2. Lock lid and cook on HIGH pressure for 30 minutes. Quick release the pressure
3. Remove lid and set the pot to sauté mode, let it sear in Medium-HIGH mode for 15 minutes until all liquid is gone. Serve and enjoy!

393. A Very Greeny Green Beans Platter

Preparation Time: 10 minutes

Cooking time: 5 minutes

Servings: 6

INGREDIENTS

- 2-3 pounds fresh green beans
- 2 tablespoons butter
- 1 garlic clove, minced
- Salt and pepper to taste
- 1 and ½ cups of water

DIRECTIONS

1. Add listed ingredients to Ninja Foodi. Lock lid and cook on HIGH pressure for 5 minutes
2. Quick release pressure

394. A Mishmash Cauliflower Mash

Preparation Time: 10 minutes

Cooking time: 5 minutes

Servings: 3

INGREDIENTS

- 1 tablespoon butter, soft
- ½ cup feta cheese
- Salt and pepper to taste
- 1 large head cauliflower, chopped into large pieces
- 1 garlic cloves, minced
- 2 teaspoons fresh chives, minced

DIRECTIONS

1. Add water to your Ninja Foodi and place steamer basket
2. Add cauliflower pieces and lock lid, cook on HIGH pressure for 5 minutes
3. Quick release pressure. Open the lid and use an immersion blender to mash the cauliflower
4. Blend until you have a nice consistency.
5. Enjoy!

395.   Zucchini and Artichoke Platter

Preparation Time: 10 minutes

Cooking time: 10 minutes

Servings: 4

INGREDIENTS

- 2 tablespoon coconut oil
- 1 bulb garlic, minced
- 1 large artichoke heart, cleaned sliced
- 2 medium zucchinis, sliced
- ½ cup vegetable broth
- Salt and pepper as needed

DIRECTIONS

1. Set your Ninja Foodi to Saute mode and add oil, allow the oil the heat up
2. Add garlic and Saute until nicely fragrant. Add rest of the Ingredients and stir

3. Lock lid and cook on HIGH pressure for 10 minutes. Quick release, serve and enjoy!

396.   Winning Broccoli Casserole

Preparation Time: 10 minutes

Cooking time: 6 hours

Servings: 4

INGREDIENTS

- 1 tablespoon extra-virgin olive oil
- 1 pound broccoli, cut into florets
- 1 pound cauliflower, cut into florets
- ¼ cup almond flour
- 2 cups of coconut milk
- ½ teaspoon ground nutmeg
- Pinch of fresh ground black pepper
- 1 and ½ cups cashew cream

DIRECTIONS

1. Grease the Ninja Foodi inner pot with olive oil. Place broccoli and cauliflower to your Ninja Foodi
2. Take a small bowl and stir in almond flour, coconut milk, pepper, 1 cup of cashew cream
3. Pour coconut milk mixture over vegetables and top casserole with remaining cashew cream
4. Cover and cook on SLOW COOK Mode (LOWfor 6 hours. Server and enjoy!

397.   Spaghetti Squash Drizzled with Sage Butter Sauce

Preparation Time: 10 minutes

Cooking time: 10 minutes

Servings: 4

INGREDIENTS

- 1 medium-sized spaghetti squash
- 1 and a ½ cup of water
- 1 bunch of fresh sage

- 3-4 garlic cloves, sliced
- 2 tablespoon of olive oil
- 1 teaspoon of salt
- 1/8 teaspoon of nutmeg

DIRECTIONS

1. Halve the squash and scoop out the seeds
2. Add water to your Ninja Foodi and lower down the squash with the squash halves facing up
3. Stack them on top of one another. Lock up the lid and cook on HIGH pressure for 3 minutes
4. Release the pressure over 10 minutes
5. Take a cold Saute pan and add sage, garlic and olive oil and cook on LOW heat, making sure to stir and fry the sage leaves. Keep it on the side
6. Release the pressure naturally and tease the squash fibers out from the shell and plop them into the Saute Pan. Stir well and sprinkle salt and nutmeg . Serve with a bit of cheese and enjoy!

398.   Uber-Keto Caper and Beet Salad

Preparation Time: 10 minutes

Cooking time: 25 minutes

Servings: 4

INGREDIENTS

- 4 medium beets
- 2 tablespoons of rice wine vinegar
- For Dressing
- Small bunch parsley, stems removed
- 1 large garlic clove
- ½ teaspoon salt
- Pinch of black pepper
- 1 tablespoon extra-virgin olive oil
- 2 tablespoons capers

DIRECTIONS

1. Pour 1 cup of water into your steamer basket and place it on the side

2. Snip up the tops of your bits and wash them well. Put the beets in your steamer basket
3. Place the steamer basket in your instant pot and lock up the lid
4. Let it cook for about 25 minutes at high pressure. Once done, release the pressure naturally
5. While it is being cooked, take a small jar and add chopped up parsley and garlic alongside olive oil, salt, pepper and capers. Shake it vigorously to prepared your dressing
6. Open up the lid once the pressure is released and check the beets for doneness using a fork
7. Take out the steamer basket to your sink and run it under cold water
8. Use your finger to brush off the skin of the beets
9. Use a plastic cutting board and slice up the beets
10. Arrange them on a platter and sprinkle some vinegar on top

399.   The Greeny And Beany Horseradish Mix

Preparation Time: 5 minutes

Cooking time: 10-15 minutes

Servings: 4

INGREDIENTS

- 2 large beets with greens, scrubbed and root ends trimmed
- 1 cup water, for steaming
- 2 tablespoons sour cream
- 1 tablespoon whole milk
- 1 teaspoon prepared horseradish
- ¼ teaspoon lemon zest
- 1/8 teaspoon salt
- 2 teaspoon unsalted butter
- 1 tablespoon minced fresh chives

DIRECTIONS

1. Trim off beet greens and keep them on the side
2. Add water to the Ninja Foodi and place steamer basket, place beets in a steamer basket
3. Lock lid and cook on HIGH pressure for 10 minutes, release pressure naturally over 10 minutes
4. While the beets are being cooked, wash greens and slice them into ½ inch thick ribbons
5. Take a bowl and whisk in sour cream, horseradish, lemon zest, 1/16 teaspoon of salt
6. Once the cooking is done, remove the lid and remove beets, let them cool
7. Use a paring knife to peel them and slice them into large bite-sized pieces
8. Remove steamer from the Ninja Foodi and pour out water
9. Set your Foodi to "Saute" mode and add butter, let it melt
10. Once the butter stops foaming, add beet greens sprinkle remaining 1/6 teaspoon salt and cook for 3-4 minutes. Return beets to the Foodi and heat for 1-2 minutes, stirring
11. Transfer beets and greens to a platter and drizzle sour cream mixture
12. Sprinkle chives and serve. Enjoy!

400.   Fully Stuffed Whole Chicken

Preparation Time: 5 minutes

Cooking time: 8 hours

Servings: 4

INGREDIENTS

- 1 cup mozzarella cheese
- 4 garlic clove, peeled
- 1 whole chicken, 2 pounds, cleaned and dried
- Salt and pepper to taste
- 2 tablespoons lemon juice

DIRECTIONS

1. Stuff chicken cavity with garlic cloves, cheese. Season with salt and pepper
2. Transfer to Ninja Foodi and drizzle lemon juice. Lock lid and SLOW COOK on LOW for 8 hours
3. Transfer to a plate, serve and enjoy!

401.   Rosemary Dredged Green Beans

Preparation Time: 5 minutes

Cooking time: 3 hours

Servings: 4

INGREDIENTS

- 1 pound green beans
- 1 tablespoon rosemary, minced
- 1 teaspoon fresh thyme, minced
- 2 tablespoons lemon juice
- 2 tablespoons water

DIRECTIONS

1. Add listed Ingredients to Ninja Foodi
2. Lock lid and cook on SLOW COOK MODE(LOW)for 3 hours . Unlock lid and stir. Enjoy!

402.   Italian Turkey Breast

Preparation Time: 5 minutes

Cooking time: 2 hours

Servings: 4

INGREDIENTS

- 1 and ½ cups Italian dressing
- 2 garlic cloves, minced
- 1 2 (poundsturkey) breast, with bone
- 2 tablespoons butter
- Salt and pepper to taste

DIRECTIONS

1. Mix in garlic cloves, salt, black pepper and rub turkey breast with mix
2. Grease Ninja Foodi pot and arrange turkey breast. Top with Italian dressing
3. Lock lid and BAKE/ROAST for 2 hours at 230 degrees F. Serve and enjoy!

403. Crazy Fresh Onion Soup

Preparation Time: 5 minutes

Cooking time: 10-15 minutes

Servings: 4

INGREDIENTS

- 2 tablespoons avocado oil
- 8 cups yellow onion
- 1 tablespoon balsamic vinegar
- 6 cups of pork stock
- 1 teaspoon salt
- 2 bay leaves
- 2 large sprigs, fresh thyme

DIRECTIONS

1. Cut up the onion in half through the root
2. Peel them and slice into thin half moons
3. Set the pot to Saute mode and add oil, one the oil is hot and add onions
4. Cook for about 15 minutes
5. Add balsamic vinegar and scrape any fond from the bottom
6. Add stock, bay leaves, salt, and thyme
7. Lock up the lid and cook on HIGH pressure for 10 minutes
8. Release the pressure naturally
9. Discard the bay leaf and thyme stems
10. Blend the soup using an immersion blender and serve!

404. Elegant Zero Crust Kale And Mushroom Quiche

Preparation Time: 5 minutes

Cooking time: 9 hours

Servings: 6

INGREDIENTS

- 6 large eggs
- 2 tablespoons unsweetened almond milk
- 2 ounces low –fat feta cheese, crumbled
- ¼ cup parmesan cheese, grated
- 1 and ½ teaspoons Italian seasoning
- 4 ounces mushrooms, sliced
- 2 cups kale, chopped

DIRECTIONS

1. Grease the inner pot of your Ninja Foodi
2. Take a large bowl and whisk in eggs, cheese, almond milk, seasoning and mix it well
3. Stir in kale and mushrooms. Pour the mix into Ninja Foodi. Gently stir
4. Place lid and cook on SLOW COOK Mode(LOWfor 8-9 hours. Serve and enjoy!

405. Delicious Beet Borscht

Preparation Time: 5 minutes

Cooking time: 45 minutes

Servings: 6

INGREDIENTS

- 8 cups beets
- ½ cup celery, diced
- ½ cup carrots, diced
- 2 garlic cloves, diced
- 1 medium onion, diced
- 3 cups cabbage, shredded
- 6 cups beef stock
- 1 bay leaf
- 1 tablespoon salt
- ½ tablespoon thyme
- ¼ cup fresh dill, chopped
- ½ cup of coconut yogurt

DIRECTIONS

1. Add the washed beets to a steamer in the Ninja Foodi
2. Add 1 cup of water. Steam for 7 minutes
3. Perform a quick release and drop into an ice bath
4. Carefully peel off the skin and dice the beets
5. Transfer the diced beets, celery, carrots, onion, garlic, cabbage, stock, bay leaf, thyme and salt to your Instant Pot. Lock up the lid and set the pot to SOUP mode, cook for 45 minutes
6. Release the pressure naturally. Transfer to bowls and top with a dollop of dairy-free yogurt
7. Enjoy with a garnish of fresh dill!

406. Pepper Jack Cauliflower Meal

Preparation Time: 5 minutes

Cooking time: 3 hours 35 minutes

Servings: 6

INGREDIENTS

- 1 head cauliflower
- ¼ cup whipping cream
- 4 ounces cream cheese
- ½ teaspoon pepper
- 1 teaspoon salt
- 2 tablespoons butter
- 4 ounces pepper jack cheese
- 6 bacon slices, crumbled

DIRECTIONS

- Grease Ninja Foodi and add listed Ingredients (except cheese and bacon
- Stir and Lock lid, cook SLOW COOK MODE (LOW)for 3 hours
- Remove lid and add cheese, stir. Lock lid again and cook for 1 hour more
- Garnish with bacon crumbles and enjoy!

407. Slow-Cooked Brussels

Preparation Time: 5 minutes

Cooking time: 4 hours

Servings: 4

INGREDIENTS

- 1 pound Brussels sprouts, bottom trimmed and cut
- 1 tablespoon olive oil
- 1 -1/2 tablespoon Dijon mustard
- ¼ cup of water
- Salt and pepper as needed
- ½ teaspoon dried tarragon

DIRECTIONS

1. Add Brussels, salt, water, pepper, mustard to Ninja Foodi
2. Add dried tarragon and stir
3. Lock lid and cook on SLOW COOK MODE (LOWfor 5 hours until the Brussels are tender
4. Stir well and add Dijon over Brussels. Stir and enjoy!

408. Slowly Cooked Lemon Artichokes

Preparation Time: 10 minutes

Cooking time: 5 hours

Servings: 4

INGREDIENTS

- 5 large artichokes
- 1 teaspoon of sea salt
- 2 stalks celery, sliced
- 2 large carrots, cut into matchsticks
- Juice from ½ a lemon
- ¼ teaspoon black pepper
- 1 teaspoon dried thyme
- 1 tablespoon dried rosemary
- Lemon wedges for garnish

DIRECTIONS

1. Remove the stalk from your artichokes and remove the tough outer shell
2. Transfer the chokes to your Ninja Foodi and add 2 cups of boiling water
3. Add celery, lemon juice, salt, carrots, black pepper, thyme, rosemary
4. Cook on Slow Cook mode (HIGHfor 4-5 hours
5. Serve the artichokes with lemon wedges. Serve and enjoy!

409. Well Dressed Brussels

Preparation Time: 10 minutes

Cooking time: 4-5 hours

Servings: 4

INGREDIENTS

- 2 pounds Brussels, halved
- 2 red onions, sliced
- 2 tablespoons apple cider vinegar
- 1 tablespoon extra-virgin olive oil
- 1 teaspoon ground cinnamon
- ½ cup pecans, chopped

DIRECTIONS

1. Add Brussels and onions to Ninja Foodi. Take a small bowl and add cinnamon, vinegar, olive oil
2. Pour mixture over sprouts and toss
3. Place lid and cook on SLOW COOK MODE (LOW)for 4-5 hours. Enjoy!

410. Cheddar Cauliflower Bowl

Preparation Time: 10 minutes

Cooking time: 5 minutes

Servings: 8

INGREDIENTS

- ¼ cup butter

- ½ sweet onion, chopped
- 1 head cauliflower, chopped
- 4 cups herbed vegetable stock
- ½ teaspoon ground nutmeg
- 1 cup heavy whip cream
- Salt and pepper as needed
- 1 cup cheddar cheese, shredded

DIRECTIONS

1. Set your Ninja Foodi to sauté mode and add butter, let it heat up and melt
2. Add onion and Cauliflower, Saute for 10 minutes until tender and lightly browned
3. Add vegetable stock and nutmeg, bring to a boil
4. Lock lid and cook on HIGH pressure for 5 minutes, quick release pressure once done
5. Remove pot and from Foodi and stir in heavy cream, puree using an immersion blender
6. Season with more salt and pepper and serve with a topping of cheddar. Enjoy!

411. A Prosciutto And Thyme Eggs

Preparation Time: 10 minutes

Cooking time: 5 minutes

Servings: 4

INGREDIENTS

- 4 kale leaves
- 4 prosciutto slices
- 3 tablespoons heavy cream
- 4 hardboiled eggs
- ¼ teaspoon pepper
- ¼ teaspoon salt
- 1 and ½ cups of water

DIRECTIONS

1. Peel eggs and wrap in kale. Wrap in prosciutto and sprinkle salt and pepper
2. Add water to your Ninja Foodi and lower trivet. Place eggs inside and lock lid
3. Cook on HIGH pressure for 5 minutes. Quick release pressure. Serve and enjoy!

412. The Authentic Zucchini Pesto Meal

Preparation Time: 10 minutes

Cooking time: 10 minutes

Servings: 4

INGREDIENTS

- 1 tablespoon olive oil
- 1 onion, chopped
- 2 and ½ pound roughly chopped zucchini
- ½ cup of water
- 1 and ½ teaspoon salt
- 1 bunch basil leaves
- 2 garlic cloves, minced
- 1 tablespoon extra-virgin olive oil
- Zucchini for making zoodles

DIRECTION

1. Set the Ninja Foodi to Saute mode and add olive oil
2. Once the oil is hot, add onion and Saute for 4 minutes
3. Add zucchini, water, and salt. Lock up the lid and cook on HIGH pressure for 3 minutes
4. Release the pressure naturally. Add basil, garlic, and leaves
5. Use an immersion blender to blend everything well until you have a sauce-like consistency
6. Take the extra zucchini and pass them through a Spiralizer to get noodle like shapes
7. Toss the Zoodles with sauce and enjoy!

413. Supreme Cauliflower Soup

Preparation Time: 10 minutes

Cooking time: 5 minutes

Servings: 4

INGREDIENTS

- ½ a small onion, chopped

- 2 tablespoons butter
- 1 large head of cauliflower, leaves and stems removed, coarsely chopped
- 2 cups chicken stock
- 1 teaspoon garlic powder
- 1 teaspoon salt
- 4 ounces cream cheese, cut into cubes
- 1 cup sharp cheddar cheese, cut
- ½ cup cream
- Extra cheddar, sour cream bacon strips, green onion for topping

DIRECTIONS

1. Peel the onion and chop up into small pieces
2. Cut the leaves of the cauliflower and steam, making sure to keep the core intact
3. Coarsely chop the cauliflower into pieces
4. Set your Ninja Foodi to Saute mode and add onion, cook for 2-3 minutes
5. Add chopped cauliflower, stock, salt, and garlic powder
6. Lock up the lid and cook on HIGH pressure for 5 minutes. Perform a quick release
7. Prepare the toppings. Use an immersion blender to puree your soup in the Ninja Foodi
8. Serve your soup with a topping of sliced green onions, cheddar, crumbled bacon. Enjoy!

414. Very Rich and Creamy Asparagus Soup

Preparation Time: 10 minutes

Cooking time: 5-10 minutes

Servings: 4

INGREDIENTS

- 1 tablespoon olive oil
- 3 green onions, sliced crosswise into ¼ inch pieces
- 1 pound asparagus, tough ends removed, cut into 1 inch pieces
- 4 cups vegetable stock

- 1 tablespoon unsalted butter
- 1 tablespoon almond flour
- 2 teaspoon salt
- 1 teaspoon white pepper
- ½ cup heavy cream

DIRECTIONS

1. Set your Ninja Foodi to "Saute" mode and add oil, let it heat up
2. Add green onions and Saute for a few minutes, add asparagus and stock
3. Lock lid and cook on HIGH pressure for 5 minutes
4. Take a small saucepan and place it over low heat, add butter, flour and stir until the mixture foams and turns into a golden beige, this is your blond roux
5. Remove from heat. Release pressure naturally over 10 minutes
6. Open the lid and add roux, salt, and pepper to the soup
7. Use an immersion blender to puree the soup
8. Taste and season accordingly, swirl in cream and enjoy!

415. Summertime Vegetable Platter

Preparation Time: 5 minutes

Cooking time: 3 hours 5 minutes

Servings: 6

INGREDIENTS

- 1 cup grape tomatoes
- 2 cups okra
- 1 cup mushrooms
- 2 cups yellow bell peppers
- 1 and ½ cup red onions
- 2 and ½ cups zucchini
- ½ cup olive oil
- ½ cup balsamic vinegar
- 1 tablespoon fresh thyme, chopped
- 2 tablespoons fresh basil, chopped

DIRECTIONS

1. Slice and chop okra, onions, tomatoes, zucchini, mushrooms
2. Add veggies to a large container and mix
3. Take another dish and add oil and vinegar, mix in thyme and basil
4. Toss the veggies into Ninja Foodi and pour marinade. Stir well
5. Close lid and cook on 3 hours on SLOW COOK MOD (HIGH), making sure to stir after every hour

416. The Creative Mushroom Stroganoff

Preparation Time: 5 minutes

Cooking time: 10 minutes

Servings: 6

INGREDIENTS

- ¼ cup unsalted butter, cubed
- 1 pound cremini mushrooms, halved
- 1 large onion, halved
- 4 garlic cloves, minced
- 2 cups vegetable broth
- ½ teaspoon salt
- ¼ teaspoon fresh black pepper
- 1 and ½ cups sour cream
- ¼ cup fresh flat-leaf parsley, chopped
- 1 cup grated parmesan cheese

DIRECTIONS

1. Add butter, mushrooms, onion, garlic, vegetable broth, salt, pepper, and paprika
2. Gently stir and lock lid. Cook on HIGH pressure for 5 minutes
3. Release pressure naturally over 10 minutes
4. Serve by stirring in sour cream and with a garnish of parsley and parmesan cheese. Enjoy!

417. Garlic And Ginger Red Cabbage Platter

Preparation Time: 10 minutes

Cooking time: 8 minutes

Servings: 6

INGREDIENTS

- 2 tablespoon coconut oil
- 1 tablespoon butter
- 3 garlic cloves, crushed
- 2 teaspoon fresh ginger, grated
- 8 cups red cabbage, shredded
- 1 teaspoon salt
- ½ a teaspoon pepper
- 1/3 cup water

DIRECTIONS

1. Set your Ninja Foodi to Saute mode and add coconut oil and butter, allow to heat up
2. Add garlic and ginger and mix. Add cabbage, pepper, salt, and water
3. Mix well and lock up the lid, cook on HIGH pressure for 5 minutes
4. Perform a quick release and mix. Serve and enjoy!

418. The Veggie Lover's Onion and Tofu Platter

Preparation Time: 8 minutes

Cooking time: 12 minutes

Servings: 4

INGREDIENTS

- 4 tablespoons butter
- 2 tofu blocks, pressed and cubed into 1-inch pieces
- Salt and pepper to taste
- 1 cup cheddar cheese, grated
- 2 medium onions, sliced

DIRECTIONS

1. Take a bowl and add tofu, season with salt and pepper

2. Set your Foodi to Saute mode and add butter, let it melt
3. Add onions and Saute for 3 minutes. Add seasoned tofu and cook for 2 minutes more
4. Add cheddar and gently stir
5. Lock the lid and bring down the Air Crisp mode, let the dish cook on "Air Crisp" mode for 3 minutes at 340 degrees F. Once done, take the dish out, serve and enjoy!

419. Feisty Maple Dredged Carrots

Preparation Time: 10 minutes

Cooking time: 4 minutes

Servings: 6

INGREDIENTS

- 2-pound carrot
- ¼ cup raisins
- Pepper as needed
- 1 cup of water
- 1 tablespoon butter
- 1 tablespoon sugar-free Keto friendly maple syrup

DIRECTIONS

1. Wash, peel the skin and slice the carrots diagonally
2. Add the carrots, raisins, water to your Ninja Foodi
3. Lock up the lid and cook on HIGH pressure for 4 minutes. Perform a quick release
4. Strain the carrots . Add butter and maple syrup to the warm Ninja Foodi and mix well
5. Transfer the strained carrots back to the pot and stir to coat with maple sauce and butter
6. Serve with a bit of pepper. Enjoy!

420. The Original Sicilian Cauliflower Roast

Preparation Time: 10 minutes

Cooking time: 10 minutes

Servings: 4

INGREDIENTS

- 1 medium cauliflower head, leaves removed
- ¼ cup olive oil
- 1 teaspoon red pepper, crushed
- ½ cup of water
- 2 tablespoons capers, rinsed and minced
- ½ cup parmesan cheese, grated
- 1 tablespoon fresh parsley, chopped

DIRECTIONS

1. Take the Ninja Foodi and start by adding water and place the cook and crisp basket inside the pot. Cut an "X" on the head of cauliflower by using a knife and slice it about halfway down
2. Take a basket and transfer the cauliflower in it
3. Then put on the pressure lid and seal it and set it on low pressure for 3 minutes
4. Add olive oil, capers, garlic, and crushed red pepper into it and mix them well
5. Once the cauliflower is cooked, do a quick release and remove the lid
6. Pour in the oil and spice mixture on the cauliflower
7. Spread equally on the surface then sprinkle some Parmesan cheese from the top
8. Close the pot with crisping lid. Set it on Air Crisp mode to 390 degrees F for 10 minutes
9. Once done, remove the cauliflower flower the Ninja Foodi transfer it into a serving plate
10. Cut it up into pieces and transfer them to serving plates. Sprinkle fresh parsley from the top
11. Serve and enjoy!

VEGETABLES

421. Asparagus Tart

Preparation time: 10 minutes

Cooking time: 25 minutes

Servings: 8

INGREDIENTS

- 7 ounces keto soda dough
- 10 ounces asparagus
- ⅓ cup walnuts
- 3 tablespoons butter
- 1 teaspoon salt
- 1 teaspoon ground black pepper
- ⅓ cup tomato paste
- 1 onion
- 1 carrot
- 1 egg yolk

DIRECTIONS

1. Roll out the dough using a rolling pin. Spread the pressure cooker with the butter inside and place the rolled dough. Chop the asparagus and transfer it to the blender.
2. Add the walnuts, salt, ground black pepper, tomato paste, and egg yolk. Peel the onion and carrot. Grate the carrot and chop the onion.
3. Add the onion in a blender and puree until smooth. Combine the asparagus mixture with the carrot and mix well. Spread the dough with the asparagus mixture. Close the pressure cooker lid Cook at "Pressure" mode for 25 minutes. When the cooking time ends, release the pressure and open the pressure cooker lid. Transfer the tart to a serving plate, cut into pieces, and serve.

NUTRITION: Calories 191, Fat 9.2, Fiber 5.4, Carbs 11.8, Protein 17.5

422. Spinach Tarts

Preparation time: 10 minutes

Cooking time: 15 minutes

Servings: 8

INGREDIENTS

- 6 ounces butter
- 1 cup coconut flour
- 1 teaspoon salt
- ½ teaspoon Erythritol
- 3 cups spinach
- ½ cup sour cream
- 1 teaspoon ground white pepper
- ½ tablespoon oregano

1 teaspoon cayenne pepper

DIRECTIONS

1. Chop the butter and combine it with the coconut flour and salt. Add Erythritol and knead the dough. Roll the dough out and place it in the pressure cooker.
2. Chop the spinach and combine it with the sour cream. Sprinkle the mixture with ground black pepper, oregano, and cayenne pepper. Mix well and spread it on the dough.
3. Close the pressure cooker lid Cook at "Pressure" mode for 15 minutes. When the cooking time ends, let the tart rest briefly. Transfer the tart to a serving plate, slice it and serve.

NUTRITION: Calories 248, Fat 22.4, Fiber 5.5, Carbs 9.5, Protein 3

423. Lettuce Warm Wraps

Preparation time: 10 minutes

Cooking time: 20 minutes

Servings: 5

INGREDIENTS

- 7 ounces lettuce
- 1 white onion
- 1 eggplant
- 5 ounces mushrooms
- 1 tablespoon olive oil
- ½ tablespoon salt
- 1 teaspoon butter
- ½ teaspoon red chile flakes
- ½ teaspoon cayenne pepper
- 1 tablespoon fresh basil

DIRECTIONS

1. Peel the onion and chop it. Chop the eggplant into tiny pieces. Combine the chopped vegetables together in a mixing bowl. Chop the mushrooms and add them to the mixture. Sprinkle the mixture with the salt, red chile flakes, and cayenne pepper and mix well.
2. Add the basil and mix again. Add the butter to the pressure cooker and add olive oil. Preheat the mixture at the "Sauté" mode for 3 minutes. Add the eggplant mixture and cook for 15 minutes on «Pressure» mode. When the vegetable mixture is cooked, remove it from the pressure cooker and let it rest. Place the vegetable mixture in the middle of the lettuce leaves and wrap it. Serve immediately.

NUTRITION: Calories 157, Fat 4.1, Fiber 8, Carbs 31.02, Protein 5

424. Spicy Asparagus Mash

Preparation time: 10 minutes

Cooking time: 10 minutes

Servings: 5

INGREDIENTS

- 3 cups beef broth
- 16 ounces asparagus
- 1 tablespoon butter
- 1 teaspoon cayenne pepper
- ½ teaspoon chile pepper
- 1 tablespoon sriracha
- 2 teaspoons salt
- ⅓ cup sour cream
- 1 teaspoon paprika

DIRECTIONS

1. Wash the asparagus and chop it roughly. Place the chopped asparagus in the pressure cooker.
2. Add cayenne pepper and beef broth. Add salt and close the pressure cooker lid. Cook the dish for 10 minutes at the "Pressure" mode. Remove the asparagus from the pressure cooker and strain it. Place the asparagus in a food processor. Add chile pepper, butter, sriracha, and sour cream. Blend the mixture until smooth. Place the cooked asparagus mash in the serving bowl.

NUTRITION: Calories 72, Fat 4.5, Fiber 2, Carbs 5.14, Protein 4

425. Creamy Vegetable Stew

Preparation time: 10 minutes

Cooking time: 25 minutes

Servings: 10

INGREDIENTS

- 2 eggplants
- 2 yellow sweet pepper
- 1 zucchini
- 1 cup green beans
- 8 ounces mushrooms
- 1 tablespoon salt
- ½ teaspoon ground black pepper
- 1 cup chicken stock
- 3 cups beef broth
- ½ cup tomato juice
- 1 tablespoon Erythritol

DIRECTIONS

1. Peel the eggplants and chop them. Sprinkle the chopped eggplants with the salt and stir the mixture. Remove the seeds from the sweet peppers. Chop the sweet peppers and zucchini. Combine all the Ingredients together in the mixing bowl.
2. Add Erythritol and mix up the mixture. Place the vegetable mixture in the pressure cooker and sauté it for 5 minutes, stirring frequently. Add tomato juice, beef broth, chicken stock, green beans, and mix well. Close the pressure cooker lid Cook at «Sauté" mode for 25 minutes. When the stew is cooked, let it rest briefly and serve.

NUTRITION: Calories 61, Fat 0.9, Fiber 5.1, Carbs 11.4, Protein 4.1

426. Crunchy Chile Peppers

Preparation time: 10 minutes

Cooking time: 10 minutes

Servings: 5

INGREDIENTS

- 5 chile peppers
- ½ cup half and half
- ⅓ cup olive oil
- 1 cup coconut flakes
- 1 teaspoon cilantro
- ¼ cup coconut flour
- 1 egg
- 1 teaspoon ground thyme

DIRECTIONS

1. Remove the seeds from the chile peppers and combine them with the coconut flour. Beat the egg in the bowl. Sprinkle the chile peppers with the whisked egg.
2. Add the coconut flakes, cilantro, and ground thyme and mix well. Pour the olive oil in the pressure cooker and preheat it well. Add the chile peppers to the pressure cooker and roast them at "Sauté" mode for

8 minutes on both sides. When the chile peppers are cooked, remove them from the pressure cooker, let it rest briefly, and serve.

NUTRITION: Calories 221, Fat 22.6, Fiber 1.9, Carbs 4.4, Protein 2.5

427. Sauteed Red Cabbage

Preparation time: 10 minutes

Cooking time: 30 minutes

Servings: 4

INGREDIENTS

- 10 oz red cabbage, shredded
- ½ cup of water
- 1 oz raisins, chopped
- 1 teaspoon paprika
- 1 teaspoon ground coriander
- 1 teaspoon ground cinnamon
- ½ teaspoon apple cider vinegar
- ½ cup heavy cream

DIRECTIONS

1. Place red cabbage in the cooker. Sprinkle it with the paprika, ground coriander, ground cinnamon, apple cider vinegar, and raisins. Add heavy cream and mix up the mixture. Then add water. Close the lid and cook the meal on saute mode for 30 minutes. Stir it from time to time. The cooked cabbage will have a soft texture.

NUTRITION: Calories 94, Fat 5.7, Fiber 2.5, Carbs 10.9, Protein 1.5

428. Oregano Croquettes

Preparation time: 10 minutes

Cooking time: 6 minutes

Servings: 6

INGREDIENTS

- 1 pound turnip, boiled
- 1 cup fresh oregano
- 1 egg
- ¼ cup coconut flour
- 1 teaspoon onion powder
- 1 tablespoon salt
- 4 tablespoons olive oil
- 1 teaspoon nutmeg
- 1 teaspoon dill

DIRECTIONS

1. Mash the turnip carefully using a fork or masher. Mince the oregano and add it to the potatoes. Beat the egg into the mixture. Sprinkle it with the coconut flour, onion powder, nutmeg, and dill. Knead the dough. Pour the olive oil in the pressure cooker and preheat it on "Steam" mode.
2. Make medium-sized croquettes from the turnip mixture and put them in the pressure cooker. Cook the croquettes for 6 minutes on each side until golden brown. Remove the croquettes from the pressure cooker, drain them on the paper towel to remove any excess oil and serve.

NUTRITION: Calories 155, Fat 11.6, Fiber 6.8, Carbs 13.6, Protein 3.1

429. Parmesan Zucchini Balls

Preparation time: 10 minutes

Cooking time: 15 minutes

Servings: 6

INGREDIENTS

- 7 ounces Parmesan
- 2 zucchini
- 1 teaspoon salt
- 1 egg
- 1 teaspoon ground black pepper
- ½ cup coconut flour
- 3 tablespoons butter

- ¼ cup parsley

DIRECTIONS

1. Grate the zucchini, sprinkle it with the salt and ground black pepper, and mix well. Grate the Parmesan cheese. Beat the egg in the separate bowl and whisk it. Add the whisked egg in the zucchini mixture and add the cheese. Chop the parsley and add it to the zucchini mixture.
2. Add the coconut flour and knead the dough that forms. Make small balls from the zucchini mixture and place them on the trivet. Transfer the trivet with the zucchini balls into the pressure cooker. Cook at "Steam" mode for 15 minutes. When the zucchini balls are cooked, remove them from the pressure cooker and serve.

NUTRITION: Calories 185, Fat 13.9, Fiber 1.3, Carbs 4.5, Protein 12.7

430. Tomato Jam

Preparation time: 10 minutes

Cooking time: 20 minutes

Servings: 5

INGREDIENTS

- 10 ounces tomatoes
- 1 tablespoon fresh basil
- ½ teaspoon cinnamon
- ½ cup Erythritol
- ½ teaspoon ground ginger
- 1 tablespoons nutmeg
- 1 tablespoons butter
- 1 teaspoon anise

DIRECTIONS

1. Wash the tomatoes carefully and chop them. Combine the basil, cinnamon, Erythritol, ground ginger, nutmeg, and anise and mix well. Put the chopped tomatoes in the pressure cooker and add the spice mixture.

2. Add the butter and mix well. Cook the dish on the "Sauté" mode for 20 minutes. When the cooking time ends, open the pressure cooker lid and stir the jam. Transfer the jam to a serving dish and let it cool before serving.

NUTRITION: Calories 39, Fat 2.9, Fiber 1.1, Carbs 3.2, Protein 0.7

431. Jalapeno Crisps

Preparation time: 10 minutes

Cooking time: 5 minutes

Servings: 5

INGREDIENTS

- 5 jalapeno peppers, sliced
- 1/3 cup coconut flour
- 2 eggs, whisked
- 1 teaspoon salt
- 1 teaspoon olive oil

DIRECTIONS

1. In the mixing bowl, combine together whisked eggs and salt. Then add sliced jalapeno peppers and mix up.
2. After this, coat jalapeno slices in the coconut flour generously. Transfer the jalapeno slices in the cooker and sprinkle with olive oil. Close the lid and cook them on air crisp mode for 5 minutes (380F). Stir them well and cook for 2-3 extra minutes if jalapeno slices are not crispy enough.

NUTRITION: Calories 71, Fat 3.7, Fiber 3.8, Carbs 6.5, Protein 3.5

432. Sliced Mushrooms with Turmeric

Preparation time: 10 minutes

Cooking time: 7 minutes

Servings: 5

INGREDIENTS

- 1 tablespoon turmeric
- 1 pound cremini mushrooms
- 1 cup sour cream
- 1 onion
- 1 tablespoon paprika
- 3 tablespoons olive oil
- 1 teaspoon salt
- ½ teaspoon cayenne pepper

DIRECTIONS

1. Peel the onions and dice them. Pour the olive oil in the pressure cooker and add the onions. Set the pressure cooker to "Sauté" mode. Sauté the onion for 3 minutes, stirring frequently. Chop the mushrooms and combine them with the paprika, salt, and cayenne pepper and mix well.
2. Add the chopped cremini mixture in the pressure cooker and cook it for 2 minutes more. Add the sour cream and mix well. Add turmeric and stir again. Close the pressure cooker Cook at "Pressure" mode for 2 minutes. When the cooking time ends, release the pressure and open the pressure cooker. Transfer the cooked dish to a serving bowl.

NUTRITION: Calories 422, Fat 14.2, Fiber 12, Carbs 75.79, Protein 11

433. Veggie Chili

Preparation time: 15 minutes

Cooking time: 25 minutes

Servings: 12

INGREDIENTS

- 5 ounces rutabaga
- ¼ teaspoon cayenne pepper
- 1 teaspoon salt
- ½ teaspoon ground black pepper
- 8 ounces tomatoes
- 1 cup black beans, cooked
- 1 carrot

- 2 eggplants
- 1 teaspoon olive oil
- 1 teaspoon oregano
- 3 cup chicken stock

DIRECTIONS

1. Peel the rutabagas and dice them. Set the pressure cooker to "Sauté" mode. Pour the olive oil in the pressure cooker. Add the rutabaga and sauté it for 5 minutes. Meanwhile, chop the tomatoes and eggplants. Combine the cayenne pepper, salt, ground black pepper, and oregano in a mixing bowl.
2. Peel the carrot and grate it. Combine all the vegetables together and sprinkle them with the spice mixture. Mix well and place it in the pressure cooker. Add the chicken stock and black beans. Mix well and close the pressure cooker lid. Cook at "Sauté" mode for 20 minutes. When the cooking time ends, remove the dish from the pressure cooker. Rest briefly and serve.

NUTRITION: Calories 94, Fat 1, Fiber 6.4, Carbs 18, Protein 4.9

434. Vegetarian Shepherd's Pie
Preparation time: 15 minutes

Cooking time: 16 minutes

Servings: 7

INGREDIENTS

- 2 white onions
- 1 carrot
- 10 ounces cauliflower mash
- 3 ounces celery stalk
- 1 tablespoon salt
- 1 teaspoon paprika
- 1 teaspoon curry
- 1 tablespoon tomato paste
- 3 tablespoons olive oil

DIRECTIONS

1. Peel the carrot and grate it. Chop the celery stalk. Combine the vegetables together and mix well. Put the vegetable mixture in the pressure cooker.
2. Add the paprika, curry, tomato paste, olive oil, and salt. Mix well and stir well. Cook at "Pressure" mode for 6 minutes, stirring frequently. Spread the vegetable mixture with the cauliflower mash and close the pressure cooker lid. Cook the dish on the "Pressure" mode for 10 minutes. When the cooking time ends, release the pressure and open the pressure cooker lid. Transfer the pie to a serving plate, cut into slices and serve.

NUTRITION: Calories 107, Fat 9.3, Fiber 2.3, Carbs 6.2, Protein 1.6

435. Fresh Thyme Burgers
Preparation time: 10 minutes

Cooking time: 15 minutes

Servings: 8

INGREDIENTS

- 1 cup black soybeans, cooked
- 1 onion
- 1 carrot
- 1 cup fresh thyme
- ⅓ cup spinach
- ¼ cup coconut flour
- 1 egg
- 1 tablespoon salt
- 1 teaspoon ground black pepper
- 1 teaspoon Dijon mustard
- 3 tablespoons starch

DIRECTIONS

1. Wash the thyme and spinach and chop them. Place the thyme and spinach in the blender and add the lentils. Blend the mixture for 1 minute. Transfer the mixture to a mixing bowl. Sprinkle it with the

coconut flour, egg, salt, ground black pepper, Dijon mustard, and starch. Peel the onion and carrot and grate the vegetables.

2. Add all the vegetables to the thyme mixture and mix well. Make medium-sized "burgers" from the mixture. Place the burgers in the trivet and transfer the trivet in the pressure cooker. Cook at "Steam" mode for 15 minutes. When the burgers are cooked, let them rest briefly, and transfer them to a serving plate.

NUTRITION: Calories 155, Fat 5.8, Fiber 5.1, Carbs 17.2, Protein 10.1

436. Celery Fries

Preparation time: 10 minutes

Cooking time: 8 minutes

Servings: 2

INGREDIENTS

- 6 oz celery root, peeled
- 1 teaspoon white pepper
- Cooking spray

DIRECTIONS

1. Cut the celery root into fries and sprinkle them with the white pepper. Mix up well the vegetables and transfer in the Foodi cooker basket.
2. Spray the fries with the cooking spray gently and close the lid. Cook the fries at 385F on air crisp mode for 8 minutes. Stir the fries after 4 minutes of cooking.

NUTRITION: Calories 38, Fat 0.3, Fiber 1.8, Carbs 8.5, Protein 1.4

437. Cinnamon Pumpkin Puree

Preparation time: 10 minutes

Cooking time: 10 minutes

Servings: 5

INGREDIENTS

- 1 pound sweet pumpkin
- 2 cups of water
- 1 tablespoon butter
- 1 teaspoon Erythritol
- 1 teaspoon cinnamon
- ½ teaspoon ground black pepper
- ¼ teaspoon nutmeg

DIRECTIONS

1. Peel the pumpkin and chop it. Put the chopped pumpkin in the pressure cooker. Add the water and ground pepper. Close the pressure cooker lid Cook at "Pressure" mode for 10 minutes. Strain the pumpkin and place it in a food processor.
2. Add Erythritol, butter, cinnamon, and nutmeg. Blend the mixture until smooth. Transfer the pumpkin puree to serving bowls.

NUTRITION: Calories 233, Fat 8.7, Fiber 2, Carbs 38.28, Protein 3

438. Onions Soup

Preparation time: 10 minutes

Cooking time: 15 minutes

Servings: 14

INGREDIENTS

- 5 onions
- 1 cup cream
- 3 cups chicken stock
- 1 tablespoon salt
- 1 teaspoon olive oil
- 2 tablespoons butter
- ½ tablespoon ground black pepper

DIRECTIONS

1. Peel the onions and grate them. Place the onions in the pressure cooker. Add the

olive oil and sauté the onion for 5 minutes, stirring frequently.

2. Add the salt, chicken stock, cream, butter, and ground black pepper. Cook at "Pressure" mode for 10 minutes. When the soup is cooked, ladle it into serving bowls. Serve.

NUTRITION: Calories 47, Fat 3.1, Fiber 0.9, Carbs 4.5, Protein 0.8

439. Carrot Bites

Preparation time: 10 minutes

Cooking time: 5 minutes

Servings: 7

INGREDIENTS

- 5 carrots
- 1 cup coconut flour
- ⅓ cup whey
- 1 teaspoon baking soda
- 1 tablespoon lemon juice
- 1 teaspoon salt
- 1 teaspoon cilantro
- ½ teaspoon turmeric
- 1 tablespoon olive oil
- 1 teaspoon nutmeg

DIRECTIONS

1. Peel the carrots and grate them. Combine the grated carrot with the coconut flour, whey, baking soda, lemon juice, salt, cilantro, turmeric, and nutmeg. Knead the dough. Make a long log and cut it into small pieces. Set the pressure cooker to "Sauté" mode. Pour the olive oil in the pressure cooker.
2. Make small pieces from the carrot mixture and put them in the pressure cooker. Sauté the carrot bites for 5 minutes or until the carrot bites are golden brown on all sides. Transfer the carrot bites to the paper towel to drain the excess oil and let them rest before serving.

NUTRITION: Calories 115, Fat 4.5, Fiber 6.9, Carbs 15.5, Protein 3

440. Vegetable Risotto

Preparation time: 10 minutes

Cooking time: 26 minutes

Servings: 5

INGREDIENTS

- 4 ounces parsnips
- 1 cup cauliflower rice
- 1 teaspoon salt
- 3 cups chicken stock
- 1 tablespoon turmeric
- ½ cup green peas
- 1 teaspoon paprika
- 2 carrots
- 1 onion
- ½ teaspoon sour cream

DIRECTIONS

1. Chop the parsnip. Peel the onion and carrots. Chop the vegetables into the tiny pieces and combine them with the parsnip. Sprinkle the vegetable mixture with the salt, turmeric, paprika, and sour cream. Place the vegetable mixture in the pressure cooker and cook it at the "Pressure" mode for 6 minutes, stirring frequently.
2. Add the cauliflower rice, green peas, and chicken stock and mix well using a wooden spoon. Close the pressure cooker Cook at "Slow Cook" mode for 20 minutes. When the cooking time ends, open the pressure cooker lid and stir well. Transfer the dish to serving bowls.

NUTRITION: Calories 65, Fat 0.8, Fiber 3.9, Carbs 13.3, Protein 2.5

441. Bacon Brussel Sprouts Balls

Preparation time: 10 minutes

Cooking time: 10 minutes

Servings: 2

INGREDIENTS

- 1 cup Brussel Sprouts
- 1 teaspoon olive oil
- ½ teaspoon ground black pepper
- 5 oz bacon, sliced

DIRECTIONS

1. Mix up together sliced bacon with olive oil and ground black pepper. Then wrap every Brussel sprout in the bacon and transfer in the Foodi cooker basket. Secure the balls with toothpicks, if needed.
2. Close the lid and set air crisp mode. Cook the meal for 10 minutes at 375F. Stir the balls during cooking from time to time. Transfer the cooked balls in the serving bowls.

NUTRITION: Calories 424, Fat 32.1, Fiber 1.8, Carbs 5.4, Protein 27.8

442.   Asparagus Sauté

Preparation time: 15 minutes

Cooking time: 35 minutes

Servings: 4

INGREDIENTS

- 2 cups asparagus, chopped
- 2 garlic cloves, diced
- ½ cup heavy cream
- ½ cu of water
- 1 teaspoon butter
- 1 teaspoon ground turmeric
- 1 teaspoon salt

DIRECTIONS

1. Place asparagus in the cooker. Add diced garlic, butter, ground turmeric, salt, and heavy cream. Mix up the mixture until it gets an orange color.

2. Then add water and stir it gently again. Close the lid and set Saute mode. Cook the asparagus saute for 35 minutes. When the time is over, switch off the cooker and let asparagus rest for 15 minutes.

NUTRITION: Calories 78, Fat 6.7, Fiber 1.6, Carbs 3.9, Protein 1.9

443.   Ratatouille

Preparation time: 15 minutes

Cooking time: 25 minutes

Servings: 9

INGREDIENTS

- 2 green zucchini
- 2 eggplants
- 1 cup tomatoes
- 3 green bell peppers
- 4 garlic cloves
- 2 red onion
- 1 cup tomato juice
- 1 teaspoon olive oil
- 1 cup chicken stock
- 1 teaspoon ground black pepper

DIRECTIONS

1. Slice the zucchini and eggplants. Slice the tomatoes. Remove the seeds from the bell peppers and slice them. Peel the onions and garlic cloves. Chop the onions and garlic. Combine tomato juice, olive oil, chicken stock, and ground black pepper together in the mixing bowl.
2. Place the sliced vegetables to the pressure cooker. Sprinkle the mixture with the onion and garlic. Pour the tomato juice mixture and close the pressure cooker lid. Cook at "Steam" mode for 25 minutes. When the cooking time ends, remove the dish from the pressure cooker. Let it rest briefly and serve.

NUTRITION: Calories 82, Fat 1.4, Fiber 6, Carbs 16.53, Protein 4

444.   Pea Stew

Preparation time: 10 minutes

Cooking time: 35 minutes

Servings: 6

INGREDIENTS

- 2 cup green peas
- 1 tablespoon salt
- 4 cups chicken stock
- 1 carrot
- 1 tablespoon olive oil
- 7 ounces ground chicken
- ⅓ cup tomato juice
- ⅓ teaspoon cilantro

DIRECTIONS

1. Peel the carrot and chop it roughly. Put the chopped carrot in the pressure cooker and sprinkle it with the olive oil. Cook the carrot at the "Pressure" mode for 5 minutes. Add the green peas. Sprinkle the mixture with the salt, chicken stock, ground chicken, tomato juice, and cilantro and mix well. Close the pressure cooker lid Cook at "Sauté" mode for 30 minutes. When the stew is cooked, let it rest briefly. Transfer the cooked stew to serving bowls.

NUTRITION: Calories 171, Fat 7.4, Fiber 3, Carbs 13.72, Protein 13

445.   Curry Squash Saute

Preparation time: 10 minutes

Cooking time: 15 minutes

Servings: 6

INGREDIENTS

- 2 cups Kabocha squash, chopped
- 1 teaspoon ground cinnamon
- 1 teaspoon curry paste
- 1 teaspoon curry powder
- ½ teaspoon dried cilantro
- 1 cup of water
- 1 tablespoon pumpkin seeds, chopped
- 1 tablespoon butter
- ¾ cup heavy cream

DIRECTIONS

1. Place squash in the cooker and sprinkle it with ground cinnamon, curry powder, and dried cilantro. Add butter, water, and pumpkin seeds. After this, in the separated bowl, mix up together heavy cream with the curry paste. Pour the liquid in the cooker and mix up well.
2. Close and seal the lid. Cook the saute for 10 minutes onHigh-pressure mode. Then allow natural pressure release for 15 minutes. Open the lid and transfer kabocha squash and gravy in the serving bowls.

NUTRITION: Calories 97, Fat 8.7, Fiber 0.8, Carbs 4.5, Protein 1.2

446.   Leek Soup

Preparation time: 10 minutes

Cooking time: 19 minutes

Servings: 7

INGREDIENTS

- 10 ounces leek
- 2 garlic cloves
- 5 cups vegetable stock
- 1 teaspoon salt
- 1 yellow onion
- 1 tablespoon olive oil
- ⅓ cup sour cream
- 1 teaspoon oregano
- 4 ounces noodles
- 1 teaspoon butter
- 1 teaspoon ground white pepper

DIRECTIONS

1. Chop the leek. Peel the garlic cloves and slice them. Peel the onion and dice it. Combine the onion and garlic. Mix well and place it in the pressure cooker. Set the pressure cooker to "Sauté" mode.
2. Add butter and sauté for 7 minutes. Add chopped leek and pour the vegetable stock. Sprinkle the soup mixture with the salt, ground white pepper, oregano, and cream.
3. Close the pressure cooker lid Cook at «Sauté» mode for 10 minutes. Open the pressure cooker lid and add the noodles. Mix the soup well and close the pressure cooker lid.
4. Cook at "Pressure" mode for 2 minutes. Release the pressure and open the pressure cooker lid. Stir the soup well, then ladle the soup into serving bowls.

NUTRITION: Calories 155, Fat 5.9, Fiber 1, Carbs 19.47, Protein 6

447.　Veggie Aromatic Stew

Preparation time: 15 minutes

Cooking time: 20 minutes

Servings: 7

INGREDIENTS

- 2 carrots
- 1 zucchini
- 8 ounces broccoli
- 4 ounces cauliflower
- 4 cups chicken stock
- ¼ cup tomato paste
- 1 teaspoon sugar
- ½ tablespoon salt
- ⅓ cup parsley
- 1 tablespoon butter
- 2 onions
- 1 teaspoon oregano

DIRECTIONS

1. Wash the broccoli and cut it into florets. Chop the zucchini and carrots. Place the vegetables in the pressure cooker.
2. Add the chicken stock and tomato paste. Sprinkle the mixture with the sugar, salt, butter, and oregano. Mix well and close the pressure cooker lid. Cook at "Sauté" mode for 10 minutes.
3. Peel the onions and chop them roughly. When the cooking time ends, open the pressure cooker lid and add the onions. Chop the parsley and add it to the stew mixture.
4. Add butter and mix well. Close the pressure cooker lid Cook at "Pressure" mode for 10 minutes. When the stew is cooked, release the pressure and open the lid. Mix the stew carefully. Add the stew to serving bowls.

NUTRITION: Calories 71, Fat 2.3, Fiber 3.2, Carbs 11.7, Protein 3

BEEF BITES

Preparation Time: 20 minutes

Servings: 8

INGREDIENTS

- 1 lb. beef meat, ground
- 1 egg; whisked.
- 1 yellow onion; chopped.
- 3 tbsp. breadcrumbs
- ½ tsp. garlic; minced.
- Cooking spray
- Salt and black pepper to the taste

DIRECTIONS

1. In a bowl mix all the Ingredients except the cooking spray, stir well and shape medium meatballs out of this mix
2. Put the meatballs in the Air Crisp basket, grease them with cooking spray, put the basket in the Foodi, set the machine on Air Crisp and cook the meatballs at 390 °F for 15 minutes. Serve the meatballs as an appetizer.

448. Beef Chili & Cornbread Casserole

Preparation Time: 60 minutes

Servings: 8

INGREDIENTS

- 2 lb. uncooked ground beef
- 3 cans 14-ounces each kidney beans, rinsed, drained
- 1 can 28-ounces crushed tomatoes
- 1 cup beef stock
- 1 large white onion, peeled, diced
- 1 green bell pepper, diced
- 1 jalapeño pepper, diced, seeds removed
- 4 cloves garlic, peeled, minced
- 2 tbsp. kosher salt
- 1 tbsp. ground black pepper
- 2 tbsp. ground cumin
- 1 tbsp. onion powder

- 1 tbsp. garlic powder
- 2 cups Cheddar Corn Bread batter, uncooked
- 1 cup shredded Mexican cheese blend
- Sour cream, for serving

DIRECTIONS

1. Place beef, beans, tomatoes, and stock into the pot, breaking apart meat. Assemble pressure lid, making sure the PRESSURE RELEASE valve is in the SEAL position. Select PRESSURE and set to HIGH. Set time to 15 minutes. Select START/STOP to begin.
2. When pressure cooking is complete, quick release the pressure by moving the PRESSURE RELEASE valve to the VENT position. Carefully remove lid when unit has finished releasing pressure
3. Select SEAR/SAUTÉ. Set temperature to MD, Select START/STOP. Add onion, green bell pepper, jalapeño pepper, garlic, and spices; stir to incorporate. Bring to a simmer and cook for 5 minutes, stirring occasionally.
4. Dollop corn bread batter evenly over the top of the chili. Close crisping lid. Select BAKE/ROAST, set temperature to 360°F, and set time to 26 minutes. Select START/STOP to begin.
5. After 15 minutes, open lid and insert a wooden toothpick into the center of the corn bread. If corn bread is not done, close lid to resume cooking for another 8 minutes
6. When corn bread is done, sprinkle it with cheese and close lid to resume cooking for 3 minutes, or until cheese is melted. When cooking is complete, top with sour cream and serve

449. Beef Soup

Preparation Time: 40 minutes

Servings: 6

INGREDIENTS

- 2 and ½ lbs. beef stew meat; cubed.
- 15 oz. canned tomatoes; chopped.
- 1 yellow onion; chopped.
- 4 carrots; chopped.
- 4 celery stalks; chopped.
- 6 cups beef stock
- 1 cup pearl barley
- 1 tsp. oregano, dried
- 1 tbsp. olive oil
- 2 tbsp. tomato paste
- A pinch of salt and black pepper

DIRECTIONS

1. Set the Foodi on sauté mode, add the oil, heat it up, add the beef, brown it for 5 minutes and transfer to a plate. Add the onion, celery, carrots, oregano, salt and pepper to the machine, stir and cook for another 5 minutes
2. Add the tomatoes, tomato paste, the barley, the stock and the beef, put the pressure lid on and cook on High for 25 minutes. Release the pressure naturally for 10 minutes, divide the soup into bowls and serve

450. Classic Brisket with Veggies

Preparation Time: 1 hour 20 minutes

Servings: 4 to 6

INGREDIENTS

- 2 lb. or larger regular brisket, rinsed and patted dry
- 2 ½ cup homemade beef broth or make from Knorr Beef Base
- 2 tbsp. olive oil
- 5 or 6 red potatoes
- 2 cup large chunks carrots
- 3 tbsp. Worcestershire Sauce
- 4 bay leaves
- Granulated garlic
- Knorr Demi-Glace sauce
- 1/2 cup dehydrated onion

- 2 stalks celery in 1 chunks
- Fresh ground black pepper
- 3 tbsp. heaping chopped garlic
- 1 large yellow onion
- 5 or 6 red potatoes

DIRECTIONS

1. Put the Ninja Foodi Multi-cooker on the sauté setting. Put in 1 tbsp. more if needed of the oil and caramelize the onions. Once golden, remove from pot, put in a bowl and set aside. But keep the Ninja Foodi Multi-cooker on the *Sauté* setting.
2. Rub the freshly ground pepper on both sides of the brisket. Do the same with the granulated garlic. Add 1 tbsp. olive oil or more and only lightly sear the brisket on all sides
3. Add back the onions, garlic, Worcestershire sauce, bay leaves, dehydrated onion and beef broth
4. High pressure for 50 minutes. Close the lid and the pressure valve and then cook for 50 minutes
5. To get 50 minutes' cook time, press *Pressure* button and use the Time Adjustment button to adjust the cook time to 50 minutes
6. While the meat is cooking, peel and cut up all the veggies. When the meat is done, use the quick pressure release feature and then remove the lid. Add all of the veggies, replace the lid and cook at high pressure for to 10 minutes.
7. To get 10 minutes' cook time, press *Steam* button
8. Pressure Release. When the time is up, turn the pot off, use the quick release again and remove the lid.
9. Finish the dish. Close crisping lid. Select ""BROIL"" and set time to 8 minutes. Check after 5 minutes, cooking for an additional 3 minutes if dish needs more browning
10. Use a platter to remove the veggies and meat. Use the *Sauté* setting and bring the broth to a boil, then add the Knorr Demi-Glace mixing with a Wisk
11. Adjust seasonings as needed. Serve with Cole Slaw or other salad, homemade rolls

or Italian garlic bread. Be sure to remove the bay leaves before serving. Serve and Enjoy

451. Mouthwatering Beef Stew

Preparation Time: 25 minutes

Servings: 4

INGREDIENTS

- 1 ½ lb. lean ground beef about 93% lean
- 1 large sweet potato about 1 lb., peeled and shredded through the large holes of a box grater
- 1 tbsp. olive oil
- 1 large yellow onion, chopped.
- 1 tsp. ground cinnamon
- 1 tsp. ground cumin
- 1/2 tsp. dried sage
- 1/2 tsp. dried oregano
- 2 ½ cups beef broth
- 2 tbsp. yellow cornmeal
- 2 tbsp. honey
- 1/2 tsp. salt
- 1/2 tsp. ground black pepper

DIRECTIONS

1. Heat the oil in the Ninja Foodi Multi-cooker turned to the Sauté function. Crumble in the ground beef; cook, stirring occasionally, until it loses its raw color and browns a bit, about 5 minutes
2. Add the onion; cook, often stirring, until softened, about 3 minutes
3. Stir in the sweet potato, cinnamon, cumin, sage, oregano, salt and pepper.
4. Cook for 1 minute, stirring constantly. Stir in the cornmeal and honey; cook for 1 minute, often stirring, to dissolve the cornmeal. Stir in the broth
5. High pressure for 5 minutes. Lock the lid on the Ninja Foodi Multi-cooker and then cook for 5 minutes.
6. To get 5 minutes' cook time, press *Pressure* button and use the Time Adjustment button to adjust the cook time to 5 minutes.

7. Pressure Release. Use the quick release method to drop the pot's pressure to normal.
8. Finish the dish. Remove the lid from the Ninja Foodi Multi-cooker. Close crisping lid. Select *Air Crisp*, set temperature to 390°F and set time to 20 minutes
9. Check after 15 minutes, cooking for an additional 15 minutes if dish needs more browning. Stir well and set aside, loosely covered, for 5 minutes before serving

452. Delightful Lamb Shanks with Pancetta

Preparation Time: 1 hour 15 minutes

Servings: 4

INGREDIENTS

- 1 28-ounce can diced tomatoes, drained about 3 ½ cups
- 4 12-ounce lamb shanks
- 1 6-ounce pancetta chunk, chopped.
- 2 cups dry, light white wine, such as Sauvignon Blanc
- 1-ounce dried mushrooms, preferably porcini, crumbled
- 2 tbsp. olive oil
- 1 small yellow onion, chopped.
- 3 tbsp. packed celery leaves, minced
- 2 tbsp. minced chives
- 2 tbsp. all-purpose flour
- 1/2 tsp. ground black pepper

DIRECTIONS

1. Heat the oil in the Ninja Foodi Multi-cooker, turned to the *Sauté* function. Add the pancetta and brown well, about 6 minutes, stirring often. Use a slotted spoon to transfer the pancetta to a large bowl
2. Add two of the shanks to the cooker; brown on all sides, turning occasionally, about 8 minutes. Transfer them to the bowl and repeat with the remaining shanks.
3. Add the onion to the pot; cook, often stirring, until softened, about 4 minutes.

Stir in the tomatoes, dried mushroom crumbles, celery leaves and chives. Cook until bubbling, about minutes, stirring often

4. Whisk the wine, flour and pepper in a medium bowl until the flour dissolves; stir this mixture into the sauce in the pot. Cook until thickened and bubbling, about 1 minute

5. Return the shanks, pancetta and their juices to the cooker.

6. High pressure for 60 minutes. Close the lid and the pressure valve and then cook for 60 minutes

7. To get 60 minutes' cook time, press *Pressure* button and use the Time Adjustment button to adjust the cook time to 60 minutes

8. Turn off the Ninja Foodi Multi-cooker or unplug it, so it doesn't jump to its keep-warm setting

9. Pressure Release. Let its pressure return to normal naturally, 20 to 30 minutes

10. Finish the dish. Remove the lid from the Ninja Foodi Multi-cooker. Close crisping lid. Select *Air Crisp*, set temperature to 375°F and set time to 18 minutes. Check after 10 minutes, cooking for an additional 8 minutes if dish needs more browning.

11. Transfer a shank to each serving bowl. Skim any surface fat from the sauce with a flatware spoon. Ladle the sauce and vegetables over the lamb shanks

12. Pork Recipes

453. Delicious Braised Pork Neck Bones

Preparation Time: 40 minutes

Servings: 6

INGREDIENTS

- 3 lb Pork Neck Bones
- 4 tbsp. Olive Oil
- 1 White Onion, sliced
- 1/2 cup Red Wine
- 2 cloves Garlic, smashed
- 1 tbsp. Tomato Paste
- 1 tsp. dried Thyme
- 1 cup Beef Broth

- Salt and Black Pepper to taste

DIRECTIONS

1. Open the lid and select Sear/Sauté mode. Warm the olive oil

2. Meanwhile season the pork neck bones with salt and pepper. After, place them in the oil to brown on all sides. Work in batches.

3. Each batch should cook in about 5 minutes. Then, remove them onto a plate.

4. Add the onion and season with salt to taste. Stir with a spoon and cook the onions until soft, for a few minutes. Then, add garlic, thyme, pepper, and tomato paste. Cook them for 2 minutes, constant stirring to prevent the tomato paste from burning

5. Next, pour the red wine into the pot to deglaze the bottom. Add the pork neck bones back to the pot and pour the beef broth over it

6. Close the lid, secure the pressure valve, and select Pressure mode on High pressure for 10 minutes. Press Start/Stop to start cooking.

7. Once the timer has ended, let the pot sit for 10 minutes before doing a quick pressure release. Close the crisping lid and cook on Broil mode for 5 minutes, until nice and tender.

8. Dish the pork neck into a serving bowl and serve with the red wine sauce spooned over and a right amount of broccoli mash .

454. Oregano Meatballs

Preparation Time: 30 minutes

Servings: 6

INGREDIENTS

- 1 lb. pork meat; minced.
- 1 cup tomato puree
- ½ tbsp. lime peel; grated.
- 1 tbsp. oregano; chopped.
- 1 tbsp. bread crumbs
- 2 tbsp. parmesan; grated.
- Salt and black pepper to the taste

DIRECTIONS

1. In a bowl mix all the Ingredients except the tomato puree, stir well and shape medium meatballs out of this mix. Set the Foodi on Sauté mode, add the meatballs and brown them for 3 minutes
2. Add the tomato puree, toss a bit, put the pressure lid on and cook on High for 15 minutes. Release the pressure naturally for 10 minutes, divide the meatballs into bowls and serve as an appetizer

455.   Paprika Pork Chops

Preparation Time: 25 minutes

Servings: 6

INGREDIENTS

- 4 medium pork chops
- 2 garlic cloves; minced.
- ¼ cup olive oil
- 1 tbsp. sweet paprika
- Salt and black pepper to the taste

DIRECTIONS

1. In a bowl mix the all the Ingredients and toss. Put the pork chops in the Foodi's basket, set the machine on Air Crisp and cook at 400 °F for 15 minutes. Divide the chops between plates and serve.

456.   Pork Shoulder Chops with Carrots

Preparation Time: 52 minutes

Servings: 4 to 6

INGREDIENTS

- 3 lb. bone in pork shoulder chops, each 1/2 to 3/4 inch thick
- 6 medium carrots
- 1/3 cup maple syrup
- 1/3 cup chicken broth
- 3 medium garlic cloves
- 1 tbsp. bacon fat
- 1/3 cup soy sauce
- 1/2 tsp. ground black pepper

DIRECTIONS

1. Melt the bacon fat in a Ninja Foodi Multi-cooker, turned to the browning function. Add about half the chops and brown well, turning once, about 5 minutes. Transfer these to a large bowl and brown the remaining chops
2. Stir the carrots and garlic into the pot; cook for 1 minute, constantly stirring. Pour in the soy sauce, maple syrup and broth, stirring to dissolve the maple syrup and to get up any browned bits on the bottom of the pot. Stir in the pepper. Return the shoulder chops and their juices to the pot. Stir to coat them in the sauce
3. High pressure for 40 minutes. Lock the lid on the Ninja Foodi Multi-cooker and then cook for 40 minutes
4. To get 40 minutes' cook time, press *Pressure* button and use the Time Adjustment button to adjust the cook time to 40 minutes.
5. Pressure Release. Let the pressure to come down naturally for at least 14 to 16 minutes, then quick release any pressure left in the pot
6. Finish the dish. Close crisping lid and select Broil, set time to 7 minutes.
7. Transfer the chops, carrots and garlic cloves to a large serving bowl. Skim the fat off the sauce and ladle it over the.

457.   Cinnamon Pork

Preparation Time: 30 minutes

Servings: 4

INGREDIENTS

- 1 lb. pork stew meat; cubed.
- 1 yellow onion; chopped.
- 1 garlic clove; minced.
- 2 tbsp. olive oil
- 3 tbsp. parsley; chopped.
- 1 tsp. cinnamon powder

- Salt and black pepper to the taste

DIRECTIONS

1. Set the Foodi on Sauté mode, add the oil and heat it up. Add the onion, stir and sauté for 5 minutes. Add the meat, garlic, cinnamon, salt and pepper, toss and sauté for 4-5 minutes more
2. Add the parsley, put the pressure lid on and cook on High for 12 minutes more. Release pre pressure naturally for 10 minutes, divide everything into bowls and serve

458. Chinese Pork

Preparation Time: 90 minutes

Servings: 8

INGREDIENTS

- 3 lbs. pork shoulder roast
- 4 garlic cloves; minced.
- ¼ cup ketchup
- ¼ cup soy sauce
- ½ cup chicken stock
- ½ cup hoisin sauce
- ½ cup honey
- 1 tsp. Chinese five spice powder
- 4 tsp. ginger; grated.

DIRECTIONS

1. Combine all the Ingredients in the Foodi machine, put the pressure lid on and cook on High for 1 hour and 20 minutes. Release the pressure naturally for 10 minutes, divide everything between plates and serve

459. Honey Mustard Pork Tenderloin Recipe

Preparation Time: 30 minutes

Servings: 4

INGREDIENTS

- 2 lb Pork Tenderloin

- 1 tbsp. Worcestershire Sauce
- 1/2 tbsp. Cornstarch
- 1/2 cup Chicken Broth
- 1/4 cup Balsamic Vinegar
- 1 clove Garlic, minced
- 2 tbsp. Olive Oil
- 1/4 cup Honey
- 1 tsp. Sage Powder
- 1 tbsp. Dijon Mustard
- 4 tbsp. Water
- Salt and Black Pepper to taste

DIRECTIONS

1. Put the pork on a clean flat surface and pat dry using paper towels. Season with salt and pepper. Select Sear/Sauté mode.
2. Heat the oil and brown the pork on both sides, for about 4 minutes in total. Remove the pork onto a plate and set aside
3. Add in honey, chicken broth, balsamic vinegar, garlic, Worcestershire sauce, mustard, and sage. Stir the Ingredients and return the pork to the pot
4. Close the lid, secure the pressure valve, and select Pressure mode on High for 15 minutes. Once the timer has ended, do a quick pressure release. Remove the pork with tongs onto a plate and wrap it in aluminum foil
5. Next, mix the cornstarch with water and pour it into the pot. Select Sear/Sauté mode, stir the mixture and cook until it thickens. Then, turn the pot off after the desired thickness is achieved.
6. Unwrap the pork and use a knife to slice it with 3 to 4-inch thickness. Arrange the slices on a serving platter and spoon the sauce all over it. Serve with a syrupy sautéed Brussels sprouts and red onion chunks

460. BBQ Pork with Ginger Coconut and Sweet Potatoes

Preparation Time: 35 minutes

Servings: 4

INGREDIENTS

- 4 frozen uncooked boneless pork chops 8-ounces each
- 3 sweet potatoes, peeled, cut in 1-inch cubes
- 1/2 cup unsweetened coconut milk
- 1 tsp. Chinese five spice powder
- 1/2 stick 1/4 cup butter
- 1 tbsp. fresh ginger, peeled, minced
- 1/4 cup hoisin sauce
- 1/3 cup honey
- 1 ½ tbsp. soy sauce
- 1 tsp. kosher salt
- 1/2 tsp. white pepper

DIRECTIONS

1. Place potatoes and coconut milk into the pot. Place reversible rack inside pot over potatoes, making sure rack is in the higher position.
2. Place pork chops on rack. Assemble pressure lid, making sure the PRESSURE RELEASE valve is in the SEAL position. Select PRESSURE and set to HIGH. Set time to 4 minutes. Select START/STOP to begin.
3. While pork chops and potatoes are cooking, whisk together hoisin sauce, honey, soy sauce, and Chinese five spice powder.
4. When pressure cooking is complete, quick release the pressure by moving the PRESSURE RELEASE valve to the VENT position. Carefully remove lid when unit has finished releasing pressure
5. Remove rack with pork from pot. Mash sweet potatoes with butter, ginger, and salt, using a mashing utensil that won't scratch the nonstick surface of the pot
6. Place rack with pork back in pot and brush top of pork generously with 1/2 of sauce mixture.
7. Close crisping lid. Select BROIL and set time to 15 minutes. Select START/STOP to begin. After 5 minutes, open lid, flip pork chops, then brush them with remaining sauce.
8. Close lid to resume cooking. Check after 10 minutes and remove if desired doneness is achieved. If not, cook up to 5 more

minutes, checking frequently. When cooking is complete, remove pork from rack and allow to rest for 5 minutes before serving with mashed potatoes

461. Special Biscuits

Preparation Time: 40 minutes

Servings: 6

INGREDIENTS

- 12 oz. pork sausage, crumbled
- 16 oz. biscuit dough
- ½ cup cheddar cheese, shredded
- 3 cups milk
- ¼ cup white flour
- 2 tbsp. butter
- A pinch of salt and black pepper

DIRECTIONS

1. Set the Foodi on Sauté mode, heat it up, add the sausage, salt and pepper, stir and cook for 5 minutes. Add the butter and the flour, whisk well and cook for 7 minutes.
2. Meanwhile, separate each biscuit and fill each with the cheese. Put the reversible rack in the Foodi, place the biscuits in on the rack and lower it into the gravy
3. Set the machine on Baking mode and cook the biscuits at 325 °F for 15 minutes. Divide the biscuits between plates, drizzle the gravy all over and serve as a side

462. Pork Loin and Apples

Preparation Time: 43 minutes

Servings: 8

INGREDIENTS

- 1 3 lb. boneless pork loin roast
- 1 large red onion, halved and thinly sliced
- 2 medium tart green apples, such as Granny Smith, peeled, cored and thinly sliced

- 1/2 cup moderately sweet white wine, such as Riesling
- 2 tbsp. unsalted butter
- 1/4 cup chicken broth
- 4 fresh thyme sprigs
- 2 bay leaves
- 1/2 tsp. salt
- 1/2 tsp. ground black pepper

DIRECTIONS

1. Melt the butter in the Ninja Foodi Multi-cooker, set on the *Sauté* function. Add the pork loin and brown it on all sides, turning occasionally, about 8 minutes in all. Transfer to a large plate.
2. Add the onion to the pot; cook, often stirring, until softened, about 3 minutes. Stir in the apple, thyme and bay leaves. Pour in the wine and scrape up any browned bits on the bottom of the pot
3. Pour in the broth; stir in the salt and pepper. Nestle the pork loin into this apple mixture; pour any juices from the plate into the pot.
4. High pressure for 30 minutes. Lock the lid on the Ninja Foodi Multi-cooker and then cook for 30 minutes.
5. To get 30 minutes' cook time, press *Pressure* button and adjust the time
6. Pressure Release. Use the quick release method to bring the pot's pressure to normal
7. Finish the dish. Close crisping lid and select Broil, set time to 7 minutes.
8. Transfer the pork to a cutting board; let stand for 5 minutes while you dish the sauce into serving bowls or onto a serving platter. Slice the loin into 1/2-inch-thick rounds and lay these over the sauce.

463.   Pork Meatballs

Preparation Time: 25 minutes

Servings: 12

INGREDIENTS

- 1 lb. pork meat, ground

- 2 garlic cloves; minced.
- ½ cup bread crumbs
- 2 cups sweet and sour sauce
- ½ cup pineapple; chopped.
- 1 cup scallions; chopped.
- 1 egg; whisked.
- 1 tbsp. ginger; grated.
- 1 tbsp. mustard
- 2 tbsp. soy sauce
- 1 tsp. coriander, ground
- Juice of 1 lime

DIRECTIONS

1. In a bowl combine all the Ingredients except the sauce, stir well and shape medium meatballs out of this mix
2. Put the meatballs in your Foodi, add the sweet and sour sauce, toss gently, put the pressure lid on and cook the meatballs on High for 15 minutes. Release the pressure naturally for 10 minutes, divide the meatballs into bowls and serve

464.   Simple Spare Ribs with Wine

Preparation Time: 30 minutes

Servings: 4

INGREDIENTS

- 1 lb. pork spare ribs, cut into pieces
- 1 tbsp. corn starch
- 1 tbsp. oil
- 1 – 2 tsp. water
- Green onions as garnish
- 1 tsp. fish sauce optional
- Black Bean Marinade:
- 3 cloves garlic, minced
- 1 tsp. sesame oil
- 1 tsp. sugar
- 1 tbsp. Shaoxing wine
- 1 tbsp. ginger, grated
- 1 tbsp. black bean sauce
- 1 tbsp. light soy sauce
- A pinch of white pepper

DIRECTIONS

1. Marinate the pork spare ribs with Black Bean Marinade in an oven-safe bowl. Then, sit it in the fridge for 25 minutes.
2. First, mix 1 tbsp. of oil into the marinated spare ribs. Then, add 1 tbsp. of cornstarch and mix well. Finally, add 1 – 2 tsp. of water into the spare ribs and mix well
3. Add 1 cup of water into the Ninja Foodi Multi-cooker. Place steam rack in the Ninja Foodi Multi-cooker. Then, put the bowl of spare ribs on the rack
4. High pressure for 15 minutes. Lock the lid on the Ninja Foodi Multi-cooker and then cook for 15 minutes.
5. To get 15 minutes' cook time, press *Pressure* Button and then adjust the time
6. Pressure Release. Let the pressure to come down naturally for at least 15 minutes, then quick release any pressure left in the pot.
7. Finish the dish. Close crisping lid. Select *Air Crisp*, set temperature to 375°F and set time to 10 minutes. Check after 5 minutes, cooking for an additional 5 minutes if dish needs more browning
8. Taste and add one tsp. of fish sauce and green onions as garnish if you like. Serve immediately.

465. Yummy Pork Chops

Preparation Time: 35 minutes

Servings: 6

INGREDIENTS

- 1 lb. pork chops
- 3 cups chicken stock
- 1 garlic clove; minced.
- 1 ½ cups heavy cream
- 2 yellow onions; chopped.
- 1 tbsp. olive oil
- 2 tbsp. sweet paprika
- 2 tbsp. dill; chopped.
- Salt and black pepper to the taste

DIRECTIONS

1. Put the pork chops in your Foodi's basket, season with salt, pepper, garlic and the paprika, rub, set the machine on Air Crisp and cook at 380 °F for 10 minutes. Transfer the pork chops to the Foodi's baking pan, add all the other Ingredients and toss
2. Place the baking pan in the machine, set it on Baking mode and cook at 370 °F for 15 minutes more. Divide everything between plates and serve hot

466. Delicious Pulled Pork Sandwiches

Preparation Time: 60 minutes

Servings: 8

INGREDIENTS

- 2 ½ – 3 lb. uncooked boneless pork shoulder, cut in 1-inch cubes
- 1 can 6-ounces tomato paste
- 2 tbsp. barbecue seasoning
- 1 cup apple cider vinegar
- 1 tbsp. garlic powder
- 2 tsp. kosher salt
- Coleslaw and Potato rolls for

DIRECTIONS

1. Add pork, spices, and vinegar to the pot. Assemble pressure lid, making sure the pressure release valve is in the SEAL position. Select PRESSURE and set to HIGH. Set time to 35 minutes. Select START/STOP to begin
2. When pressure cooking is complete, quick release the pressure by turning the pressure release valve to VENT position. Carefully remove lid when unit has finished releasing pressure.
3. Select SEAR/SAUTÉ and set to MEDIUM-HIGH. Select START/STOP to begin
4. Add tomato paste and stir to incorporate. Allow pork to simmer for 10 minutes, or until the liquid has reduced by half, as shown above, stirring occasionally with a

wooden spoon or silicone tongs to shred the pork.

5. Serve pulled pork on potato rolls topped with coleslaw.

467. Garlic Pork Chops

Preparation Time: 30 minutes

Servings: 4

INGREDIENTS

- 4 pork chops
- 4 garlic cloves; minced.
- 2 tbsp. rosemary; chopped.
- 2 tbsp. olive oil
- Salt and black pepper to the taste

DIRECTIONS

1. In a bowl mix all the Ingredients and toss them well. Put the reversible rack in the Foodi and add the basket inside
2. Add the pork chops to the basket, set the machine on Air Crisp and cook at 400 °F for 20 minutes. Serve with a side salad.

468. Buttery Pork Steaks

Preparation Time: 24 minutes

Servings: 4

INGREDIENTS

- 4 pork steaks
- 2 tbsp. butter, melted
- 1 tbsp. smoked paprika
- Salt and black pepper to the taste

DIRECTIONS

1. In a bowl mix all the Ingredients and toss them. Put the steaks in the Foodi's basket, set the machine on Air Crisp and cook at 390 °F for 7 minutes on each side. Divide the steaks between plates and serve

469. Garlic Pork

Preparation Time: 35 minutes

Servings: 4

INGREDIENTS

- 1 ½ lbs. pork stew meat; cubed.
- 1 tbsp. smoked paprika
- 3 tbsp. olive oil
- 3 tbsp. garlic; minced.
- Salt and black pepper to the taste

DIRECTIONS

1. In the Foodi's baking pan, combine all the Ingredients and toss. Put the reversible rack in the machine, add the baking pan inside, set the pot on Roast mode and cook at 390 °F for 25 minutes.
2. Divide everything between plates and serve with a side salad

470. Pork Chops

Preparation Time: 25 minutes

Servings: 4

INGREDIENTS

- 2 lbs. pork chops, boneless
- 1 green cabbage head, shredded
- 2 cups chicken stock
- A pinch of salt and black pepper
- 2 tbsp. butter, melted

DIRECTIONS

1. Put all the Ingredients in the Foodi machine, put the pressure lid on and cook on High for 15 minutes. Release the pressure naturally for 10 minutes, divide everything between plates and serve

471. Rosemary Sausage and Onion

Preparation Time: 35 minutes

Servings: 4

INGREDIENTS

- 6 pork sausage links, halved
- 2 yellow onion, sliced
- 2 garlic cloves; minced.
- 1 tbsp. rosemary; chopped.
- 1 tbsp. olive oil
- 1 tbsp. sweet paprika
- Salt and black pepper to the taste

DIRECTIONS

1. In your Foodi's baking pan, combine all the Ingredients and toss. Put the reversible rack in the Foodi, add the baking pan, set the machine on Baking mode and cook at 370 °F for 25 minutes. Divide between plates and serve

472. Pork Carnitas

Preparation Time: 55 minutes

Servings: 4

INGREDIENTS

- 2 lbs. pork butt; cubed.
- 1 yellow onion; chopped.
- 6 garlic cloves; minced.
- ½ cup chicken stock
- Juice of 1 orange
- A pinch of salt and black pepper
- ½ tsp. oregano, dried
- ½ tsp. cumin, ground

DIRECTIONS

1. Put all the Ingredients in the Ninja Foodi machine, put the pressure lid on and cook on High for 20 minutes.
2. Release the pressure fast for 4 minutes, set the machine on Sauté mode and cook everything for 15 minutes more. Set the Foodi on Broil mode, cook everything for 8 more minutes. Divide everything into bowls and serve

473. Ninja Pulled Pork

Preparation Time: 1 hour 33 minutes

Servings: 10

INGREDIENTS

- 1 4- to 4½ lb. bone in skinless pork shoulder, preferably pork butt
- Up to 1 ½ cups light-colored beer, preferably a pale ale or amber lager
- 1/2 tsp. garlic powder
- 1/2 tsp. ground cloves
- 1/2 tsp. ground cinnamon
- 2 tbsp. smoked paprika
- 2 tbsp. packed dark brown sugar
- 1 tbsp. ground cumin
- 1/2 tbsp. dry mustard
- 1 tsp. ground coriander
- 1 tsp. dried thyme
- 1 tsp. onion powder
- 1 tsp. salt
- 2 tsp. ground black pepper

DIRECTIONS

1. Mix the smoked paprika, brown sugar, cumin, pepper, mustard, coriander, thyme, onion powder, salt, garlic powder, cloves and cinnamon in a small bowl. Massage the mixture all over the pork.
2. Set the pork in the Ninja Foodi Multi-cooker. Pour 1cup beer into the electric cooker without knocking the spices off the meat
3. High pressure for 80 minutes. Lock the lid on the Ninja Foodi Multi-cooker and then cook for 80 minutes.
4. To get 80 minutes' cook time, press *Pressure* button and use the Time Adjustment button to adjust the cook time to 80 minutes.
5. Pressure Release. Let its pressure fall to normal naturally, 25 to 35 minutes
6. Finish the dish. Close crisping lid and select Broil, set time to 7 minutes
7. Transfer the meat to a large cutting board. Let stand for 5 minutes. Use a spoon to

skim as much fat off the sauce in the pot as possible

8. Set the *Sauté* function. Bring the sauce to a simmer, stirring occasionally; continue boiling the sauce, often stirring, until reduced by half, 7 to 10 minutes.

9. Use two forks to shred the meat off the bones; discard the bones and any attached cartilage. Pull any large chunks of meat apart with the forks and stir the meat back into the simmering sauce to reheat. Serve and Enjoy!

474. Amazing Pork Chops with Applesauce

Preparation Time: 30 minutes

Servings: 4

INGREDIENTS

- 2 to 4 pork loin chops we used center cut, bone-on
- 2 gala apples, thinly sliced
- 1 tsp. cinnamon powder
- 1 tbsp. honey
- 1/2 cup unsalted homemade chicken stock or water
- 1 tbsp. grapeseed oil or olive oil
- 1 small onion, sliced
- 3 cloves garlic, roughly minced
- 2 tbsp. light soy sauce
- 1 tbsp. butter
- Kosher salt and ground black pepper to taste
- 2 pieces whole cloves optional
- 1 ½ tbsp. cornstarch mixed with 2 tbsp. water optional

DIRECTIONS

1. Make a few small cut around the sides of the pork chops so they will stay flat and brown evenly
2. Season the pork chops with a generous amount of kosher salt and ground black pepper.

3. Heat up your Ninja Foodi Multi-cooker. Add grapeseed oil into the pot. Add the seasoned pork chops into the pot, then let it brown for roughly 2 – 3 minutes on each side. Remove and set aside.
4. Add the sliced onions and stir. Add a pinch of kosher salt and ground black pepper to season if you like. Cook the onions for roughly 1 minute until softened. Then, add garlic and stir for 30 seconds until fragrance
5. Add in the thinly sliced gala apples, whole cloves optional and cinnamon powder, then give it a quick stir. Add the honey and partially deglaze the bottom of the pot with a wooden spoon
6. Add chicken stock and light soy sauce, then fully deglaze the bottom of the pot with a wooden spoon. Taste the seasoning and add more salt and pepper if desired
7. Place the pork chops back with all the meat juice into the pot
8. High pressure for 10 minutes. Lock the lid on the Ninja Foodi Multi-cooker and then cook for 10 minutes.
9. To get 10 minutes' cook time, press *Pressure* button and use the Time Adjustment button to adjust the cook time to 10 minutes
10. Pressure Release. Let it fully natural release roughly 10 minutes. Open the lid carefully.
11. Finish the dish. Close crisping lid. Select *Air Crisp*, set temperature to 375°F and set time to 10 minutes. Check after 10 minutes, cooking for an additional 5 minutes if dish needs more browning
12. Remove the pork chops and set aside. Turn the Multi-cooker to the Sauté setting. Remove the cloves and taste the seasoning one more time.
13. Add more salt and pepper if desired. Add butter and stir until it has fully dissolved into the sauce
14. Mix the cornstarch with water and mix it into the applesauce one third at a time until desired thickness.
15. Drizzle the applesauce over the pork chops and serve immediately with side dishes!

475. Peppers and Pork Stew

Preparation Time: 18 minutes

Servings: 4

INGREDIENTS

- 1 large yellow or white onion, chopped.
- 1 large green bell pepper, stemmed, cored and cut into 1/4-inch-thick strips
- 1 lb. boneless center-cut pork loin chops, cut into 1/4-inch-thick strips
- 1 large red bell pepper, stemmed, cored and cut into 1/4-inch-thick strips
- 1 14-ounce can diced tomatoes, drained about 1 3/4 cups
- 2 tsp. minced, seeded fresh jalapeño chile
- 2 tsp. dried oregano
- 2 tbsp. olive oil
- 2 tsp. minced garlic
- 2 ½ cups canned hominy drained and rinsed
- 1 cup chicken broth

DIRECTIONS

1. Heat the oil in a Ninja Foodi Multi-cooker, turned to the Sauté function. Add the onion and both bell peppers; cook, often stirring, until the onion softens, about 4 minutes.
2. Add the garlic, jalapeño and oregano; stir well until aromatic, less than 20 seconds. Add the hominy, tomatoes, broth and pork; stir over the heat for 1 minute
3. High pressure for 12 minutes. Lock the lid on the Ninja Foodi Multi-cooker and then cook for 12 minutes.

4. To get 12 minutes' cook time, press *Pressure* button and use the Time Adjustment button to adjust the cook time to 12 minutes.
5. Pressure Release. Use the quick release method to bring the pot's pressure back to normal. Unlock and open the cooker. Stir well before serving

476. Smoked Pork

Preparation Time: 40 minutes

Servings: 6

INGREDIENTS

- 2 and ½ lbs. pork loin, boneless and cubed
- ¾ cup beef stock
- 1 tbsp. smoked paprika
- 2 tbsp. olive oil
- ½ tbsp. garlic powder
- 1 tsp. oregano, dried
- 1 tsp. basil, dried
- Salt and black pepper to the taste

DIRECTIONS

1. In your Foodi's baking pan, combine all the Ingredients and toss. Put the reversible rack in the machine, add the baking pan, set the pot on Roast mode and cook at 370 °F for 30 minutes. Divide everything between plates and serve

SOUPS AND STEWS

477. Chicken Noodle Soup Recipe

Preparation Time: 30 minutes

Servings: 6

INGREDIENTS

- 2 large bone in skinless chicken breasts about 1 lb. each
- 1 medium red onion; halved
- 6 cups chicken broth
- 2 medium carrots
- 2 fresh thyme sprigs
- 2 fresh sage sprigs
- 2 medium garlic cloves; peeled
- 4-ounces wide egg noodles
- 1 tbsp. minced fresh dill fronds
- 2 tbsp. olive oil
- 1/2 tsp. salt

DIRECTIONS

1. Heat the oil in the Ninja Foodi Multi-cooker, turned to the sauté function. Add the chicken and brown well on both sides, about 4 minutes in all, turning once.
2. Pour in the broth; add the onion, carrots, salt, thyme, sage and garlic
3. High pressure for 18 minutes. Lock the lid on the Ninja Foodi Multi-cooker and then cook for 18 minutes.
4. To get 18 minutes' cook time, press *Pressure* button and use the Time Adjustment button to adjust the cook time to 18 minutes.
5. Pressure Release. Use the quick release method to return the pot's pressure to normal
6. Unlock and open the cooker. Transfer the chicken to a cutting board. Cool for a few minutes, then debone and chop the meat into bite size bits; set aside
7. Discard the onion, carrots, thyme, sage and garlic from the pot. Stir in the noodles and dill

8. High pressure for 4 minutes. Lock the lid on the Ninja Foodi Multi-cooker and then cook for 4 minutes.
9. To get 4 minutes' cook time, press *pressure* button and use the Time Adjustment button to adjust the cook time to 4 minutes
10. Pressure Release. Use the quick release method to return the pot's pressure to normal
11. Finish the dish. Unlock and open the cooker. Stir in the chopped chicken. Cover loosely and set aside for a couple of minutes to warm through

478. Beef Stock Recipe

Preparation Time: 120 minutes

Servings: 6

INGREDIENTS

- 2 lb beef soup bones
- 1 large onion; quartered, skin on
- 2 tsp. ground pepper
- 1 tsp. ground Himalayan salt
- 2 tbsp. garlic; minced
- 3 tbsp. apple cider vinegar
- 3 large carrots
- 1 bay leaf
- 3 celery sticks
- Handful fresh parsley
- Water

DIRECTIONS

1. Ideally, baking the bones at 375°F for 30 minutes prior to pressure cooking them helps draw out the marrow, but if you only have access to your Multi-cooker, it will still get the job done.
2. To start the stock, place the bones, veggies and seasonings into the Ninja Foodi Multi-cooker
3. Pour in the apple cider vinegar and cover with water. The amount of water will vary based on the size and quantities of your

vegetables. You can add in extra greens if you want

4. High pressure for 90 minutes. Lock the lid on the Ninja Foodi Multi-cooker and then cook for 90 minutes

5. To get 90 minutes' cook time, press *Pressure* button and use the time adjustment button to adjust the cook time to 90 minutes

6. Pressure Release. Once complete, quick release the pressure valve, allowing the steam to escape

479. Potato, Carrot and Leek Soup Recipe

Prep + Cooking Time:20 minutes

Servings: 4

INGREDIENTS

- 1 lb. carrots; coarsely chopped.
- 1 bouquet garni parsley sprigs; bay leaf, a sprig of thyme, tied tightly with string or in cheesecloth
- 1 large potato; peeled and coarsely chopped.
- 1 medium leek; white and pale green parts only, coarsely chopped.
- 1 tbsp. olive oil
- 2 tbsp. unsalted butter
- 2 tsp. salt
- 4 cups salt free Chicken Stock
- Freshly ground black pepper
- 1/4 cup heavy cream
- 1/8 tsp. freshly grated nutmeg
- Fresh thyme sprigs or chopped fresh chives; for serving

DIRECTIONS

1. Heat the Ninja Foodi Multi-cooker using the *Sauté* function, add the oil and butter and cook until the butter has melted. Stir in the chopped leeks and salt and sauté, infrequently stirring, until the leeks have softened about 5 minutes

2. Add the carrots and cook, infrequently stirring, until they are golden on one side, about 5 more minutes. Add the potato,

stock, pepper to taste and the bouquet garni

3. High pressure for 10 minutes. Lock the lid on Ninja Foodi Multi-cooker and then cook for 10 minutes.

4. To get 10 minutes' cook time, press *Pressure* button and use the Time Adjustment button to adjust the cook time to 10 minutes.

5. Pressure Release When the time is up, open the cooker with the Normal Release method.

6. Finish the dish. Fish out and discard the bouquet garni. Using an immersion blender, puree the soup in the cooker

7. Stir in the cream and nutmeg. Ladle into bowls and dot each serving with a thyme sprig or a few chopped chives

480. Tomato Soup Recipe

Preparation Time: 15 minutes

Servings: 2 to 4

INGREDIENTS

- 1 14.5-ounce can fire roasted tomatoes
- 1 small roasted red bell pepper; cut into chunks about 1/4 cup
- 1/2 cup sliced onion
- 3/4 cup Chicken Stock or low sodium broth
- 1/4 cup dry or medium dry sherry
- 3 tbsp. olive oil
- 1 tbsp. heavy whipping cream optional
- 1 medium garlic clove; sliced or minced
- 1/8 tsp. ground cumin
- 1/8 tsp. freshly ground black pepper
- Kosher salt

DIRECTIONS

1. Set the Ninja Foodi Multi-cooker to sauté, heat the olive oil until it shimmers and flows like water. Add the onions and sprinkle with a pinch or two of kosher salt. Cook for about 5 minutes, stirring until the onions just begin to brown. Add the garlic and cook for 1 to 2 minutes more or until fragrant

2. Pour in the sherry and simmer for 1 to 2 minutes or until the sherry is reduced by half, scraping up any browned bits from the bottom of the pan. Add the tomatoes, roasted red bell pepper and Chicken Stock to the Ninja Foodi Multi-cooker.

3. High pressure for 10 minutes. Lock the lid on the Ninja Foodi Multi-cooker and then cook for 10 minutes.

4. To get 10 minutes' cook time, press *Pressure* button and use the Time Adjustment button to adjust the cook time to 10 minutes.

5. Pressure Release. Use the quick release method. Finish the dish. For a smooth soup, blend using an immersion or standard blender. Add the cumin and pepper and adjust the salt, if necessary. If you like a creamier soup, stir in the heavy cream

6. If using a standard blender, be careful. Steam can build up and blow the lid off if the soup is very hot. Hold the lid on with a towel and blend in batches, if necessary; don't fill the jar more than halfway full

481. Turkey Meatballs in Tomato Sauce

Preparation Time: 15 minutes

Servings: 4

INGREDIENTS

- 1 lb. ground turkey
- 1 large egg, at room temperature and beaten in a small bowl
- 1 28-ounce can whole tomatoes, drained and roughly chopped. about 3 ½ cups
- 1 medium yellow onion, chopped.
- 2 medium celery stalks, thinly sliced
- 1/2 cup plain dried breadcrumbs
- 1/4 cup finely grated Parmesan cheese about 1/2-ounce
- 2 tbsp. unsalted butter
- 1/2 cup chicken broth
- 1 tbsp. packed fresh oregano leaves, minced
- 1/4 tsp. grated nutmeg
- 1/4 cup heavy cream
- 1/2 tsp. dried oregano

- 1/2 tsp. dried rosemary
- 1/2 tsp. ground black pepper
- 1/2 tsp. salt

DIRECTIONS

1. Mix the ground turkey, egg, breadcrumbs, cheese, oregano, rosemary, pepper and 1/4 tsp. salt in a large bowl until well combined. Form the mixture into 12 balls

2. Melt the butter in the Ninja Foodi Multi-cooker turned to the sauté function. Add the onion and celery; cook, often stirring, until the onion turns translucent, about 3 minutes.

3. Stir in the tomatoes, broth, oregano and the remaining 1/4 tsp. salt. Drop the meatballs into the sauce.

4. High pressure for 10 minutes. Lock the lid on the Ninja Foodi Multi-cooker and then cook for 10 minutes.

5. To get 10 minutes' cook time, press *Pressure* button and use the Time Adjustment button to adjust the cook time to 10 minutes.

6. Pressure Release. Use the quick release method to drop the pot's pressure to normal

7. Finish the dish. Unlock and open the cooker. Turn the Ninja Foodi Multi-cooker to its sauté function.

8. Stir in the cream and nutmeg; simmer, stirring all the while, for 1 minute to reduce the cream a little and blend the flavors

482. Chicken Strips

Preparation Time: 25 minutes

Servings: 4

INGREDIENTS

- 2 chicken breasts, skinless, boneless and cut into strips
- 2 eggs; whisked.
- 1 cup rice flour
- 3 cups cereal, crushed
- A pinch of salt and black pepper

DIRECTIONS

1. In a bowl mix the flour with salt and pepper. Put the eggs in a second bowl and the cereal mixed with salt and pepper in a third one
2. Dredge each chicken strip in flour, egg and cereal and place all the pieces in the Foodi's basket
3. Set the machine on Air Crisp and cook at 390 °F for 15 minutes. Divide the strips between plates and serve.

483. Olive and Lemon Ligurian Chicken

Preparation Time: 35 minutes

Servings: 6 to 8

INGREDIENTS

- 3.5-ounce 100g Black Gourmet Salt-Cured Olives Taggiesche, French or Kalamata
- 3 sprigs of Fresh Rosemary two for chopping, one for garnish
- 1 whole chicken, cut into parts or package of bone in chicken pieces, skin removed or not 1/2 cup 125ml dry white wine
- 2 garlic cloves, chopped.
- 2 sprigs of Fresh Sage
- 1/2 bunch of Parsley Leaves and stems
- 3 lemons, juiced about a 3/4 cup or 180ml
- 4 tbsp. extra virgin olive oil
- 1 tsp. sea salt
- 1/4 tsp. pepper
- 1 fresh lemon, for garnish optional

DIRECTIONS

1. Prepare the marinade by finely chopping together the garlic, rosemary, sage and parsley. Place them in a container and add the lemon juice, olive oil, salt and pepper. Mix well and set aside
2. Remove the skin from the chicken save it for a chicken stock
3. In the preheated Ninja Foodi Multi-cooker, with the lid off, add a swirl of olive oil and brown the chicken pieces on all sides for about 5 minutes.
4. De-glaze cooker with the white wine until it has almost all evaporated about 3 minutes
5. Add the chicken pieces back in this time being careful with the order. Put all dark meat wings, legs, thighs first and then the chicken breasts on top so that they do not touch the bottom of the Ninja Foodi Multi-cooker.
6. Pour the remaining marinade on top. Don't worry if this does not seem like enough liquid the chicken will also release its juices into the cooker, too
7. High pressure for 10 minutes. Lock the lid on the Ninja Foodi Multi-cooker and then cook for 10 minutes.
8. To get 10 minutes' cook time, press *Pressure* button and adjust the time
9. Pressure Release. When time is up, open the cooker by releasing the pressure using the Quick Release Method.
10. Finish the dish. Close crisping lid. Select *Air Crisp*, set temperature to 390°F and set time to 10 minutes. Check after 5 minutes, cooking for an additional 5 minutes if dish needs more browning
11. Take the chicken pieces out of the cooker and place on a serving platter tightly covered with foil
12. Reduce the cooking liquid in the Ninja Foodi Multi-cooker, if necessary, with the lid off to 1/4 of its amount or until it becomes thick and syrupy.
13. Put all of the chicken pieces back into the Ninja Foodi Multi-cooker to warm up. Mix and spoon the thick glaze onto the chicken pieces and simmer it in the glaze for a few minutes before serving
14. Sprinkle with fresh rosemary, olives and lemon slices. When serving, caution your guests that the olives still have their pits!

484. Chicken Drumsticks

Preparation Time: 30 minutes

Servings: 4

INGREDIENTS

- 10 chicken drumsticks
- 1 cup coconut milk
- ¼ cup cilantro; chopped.
- A bunch of spring onions; chopped.
- 4 garlic cloves; minced.
- 1 tbsp. lime juice
- 2 tbsp. oyster sauce
- 1 tbsp. ginger; grated.
- 1 tsp. Chinese five spice
- 1 tsp. olive oil
- Salt and black pepper to the taste

DIRECTIONS

1. In a blender, mix the spring onions with ginger, garlic, oyster sauce, five spice, salt, pepper, oil and coconut milk and pulse well. Put the chicken drumsticks in the Foodi's baking pan and spread the spring onions mix all over
2. Put the reversible rack in the machine, add the baking pan, set the pot on Baking mode and cook at 370 °F for 20 minutes. Divide the chicken mix between plates, sprinkle the cilantro on top, drizzle the lime juice all over and serve

485.   Spicy Chicken

Preparation Time: 40 minutes

Servings: 6

INGREDIENTS

- 3 and ½ lbs. chicken breasts
- 1 ¼ cups yellow onion; chopped.
- 1 cup chicken stock
- 1 tbsp. olive oil
- 1 tbsp. lemon juice
- 2 tbsp. green onions; chopped.
- 2 tsp. hot paprika
- 2 tsp. red pepper flakes
- Salt and black pepper to the taste

DIRECTIONS

1. Set the Foodi on Sauté mode, add the oil and heat it up. Add the yellow onion, stir and sauté for 2 minutes. Add all the Ingredients toss, put the pressure lid on and cook on High for 18 minutes
2. Release the pressure naturally for 10 minutes, divide everything into bowls and serve. Add the chicken and the stock, toss, simmer for 1 more minute, transfer the pan to your air fryer and cook at 370 °F for 12 minutes. Divide between plates and serve

486.   Pesto Chicken Breasts

Preparation Time: 40 minutes

Servings: 4

INGREDIENTS

1. 2 chicken breasts, boneless, skinless and halved
2. 4 garlic cloves; minced.
3. 1 cup parsley; chopped.
4. ½ cup olive oil
5. ¼ cup red wine
6. A pinch of salt and black pepper

DIRECTIONS

1. In a blender, mix the parsley with garlic, salt, pepper, oil and wine and pulse well. In the Foodi's baking pan, combine the chicken with the parsley pesto and toss well
2. Put the reversible rack in the Foodi, add the baking pan, set the pot on Baking mode and cook at 370 °F for 30 minutes. Divide everything between plates and serve

487.   Crispy Chicken Thighs with Carrots and Rice Pilaf

Preparation Time: 25 minutes

Servings: 4

INGREDIENTS

- 4 uncooked boneless skin-on chicken thighs
- 1 box 6-ounces rice pilaf
- 2 tbsp. honey, warmed
- 1/2 tsp. smoked paprika
- 1 3/4 cups water
- 1 tbsp. butter
- 4 carrots, peeled, cut in half, lengthwise
- 2 tsp. kosher salt, divided.
- 1 tbsp. extra-virgin olive oil
- 2 tsp. poultry spice
- 1/2 tsp. ground cumin

DIRECTIONS

1. Place rice pilaf, water, and butter into pot; stir to incorporate
2. Place reversible rack in the pot, making sure rack is in the higher position. Place carrots in center of rack. Arrange chicken thighs, skin side up, around the carrots. Assemble pressure lid, making sure the PRESSURE RELEASE valve is in the SEAL position. Select PRESSURE and set to HIGH. Set time to 4 minutes. Select START/STOP to begin.
3. While chicken and rice are cooking, stir together warm honey, smoked paprika, cumin, and 1 tsp. salt. Set aside
4. When pressure cooking is complete, quick release the pressure by moving the PRESSURE RELEASE valve to the VENT position. Carefully remove lid when unit has finished releasing pressure
5. Brush carrots with seasoned honey. Brush chicken with olive oil, then season evenly with poultry spice and remaining salt.
6. Close crisping lid. Select BROIL and set time to 10 minutes. Select START/STOP to begin. When cooking is complete, serve chicken with carrots and rice

488. Chicken And Mushrooms Mix

Preparation Time: 30 minutes

Servings: 4

INGREDIENTS

- 2 lbs. chicken breasts, skinless, boneless and cubed
- 12 brown mushrooms, halved
- 1 sweet onion; chopped.
- 2 garlic cloves; minced.
- 1 red bell pepper; chopped.
- 2 tbsp. cheddar cheese, shredded
- 2 tbsp. canola oil
- Salt and black pepper to the taste

DIRECTIONS

1. Set the Foodi on Sauté mode, add the oil and heat it up. Add the onion, garlic, salt and pepper, toss and sauté for 3-4 minutes
2. Add the chicken pieces, toss and brown for 2-3 minutes more. Add all the other Ingredients except the cheese, toss, put the pressure lid on and cook on High for 10 minutes
3. Release the pressure naturally for 10 minutes, divide the chicken and mushrooms mix between plates, sprinkle the cheese on top and serve.

489. Turmeric Chicken

Preparation Time: 25 minutes

Servings: 4

INGREDIENTS

- 2 chicken breasts, skinless, boneless and cubed
- 2 tbsp. canola oil
- 1 tbsp. turmeric powder
- 1 tbsp. lemon juice
- 1 tbsp. ginger; grated.
- 1 tbsp. sweet paprika
- Salt and black pepper to the taste

DIRECTIONS

1. Set the Foodi on Sauté mode, add the oil and heat it up. Add the chicken, toss and brown for 4-5 minutes

2. Add the rest of the Ingredients toss, put the pressure lid on and cook on High for 10 minutes. Release the pressure naturally for 10 minutes, divide everything into bowls and serve

490. Sweet Chipotle Chicken Wings

Preparation Time: 25 minutes

Servings: 2

INGREDIENTS

- 3 tbsp. Mexican hot sauce such as Valentina brand
- 1 tsp. minced canned chipotle in adobo sauce
- 1 cup water, for steaming
- 2 tbsp. honey

DIRECTIONS

1. If using whole wings, cut off the tips and discard. Cut the wings at the joint into two pieces each the *drumette and the flat.
2. Add the water and insert the steamer basket or trivet. Place the wings on the steamer insert
3. High pressure for 10 minutes. Close the lid and the pressure valve and then cook for 10 minutes.
4. To get 10 minutes' cook time, press *Pressure* button and the time selector
5. Pressure Release. Use the quick release method. Finish the dish. While the wings are cooking, make the sauce. In a large bowl, whisk together the hot sauce, honey and minced chipotle.
6. Close crisping lid. Select *Air Crisp*, set temperature to 390°F and set time to 10 minutes. Select START/STOP to begin. Serve!

491. Spicy Turkey Chili

Preparation Time: 60 minutes

Servings: 4

INGREDIENTS

- 1 lb. ground turkey
- 1/4 cup your favorite hot sauce
- 1 15-ounce can fire roasted diced tomatoes
- 1 15-ounce can kidney beans, including their liquid
- 1 medium yellow onion, diced
- 2 green bell peppers, seeded and diced
- 2 fresh cayenne peppers, chopped. seeds included
- 4 cloves garlic, chopped.
- 1 cup grated Monterey Jack cheese
- 1 tbsp. olive oil
- 1 tsp. ground cumin
- 1/2 tsp. dried oregano leaves
- 1/4 cup chopped cilantro

DIRECTIONS

1. Set the Ninja Foodi Multi-cooker to its *Sauté* setting and add the oil. Add the onions, peppers and garlic and sauté until the onions soften and begin to brown, about 10 minutes. Add the cumin and oregano and sauté two more minutes, until aromatic.
2. Add the ground turkey, breaking it up with a spoon or spatula. Sauté until opaque and cooked through, about 5 minutes
3. Add the hot sauce, canned tomatoes and kidney beans and stir to combine
4. High pressure for 45 minutes. Lock the lid on the Ninja Foodi Multi-cooker and then cook for 45 minutes.
5. To get 45 minutes' cook time, press *pressure* button and use the adjust button to adjust the cook time to 45 minutes.
6. Pressure Release. Use natural release method.
7. Finish the dish. Top with grated cheese and cilantro and serve with rice or cornbread, if desired

492. Delicious Frozen Chicken Dinner

Preparation Time: 50 minutes

Servings: 2

INGREDIENTS

- 2 frozen chicken breasts 8 - 10 ounces each
- 2 tbsp. olive oil, divided.
- 1 small onion, peeled, diced
- 3/4 cup chicken stock
- 1 bag 12-ounces green beans, trimmed
- 1 tsp. black pepper, divided.
- 1/4 cup fresh parsley, chopped.
- 1 cup wild rice blend
- 3 tsp. kosher salt, divided.
- 1 tbsp. Moroccan seasoning "Ras el Hanout"
- 1/4 cup honey mustard sauce

DIRECTIONS

1. Select SEAR/SAUTÉ and set to HIGH. Allow to preheat for 5 minutes.
2. After 5 minutes, add 1 tbsp. oil and onion. Cook, stirring occasionally, for 3 minutes, until onions are fragrant. Add wild rice, 2 tsp. salt, and Moroccan seasoning. Cook, stirring frequently, until the rice is coated with oil and very shiny. Add chicken stock and stir to incorporate
3. Place frozen chicken breasts on reversible rack, making sure rack is in the higher position. Place rack inside pot over rice mixture.
4. Assemble pressure lid, making sure the PRESSURE RELEASE valve is in the SEAL position. Select PRESSURE and set to HIGH. Set time to 22 minutes. Select START/STOP to begin
5. While chicken and rice are cooking, toss green beans in a bowl with the remaining oil, salt, and pepper
6. When pressure cooking is complete, allow pressure to naturally release for 10 minutes. After 10 minutes, quick release any remaining pressure by turning the PRESSURE RELEASE valve to the VENT position. Carefully remove lid when unit has finished releasing pressure.

7. Lift reversible rack out of the pot. Stir parsley into rice, then add green beans directly on top of the rice
8. Brush chicken breasts on all sides with honey mustard sauce, then return the reversible rack to the pot over rice and green beans. Close crisping lid. Select BROIL and set time to 10 minutes. Select START/STOP to begin.
9. Cooking is complete when internal temperature reaches 165°F. Serve chicken with green beans and rice

493. Asian Chicken Delight
Preparation Time: 40 minutes

Servings: 4

INGREDIENTS

- 2 chicken breasts, skinless, boneless and cubed
- 14 oz. water
- 2 red chilies; chopped.
- 1 bunch spring onions; chopped.
- 1 tbsp. ginger; grated.
- 1 tbsp. rice wine
- 1 tbsp. olive oil
- 1 tbsp. soy sauce
- 1 tsp. sesame oil

DIRECTIONS

1. Set the Foodi on Sauté mode, add the olive oil and the sesame seed oil and heat them up. Add the chilies, spring onions and the ginger, stir and cook for 2-3 minutes
2. Add all the other Ingredients toss, put the pressure lid on and cook on High for 25 minutes. Release the pressure naturally for 10 minutes, divide everything into bowls and serve

494. Turkey Gluten Free Gravy
Preparation Time: 60 minutes

Servings: 6

INGREDIENTS

- 1 4 - 5 lb. bone in, skin on turkey breast
- 2 tbsp. ghee or butter use coconut oil for AIP
- 1 medium onion, cut into medium dice
- 1 large carrot, cut into medium dice
- 1 celery rib, cut into medium dice
- 1 garlic clove, peeled and smashed
- 1 ½ cups bone broth preferably from chicken or turkey bones
- Black pepper omit for AIP
- 2 tsp. dried sage
- 1/4 cup dry white wine
- 1 bay leaf
- 1 tbsp. tapioca starch optional
- Salt to taste

DIRECTIONS

1. Set the *Sauté* function. Pat turkey breast dry and generously season with salt and pepper. Melt cooking fat in the Ninja Foodi Multi-cooker.
2. Brown turkey breast, skin side down, about 5 minutes and transfer to a plate, leaving fat in the pot
3. Add onion, carrot and celery to pot and cook until softened, about 5 minutes. Stir in garlic and sage and cook until fragrant, about 30 seconds
4. Pour in wine and cook until slightly reduced about 3 minutes. Stir in broth and bay leaf. Using a wooden spoon, scrape up all browned bits stuck on the bottom of pot.
5. Place turkey skin side up in the pot with any accumulated juices.
6. High pressure for 35 minutes. Lock the lid on the Ninja Foodi Multi-cooker and then cook for 35 minutes.
7. To get 35 minutes' cook time, press *Pressure* button and use the Time Adjustment button to adjust the cook time to 35
8. Pressure Release. Use quick release method and carefully remove lid
9. Finish the dish. Close crisping lid. Select *Air Crisp*, set temperature to 375°F and set time to 10 minutes. Check after 5 minutes,

cooking for an additional 5 minutes if dish needs more browning.
10. Transfer turkey breast to carving board or plate and tent loosely with foil, allowing it to rest while you prepare the gravy.
11. Use an immersion blender or carefully transfer cooking liquid and vegetables to blender and puree until smooth. Return to heat and cook until thickened and reduced to about 2 cups. Adjust seasoning to taste. Slice turkey breast and serve with hot gravy. Enjoy!

495. Cheddar Chicken Breast
Preparation Time: 30 minutes

Servings: 4

INGREDIENTS

- 16 oz. salsa
- 1 lb. chicken breast, boneless and skinless
- 1 ½ cup cheddar cheese; grated.
- ¼ cup cilantro; chopped.
- 1 tsp. sweet paprika
- 1 tbsp. olive oil
- Salt and black pepper to the taste

DIRECTIONS

1. In your Foodi's baking pan, combine all the Ingredients except the cheese. Sprinkle the cheese over the chicken
2. Put the reversible rack in the machine, add the baking pan inside, set the pot on Baking mode and cook at 380 °F for 20 minutes. Divide between plates and serve

496. Chicken Pot Pie Recipe
Preparation Time: 35 minutes

Servings: 6

INGREDIENTS

- 2 lb. uncooked boneless skinless chicken breasts, cut in 1-inch cubes
- 1/2 stick 1/4 cup unsalted butter

- 1/2 large onion, peeled, diced
- 1 large carrot, peeled, diced
- 2 cloves garlic, peeled, minced
- 1 stalk celery, diced
- 1/2 cup frozen peas
- 1 ½ tsp. fresh thyme, minced
- 2 tsp. kosher salt
- 1/2 tsp. black pepper
- 1/2 cup heavy cream
- 1 cup chicken broth
- 1 tbsp. fresh Italian parsley, minced
- 1/4 cup all-purpose flour

DIRECTIONS

1. Select SEAR/SAUTÉ and set to MD:HI. Select START/STOP to begin. Allow to preheat for 5 minutes. After 5 minutes, add butter to pot. Once it melts, add onion, carrot, and garlic, and SAUTÉ until softened, about 3 minutes
2. Add chicken and broth to the pot. Assemble pressure lid, making sure the PRESSURE RELEASE valve is in the SEAL position. Select PRESSURE and set to HIGH. Set time to 5 minutes. Select START/STOP to begin
3. When pressure cooking is complete, quick release the pressure by moving the PRESSURE RELEASE valve to the VENT position. Carefully remove lid when unit has finished releasing pressure
4. Select SEAR/SAUTÉ and set to MD:HI. Select START/STOP to begin. Add remaining ingredients to pot, except pie crust. Stir until sauce thickens and bubbles, about 3 minutes
5. Lay pie crust evenly on top of the filling mixture, folding over edges if necessary. Make a small cut in center of pie crust so that steam can escape during baking. Close the crisping lid. Select BROIL and set time to 10 minutes. Select START/STOP to begin.
6. When cooking is complete, remove pot from unit and place on a heat-resistant surface. Let rest 10 to 15 minutes before serving

497. Chicken Casserole

Preparation Time: 40 minutes

Servings: 4

INGREDIENTS

- 1 lb. chicken meat, ground
- 12 eggs; whisked.
- 1 cup baby spinach
- ½ tsp. sweet paprika
- 1 tbsp. olive oil
- Salt and black pepper to the taste

DIRECTIONS

1. In a bowl mix all the Ingredients except the oil and toss them. Put the reversible rack in the Foodi, place the baking pan inside, add the oil and spread
2. Pour the chicken mix in the pan and cook the casserole for 30 minutes on Baking mode at 350 °F. Divide between plates and serve for breakfast.

498. Cream of Sweet Potato Soup Recipe

Preparation Time: 11 minutes

Servings: 6

INGREDIENTS

- 2 lb. sweet potatoes about 2 large; peeled and cut into 2-inch pieces
- 8 tbsp. 1 stick unsalted butter; cut into small pieces
- 1/2 tsp. ground cinnamon
- 1/2 tsp. ground ginger
- 1/4 tsp. baking soda
- 2 ½ cups chicken broth
- 1/2 cup heavy cream
- 1 tsp. salt

DIRECTIONS

1. Melt the butter in a Ninja Foodi Multi-cooker turned to the browning function. Stir in the sweet potatoes, salt, cinnamon,

ginger and baking soda. Pour 1/2 cup water over everything

2. High pressure for 15 minutes. Lock the lid on the Ninja Foodi Multi-cooker and then cook for 15 minutes.
3. To get 15 minutes' cook time, press *Pressure* button and then adjust the time
4. Pressure Release. Use the quick release method to bring the pot's pressure back to normal
5. Finish the dish. Unlock and open the pot. Stir in the broth and cream. Use an immersion blender to puree the soup in the pot or ladle the soup in batches into a blender, remove the knob from the blender's lid, cover the hole with a clean kitchen towel and blend until smooth

499. Butternut Squash Soup with Chicken

Preparation Time: 30 minutes

Servings: 6

INGREDIENTS

- 1 ½ lb. of fresh baked butternut squash; peeled and cubed
- 1 cup chicken breast; seasoned, cooked and diced
- 1 onion; diced
- 1 garlic clove; minced
- 2 cans chicken broth
- 1 cup orzo; cooked
- 1/2 cup celery; diced
- 1/2 cup carrots; diced
- 2 tbsp. red pepper flakes
- 2 tbsp. dried parsley flakes
- 1 tomato diced
- 3 tbsp. butter
- 1/4 tsp. freshly ground black pepper

DIRECTIONS

1. Set the Ninja Foodi Multi-cooker to sauté and melt butter to sauté the onion, garlic clove, celery and carrots
2. Then add the chicken broth, red pepper flakes, dried parsley flakes, black pepper,

baked butternut squash and tomato diced to the Ninja Foodi Multi-cooker.

3. High pressure for 15 minutes. Lock the lid on the Ninja Foodi Multi-cooker and then cook for 15 minutes.
4. To get 15 minutes' cook time, press *Pressure* Button
5. Pressure Release. Use the quick release method
6. Blend/puree until mixture is smooth.
7. High pressure for 5 minutes. Then add it back to your Ninja Foodi Multi-cooker along with the chicken breast and orzo and cook for another 5 minutes
8. To get 5 minutes' cook time, press *Pressure* button and adjust the time.
9. Pressure Release. Use the quick release method. Serve with fresh dinner rolls and butter on the side

500. Tasty Chicken Soup

Preparation Time: 45 minutes

Servings: 8

INGREDIENTS

- 3 peeled carrots chopped into similar size as potatoes for even cooking time
- 4 cups of water and chicken concentrate/bullion of your choice to equal 32-ounces – or if you have it, use chicken stock
- 2 frozen boneless skinless chicken breasts
- 4 washed medium size diced potatoes I did not peel you can if you want
- 1/2large onion diced
- Salt and pepper to taste flavors will intensify while under pressure

DIRECTIONS

1. Mix the broth, chicken, potatoes, onion, carrots, salt and pepper in the Ninja Foodi Multi-cooker
2. High pressure for 35 minutes. Lock the lid on the Ninja Foodi Multi-cooker and then cook for 35 minutes

3. To get 35 minutes' cook time, press *pressure* button and use the Time Adjustment button to adjust the cook time to 35 minutes

4. Pressure Release Let the pressure to come down naturally for at least 15 minutes, then quick release any pressure left in the pot. Open when all pressure is released stir and enjoy.

501. Colombian Style Chicken Soup Recipe

Preparation Time: 20 minutes

Servings: 4

INGREDIENTS

- 3 bone in chicken breasts about 2 lb. or 907 g
- 5 cups 1.2 L water
- 1 ½ tsp. kosher salt
- 1 ½ lb. Yukon gold potatoes, cut into 1/2-inch 13 mm pieces
- 1 ear corn, cut into 4 pieces
- 1 medium yellow onion, cut in half
- 2 medium carrots, cut in half crosswise
- 2 ribs celery, cut in half crosswise
- 1/4 cup sour cream
- 1 tbsp. capers, rinsed
- 1/4 tsp. freshly ground black pepper
- 1 avocado
- 1 tsp. dried oregano
- 1 lime; quartered
- 8 sprigs fresh cilantro

DIRECTIONS

1. To the Ninja Foodi Multi-cooker, add the onion, carrots, celery, chicken, water and salt

2. High pressure for 15 minutes. Lock the lid on the Ninja Foodi Multi-cooker and then cook for 15 minutes.

3. To get 15 minutes' cook time, press *Pressure* Button and then adjust the time

4. Pressure Release. Use the *Quick Release* method to vent the steam, then open the lid. Transfer the chicken to a large bowl. When cool enough to handle, shred into pieces, discarding the skin and bones

5. Discard the onion, carrots and celery. Add the potatoes and corn to the broth.

6. High pressure for 2 minutes. Lock the lid on the Ninja Foodi Multi-cooker and then cook for 2 minutes

7. To get 2 minutes' cook time, press *Pressure* button and use the Time Adjustment button to adjust the cook time to 2 minutes.

8. Pressure Release. Use the *Quick Release* method to vent the steam, then open the lid

9. Finish the dish. Stir in the chicken and pepper.

10. Divide the soup among bowls. Peel, pit and slice the avocado. Top the soup with the avocado, sour cream, capers, oregano and cilantro.

11. Serve with the lime quarters for squeezing

502. French Onion Soup Recipe

Preparation Time: 40 minutes

Servings: 4

INGREDIENTS

- 1-ounce Gruyère or other Swiss-style cheese; coarsely grated about 1/3 cup
- 1/4 cup dry sherry
- 2 cups low sodium chicken broth
- 1/2 cup Beef Stock; Mushroom Stock or low sodium broth
- 4 cups thinly sliced white or yellow onions; divided.
- 2 thin slices French or Italian bread
- 1/2 tsp. kosher salt; plus additional for seasoning
- 1/2 tsp. Worcestershire sauce
- 2 tbsp. unsalted butter; divided.
- 1/4 tsp. dried thyme
- 1 tsp. sherry vinegar or red wine vinegar; plus additional as needed

DIRECTIONS

1. Set the Ninja Foodi Multi-cooker to *Sauté*, heat 1 tbsp. of butter until it stops foaming and then add 1 cup of onions. Sprinkle with a pinch or two of kosher salt and stir to coat with the butter. Cook the onions in a single layer for about 4 minutes or until browned

2. Resist the urge to stir them until you see them browning. Stir them to expose the other side to the heat and cook for 4 minutes more. The onions should be quite browned but still slightly firm. Remove the onions from the pan and set aside

3. Pour the sherry into the pot and stir to scrape up the browned bits from the bottom. When the sherry has mostly evaporated, add the remaining 1 tbsp. of butter and let it melt

4. Stir in the remaining 3 cups of onions and sprinkle with 1/2 tsp. of kosher salt

5. High pressure for 25 minutes. Lock the lid on the Ninja Foodi Multi-cooker and then cook for 25 minutes.

6. To get 25 minutes' cook time, press *Pressure* button and use the Time Adjustment button to adjust the cook time to 25 minutes.

7. Pressure Release Use the quick release method. Unlock and remove the lid.

8. The onions should be pale and very soft, with a lot of liquid in the pot. Add the chicken broth, Beef Stock, Worcestershire sauce and thyme

9. High pressure for 10 minutes. Lock the lid on the Ninja Foodi Multi-cooker and then cook for 10 minutes.

10. To get 10 minutes' cook time, press *Pressure* button and use the Time Adjustment button to adjust the cook time to 10 minutes.

11. Pressure Release Use the quick release method

12. Finish the dish. Unlock and remove the lid. Stir in the sherry vinegar and taste. The soup should be balanced between the sweetness of the onions the savory stock and the acid from the vinegar. If it seems bland, add a pinch or two of kosher salt or a little more vinegar

13. Stir in the reserved cup of onions and keep warm while you prepare the cheese toasts

14. Preheat the broiler. Reserve 2 tbsp. of the cheese and sprinkle the remaining cheese evenly over the 2 bread slices. Place the bread slices on a sheet pan under the broiler for 2 to 3 minutes or until the cheese melts

15. Place 1 tbsp. of the reserved cheese in each of 2 bowls. Ladle the soup into the bowls, float a toast slice on top of each and serve.

SNACKS

503. Chicken Wings

Preparation Time: 60 Minutes

Servings: 4

INGREDIENTS

- 2 lb. chicken wings, frozen
- ½ (1-ounceranch salad mix
- ½ cup sriracha sauce
- ½ cup water
- 2 tablespoon butter, melted
- 1 tablespoon lemon juice
- ½ teaspoon paprika
- Non-stick cooking spray

DIRECTIONS

1. Mix the water, sriracha, butter and lemon juice or vinegar in the pot. In the Crisping Basket, put the wings, and then the basket into the pot.
2. Seal the pressure lid, choose Pressure, set to High, set the timer at 5 minutes, and press Start. When the timer is done reading, perform a quick pressure release, and carefully open the lid.
3. Pour the paprika and ranch dressing all over the chicken and oil with cooking spray. Cover the crisping lid. Choose Air Crisp, set the temperature to 370 F, and the timer to 15 minutes. Choose Start to commence frying.
4. After half the cooking time, open the lid, remove the basket and shake the wings. Oil the chicken again with cooking spray and return the basket to the pot. Close the lid and continue cooking until the wings are crispy to your desire.

504. Creamy Tomato Parsley Dip

Preparation Time: 18 Minutes

Servings: 6

INGREDIENTS

- 10 oz. shredded Parmesan cheese
- 10 oz. cream cheese
- ½ cup heavy cream
- 1 cup chopped tomatoes
- 1 cup water
- ¼ cup chopped parsley

DIRECTIONS

1. Open the Ninja Foodi and pour in the tomatoes, parsley, heavy cream, cream cheese, and water. Close the lid, secure the pressure valve, and select Pressure for 3 minutes at High. Press Start/Stop.
2. Once the timer has ended, do a natural pressure release for 10 minutes.
3. Stir the mixture with a spoon while mashing the tomatoes with the back of the spoon. Add the parmesan cheese and Close the crisping lid.
4. Select Bake/Roast mode, set the temperature to 370 degrees F and the time to 3 minutes. Dish the dip into a bowl and serve with chips or veggie bites.

505. Turkey Scotch Eggs

Preparation Time: 20 Minutes

Servings: 6

INGREDIENTS

- 10 oz. ground turkey
- 4 eggs, soft boiled, peeled
- 2 garlic cloves, minced
- 2 eggs, lightly beaten
- 1 white onion; chopped
- ½ cup flour
- ½ cup breadcrumbs
- 1 teaspoon dried mixed herbs
- Salt and pepper to taste
- Cooking spray

DIRECTIONS

1. Mix together the onion, garlic, salt, and pepper. Shape into 4 balls. Wrap the turkey mixture around each egg, and ensure the eggs are well covered.
2. Dust each egg ball in flour, then dip in the beaten eggs and finally roll in the crumbs, until coated. Spray with cooking spray.
3. Lay the eggs into your Ninja Foodi's basket. Set the temperature to 390 degrees F, close the crisping lid and cook for 15 minutes. After 8 minutes, turn the eggs. Slice in half and serve warm.

506. Fried Pin Wheels

Preparation Time: 50 Minutes

Servings: 6

INGREDIENTS

- 1 sheet puff pastry
- 1 ½ cups Gruyere cheese, grated
- 8 ham slices
- 4 teaspoon Dijon mustard

DIRECTIONS

1. Place the pastry on a lightly floured flat surface. Brush the mustard over and arrange the ham slices; top with cheese. Start at the shorter edge and roll up the pastry.
2. Wrap it in a plastic foil and place in the freezer for about half an hour, until it becomes firm and comfortable to cut.
3. Meanwhile, slice the pastry into 6 rounds. Line the Ninja Foodi basket with parchment paper, and arrange the pinwheels on top.
4. Close the crisping lid and cook for 10 minutes on Air Crisp mode at 370 F. Leave to cool on a wire rack before serving.

507. Cheesy Cauliflower Tater Tots

Preparation Time: 35 Minutes

Servings: 10

INGREDIENTS

- 2 lb. cauliflower florets, steamed
- 5 oz. cheddar cheese
- 1 egg, beaten
- 1 onion; diced
- 1 cup breadcrumbs
- 1 teaspoon chopped chives
- 1 teaspoon garlic powder
- 1 teaspoon chopped parsley
- 1 teaspoon chopped oregano
- Salt and pepper, to taste

DIRECTIONS

1. Mash the cauliflower and place it in a large bowl. Add the onion, parsley, oregano, chives, garlic powder, salt, and pepper, and cheddar cheese. Mix with hands until thoroughly combined.
2. Form 12 balls out of the mixture. Line a baking sheet with paper. Dip half of the tater tots into the egg and then coat with breadcrumbs.
3. Arrange them on the baking sheet, close the crisping lid and cook in the Ninja Foodi at 350 F for 15 minutes on Air Crisp mode. Repeat with the other half.

508. Zesty Brussels Sprouts with Raisins

Preparation Time: 45 Minutes

Servings: 4

INGREDIENTS

- 14 oz. Brussels sprouts, steamed
- 2 oz. toasted pine nuts
- 2 oz. raisins
- 1 tablespoon olive oil
- Juice and zest of 1 orange

DIRECTIONS

1. Soak the raisins in the orange juice and let sit for about 20 minutes. Drizzle the Brussels sprouts with the olive oil, and place them in the basket of the Ninja Foodi.

2. Close the crisping lid and cook for 15 minutes on Air Crisp mode at 370 F. Remove to a bowl and top with pine nuts, raisins, and orange zest.

509. Rosemary Potato Fries

Preparation Time: 30 Minutes

Servings: 4

INGREDIENTS

- 4 russet potatoes, cut into sticks
- 2 garlic cloves, crushed
- 2 tablespoon butter, melted
- 1 teaspoon fresh rosemary; chopped
- Salt and pepper, to taste

DIRECTIONS

1. Add butter, garlic, salt, and pepper to a bowl; toss until the sticks are well-coated. Lay the potato sticks into the Ninja Foodi's basket. Close the crisping lid and cook for 15 minutes at 370 F. Shake the potatoes every 5 minutes.
2. Once ready, check to ensure the fries are golden and crispy all over if not, return them to cook for a few minutes.
3. Divide standing up between metal cups lined with nonstick baking paper, and serve sprinkled with rosemary.

510. Chicken and Cheese Bake

Preparation Time: 1 hour 18 Minutes

Servings: 6

INGREDIENTS

- 1 lb. chicken breast
- 10 oz. Cheddar cheese
- 10 oz. cream cheese
- ½ cup sour cream
- ½ cup breadcrumbs
- ½ cup water

DIRECTIONS

1. Open the Ninja Foodi and add the chicken, water, and cream cheese. Close the lid, secure the pressure valve, and select Pressure mode on High for 10 minutes. Press Start/Stop.
2. Once the timer has ended, do a quick pressure release, and open the pot.
3. Shred the chicken with two forks and add the cheddar cheese. Sprinkle with breadcrumbs, and close the crisping lid. Select Bake/Roast, set the temperature to 380 degrees F and the timer to 3 minutes. Serve warm with veggie bites.

511. Cheesy Brazilian Balls

Preparation Time: 35 Minutes

Servings: 4

INGREDIENTS

- 2 cups flour
- 2 cups grated mozzarella cheese
- ½ cup olive oil
- 1 cup milk
- 2 eggs, cracked into a bowl
- A pinch of salt

DIRECTIONS

1. Grease the crisp basket with cooking spray and set aside. Put the Ninja Foodi on Medium and select Sear/Sauté mode. Add the milk, oil, and salt, and let boil. Add the flour and mix it vigorously with a spoon.
2. Let the mixture cool. Once cooled, use a hand mixer to mix the dough well, and add the eggs and cheese while still mixing. The dough should be thick and sticky.
3. Use your hands to make 14 balls out of the mixture, and put them in the greased basket. Put the basket in the pot and close the crisping lid.
4. Select Air Crisp, set the temperature to 380 degrees F and set the timer to 15 minutes. At the 7-minute mark, shake the balls.

Serve with lemon aioli, garlic mayo or ketchup.

512. Teriyaki Chicken Wings

Preparation Time: 30 Minutes

Servings: 6

INGREDIENTS

- 2 lb. chicken wings
- 1 cup teriyaki sauce
- 1 tablespoon honey
- 2 tablespoon cornstarch
- 2 tablespoon cold water
- 1 teaspoon finely ground black pepper
- 1 teaspoon sesame seeds

DIRECTIONS

1. In the pot, combine honey, teriyaki sauce and black pepper until the honey dissolves completely; toss in chicken to coat. Seal the pressure lid, choose Pressure, set to High, and set the timer to 10 minutes. Press Start.
2. When ready, release the pressure quickly. Transfer chicken wings to a platter. Mix cold water with the cornstarch.
3. Press Sear/Sauté and stir in cornstarch slurry into the sauce and cook for 3 to 5 minutes until thickened. Top the chicken with thickened sauce. Add a garnish of sesame seeds, and serve.

513. Cheesy Cabbage Side Dish

Preparation Time: 30 Minutes

Servings: 4

INGREDIENTS

- ½ head of cabbage, cut into 4 wedges
- 2 cup Parmesan cheese
- 4 tablespoon butter, melted
- 1 teaspoon smoked paprika
- Salt and pepper, to taste

DIRECTIONS

1. Line the basket with parchment paper. Brush the butter over the cabbage wedges; season with salt and pepper. Coat the cabbage with the Parmesan cheese. Arrange in the basket and sprinkle with paprika.
2. Close the crisping lid and cook for 15 minutes on Air Crisp mode, flip over and cook for an additional 10 minutes; at 330 F.

514. Cheesy Bacon Dip

Preparation Time: 10 Minutes

Servings: 10

INGREDIENTS

- 10 bacon slices; chopped roughly
- 4 chopped tomatoes
- 1 cup water
- 1¼ cup cream cheese
- 1¼ cup shredded Monterey Jack cheese

DIRECTIONS

1. Turn on the Ninja Foodi and select Air Crisp mode. Set the temperature to 370 degrees F and the time to 8 minutes. Add the bacon pieces and close the crisping lid. Press Start/Stop.
2. When ready, open the lid and add the water, cream cheese, and tomatoes. Do Not Stir. Close the lid, secure the pressure valve, and select Pressure mode on High for 5 minutes. Press Start/Stop.
3. Once the timer has ended, do a quick pressure release, and open the lid. Stir in the cheddar cheese and mix to combine. Serve with a side of chips.

515. Spinach Hummus

Preparation Time: 1 hr 10 Minutes

Servings: 12

INGREDIENTS

- 2 cups spinach; chopped
- ½ cup tahini
- 2 cups dried chickpeas
- 8 cups water
- 5 garlic cloves, crushed
- 5 tablespoon grapeseed oil
- 2 teaspoon salt; divided
- 5 tablespoon lemon juice

DIRECTIONS

1. In the pressure cooker, mix 2 tablespoon oil, water, 1 teaspoon salt, and chickpeas. Seal the pressure lid, choose Pressure, set to High, and set the timer to 35 minutes. Press Start. When ready, release the pressure quickly. In a small bowl, reserve ½ cup of the cooking liquid and drain chickpeas.
2. Mix half the reserved cooking liquid and chickpeas in a food processor and puree until no large chickpeas remain; add remaining cooking liquid, spinach, lemon juice, remaining teaspoon salt, garlic, and tahini.
3. Process hummus for 8 minutes until smooth. Stir in the remaining 3 tablespoon of olive oil before serving.

516. Wrapped Asparagus in Bacon

Preparation Time: 30 Minutes

Servings: 6

INGREDIENTS

- 1 lb. bacon; sliced
- 1 lb. asparagus spears, trimmed
- ½ cup Parmesan cheese, grated
- Cooking spray
- Salt and pepper, to taste

DIRECTIONS

1. Place the bacon slices out on a work surface, top each one with one asparagus spear and half of the cheese. Wrap the bacon around the asparagus.
2. Line the Ninja Foodi basket with parchment paper. Arrange the wraps into the basket, scatter over the remaining cheese, season with salt and black pepper, and spray with cooking spray. Close the crisping lid and cook for 8 to 10 minutes on Roast mode at 370 F. If necessary work in batches. Serve hot!

517. Cheese bombs wrapped in Bacon.

Preparation Time: 20 Minutes

Servings: 8

INGREDIENTS

- 8 bacon slices, cut in half
- 16 oz. Mozzarella cheese, cut into 8 pieces
- 3 tablespoon butter, melted

DIRECTIONS

1. Wrap each cheese string with a slice of bacon and secure the ends with toothpicks. Set aside. Grease the crisp basket with the melted butter and add in the bombs.
2. Close the crisping lid, select Air Crisp mode, and set the temperature to 370 degrees F and set the time to 10 minutes.
3. At the 5-minute mark, turn the bombs. When ready, remove to a paper-lined plate to drain the excess oil. Serve on a platter with toothpicks and tomato dip.

518. Mouthwatering Meatballs

Preparation Time: 30 Minutes

Servings: 6

INGREDIENTS

- 2 lb. ground beef
- 1 potato, shredded
- 2 eggs, beaten
- ½ cup Parmesan cheese, grated
- 2 cups tomato sauce to serve

- 2 tablespoon chopped chives
- ¼ teaspoon pepper
- ½ teaspoon garlic powder
- ½ teaspoon salt
- 1 package cooked spaghetti to serve
- Basil leaves to serve
- Cooking spray

DIRECTIONS

1. In a large bowl, combine the potato, salt, pepper, garlic powder, eggs, and chives. Form 12 balls out of the mixture. Spray with cooking spray. Arrange half of the balls onto a lined Ninja Foodi basket.
2. Close the crisping lid and cook for 14 minutes on Air Crisp mode at 330 F. After 7 minutes, turn the meatballs.
3. Repeat with the other half. Serve over cooked spaghetti mixed with tomato sauce, sprinkled with Parmesan cheese and basil leaves.

519.   Rosemary and Garlic Mushrooms

Preparation Time: 20 Minutes

Servings: 4

INGREDIENTS

- 12 oz. button mushrooms
- 2 rosemary sprigs
- 3 garlic cloves, minced
- ¼ cup melted butter
- ½ teaspoon salt
- ¼ teaspoon black pepper

DIRECTIONS

1. Wash and pat dry the mushrooms and cut them in half. Place in a large bowl. Add the remaining Ingredients to the bowl and toss well to combine.
2. Transfer the mushrooms to the basket of the Ninja Foodi. Close the crisping lid and cook for 12 minutes on Air Crisp mode, shaking once halfway through; at 350 F.

520.   Sweet Pickled Cucumbers

Preparation Time: 5 Minutes

Servings: 6

INGREDIENTS

- 1 pound small cucumbers; sliced into rings
- 1/4 cup green garlic, minced
- 2 cups white vinegar
- 1 cup sugar
- 1 cup water
- 2 tablespoon Dill Pickle Seasoning
- 2 teaspoon salt
- 1 teaspoon cumin

DIRECTIONS

1. Into the pot, add sliced cucumber, vinegar and pour water on top. Sprinkle sugar over cucumbers. Add cumin, dill pickle seasoning, and salt.
2. Stir well to dissolve the sugar. Seal the pressure lid, choose Pressure, set to High, and set the timer to 4 minutes. Press Start.
3. When ready, release the pressure quickly. Ladle cucumbers into a large storage container and pour cooking liquid over the top. Chill for 1 hour.

521.   Cheesy Tomato Bruschetta

Preparation Time: 15 Minutes

Servings: 2

INGREDIENTS

- Italian Ciabatta Sandwich Bread
- tomatoes; chopped
- garlic cloves, minced
- cup grated mozzarella cheese
- Olive oil to brush
- Basil leaves; chopped
- Salt and pepper to taste

DIRECTIONS

1. Cut the bread in half, lengthways, then each piece again in half. Drizzle each bit with olive oil and sprinkle with garlic. Top with the grated cheese, salt, and pepper.
2. Place the bruschetta pieces into the Ninja Foodi basket, close the crisping lid and cook for 12 minutes on Air Crisp mode at 380 F. At 6 minutes, check for doneness.
3. Once the Ninja Foodi beeps, remove the bruschetta to a serving platter, spoon over the tomatoes and chopped basil to serve.

522.   Chicken Meatballs with Ranch Dip

Preparation Time: 34 Minutes

Servings: 4

INGREDIENTS

- 1 lb. ground chicken
- 1 egg, beaten
- Green onions for garnish
- 2 tablespoon minced garlic
- 2 tablespoon olive oil
- 2 tablespoon chopped green onions
- 5 tablespoon Hot sauce
- 2 tablespoon Buffalo wing sauce
- Salt and pepper, to taste

For the dip:

- ½ cup Roquefort cheese, crumbled
- 2 tablespoon olive oil
- 2 tablespoon mayonnaise
- ¼ tablespoon heavy cream
- Juice from ½ lemon

DIRECTIONS

1. Mix all salsa Ingredients in a bowl until uniform and creamy, and refrigerate. Add the ground chicken, salt, garlic, and two tablespoons of green onions. Mix well with your hands.
2. Rub your hands with some oil and form bite-size balls out of the mixture. Lay onto

your crisp basket fryer basket. Spray with cooking spray.
3. Select Air Crisp, set the temperature to 385 degrees F and the time to 14minutes. At the 7-minute mark, turn the meatballs.
4. Meanwhile, add the hot sauce and butter to a bowl and microwave them until the butter melts. Mix the sauce with a spoon.
5. Pour the hot sauce mixture and a half cup of water over the meatballs.
6. Close the lid, secure the pressure valve, and select Sear/Sauté mode on High Pressure for 10 minutes. Press Start/Stop.
7. Once the timer has ended, do a quick pressure release. Dish the meatballs. Garnish with green onions, and serve with Roquefort sauce.

523.   Crispy Cheesy Straws

Preparation Time: 45 Minutes

Servings: 8

INGREDIENTS

- 2 cups cauliflower florets, steamed
- 5 oz. cheddar cheese
- 3 ½ oz. oats
- 1 egg
- 1 red onion; diced
- 1 teaspoon mustard
- Salt and pepper, to taste

DIRECTIONS

1. Add the oats in a food processor and process until they resemble breadcrumbs. Place the steamed florets in a cheesecloth and squeeze out the excess liquid.
2. Put the florets in a large bowl, and add the rest of the Ingredients to the bowl.
3. Mix well with your hands, to combine the Ingredients thoroughly.
4. Take a little bit of the mixture and twist it into a straw. Place in the lined Ninja Foodi basket; repeat with the rest of the mixture.
5. Close the crisping lid and cook for 10 minutes on Air Crisp mode at 350 F. After 5

minutes, turn them over and cook for an additional 10 minutes.

524. Green Vegan Dip

Preparation Time: 20 Minutes

Servings: 4

INGREDIENTS

- 10 ounces canned green chiles, drained with liquid reserved
- 2 cups broccoli florets
- ¼ cup raw cashews
- ¼ cup soy sauce
- 1 cup water
- ¾ cup green bell pepper; chopped
- ¼ teaspoon garlic powder
- ½ teaspoon sea salt
- ¼ teaspoon chili powder

DIRECTIONS

1. In the cooker, add cashews, broccoli, green bell pepper, and water. Seal the pressure lid, choose Pressure, set to High, and set the timer to 5 minutes. Press Start. When ready, release the pressure quickly.
2. Drain water from the pot; add reserved liquid from canned green chilies, sea salt, garlic powder, chili powder, soy sauce, and cumin.
3. Use an immersion blender to blend the mixture until smooth; set aside in a mixing bowl. Stir green chilies through the dip; add your desired optional additions.

525. Egg Brulee

Preparation Time: 12 Minutes

Servings: 8

INGREDIENTS

- 8 large eggs
- 1 cup water
- Salt to taste
- Ice bath

DIRECTIONS

1. Open the Ninja Foodi, pour the water in, and fit the reversible rack in it. Put the eggs on the rack in a single layer, close the lid, secure the pressure valve, and select Pressure on High Pressure for 5 minutes. Press Start/Stop.
2. Once the timer has ended, do a quick pressure release, and open the pot.
3. Remove the eggs into the ice bath and peel the eggs. Put the peeled eggs in a plate and slice them in half.
4. Sprinkle a bit of salt on them and then followed by the sugar. Lay onto your crisp basket fryer basket. Select Air Crisp mode, set the temperature to 390 degrees F and the time to 3 minutes.

526. Cumin Baby Carrots

Preparation Time: 25 Minutes

Servings: 4

INGREDIENTS

- 1 ¼ lb. baby carrots
- 1 handful cilantro; chopped
- 2 tablespoon olive oil
- ½ teaspoon cumin powder
- ½ teaspoon garlic powder
- 1 teaspoon cumin seeds
- 1 teaspoon salt
- ½ teaspoon black pepper

DIRECTIONS

Place the baby carrots in a large bowl. Add cumin seeds, cumin, olive oil, salt, garlic powder, and pepper, and stir to coat them well.

Put the carrots in the Ninja Foodi's basket, close the crisping lid and cook for 20 minutes on Roast mode at 370 F. Remove to a platter and sprinkle with chopped cilantro, to serve.

527. Balsamic Parsnips Chips

Preparation time: 30 minutes

Servings: 4

INGREDIENTS

- 4 parsnips; thinly sliced
- 2 tablespoons balsamic vinegar
- 2 tablespoons olive oil
- Salt and black pepper to the taste

DIRECTIONS

1. Put the Foodi's basket inside and mix all the Ingredients in it. Cook the chips on Air Crisp at 380°F for 20 minutes. Divide into cups and serve as a snack.

528. Minty Turkey Bites

Preparation time: 30 minutes

Servings: 4

INGREDIENTS

- 1 big turkey breast; skinless, boneless and cubed
- 1/3 cup red wine
- 1 tablespoons mint; chopped.
- 2 tablespoons olive oil

DIRECTIONS

1. In your Foodi, combine all the Ingredients toss, set the machine on Baking mode and cook at 390°F for 20 minutes. Divide into bowls and serve as a snack.

529. Pork Bites

Preparation time: 26 minutes

Servings: 9

INGREDIENTS

- 5 ounces pork stew meat; cubed
- 1 yellow onion; chopped.
- 3 tablespoons red wine
- 1 tablespoon olive oil
- 1/2 teaspoon garlic; minced

- Salt and black pepper to the taste

DIRECTIONS

1. Set the Foodi on Sauté mode, add the oil, heat it up, add the garlic, onion, salt and pepper and sauté for 3 minutes.
2. Add the meat cubes and the wine, toss, put the pressure lid on and cook on High for 15 minutes. Release the pressure fast for 6 minutes, divide the bites into bowls and serve.

530. Buttery Chicken Bites

Preparation time: 20 minutes

Servings: 4

INGREDIENTS

- 1 pound chicken breast; skinless, boneless and cubed
- 2 teaspoons butter; melted
- 2 teaspoons garlic powder
- Salt and black pepper to the taste

DIRECTIONS

1. In a bowl, mix all the Ingredients and transfer to your Foodi's basket. Cook the chicken bites on Air Crisp at 380°F for 15 minutes. Divide into bowls and serve as a snack.

531. Coconut Carrot Chips

Preparation time: 25 minutes

Servings: 4

INGREDIENTS

- 1 pound carrots; thinly sliced
- 2 cups coconut; shredded
- 2 eggs; whisked
- Salt and black pepper to the taste

DIRECTIONS

1. Put the coconut in a bowl and the eggs mixed with salt and pepper in another one.
2. Dredge the carrot chips in eggs and then in coconut and put them in your Foodi's basket. Cook the chips on Air Crisp at 380°F for 20 minutes and serve as a snack.

532.   Oregano Chickpeas Spread

Preparation time: 30 minutes

Servings: 4

INGREDIENTS

- 2 cups canned chickpeas; drained
- 2 garlic cloves; minced
- 2 tablespoons veggie stock
- 2 tablespoons apple cider vinegar
- 1 teaspoon oregano; dried
- Slat and black pepper to the taste

DIRECTIONS

1. In your Foodi, mix all the Ingredients toss, put the pressure lid on and cook on High for 20 minutes. Release the pressure naturally for 10 minutes, blend the mix using an immersion blender, divide into bowls and serve as a party spread.

533.   Carrot Sticks

Preparation time: 20 minutes

Servings: 8

INGREDIENTS

- 8 carrots; cut into sticks
- 1 cup bread crumbs
- A drizzle of olive oil
- 2 eggs; whisked
- 1 tablespoon Italian seasoning
- Salt and black pepper to the taste

DIRECTIONS

1. In a bowl, mix the bread crumbs with seasoning, salt and pepper and toss. Put the eggs in a separate bowl. Dredge the carrots sticks in the egg and then coat in bread crumbs.
2. Put the sticks in your Foodi's basket and cook them on Air Crisp mode at 390°F for 15 minutes. Serve as a snack.

534.   Chives Chips

Preparation time: 30 minutes

Servings: 4

INGREDIENTS

- 4 gold potatoes; thinly sliced
- 1 tablespoon chives; chopped.
- 2 teaspoons olive oil
- Salt and black pepper to the taste

DIRECTIONS

1. In a bowl, mix all the Ingredients and toss. Put the Foodi's basket in the machine, put the chips inside and cook on Air Crisp at 380°F for 20 minutes. Serve as a snack.

535.   Balsamic Tomatoes

Preparation time: 20 minutes

Servings: 8

INGREDIENTS

- 1½ pounds mixed tomatoes; halved
- 1 yellow onion; chopped.
- 2 tablespoons olive oil
- 1 tablespoon balsamic vinegar
- A pinch of cayenne pepper
- Salt and black pepper to the taste

DIRECTIONS

1. Put the reversible rack in the Foodi, add the baking pan inside and mix all the Ingredients in it.
2. Set the machine on Baking mode and cook the tomatoes at 370°F for 15 minutes. Arrange the tomatoes on a platter and serve as an appetizer.

536. Lime Carrot Sticks

Preparation time: 21 minutes

Servings: 4

INGREDIENTS

- 4 carrots; cut into sticks
- 1 teaspoon garlic powder
- 3 tablespoons lime juice
- Cooking spray
- Salt and black pepper to the taste

DIRECTIONS

1. In a bowl, mix all the Ingredients and transfer to your Foodi's basket. Grease the sticks with cooking spray and cook them on Air Crisp at 390°F for 15 minutes. Serve as a snack right away.

537. Celery Dip

Preparation time: 25 minutes

Servings: 6

INGREDIENTS

- 28 ounces canned tomatoes; crushed
- 1/4 cup veggie stock
- 1 yellow onion; chopped.
- 4 garlic cloves; minced
- 4 celery ribs; chopped.
- Cooking spray
- A pinch of basil; dried
- Salt and black pepper to the taste

DIRECTIONS

1. Put the reversible rack in the Foodi, add the baking pan inside and grease it with cooking spray.
2. Combine all the Ingredients inside, set the machine on Baking mode and cook at 380°F for 20 minutes. Divide into bowls and serve as a snack.

538. Paprika Potato Chips

Preparation time: 30 minutes

Servings: 4

INGREDIENTS

- 4 potatoes; thinly sliced
- 1/2 teaspoon turmeric powder
- 1 teaspoon olive oil
- Salt and black pepper to the taste

DIRECTIONS

1. In a bowl, mix all the Ingredients and toss. Put the Foodi's basket inside, put the potato chips in it and cook them on Air Crisp at 380°F for 20 minutes. Serve as a snack.

539. Peppers and Tomatoes Dip

Preparation time: 18 minutes

Servings: 4

INGREDIENTS

- 5 ounces canned tomatoes; chopped.
- 3 cups bell peppers; chopped.
- 4 tablespoons veggie stock

DIRECTIONS

1. In your Foodi, mix all the Ingredients put the pressure lid on and cook on High for 15 minutes. Release the pressure fast for 3 minutes, blend using an immersion blender, divide the mix into bowls and serve.

540. Turkey Dip

Preparation time: 35 minutes

Servings: 6

INGREDIENTS

- 1½ pound turkey meat; ground
- 1 yellow onion; chopped.
- 4 garlic cloves; minced
- 2 cups tomato puree
- 2 carrots; chopped.
- 1 tablespoon olive oil
- Salt and black pepper to the taste

DIRECTIONS

1. Set the Foodi on Sauté mode, add the oil, heat it up, add the onion and the garlic and sauté for 5 minutes. Add the rest of the Ingredients put the pressure lid on and cook on High for 20 minutes.
2. Release the pressure naturally for 10 minutes, divide everything into bowls and serve. Serve with your favorite pasta.

541. Basil Beet Chips

Preparation time: 30 minutes

Servings: 6

INGREDIENTS

- 1 pound beets; thinly sliced
- 4 garlic cloves; minced
- 1/3 cup olive oil
- 1 bunch basil; chopped.

DIRECTIONS

1. In a bowl, mix all the Ingredients and toss. Put the chips in your Foodi's basket and cook them on Air Crisp at 390°F for 20 minutes. Serve as a snack.

542. Cauliflower Dip

Preparation time: 25 minutes

Servings: 4

INGREDIENTS

- 12 ounces cauliflower florets
- 1 yellow onion; chopped.
- 1½ cups coconut cream
- 1 tablespoon butter; melted
- A pinch of salt and black pepper

DIRECTIONS

1. Set the Foodi on Sauté mode, add the butter, heat it up, add the onion and sauté for 2 minutes.
2. Add the rest of the Ingredients cover and cook on High for 12 minutes. Release the pressure naturally for 10 minutes, blend the mix with an immersion blender, divide into bowls and serve.

543. Black Olives Spread

Preparation time: 9 minutes

Servings: 4

INGREDIENTS

- 12 black olives; pitted and minced
- 4 ounces cream cheese
- 2 tablespoons basil pesto
- Salt and black pepper to the taste

DIRECTIONS

1. In your Foodi, mix all the Ingredients toss, put the pressure lid on and cook on High for 5 minutes.
2. Release the pressure fast for 4 minutes, blend the mix a bit using an immersion blender, divide into bowls and serve.

544. Basil Shrimp

Preparation time: 13 minutes

Servings: 6

INGREDIENTS

- 1 pound shrimp; peeled and deveined
- 1 tablespoon basil; chopped.
- 2 teaspoons olive oil
- Salt and black pepper to the taste

DIRECTIONS

1. In your Foodi's basket, mix all the Ingredients toss, set the machine on Air Crisp and cook the shrimp at 370°F for 8 minutes. Divide into bowls and serve as an appetizer.

545. Hot Beef Dip

Preparation time: 25 minutes

Servings: 6

INGREDIENTS

- 1 pound beef meat; ground
- 1¼ cups apple cider vinegar
- 1/2 cup tomato sauce
- 10 ounces hot peppers; chopped.
- 2 tablespoons olive oil
- Salt and black pepper to the taste

DIRECTIONS

1. Set the Foodi on Sauté mode, add the oil, heat it up, add the meat and brown for 5 minutes.
2. Add the rest of the Ingredients put the pressure lid on and cook on High for 20 minutes. Release the pressure fast for 5 minutes, divide the dip into bowls and serve as a party mix.

546. Orange Cherries Dip

Preparation time: 18 minutes

Servings: 4

INGREDIENTS

- 1 pound cherries; pitted

- 2 ounces orange juice
- 1/2 cup sugar

DIRECTIONS

1. In your Foodi, combine all the Ingredients put the pressure lid on and cook on High for 8 minutes. Release the pressure naturally for 10 minutes, blend using an immersion blender, divide into bowls and serve as a sweet party dip.

547. Lentils Salsa

Preparation time: 25 minutes

Servings: 4

INGREDIENTS

- 2 cups canned lentils; drained
- 2 garlic cloves; minced
- 1 cup tomato puree
- 1 yellow onion; chopped.
- 1 tablespoon olive oil
- 4 tablespoons white vinegar
- 1 teaspoon Tabasco sauce
- Salt and black pepper to the taste

DIRECTIONS

1. In your Foodi, mix all the Ingredients put the pressure lid on and cook on High for 15 minutes. Release the pressure naturally for 10 minutes, divide the mix into bowls and serve as an appetizer.

548. Crispy Turkey Bites

Preparation time: 30 minutes

Servings: 4

INGREDIENTS

- 1 pound turkey breast; skinless, boneless and cubed
- 3/4 cup white flour
- 1 cup bread crumbs
- 1 egg; whisked

- Cooking spray
- Salt and black pepper to the taste

DIRECTIONS

1. In a bowl, mix the flour with salt and pepper and stir. Put the egg in another bowl and the breadcrumbs in a third one.
2. Dredge the turkey bites in flour, egg and breadcrumbs, arrange all the bites in your Foodi's basket and grease them with some cooking spray. Cook on Air Crisp mode at 380°F for 20 minutes, divide into bowls and serve.

549.   Peppers Salsa

Preparation time: 17 minutes

Servings: 4

INGREDIENTS

- 1 orange bell pepper; cut into strips
- 1 yellow bell pepper; cut into strips
- 2 ounces tomato sauce
- 1 green onion; chopped.
- 2 tablespoons oregano; chopped.
- Salt and black pepper to the taste

DIRECTIONS

1. In your Foodi, mix all the Ingredients toss, put the pressure lid on and cook on High for 12 minutes. Release the pressure fast for 5 minutes, divide the salsa into bowls and serve as an appetizer.

550.   Zucchini and Dill Spread

Preparation time: 20 minutes

Servings: 6

INGREDIENTS

- 1/2 cup dill; chopped.
- 2 garlic cloves; minced
- 3 zucchinis; grated
- 2 eggs; whisked

- Cooking spray
- Salt and black pepper to the taste

DIRECTIONS

1. Put the reversible rack in the Foodi, add the baking pan inside and grease it with cooking spray.
2. Add all the Ingredients inside, set the machine on Baking mode and cook the mix at 370°F for 15 minutes. Divide into cups and serve warm as a spread.

551.   Celeriac Sticks

Preparation time: 25 minutes

Servings: 4

INGREDIENTS

1 big celeriac; cut into medium sticks

1 tablespoon olive oil

Salt and black pepper to the taste

DIRECTIONS

1. In your Foodi's basket, mix all the Ingredients toss, set the machine on Air Crisp and cook at 380°F for 20 minutes. Divide the sticks into bowls and serve as a snack.

552.   Mango Spread

Preparation time: 20 minutes

Servings: 4

INGREDIENTS

- 1 shallot; chopped.
- 2 mangos; chopped.
- 1 apple; cored and chopped.
- 1¼ cup sugar
- 1 tablespoon olive oil
- 1/2 teaspoon cinnamon powder

DIRECTIONS

1. Set the Foodi on Sauté mode, add the oil, heat it up,
2. Add the shallot and sauté for 2 minutes.
3. Add all the other Ingredients toss,
4. Put the pressure lid on and cook on High for 8 minutes.
5. Release the pressure naturally for 10 minutes,
6. Blend using an immersion blender
7. Serve as a spread.

553. Chickpeas Salad

Preparation time: 30 minutes

Servings: 4

INGREDIENTS

- 20 ounces canned tomatoes; crushed
- 1/4 cup veggie stock
- 1 cup baby spinach
- 2 cups canned chickpeas; drained
- 3 garlic cloves; minced
- Salt and black pepper to the taste

DIRECTIONS

1. In your Foodi, combine all the Ingredients except the spinach, put the pressure lid on and cook on High for 20 minutes.
2. Release the pressure naturally for 10 minutes. Divide the spinach into bowls, also divide the chickpeas salsa, toss and serve as an appetizer.

554. Chinese Beet Slices

Preparation time: 30 minutes

Servings: 4

INGREDIENTS

- 4 beets; thinly sliced
- 2 tablespoons soy sauce
- 2 teaspoons olive oil
- 1 teaspoon sweet paprika

DIRECTIONS

1. In a bowl, mix all the Ingredients and toss.
2. Put the beet slices in your Foodi's basket and cook on Air Crisp at 390°F for 20 minutes.
3. Serve as a snack.

555. Carrot Spread

Preparation time: 30 minutes

Servings: 4

INGREDIENTS

- 1½ pounds carrots; chopped.
- 1 yellow onion; chopped.
- 1/2 cup chicken stock
- 1 bunch mint; chopped.
- 2 garlic cloves; minced
- 1 tablespoon olive oil
- Salt and white pepper to the taste

DIRECTIONS

1. In your Foodi, mix all the Ingredients cover and cook on High for 20 minutes.
2. Release the pressure naturally for 10 minutes,
3. Blend using an immersion blender,
4. Divide the spread into bowls and serve.

556. Orange Cranberry Dip

Preparation time: 25 minutes

Servings: 4

INGREDIENTS

- 12 ounces cranberries
- 1/4 cup orange juice
- 2½ teaspoons orange zest.
- 4 tablespoons maple syrup

DIRECTIONS

1. In your Foodi, mix all the Ingredients put the pressure lid on and cook on High for 15 minutes.

2. Release the pressure naturally for 10 minutes, blend the dip with an immersion blender,
3. Divide into bowls and serve.

DESSERTS

557. Lemon Cheesecake with Strawberries

Preparation Time: 3 hr

Servings: 8

INGREDIENTS

Crust:

- 4 ounces graham crackers
- 3 tablespoon butter, melted
- 1 teaspoon ground cinnamon

Filling:

- 1 pound mascarpone cheese, at room temperature
- 2 cups water
- 1 cup strawberries, halved
- ¾ cup sugar
- ¼ cup sour cream, at room temperature
- 2 eggs, at room temperature
- 1 tablespoon lemon juice
- 1 teaspoon vanilla extract
- 1 teaspoon lemon zest
- 1 pinch salt

DIRECTIONS

1. In a food processor, beat cinnamon and graham crackers to attain a texture almost same as sand; mix in melted butter. Press the crumbs into the bottom of a 7-inch springform pan in an even layer.
2. In a stand mixer, beat sugar, mascarpone cheese, and sour cream for 3 minutes to combine well and have a fluffy and smooth mixture. Scrape the bowl's sides and add eggs, lemon zest, salt, lemon juice, and vanilla extract. Carry on to beat the mixture until you obtain a consistent color and all I Ingredients are completely combined. Pour filling over crust.

3. Into the inner pot of your Foodi, add water and set in the reversible rack. Insert the springform pan on the rack. Close the crisping lid and select Bake/Roast; adjust the temperature to 250°F and the cook time to 40 minutes. Press Start.
4. Remove cheesecake and let cool for 1 hour. Refrigerate for 2 hours. Transfer to a serving plate and garnish with strawberry halves on top. Use a paring knife to run along the edges between the pan and cheesecake to remove the cheesecake and set to the plate.

558. Filling Coconut and Oat Cookies

Preparation Time: 30 Minutes

Servings: 4

INGREDIENTS

- 5 ½ oz. flour
- 3 oz. sugar
- 1 small egg, beaten
- ¼ cup coconut flakes
- ½ cup oats
- 1 teaspoon vanilla extract

Filling:

- 4 oz. powdered sugar
- 1 oz. white chocolate, melted
- 2 oz. butter
- 1 teaspoon vanilla extract

DIRECTIONS

1. Beat all cookie Ingredients with an electric mixer, except the flour. When smooth, fold in the flour. Drop spoonfuls of the batter onto a prepared cookie sheet. Close the crisping lid and cook in the Foodi at 350 F for about 18 minutes on Air Crisp mode; let cool.
2. Prepare the filling by beating all Ingredients together. Spread the mixture on half of the

cookies. Top with the other halves to make cookie sandwiches.

559. Raspberry Cream Tart

Preparation Time: 55 min+ Chilling time

Servings: 4

INGREDIENTS

- 1 refrigerated piecrust, for the raspberries
- 2½ cups fresh raspberries; divided
- ¼ cup sugar
- 2 tablespoons water
- 1 tablespoon arrowroot starch
- 1 teaspoon lemon juice
- ¼ teaspoon grated lemon zest
- Pinch salt

For The Filling

- 8 ounces cream cheese, at room temperature
- ¼ cup heavy cream
- ½ cup confectioners' sugar
- 1 teaspoon vanilla extract

DIRECTIONS

1. Roll out the pie crust and fit into a tart pan. Do not stretch the dough to prevent shrinking when cooking. Use a fork to prick all over the bottom of the dough. Place the reversible rack in the pot in the lower position of the pot and put the tart pan on top.
2. Close the crisping lid, choose Bake/Roast; adjust the temperature to 250°F, and the cook time to 15 minutes. Press Start. When done baking, open the lid and check the crust. It should be set and lightly brown around the edges.
3. Close the crisping lid again. Adjust the temperature to 375°F and the cook time to 4 minutes. Press Start to begin baking.
4. After 3 minutes, check the crust, which should be a deep golden brown color by now. If not, cook for the remaining 1 minute. Remove the rack and set the crust aside to cool.
5. Fetch out 1 cup of berries into the inner pot. In a small bowl, whisk the arrowroot starch and water until smoothly mixed. Pour the slurry on the raspberries along with the sugar, lemon zest, lemon juice, and salt. Mix to distribute the slurry among the raspberries.
6. Seal the pressure lid, choose Pressure; adjust the pressure to High and the cook time to 2 minutes. Press Start.
7. Once done cooking, perform a quick pressure release and carefully open the lid. The raspberries will have softened. Add the remaining 1½ cups of raspberries, stirring to coat with the cooked mixture. Then, allow cooling.
8. To make the cream filling, in a bowl and with a hand mixer, whisk the vanilla extract and cream cheese until evenly combined and smooth. Mix in the confectioners' sugar and whisk again until the sugar has fully incorporated and the mixture is light and smooth.
9. With clean whisks and in another bowl, beat the heavy cream until soft peaks form. Fold the heavy cream into the vanilla mixture until both are evenly combined. To assemble, spoon the cream filling into the piecrust and scatter the remaining raspberries on the cream. Chill for 30 minutes before cutting and serving.

560. Vanilla Cheesecake

Preparation Time: 60 Minutes

Servings: 6

INGREDIENTS

- 16 ounces cream cheese, at room temperature
- 2 eggs
- ¼ cup sour cream
- 1½ cups finely crushed graham crackers
- 1 cup water
- ½ cup brown sugar
- 2 tablespoons sugar

- 1 tablespoon all-purpose flour
- 4 tablespoons unsalted butter, melted
- 1½ teaspoons vanilla extract
- ½ teaspoon salt
- Cooking spray

DIRECTIONS

1. Grease a spring form pan with cooking spray, then line the pan with parchment paper, grease with cooking spray again, and line with aluminium foil. This is to ensure that there are no air gaps in the pan. In a medium mixing bowl, mix the graham cracker crumbs, sugar, and butter. Spoon the mixture into the pan and press firmly into with a spoon.
2. In a deep bowl and with a hand mixer, beat the beat the cream cheese and brown sugar until well-mixed. Whisk in the sour cream to be smooth and stir in the flour, vanilla, and salt.
3. Crack the eggs in and beat but not to be overly smooth. Pour the mixture into the pan over the crumbs. Next, pour the water into the pot. Put the spring form pan on the reversible rack and put the rack in the lower positon of the pot.
4. Seal the pressure lid, choose Pressure, set to High, and set the time to 35 minutes. Choose Start/Stop to begin. Once done baking, perform a natural pressure release for 10 minutes, then a quick pressure release to let out any remaining pressure. Carefully open the lid.
5. Remove the pan from the rack and allow the cheesecake to cool for 1 hour. Cover the cheesecake with foil and chill in the refrigerator for 4 hours.

561. Berry Vanilla Pudding

Preparation Time: 35 min + 6h for refrigeration

Servings: 4

INGREDIENTS

- 4 raspberries
- 4 blueberries
- 4 egg yolks
- ½ cup sugar
- ½ cup milk
- 1 cup heavy cream
- 1 teaspoon vanilla extract
- 4 tablespoon water + 1 ½ cups water

DIRECTIONS

1. Turn on your Foodi and select Sear/Sauté mode on Medium. Add four tablespoons for water and the sugar. Stir it constantly until it dissolves. Press Stop. Add milk, heavy cream, and vanilla. Stir it with a whisk until evenly combined.
2. Crack the eggs into a bowl and add a tablespoon of the cream mixture. Whisk it and then very slowly add the remaining cream mixture while whisking. Fit the reversible rack at the bottom of the pot, and pour one and a half cup of water in it. Pour the mixture into four ramekins and place them on the rack.
3. Close the lid of the pot, secure the pressure valve, and select Pressure mode on High Pressure for 4 minutes. Press Start/Stop. Once the timer has gone off, do a quick pressure release, and open the lid.
4. With a napkin in hand, carefully remove the ramekins onto a flat surface. Let cool for about 15 minutes and then refrigerate them for 6 hours.
5. After 6 hours, remove them from the refrigerator and garnish them with the raspberries and blueberries. Enjoy immediately or refrigerate further until dessert time is ready.

562. Molten Lava Cake

Preparation Time: 20 Minutes

Servings: 4

INGREDIENTS

- 3 ½ oz. butter, melted
- 3 ½ oz. dark chocolate, melted
- 2 eggs
- 3 ½ tablespoon sugar

- 1 ½ tablespoon self-rising flour

DIRECTIONS

1. Grease 4 ramekins with butter. Beat the eggs and sugar until frothy. Stir in the butter and chocolate.
2. Gently fold in the flour. Divide the mixture between the ramekins and bake in the Foodi for 10 minutes on Air Crisp mode at 370 F. Let cool for 2 minutes before turning the lava cakes upside down onto serving plates.

563. Apple Vanilla Hand Pies

Preparation Time: 40 Minutes

Servings: 8

INGREDIENTS

- 2 apples, peeled, cored, and diced
- 1 (2-crustpackage refrigerated piecrusts, at room temperature
- 1 lemon, juiced
- 3 tablespoons sugar
- ¼ teaspoon salt
- 1 teaspoon vanilla extract
- 1 teaspoon corn-starch
- Cooking spray

DIRECTIONS

1. In a large mixing bowl, combine the apples, sugar, lemon juice, salt, and vanilla. Allow the mixture to stand for 10 minutes, then drain, and reserve 1 tablespoon of the liquid. In a small bowl, whisk the corn-starch into the reserved liquid and then, mix with the apple mixture. Put the crisping basket in the pot and close the crisping lid. Choose Air Crisp, set the temperature to 350°F, and the time to 5 minutes. Press Start/Stop to preheat.
2. Put the piecrusts on a lightly floured surface and cut into 8 (4-inch-diametercircles. Spoon a tablespoon of apple mixture in the center of the circle, with ½ an inch's border around the dough.

Brush the edges with water and fold the dough over the filling. Press the edges with a fork to seal.

3. Cut 3 small slits on top of each pie and oil with cooking spray. Arrange the pies in a single layer in the preheated basket. Close the crisping lid. Choose Air Crisp, set the temperature to 350°F, and set the time to 12 minutes. Press Start/Stop to begin baking. Once done baking, remove, and place the pies on a wire rack to cool. Repeat with the remaining hand pies.

564. Caramel Walnut Brownies

Preparation Time: 60 min+ cooling time

Servings: 4

INGREDIENTS

- 2 large eggs, at room temperature
- 8 ounces white chocolate
- 1 cup sugar
- ½ cup caramel sauce
- ½ cup toasted walnuts
- ¾ cup all-purpose flour
- 8 tablespoons unsalted butter
- 2 teaspoons almond extract
- A pinch of salt
- Cooking spray

DIRECTIONS

1. Put the white chocolate and butter in a small bowl and pour 1 cup of water into the inner pot. Place the reversible rack in the lower position of the pot and put the bowl on top.
2. Close the crisping lid. Choose Bake/Roast; adjust the temperature to 375°F and the cook time to 10 minutes to melt the white chocolate and butter. Press Start. Check after 5 minutes and stir. As soon as the chocolate has melted, remove the bowl from the pot.
3. Use a small spatula to transfer the chocolate mixture into a medium and stir in the almond extract, sugar, and salt. One after another, crack each egg into the bowl

and whisk after each addition. Mix in the flour until smooth, about 1 minute.

4. Grease a round cake pan with cooking spray or line the pan with parchment paper. Pour the batter into the prepared pan and place on the rack.

5. Close the crisping lid and Choose Bake/Roast; adjust the temperature to 250°F and the cook time to 25 minutes. Press Start. Once the time is up, open the lid and check the brownies. The top should be just set. Blot out the butter that may pool to the top using a paper towel.

6. Close the crisping lid again and adjust the temperature to 300°F and the cook time to 15 minutes. Press Start. Once the time is up, open the lid and check the brownies. A toothpick inserted into the center should come out with crumbs sticking to it but no raw batter.

7. Generously drizzle the caramel sauce on top of the brownies and scatter the walnuts on top. Close the crisping lid again and adjust the temperature to 325°F and the cook time to 8 minutes; press Start.

8. When the nuts are brown and the caramel is bubbling, take out the brownies, and allow cooling for at least 30 minutes and cut into squares.

565. Strawberry and Lemon Ricotta Cheesecake

Preparation Time: 35 Minutes

Servings: 6

INGREDIENTS

- 10 strawberries, halved to decorate
- 10 oz. cream cheese
- 1 ½ cups water
- ¼ cup sugar
- ½ cup Ricotta cheese
- One lemon, zested and juiced
- 2 eggs, cracked into a bowl
- 3 tablespoon sour cream
- 1 teaspoon lemon extract

DIRECTIONS

1. In the electric mixer, add the cream cheese, quarter cup of sugar, ricotta cheese, lemon zest, lemon juice, and lemon extract. Turn on the mixer and mix the Ingredients until a smooth consistency is formed. Adjust the sweet taste to liking with more sugar.

2. Reduce the speed of the mixer and add the eggs. Fold it in at low speed until it is fully incorporated. Make sure not to fold the eggs in high speed to prevent a cracker crust. Grease the spring form pan with cooking spray and use a spatula to spoon the mixture into the pan. Level the top with the spatula and cover it with foil.

3. Open the Foodi, fit in the reversible rack, and pour in the water. Place the cake pan on the rack. Close the lid, secure the pressure valve, and select Pressure mode on High pressure for 15 minutes. Press Start/Stop.

4. Meanwhile, mix the sour cream and one tablespoon of sugar. Set aside. Once the timer has gone off, do a natural pressure release for 10 minutes, then a quick pressure release to let out any extra steam, and open the lid.

5. Remove the rack with pan, place the spring form pan on a flat surface, and open it. Use a spatula to spread the sour cream mixture on the warm cake. Refrigerate the cake for 8 hours. Top with strawberries; slice it into 6 pieces and serve while firming.

566. Dark Chocolate Brownies

Preparation Time: 40 Minutes

Servings: 6

INGREDIENTS

- 1 cup water
- 2 eggs
- ¼ cup olive oil
- ⅓ cup flour
- ⅓ cup cocoa powder
- ⅓ cup dark chocolate chips
- ⅓ cup chopped Walnuts

- ⅓ cup granulated sugar
- 1 tablespoon vanilla extract
- 1 tablespoon milk
- ½ teaspoon baking powder
- A pinch salt

DIRECTIONS

1. In the Foodi, add water and set in the reversible rack. Line a parchment paper on. a springform pan. In a bowl, beat eggs and sugar to mix until smooth; stir in olive oil, cocoa powder, milk, salt baking powder, chocolate chips, flour, walnuts, vanilla, and sea salt.
2. Transfer the batter to the prepared springform pan and place the pan in the pot on the rack. Close the crisping lid and select Bake/Roast; adjust the temperature to 250°F and the cook time to 20 minutes. Press Start.
3. When the time is up, open the lid and. and allow the brownie to cool for 10 minutes before cutting. Use powdered sugar to dust the brownies before serving lightly.

567.   Créme Brulee

Preparation Time: 30 min + 6 hours of cooling

Servings: 4

INGREDIENTS

- 3 cups heavy whipping cream
- 7 large egg yolks
- 2 cups water
- 6 tablespoon sugar
- 2 tablespoon vanilla extract

DIRECTIONS

1. In a mixing bowl, add the yolks, vanilla, whipping cream, and half of the swerve sugar. Use a whisk to mix them until they are well combined. Pour the mixture into the ramekins and cover them with aluminium foil.
2. Open the Foodi, fit the reversible rack into the pot, and pour in the water.

3. Place 3 ramekins on the rack and place the remaining ramekins to sit on the edges of the ramekins below.
4. Close the lid, secure the pressure valve, and select Pressure mode on High for 8 minutes. Press Start/Stop.
5. Once the timer has stopped, do a natural pressure release for 10 minutes, then a quick pressure release to let out the remaining pressure.
6. With a napkin in hand, remove the ramekins onto a flat surface and then into a refrigerator to chill for at least 6 hours. After refrigeration, remove the ramekins and remove the aluminium foil.
7. Equally, sprinkle the remaining sugar on it and return to the pot. Close the csisping lid, select Bake/Roast mode, set the timer to 4 minutes on 380 degrees F. Serve the crème brulee chilled with whipped cream.

568.   Chocolaty Fudge

Preparation Time: 55 Minutes

Servings: 8

INGREDIENTS

- 1 oz. cocoa powder
- 4 oz. butter
- 7 oz. flour, sifted
- 1 cup sugar
- ¼ cup milk
- 2 eggs
- 1 tablespoon honey
- 1 teaspoon vanilla extract
- 1 orange, juice and zest

Icing:

- 4 oz. powdered sugar
- 1 oz. butter, melted
- 1 tablespoon milk
- 1 tablespoon brown sugar
- 2 teaspoon honey

DIRECTIONS

1. In a bowl, mix the dry Ingredients for the fudge. Mix the wet Ingredients separately. Combine the two mixtures gently. Transfer the batter to a prepared Foodi basket. Close the crisping lid and cook for about 35 minutes on Roast mode at 350 F.
2. Once the timer beeps, check to ensure the cake is cooked. For the Topping: whisk together all of the icing Ingredients When the cake is cooled, coat it with the icing. Let set before slicing the fudge.

569. Lime Muffins

Preparation Time: 30 Minutes

Servings: 6

INGREDIENTS

- 2 eggs plus 1 yolk
- 1 cup yogurt
- ¼ cup superfine sugar
- Juice and zest of 2 limes
- 8 oz. cream cheese
- 1 teaspoon vanilla extract

DIRECTIONS

1. With a spatula, gently combine the yogurt and cheese. In another bowl, beat together the rest of the Ingredients
2. Gently fold the lime with the cheese mixture. Divide the batter between 6 lined muffin tins. Close the crisping lid and cook in the Foodi for 10 minutes on Air Crisp mode at 330 F.

570. Lemon and Blueberries Compote

Preparation Time: 10 min + chilling time

Servings: 4 |

INGREDIENTS

- 2 cups Blueberries
- ½ cup Water + 2 tbsp.

- ¾ cups Coconut Sugar
- 2 tablespoon Cornstarch
- Juice of ½ Lemon

DIRECTIONS

1. Place blueberries, lemon juice, ½ cup water, and coconut sugar in your cooker. Seal the pressure lid, choose Steam and set the timer to 3 minutes at High pressure. Press Start. Once done, do a quick pressure.
2. Meanwhile, combine the cornstarch and water, in a bowl. Stir in the mixture into the blueberries and cook until the mixture thickens, pressure lid off, on Sear/Sauté. Transfer the compote to a bowl and let cool completely before refrigerating for 2 hours.

571. Mixed Berry Cobbler

Preparation Time: 40 Minutes

Servings: 4

INGREDIENTS

- 2 bags frozen mixed berries
- 1 cup sugar
- 3 tablespoons arrowroot starch
- For the topping
- 1 cup self-rising flour
- ⅔ cup crème fraiche, plus more as needed
- 1 tablespoon melted unsalted butter
- 1 tablespoon whipping cream
- 5 tablespoons powdered sugar; divided
- ¼ teaspoon cinnamon powder

DIRECTIONS

1. To make the base, pour the blackberries into the inner pot along with the arrowroot starch and sugar. Mix to combine. Seal the pressure lid, choose Pressure; adjust the pressure to High and the cook time to 3 minutes; press Start. After cooking, perform a quick pressure release and carefully open the lid.
2. To make the topping, in a small bowl, whisk the flour, cinnamon powder, and 3 tablespoons of sugar. In a separate small

bowl, whisk the crème fraiche with the melted butter.

3. Pour the cream mixture on the dry Ingredients and combine evenly. If the mixture is too dry, mix in 1 tablespoon of crème fraiche at a time until the mixture is soft.

4. Spoon 2 to 3 tablespoons of dough on top over the peaches and spread out slightly on top. Brush the topping with the whipping cream and sprinkle with the remaining sugar.

5. Close the crisping lid and Choose Bake/Roast; adjust the temperature to 325°F and the cook time to 12 minutes. Press Start. Check after 8 minutes; if the dough isn't cooking evenly, rotate the pot about 90 degrees, and continue cooking.

6. When ready, the topping should be cooked through and lightly browned. Allow cooling before slicing. Serve warm.

572. Raspberry Crumble

Preparation Time: 40 Minutes

Servings: 6

INGREDIENTS

- 1 (16-ouncepackage frozen raspberries
- ½ cup rolled oats
- ⅓ cup cold unsalted butter; cut into pieces
- ½ cup all-purpose flour
- ⅔ cup brown sugar
- ½ cup water, plus 1 tablespoon
- 2 tablespoons arrowroot starch
- 5 tablespoons sugar; divided
- 1 teaspoon freshly squeezed lemon juice
- 1 teaspoon cinnamon powder

DIRECTIONS

1. Place the raspberries in the baking pan. In a small mixing bowl, combine the arrowroot starch, 1 tablespoon of water, lemon juice, and 3 tablespoons of sugar. Pour the mixture all over the raspberries.

2. Put the reversible rack in the lower position of the pot. Cover the pan with foil and pour the remaining water into the pot. Put the pan on the rack in the pot. Put the pressure lid together, and lock in the Seal position. Choose Pressure, set to High, and set the time to 10 minutes, then Choose Start/Stop to begin.

3. In a bowl, mix the flour, brown sugar, oats, butter, cinnamon, and remaining sugar until crumble forms. When done pressure-cooking, do a quick release and carefully open the lid.

4. Remove the foil and stir the fruit mixture. After, spread the crumble evenly on the berries. Close the crisping lid; choose Air Crisp, set the temperature to 400°F, and the time to 10 minutes. Choose Start/Stop to begin crisping. Cook until the top has browned and the fruit is bubbling. When done baking, remove the rack with the pan from the pot, and serve.

573. Apple Cider

Preparation Time: 45 Minutes

Servings: 6

INGREDIENTS

- 6 green apples, cored and chopped
- 1/4 cup orange juice
- 3 cups water
- 2 cinnamon sticks

DIRECTIONS

1. In a blender, add orange juice, apples, and water and blend until smooth; use a fine-mesh strainer to strain and press using a spoon. Get rid of the pulp. In the cooker, mix the strained apple puree, and cinnamon sticks.

2. Seal the pressure lid, choose Pressure, set to High, and set the timer to 10 minutes. Press Start. Release the pressure naturally for 15 minutes, then quick release the remaining pressure. Strain again and do away with the solids.

574.   Vanilla Hot Lava Cake

Preparation Time: 40 Minutes

Servings: 8

INGREDIENTS

- 1 ½ cups chocolate chips
- 1 ½ cups sugar
- 1 cup butter
- 1 cup water
- 5 eggs
- 7 tablespoon flour
- 4 tablespoon milk
- 4 teaspoon vanilla extract
- Powdered sugar to garnish

DIRECTIONS

1. Grease the cake pan with cooking spray and set aside. Open the Foodi, fit the reversible rack at the bottom of it, and pour in the water. In a medium heatproof bowl, add the butter and chocolate and melt them in the microwave for about 2 minutes. Remove it from the microwave.
2. Add sugar and use a spatula to stir it well. Add the eggs, milk, and vanilla extract and stir again. Finally, add the flour and stir it until even and smooth.
3. Pour the batter into the greased cake pan and use the spatula to level it. Place the pan on the trivet in the pot, close the lid, secure the pressure valve, and select Pressure on High for 15 minutes. Press Start/Stop.
4. Once the timer has gone off, do a natural pressure release for 10 minutes, then a quick pressure release, and open the lid.
5. Remove the rack with the pan on it and place the pan on a flat surface. Put a plate over the pan and flip the cake over into the plate. Pour the powdered sugar in a fine sieve and sift it over the cake. Use a knife to cut the cake into 8 slices and serve immediately (while warm).

575.   Pineapple Cake

Preparation Time: 50 Minutes

Servings: 4

INGREDIENTS

- 2 oz. dark chocolate, grated
- 4 oz. butter
- 7 oz. pineapple chunks
- 8 oz. self-rising flour
- ½ cup sugar
- 1 egg
- ½ cup pineapple juice
- 2 tablespoon milk

DIRECTIONS

1. Preheat the Foodi to 390 F. Place the butter and flour into a bowl and rub the mixture with your fingers until crumbed. Stir in the pineapple, sugar, chocolate, and juice. Beat the eggs and milk separately, and then add them to the batter.
2. Transfer the batter to a previously prepared (greased or linedcake pan, and cook for 40 minutes on Roast mode. Let cool for at least 10 minutes before serving.

576.   Grated Pie

Preparation time: 25 minutes

Cooking time: 25 minutes

Servings: 7

INGREDIENTS

- 1 cup strawberries, mashed
- 7 ounces butter
- 1 teaspoon salt
- 1 cup almond flour
- 1 teaspoon vanilla extract
- 1 tablespoon lemon zest
- 1 tablespoon turmeric
- 1 teaspoon nutmeg
- ½ teaspoon ground ginger

DIRECTIONS

1. Grate the butter in a mixing bowl. Sprinkle it with the salt, vanilla extract, lemon zest, turmeric, nutmeg, and ground ginger. Sift the almond flour into the bowl and knead the dough using your hands. Place the dough in the freezer for 15 minutes.
2. Remove the dough from the freezer and cut it in half. Grate the one part of the dough in the pressure cooker. Sprinkle the grated dough with the strawberries.
3. Flatten it well to make a layer. Grate the second part of the dough in the pressure cooker. Close the lid and cook at "Pressure" mode for 25 minutes. When the cooking time ends, transfer the pie to a serving plate and let it rest. Cut into slices and serve.

NUTRITION: Calories 309, Fat 31.3, Fiber 2.5, Carbs 6.2, Protein 3.9

577. Condensed Cream

Preparation time: 10 minutes

Cooking time: 40 minutes

Servings: 7

INGREDIENTS

- 3 cups cream
- 5 egg yolks
- 1 cup Erythritol
- 1 teaspoon vanilla extract

DIRECTIONS

1. Whisk the yolks in a mixing bowl. Combine the cream and Erythritol together in the pressure cooker. Set the pressure cooker to "Sauté" mode.
2. Add the vanilla extract and cook for 10 minutes, stirring frequently. Mix the Ingredients and add the egg yolks slowly and stir well. Close the pressure cooker and cook at "Pressure" mode for 30 minutes.

When the cooking time ends, remove the milk and refrigerate immediately.

NUTRITION: Calories 106, Fat 8.9, Fiber 0, Carbs 3.7, Protein 2.8

578. Crème Brule

Preparation time: 10 minutes

Cooking time: 20 minutes

Servings: 6

INGREDIENTS

- 5 tablespoon Erythritol
- 2 cup cream
- ½ teaspoon salt
- 10 egg yolks

DIRECTIONS

1. Put the egg yolks in a mixing bowl and use a hand mixer to combine for a minute. Add salt and continue to blend the egg mixture for another minute.
2. When the mixture becomes fluffy, add cream. Mix well for another minute. Sprinkle the glass ramekins with Erythritol and pour the cream mixture into each one.
3. Pour the water in the pressure cooker and place the trivet there. Transfer the ramekins in the trivet to the pressure cooker and close the lid. Cook at "Steam" mode for 20 minutes. When the dish is cooked, let it rest before serving, which should be done warm.

NUTRITION: Calories 141, Fat 12, Fiber 0, Carbs 3.5, Protein 5.1

579. Macaroons

Preparation time: 10 minutes

Cooking time: 3 minutes

Servings: 5

INGREDIENTS

- 3 egg whites
- 2 tablespoons Erythritol
- 1 teaspoon vanilla protein powder
- ½ cup almond flour
- ½ cup coconut shred
- 1 teaspoon baking powder

DIRECTIONS

1. Whisk the eggs whites in the mixing bowl. Add Erythritol, vanilla protein powder, almond flour, coconut shred, and baking powder. Stir the mixture well.
2. Make the medium size balls from the mixture and press them gently. Place the pressed balls (macaroonsin the Foodie basket. Close the lid and cook on Air fryer mode at 360F for 3 minutes or until thedessert is light brown. Chill little before serving.

NUTRITION: Calories 118, Fat 9.4, Fiber 2, Carbs 9.3, Protein 5.5

580. Coconut Bars

Preparation time: 10 minutes

Cooking time: 6 minutes

Servings: 8

INGREDIENTS

- 1 cup coconut shred
- 1/3 cup coconut flour
- 2 eggs, whisked
- 3 tablespoons swerve
- 1 teaspoon vanilla extract
- ¼ cup pecans, chopped
- 2 tablespoons butter

DIRECTIONS

1. Mix up together coconut shred, coconut flour, whisked eggs, swerve, vanilla extract, and chopped pecans. Then add butter and stir the mass until homogenous.

2. Line the Foodie with baking paper from inside and place coconut mixture on it. Flatten it to get the smooth layer. Close the lid and cook coconut mixture for 6 minutes on High-Pressure mode.
3. Then make quick pressure release. Open the lid and transfer cooked coconut mixture on the plate. Cut it into the serving bars.

NUTRITION: Calories 182, Fat 15.5, Fiber 4.4, Carbs 13.6, Protein 3.4

581. Avocado Mousse

Preparation time: 10 minutes

Cooking time: 25 minutes

Servings: 4

INGREDIENTS

- ½ cup almond milk
- 2 egg yolks
- 2 tablespoons swerve
- 2 avocado, peeled
- 1 teaspoon coconut flakes
- 1 teaspoon vanilla extract

DIRECTIONS

1. Pour almond milk in the Foodie. Whisk yolks with swerve and vanilla extract. Transfer the mixture in the Foodie. Close the lid and cook on Pressure mode (high pressurefor 3 minutes.
2. Meanwhile, blend the avocado until soft and smooth. Chill the cooked almond milk mixture little. Mix up together blended avocado and almond milk mixture. Stir well.
3. Transfer the dessert into the serving bowls and sprinkle with coconut flakes.

NUTRITION: Calories 308, Fat 29.2, Fiber 7.4, Carbs 11.8, Protein 4

582. Ricotta Pie

Preparation time: 10 minutes

Cooking time: 20 minutes

Servings: 8

INGREDIENTS

- 14 ounces ricotta cheese
- 4 eggs
- 1/3 cup Erythritol
- 1 cup coconut flour
- 1 teaspoon salt
- 1 tablespoon butter
- 1 teaspoon nutmeg
- 1 tablespoon vanilla extract
- ¼ teaspoon sage

DIRECTIONS

1. Whisk the eggs in a mixing bowl and combine it with the ricotta. Stir the mixture and sprinkle it with the salt, nutmeg, Erythritol, vanilla extract, and butter.
2. Mix well and sift the coconut flour into the bowl. Mix the batter until smooth. Pour the batter into the pressure cooker. Flatten it gently using a spatula.
3. Close the lid and cook at "Pressure" mode for 20 minutes. When the cooking time ends, release the pressure and let the pie rest for 10 minutes. Transfer the pie to a serving plate. Slice and serve.

NUTRITION: Calories 126, Fat 7.9, Fiber 0.7, Carbs 12.1, Protein 8.7

583.   "Apple" Crumble

Preparation time: 10 minutes

Cooking time: 25 minutes

Servings: 6

INGREDIENTS

- ⅓ cup Erythritol
- 1 cup almond flour
- 8 ounces butter
- 1 teaspoon cinnamon

- 1 tablespoon nutmeg
- 1 zucchini, chopped
- 1 tablespoon vanilla extract
- ½ cup whipped cream

DIRECTIONS

1. Place zucchini in the pressure cooker. Set the pressure cooker to "Sauté" mode. Sprinkle the zucchini with Erythritol and nutmeg. Mix well and sauté it for 10 minutes.
2. Slice the butter. Combine the cinnamon, vanilla extract, and almond flour together. Add the butter and mix well using your hands. Rub the dough using your fingers until a crumbly mixture is achieved. Sprinkle the sautéed zucchini with the crumble dough and close the pressure cooker lid.
3. Cook at "Pressure" mode for 15 minutes. Release the pressure and let the dish rest. Transfer the dish to a serving plate and add whipped cream.

NUTRITION: Calories 423, Fat 43.5, Fiber 2.7, Carbs 6.1, Protein 4.9

584.   Blackberry Compote

Preparation time: 8 minutes

Cooking time: 5 minutes

Servings: 5

INGREDIENTS

- 1 ½ cup blackberries
- 3 tablespoons Erythritol
- 1 teaspoon vanilla extract
- ¼ cup of water

DIRECTIONS

1. Mash the blackberries gently and place in Foodie. Add Erythritol, vanilla extract, and water. Stir the berries with the help of a wooden spatula. Close the lid and seal it.

2. Cook compote on Pressure mode (High pressurefor 5 minutes. Release the pressure naturally and chill dessert.

NUTRITION: Calories 21, Fat 0.2, Fiber 2.3, Carbs 11.5, Protein 0.6

585. Sponge Cake
Preparation time: 15 minutes

Cooking time: 30minutes

Servings: 8

INGREDIENTS

- 6 eggs
- 2 cups coconut flour
- 1 cup whipped cream
- ½ cup Erythritol
- 1 tablespoon vanilla extract

DIRECTIONS

1. Separate the egg yolks and egg whites. Combine the egg yolks with Erythritol and mix well using a hand mixer until fluffy. Whisk the egg whites until you get firm peaks. Sift the coconut flour and vanilla extract into the egg yolk mixture and stir well.
2. Add the egg whites and fold them in gently using a spatula. Add the sponge cake batter to the pressure cooker. Level the batter using the spatula and close the lid. Cook the cake at the "Pressure" mode for 30 minutes.
3. When the dish is cooked, let it rest before serving. Cut the sponge cake in half crossways and spread one part of the sponge cake with the whipped cream. Cover it with the second part of the cake and serve.

NUTRITION: Calories 111, Fat 8.4, Fiber 1.3, Carbs 2.9, Protein 5

586. Zucchini Crisp
Preparation time: 10 minutes

Cooking time: 20 minutes

Servings: 6

INGREDIENTS

- 1 pound zucchini
- 2 cups almond flour
- 1/3 cup Erythritol
- 1 tablespoon cinnamon
- 1 teaspoon vanilla extract
- ⅓ teaspoon baking soda
- 7 ounces butter
- 1 cup of water
- ½ cup flax meal
- 11 tablespoon lemon juice

DIRECTIONS

1. Chop the zucchini. Place them in the pressure cooker. Combine Erythritol, cinnamon, and 1 cup of the almond flour together. Sprinkle the chopped zucchini with Erythritol mixture.
2. Pour the water over the zucchini mixture. Combine the vanilla extract, the remaining flour, flax meal, baking soda, lemon juice, and butter in a mixing bowl.
3. Combine untilcrumble forms from the mixture. Sprinkle the apple mixture with the crumbles and close the pressure cooker lid. Cook at "Pressure" mode for 20 minutes. When the cooking time ends, let the apple crisp rest before serving.

NUTRITION: Calories 514, Fat 49.2, Fiber 8.2, Carbs 25.5, Protein 11.5

587. Cottage Cheese Prune Soufflé
Preparation time: 10 minutes

Cooking time: 10 minutes

Servings: 6

INGREDIENTS

- 6 ounces prunes
- 1 cup cottage cheese

- ½ cup sour cream
- 5 whole eggs
- 1 teaspoon ground ginger
- 3 egg yolks

DIRECTIONS

1. Beat the whole eggs in the bowl and add egg yolks. Add the cottage cheese and sour cream and mix for 3 minutes. Add ground ginger and mix well. Chop the prunes and add them to the cheese mixture.
2. Add the cheese mixture in the ramekins and place the ramekins in the pressure cooker trivet. Pour water in the pressure cooker and transfer the trivet to the pressure cooker.
3. Close the pressure cooker lid and cook at "Pressure" mode for 10 minutes. When the soufflé is cooked, let it rest before serving.

NUTRITION: Calories 208, Fat 10.9, Fiber 2.1, Carbs 21.2, Protein 9.3

588.   Walnuts Bars

Preparation time: 10 minutes

Cooking time: 15 minutes

Servings: 8

INGREDIENTS

- 1 cup walnuts
- ⅓ cup cream
- 1 tablespoon starch
- ⅓ cup Erythritol
- 5 tablespoon butter
- 1 cup almond flour
- 1 teaspoon baking soda
- 1 teaspoon lemon juice
- 1 egg
- ¼ teaspoon salt
- 1 teaspoon turmeric

DIRECTIONS

1. Place the butter, baking soda, lemon juice, egg, and flour in a food processor. Blend the mixture until smooth. Place the dough into the silicone form and flatten it using a spatula. Place the form in the pressure cooker and close the lid. Cook at "Pressure" pressure for 10 minutes.
2. Combine the starch, cream, Erythritol, and turmeric and mix well using a hand mixer until the volume to expand twice its size. Crush the walnuts and add them to the batter and stir well.
3. When the cooking time ends, release the pressure and chill the crust. Spread it with the cream mixture and transfer it to the pressure cooker again. Cook for 5 minutes. Let the dish rest, cut it into the bars, and serve.

NUTRITION: Calories 265, Fat 24.2, Fiber 2.6, Carbs 6.4, Protein 7.6

589.   Pineapple Pie

Preparation time: 10 minutes

Cooking time: 20 minutes

Servings: 8

INGREDIENTS

- 9 ounces fresh pineapple
- 1 tablespoon apple cider vinegar
- 4 tablespoons liquid stevia
- 8 tablespoon butter
- 1 cup coconut flour
- ½ cup ground flax meal
- 1 teaspoon olive oil
- ¼ teaspoon ground ginger

DIRECTIONS

1. Slice the pineapple. Combine the coconut flour, ground flax meal, butter, Erythritol, ground ginger, and baking soda in a mixing bowl. Sprinkle the mixture with the apple cider vinegar and knead the dough until

smooth. Transfer the dough to the freezer for 10 minutes.

2. Remove the frozen dough from the freezer and grate it. Sprinkle the pressure cooker with olive oil. Add half of the grated dough. Make a layer of the sliced pineapple and sprinkle them with the second part of the grated dough. Close the pressure cooker lid cook at "Sauté" mode for 10 minutes. Turn the pie on the other side and sauté for 10 minutes. Let the pie rest before slicing and serving.

NUTRITION: Calories 218, Fat 16.2, Fiber 8.5, Carbs 16.8, Protein 3.8

590. Sweet Carrot Slow Cook

Preparation time: 10 minutes

Cooking time: 20 minutes

Servings: 7

INGREDIENTS

- 3 cups of coconut milk
- 2 carrots
- 1 tablespoon Erythritol
- 1 teaspoon ground ginger
- ¼ teaspoon salt

DIRECTIONS

1. Peel the carrot and dice it. Transfer it to the pressure cooker. Add the coconut milk, ground ginger, and salt. Stir well and close the pressure cooker lid. Cook at "Slow Cook" mode for 15 minutes.
2. Open the pressure cooker lid and add Erythritol. Stir well and cook at "Pressure" mode for 5 minutes. When the cooking time ends, chill the Slow Cook in the refrigerator before serving.

NUTRITION: Calories 245, Fat 24.5, Fiber 2.7, Carbs 7.6, Protein 2.5

591. Sweet Poppy Bun

Preparation time: 15 minutes

Cooking time: 30 minutes

Servings: 8

INGREDIENTS

- ¼ cup poppy seeds
- 1 tablespoon baking powder
- 1 cup almond milk
- 1 teaspoon salt
- ⅓ cup Erythritol
- 1 teaspoon vanilla extract
- 1 egg
- 2 cups coconut flour
- 1 teaspoon olive oil

DIRECTIONS

1. Combine the baking powder, salt, and Erythritol in a mixing bowl and stir well. Add the almond milk and 1 cup of the coconut flour. Mix until smooth. Whisk the egg and combine it with the vanilla extract. Add the egg mixture to the baking powder mixture.
2. Stir well and add the second cup of the flour. Knead the dough until smooth, adding more flour, if desired. Combine the poppy seeds and Erythritol in another mixing bowl, stirring well. Separate the dough into 3 parts. Spray the pressure cooker with the olive oil.
3. Dip every piece of dough partially into the poppy seed mixture and place the dough in the pressure cooker to form one large bun. Close the pressure cooker lid and cook at "Pressure" mode for 30 minutes. Release the pressure and open the pressure cooker lid. Transfer the poppy bun to a serving plate and let it rest before cutting into serving pieces.

NUTRITION: Calories 228, Fat 13.2, Fiber 13.1, Carbs 23.6, Protein 6.1

592. Caramel Bites

Preparation time: 10 minutes

Cooking time: 9 minutes

Servings: 10

INGREDIENTS

- 7 ounces puff pastry
- 1 tablespoon butter
- 1 teaspoon cinnamon
- 1 egg yolk
- 1 teaspoon olive oil
- 4 tablespoons low carb caramel drops

DIRECTIONS

1. Roll the puff pastry using a rolling pin. Make the circles from the dough using a cutter. Whisk the egg yolk and sprinkle the dough circles with it.
2. Put the butter and caramel in the center of the puff pastry circle and make small puffs. Spray the pressure cooker with the olive oil. Add the puff pastry bites to the pressure cooker and cook at "Sauté" mode for 3 minutes on each side until all sides are light brown. Place the caramel bites on a paper towel to drain any excess oil and serve warm.

NUTRITION: Calories 173, Fat 12.4, Fiber 1.2, Carbs 16, Protein 2.1

593. Puff Pastry Cups

Preparation time: 15 minutes

Cooking time: 25 minutes

Servings: 8

INGREDIENTS

- 10 ounces puff pastry
- 3 tablespoons pumpkin puree
- 1 teaspoon butter
- 1 tablespoon almond flour
- 1 tablespoon Erythritol
- 1 teaspoon cinnamon
- 1 cup water, for pressure cooker
- 1 teaspoon olive oil

DIRECTIONS

1. Roll out the puff pastry and cut it into the circles. Sprinkle the ramekins with the olive oil inside and place the puff pastry squares inside them. The puff pastry squares should be bigger than ramekins to be able to wrap the dough. Combine the pumpkin puree, almond flour, Erythritol, and cinnamon together and stir well. Fill the ramekins with the pumpkin puree mixture and wrap the puff pastry gently. Pour water in the pressure cooker. Place the ramekins on the trivet and transfer the trivet in the pressure cooker. Cook at "Steam" mode for 25 minutes. When the puff pastry cups are cooked, remove them from the pressure cooker and remove them from the ramekins. Serve warm.

NUTRITION: Calories 212, Fat 15, Fiber 0.9, Carbs 16.9, Protein 2.9

594. Cream Cheese Mousse

Preparation time: 15 minutes

Cooking time: 4 minutes

Servings: 6

INGREDIENTS

- 2 cups cream cheese
- 1 oz chocolate
- 1 teaspoon vanilla extract
- ½ cup cream
- ½ cup Erythritol
- 1 teaspoon of cocoa powder

DIRECTIONS

1. Combine the chocolate, vanilla extract, sugar, cocoa powder, and cream together. Mix well using a hand mixer. Set the pressure cooker to "Sauté" mode.
2. Place the cream mixture in the pressure cooker and sauté it for 4 minutes. Chill the mixture briefly and add the cream cheese. Whisk the mixture until smooth. Transfer

the cooked mousse to the freezer and chill for 10 minutes before serving.

NUTRITION: Calories 311, Fat 29.5, Fiber 0.3, Carbs 5.7, Protein 6.4

595. Carrot Cake

Preparation time: 10 minutes

Cooking time: 35 minutes

Servings: 8

INGREDIENTS

- 1 cup almond flour
- 1 teaspoon baking soda
- 1 teaspoon lemon juice
- 1 carrot
- 1 teaspoon apple juice
- ½ cup yogurt
- ½ cup of coconut milk
- 1 teaspoon pumpkin pie spices
- 2 eggs
- 4 tablespoons Erythritol

DIRECTIONS

1. Peel the carrot and grate it. Combine the eggs with the grated carrot and whisk the mixture. Add the yogurt and milk. Sprinkle the mixture with the apple juice, lemon juice, baking soda, pumpkin pie spices, semolina, and flour. Knead the dough until smooth.
2. Pour the carrot batter in the pressure cooker form. Pour water in the pressure cooker and place the trivet inside. Put the pressure cooker form in the trivet and close the lid.
3. Cook the carrot cake at the "Pressure" mode for 35 minutes. When the carrot cake is cooked, remove it from the pressure cooker and let it rest. Cut into slices and serve.

NUTRITION: Calories 159, Fat 11.9, Fiber 2.1, Carbs 9.4, Protein 5.7

596. Strawberry Jam

Preparation time: 10 minutes

Cooking time: 20 minutes

Servings: 7

INGREDIENTS

- ½ cup Erythritol
- 2 cups strawberries
- 1 teaspoon lemon zest
- ½ teaspoon ground cardamom

DIRECTIONS

1. Chop the strawberries and sprinkle them with Erythritol. Set the pressure cooker to "Sauté" mode. Stir the mixture and transfer it to the pressure cooker. Sauté the mixture for 5 minutes. Stir frequently using a wooden spoon. Sprinkle the strawberry mixture with ground cardamom and lemon zest. Stir well and sauté the mixture for 15 minutes until it reduces by half. Remove the jam from the pressure cooker and chill in the refrigerator for few hours before using.

NUTRITION: Calories 14, Fat 0.1, Fiber 0.9, Carbs 14.8, Protein 0.3

597. Sweet Yogurt

Preparation time: 25 minutes

Cooking time: 9 hours 15 minutes

Servings: 7

INGREDIENTS

- 5 cups almond milk
- 3 tablespoons yogurt starter
- 1 cup strawberries, chopped
- ½ cup blueberries

DIRECTIONS

1. Pour almond milk in the pressure cooker and close the lid. Set the "Slow Cook" mode and cook for 15 minutes, stirring periodically.
2. Open the pressure cooker lid and let the almond milk sit for 15 minutes. Add the yogurt starter and stir well using a wooden spoon.
3. Close the pressure cooker lid and cook for 9 hours. Remove from the pressure cooker and chill in the refrigerator for several hours. Transfer the yogurt to serving bowls and sprinkle them with the strawberries.

NUTRITION: Calories 407, Fat 41, Fiber 4.4, Carbs 12.6, Protein 4.2

598. Brownie Cups

Preparation time: 10 minutes

Cooking time: 4 minutes

Servings: 2

INGREDIENTS

- 1 oz dark chocolate, melted
- 2 eggs, whisked
- 4 tablespoons butter
- 2 tablespoons almond flour
- 1 teaspoon vanilla extract
- 5 drops liquid stevia

DIRECTIONS

1. In the mixing bowl, mix up together melted chocolate, whisked eggs, butter, almond flour, and vanilla extract. Add liquid stevia and mix the mixture until smooth.
2. Pour the brownie mixture in the brownie cups. Insert trivet in Foodi and pour 1 cup of water. Place the cups on the trivet and close the lid. Cook the brownie cups for 4 minutes on Pressure. Release the pressure and chill the cooked dessert little before serving.

NUTRITION: Calories 388, Fat 35.1, Fiber 1.2, Carbs 10.6, Protein 8.4

599. Cream Mousse with Strawberries

Preparation time: 15 minutes

Cooking time: 7 minutes

Servings: 10

INGREDIENTS

- 1 cup cream cheese
- 1 cup whipped cream
- 3 egg yolks
- ½ cup Erythritol
- 1 tablespoon cocoa powder
- 1 tablespoon butter

DIRECTIONS

1. Whisk the egg yolks with Erythritol and combine the mixture with the cream cheese. Set the pressure cooker to "Sauté" mode.
2. Transfer the mixture to the pressure cooker and cook for 7 minutes. Stir the cream cheese mixture constantly. Transfer the cream cheese mixture to a mixing bowl.
3. Add the whipped cream and cocoa powder. Add the butter and mix it well using a hand blender. Transfer the mousse to serving glasses.

NUTRITION: Calories 144, Fat 14.4, Fiber 0.2, Carbs 13.5, Protein 2.9

600. Butter Cake

Preparation time: 20 minutes

Cooking time: 25 minutes

Servings: 8

INGREDIENTS

- 2 egg whites
- 10 tablespoon butter

- 2 cups almond flour
- ½ cup almond milk
- ½ cup Erythritol
- 1 teaspoon vanilla extract
- 1 teaspoon baking soda
- 1 tablespoon lemon juice
- ½ teaspoon ground cardamom

DIRECTIONS

1. Melt the butter and combine it with the almond milk, almond flour, Erythritol, vanilla extract, baking soda, lemon juice, and ground cardamom. Knead the dough until smooth and place it in the pressure cooker form.
2. Pour water in the pressure cooker and add the trivet with the butter dough form. Close the lid and cook at "Pressure" mode for 25 minutes. Open the pressure cooker lid and check if it is done using a toothpick. Transfer the cake to a plate and let it rest.
3. Whisk the egg whites white peaks form. Sprinkle the butter cake with the icing and let it cool before serving.

NUTRITION: Calories 71, Fat 5.8, Fiber 1, Carbs 17.8, Protein 2.4

601. Zucchini Tacos

Preparation time: 15 minutes

Cooking time: 5 minutes

Servings: 7

INGREDIENTS

- 2 zucchini
- 2 tablespoons liquid stevia
- 1 teaspoon cinnamon
- ½ teaspoon ginger
- 6 ounces almond flour tortillas (keto tortilla

DIRECTIONS

1. Peel the zucchini and chop them. Sprinkle the chopped zucchini with the cinnamon,

and ginger. Mix well and let the zucchini for 5 minutes or until they give off some juice.
2. Place the zucchini in the pressure cooker and cook them at the "Pressure" mode for 4 minutes. Sprinkle the tortillas with the liquid stevia.
3. Remove the cooked zucchini from the pressure cooker and let them rest briefly. Place the zucchini mixture in the tortillas, wrap them and serve.

NUTRITION: Calories 140, Fat 7.1, Fiber 4.3, Carbs 9.2, Protein 11.1

602. Lemon Loaf

Preparation time: 10 minutes

Cooking time: 30 minutes

Servings: 8

INGREDIENTS

- 1 cup lemon juice
- 3 tablespoons lemon zest
- 3 cups almond flour
- ½ cup cream
- 1 egg
- 1 teaspoon baking soda
- ½ teaspoon baking powder
- 2 tablespoons Erythritol
- 1 teaspoon turmeric

DIRECTIONS

1. Combine the almond flour, baking powder, baking soda, turmeric, and Erythritol in a mixing bowl. Stir the mixture and add the lemon juice and cream.
2. Add the egg and lemon zest. Knead the dough until smooth and place the dough in the loaf form. Pour water in the pressure cooker and put the trivet. Transfer the loaf form with the dough in the pressure cooker and close the pressure cooker lid.
3. Cook at "Pressure" mode for 30 minutes. Open the pressure cooker lid and remove the form from the machine. Let it cool, slice it and serve.

NUTRITION: Calories 88, Fat 6.9, Fiber 1.5, Carbs 7.9, Protein 3.4

603. Sweet Spaghetti Casserole

Preparation time: 10 minutes

Cooking time: 20 minutes

Servings: 7

INGREDIENTS

- 8 ounces black bean pasta, cooked
- 1 cup cottage cheese
- 6 eggs
- ¼ cup cream
- 1 tablespoon olive oil
- 1 teaspoon salt
- 1/3 cup Erythritol
- 1 teaspoon vanilla extract
- 1 teaspoon nutmeg

DIRECTIONS

1. Combine the cottage cheese, cream, eggs, and Erythritol together in a blender. Blend the mixture well until smooth. Transfer the cottage cheese mixture to a mixing bowl, add the cooked pasta, nutmeg, and vanilla extract and mix well. Pour the olive oil in the pressure cooker and transfer the cottage cheese mixture. Close the lid and cook at "Slow Cook" mode for 20 minutes.
2. When the dish is cooked, let it cool and remove from the pressure cooker. Cut it into pieces and serve.

NUTRITION: Calories 2,13 Fat 8.1, Fiber 7, Carbs 23.2, Protein 23.7

604. Vanilla Cake

Preparation time: 10 minutes

Cooking time: 45 minutes

Servings: 12

INGREDIENTS

- 5 eggs
- 1 teaspoon vanilla extract
- ½ cup almond flour
- ½ cup Erythritol
- 3 cups almond milk
- 6 ounces butter

DIRECTIONS

1. Melt the butter and combine it with the vanilla extract, Erythritol, almond milk, almond flour, and eggs. Whisk the mixture well. Pour a half cup of water in the pressure cooker.
2. Pour the butter mixture into the glass form. Place the trivet in the pressure cooker. Transfer the glass form in the trivet and close the pressure cooker lid. Cook at "Pressure" mode for 45 minutes.
3. When the cooking time ends, open the pressure cooker lid and chill the cake. Transfer the cake to a serving plate.

NUTRITION: Calories 273, Fat 28.2, Fiber 1.5, Carbs 13.8, Protein 4.1

605. Caramel Pudding

Preparation Time: 22 minutes

Servings: 6

INGREDIENTS

- 8 oz. cream cheese, soft
- 3 eggs
- 1/3 cup sugar
- 2 tbsp. caramel syrup
- 2 tbsp. butter, melted

DIRECTIONS

1. In your blender, combine all the Ingredients pulse well and divide into 6 ramekins. Put the reversible rack in the Foodi, add the ramekins inside, set the machine on Baking mode and cook at 320 °F for 12 minutes. Leave aside to cool down and serve

606. Egg Pudding

Preparation Time: 35 minutes

Servings: 6

INGREDIENTS

- 6 egg yolks; whisked.
- 2 cups heavy cream
- 6 tbsp. white sugar
- Zest of 1 lemon; grated.

DIRECTIONS

1. In a bowl mix all the Ingredients whisk well and divide into 6 ramekins. Put the reversible rack in the Foodi, arrange the ramekins inside, set the machine on Baking mode and cook at 340 °F for 25 minutes. Cool down and serve

607. Buttery Rolls

Preparation Time: 2 hours 10 minutes

Servings:8

INGREDIENTS

- 1 lb. bread dough
- ¼ cup butter, melted
- ¾ cup brown sugar

DIRECTIONS

1. Roll the dough on a floured working surface, shape a rectangle and brush with the butter. Sprinkle the sugar all over, roll the dough into a log and cut into 8 pieces
2. Leave the rolls to rise in a warm place for 2 hours. Put the Air Crisp basket in the Foodi and put the rolls in the basket. Set the machine on Air Crisp, cook at 350 °F for 10 minutes Serve warm

608. Sweet Bread

Preparation Time: 25 minutes

Servings: 4

INGREDIENTS

- 8 oz. flour
- 4 oz. milk
- 1 egg
- 2 tbsp. butter
- 2 tbsp. white sugar
- 1 tsp. baking powder

DIRECTIONS

1. In a bowl mix all the Ingredients and stir well. Transfer the dough to a loaf pan that fits the Foodi. Put the reversible rack in the Foodi and put the loaf pan inside
2. Set the machine on Baking mode and cook at 360 °F for 15 minutes. Slice the sweet bread and serve it warm.

609. Butter Brownies

Preparation Time: 35 minutes

Servings: 12

INGREDIENTS

- 2 eggs
- 2 cups white flour
- 1 cup butter, melted
- ½ cup chocolate chips; chopped.
- 4 tbsp. sugar
- 1 tsp. vanilla extract

DIRECTIONS

1. In a bowl mix all the Ingredients whisk well and pour into your Foodi's cake pan. Put the reversible rack in the Foodi, put the cake pan inside, set the machine on Baking mode and cook at 330 °F for 25 minutes. Cool down, slice and serve

610. Awesome Cake

Preparation Time: 35 minutes

Servings: 8

INGREDIENTS

- 15 oz. cake mix
- ½ cup chocolate chips.
- Cooking spray

DIRECTIONS

1. In a bowl combine all the Ingredients and whisk well. Grease the Foodi's cake pan with cooking spray and pour the cake mix in it
2. Put the reversible rack in the Foodi, add the cake pan inside, set the machine on Baking mode and cook the cake at 350 °F for 25 minutes. Cool the cake down, slice and serve.

611. Apple Cake

Preparation Time: 60 minutes

Servings: 4

INGREDIENTS

- 40 oz. apple flesh
- 14 oz. cake mix
- 8 oz. butter, soft
- 1 tsp. cinnamon powder
- Cooking spray

DIRECTIONS

1. Grease your Foodi's cake pan with the cooking spray and layer the apple flesh on the bottom. In a bowl mix the butter with the cooking spray and spread this over the apple mix
2. Sprinkle the cinnamon on top, put the cake pan in the Foodi, set the machine on Baking mode and cook at 360 °F for 50 minutes. Cool the cake down, slice and serve

612. Chocolate Cream

Preparation Time: 25 minutes

Servings: 6

INGREDIENTS

- 12 oz. chocolate chips
- 1 cup heavy cream
- 1 cup sugar
- ½ cup butter, melted

DIRECTIONS

1. In a bowl mix all the Ingredients whisk well and divide everything into 6 ramekins. Put the reversible rack in the Foodi, put the ramekins inside, set the machine on Baking mode and cook at 350 °F for 15 minutes. Serve the cream cold

613. Pumpkin Cake

Preparation Time: 60 minutes

Servings: 12

INGREDIENTS

- 14 oz. cake mix
- 2 oz. chocolate chips
- 12 oz. pumpkin puree
- 1 cup cranberries, dried
- 1 tbsp. pumpkin pie spice

DIRECTIONS

1. In a bowl combine all the Ingredients stir well and pour into your Foodi's cake pan. Put the reversible rack in the Foodi, add the cake pan inside, set the machine on Baking mode and cook at 350 °F for 50 minutes. Slice the cake and serve

614. Black Beans Brownies

Preparation Time: 30 minutes

Servings: 12

INGREDIENTS

- 4 oz. chocolate; chopped.
- 4 eggs; whisked.
- 1 cup white flour

- ½ cup canned black beans; drained. and blended
- ½ cup butter, melted
- ¼ cup brewed black coffee
- 1 ¼ cups sugar
- 1 tsp. vanilla extract
- Cooking spray

DIRECTIONS

1. In a bowl combine all the Ingredients except the cooking spray and whisk well. Grease a cake pan with the cooking spray and pour the batter in it
2. Put the reversible rack in the Foodi, add the cake pan inside, set the machine on Baking mode and cook at 350 °F for 20 minutes. Slice the brownies and serve

615. Cocoa And Orange Pudding

Preparation Time: 30 minutes

Servings: 4

INGREDIENTS

- 1 egg
- 2 tbsp. orange juice
- 4 tbsp. white flour
- 1 tbsp. cocoa powder
- 4 tbsp. sugar
- 2 tbsp. coconut oil, melted
- 4 tbsp. milk
- ½ tsp. baking powder
- ½ tsp. lime zest; grated.

DIRECTIONS

1. In a bowl mix all the Ingredients, stir well and divide into 4 ramekins. Put the reversible rack in the Foodi, put the ramekins inside, set the machine on Baking mode and cook 320 °F for 20 minutes. Serve the pudding warm

616. Apple Pie

Preparation Time: 60 minutes

Servings: 8

INGREDIENTS

- 2 apples, cored, peeled and sliced
- 2 eggs; whisked.
- ¾ cup milk
- 2/3 cup white flour
- 1/3 cup sugar
- Cooking spray
- 2 tbsp. flavored liqueur
- 1 tsp. cinnamon powder

DIRECTIONS

1. In a bowl mix the sugar with the cinnamon, flour, eggs, milk and the liqueur and stir well. Grease the Foodi's cake pan with cooking spray and arrange the apples into the pan
2. Pour the batter over the apples and put the pan in the Foodi. Set the machine on Baking mode and cook at 400 °F for 55 minutes. Cool the pie down, slice and serve.

617. Apples Jam

Preparation Time: 30 minutes

Servings: 6

INGREDIENTS

- 1 lb. apples, peeled, cored and chopped
- 2 lbs. sugar
- 2 cups apple juice
- Juice of 2 limes

DIRECTIONS

1. In your Foodi, combine all the Ingredients toss, put the pressure lid on and cook on High for 20 minutes. Blend the mix using an immersion blender, divide into cups and serve cold

618. Pineapple and Yogurt Cake

Preparation Time: 50 minutes

Servings: 6

INGREDIENTS

- 5 oz. flour
- 1 egg; whisked.
- ½ cup sugar
- 1/3 cup coconut flakes, shredded
- ¼ cup pineapple juice
- 4 tbsp. vegetable oil
- 3 tbsp. yogurt
- ¾ tsp. baking powder
- ½ tsp. baking soda
- ½ tsp. cinnamon powder
- Cooking spray

DIRECTIONS

1. In a bowl mix all the Ingredients except the cooking spray and whisk well. Grease the Foodi's cake pan with cooking spray and pour the cake batter inside
2. Put the reversible rack in the Foodi, put the cake pan on the rack, set the machine on baking mode and cook the cake at 320 °F for 40 minutes. Cool down, cut and serve it.

619.   Creamy Orange Cake

Preparation Time: 40 minutes

Servings: 10

INGREDIENTS

- 9 oz. white flour
- 2 oz. sugar
- 4 oz. cream cheese
- 6 eggs; whisked.
- 1 orange, peeled and pureed
- 1 tsp. vanilla extract
- 1 tsp. baking powder

DIRECTIONS

1. In a food processor, combine all the Ingredients pulse well and spread into the Foodi's cake pan.

2. Put the reversible rack in the Foodi, put the cake pan inside, set the machine on Baking mode and cook at 340 °F for 30 minutes. Cool the cake down, slice and serve

620.   Raisins Pudding

Preparation Time: 60 minutes

Servings: 4

INGREDIENTS

- ½ cups cherries, pitted and halved.
- 4 egg yolks
- 1 ½ cups coconut cream
- ¼ cup sugar
- ½ cup chocolate chips
- 1 cup raisins

DIRECTIONS

1. In a bowl mix all the Ingredients stir well and pour everything into a ramekin. Put the reversible rack in the Foodi and place the ramekin inside
2. Set the machine on Baking mode, cook the pudding at 310 °F for 50 minutes, cool down and serve.

621.   Cream Cheese Cake

Preparation Time: 25 minutes

Servings: 10

INGREDIENTS

- 6 oz. coconut oil, melted
- 3 oz. cocoa powder
- 4 oz. cream cheese, soft
- 6 eggs
- 5 tbsp. sugar
- 2 tsp. vanilla extract
- ½ tsp. baking powder

DIRECTIONS

1. In a blender, combine all the Ingredients pulse well and pour this into your Foodi's cake pan.
2. Put the reversible rack in the Foodi machine, add the cake pan inside, set the pot on Baking mode and cook at 320 °F, bake for 15 minutes. Slice and serve

622. Banana Cupcakes

Preparation Time: 30 minutes

Servings: 12

INGREDIENTS

- 14 oz. cake mix
- 3 bananas, peeled and mashed
- Cooking spray

DIRECTIONS

1. In a bowl combine all the Ingredients and stir well. Grease a cupcake pan with cooking spray and pour the cake mix into the pan
2. Put the reversible rack in the Foodi, put the cupcake pan inside, set the machine on Baking mode and cook at 350 °F for 20 minutes. Serve the cupcakes cold

623. Dark Chocolate Creamy Pudding

Preparation Time: 22 minutes

Servings: 4

INGREDIENTS

- 4 oz. dark chocolate, cut into chunks and melted
- 4 oz. heavy cream

DIRECTIONS

1. In 4 ramekins, combine the Ingredients and whisk well. Put the reversible rack in the Foodi, put the ramekins inside, set the machine on Baking mode and cook at 300 °F for 12 minutes. Serve cold

624. Mango Bowls

Preparation Time: 30 minutes

Servings: 4

INGREDIENTS

- 4 mangos, peeled and roughly cut into cubes
- ¼ cup brown sugar
- 2 tsp. cinnamon powder
- 4 tbsp. butter, melted

DIRECTIONS

1. In your Foodi's baking pan, combine all the Ingredients and toss. Put the reversible rack in the Foodi, add the baking pan inside, set the machine on Baking mode and cook at 300 °F for 20 minutes. Divide the mix into bowls and serve

CONCLUSION

Thank you for reaching the end of this book. Now that you have convinced yourself that the Ninja Foodi cooker is so much more than oil-free frying, the next step is to prepare these recipes, modify them to your liking, and create your own unique air fried delicacies.

Made in the USA
Columbia, SC
08 June 2020